Routledge Revivals

New Zealand in the Making

First published in 1930, *New Zealand in the Making* is an economic history of the democratic experiments in New Zealand. The geography, population, government ownership of public utilities, compulsory arbitration, pensions and all other factors have been covered in detail. The book will be of interest to anyone keen on learning about New Zealand as well as to students of economy, history, agriculture, and government.

New Zealand in the Making

A Survey of Economic and Social Development

J. B. Condliffe

Routledge
Taylor & Francis Group
Routledge Revivals

First published in 1930
By George Allen & Unwin

This edition first published in 2023 by Routledge
4 Park Square, Milton Park, Abingdon, Oxon, OX14 4RN
and by Routledge
605 Third Avenue, New York, NY 10017

Routledge is an imprint of the Taylor & Francis Group, an informa business

Publisher's Note
The publisher has gone to great lengths to ensure the quality of this reprint but points out that some imperfections in the original copies may be apparent.

Disclaimer
The publisher has made every effort to trace copyright holders and welcomes correspondence from those they have been unable to contact.

A Library of Congress record exists under LCCN: 30025376

ISBN: 978-1-032-52177-0 (hbk)
ISBN: 978-1-003-40706-5 (ebk)
ISBN: 978-1-032-52533-4 (pbk)

Book DOI 10.4324/9781003407065

NEW ZEALAND
IN THE MAKING

A Survey of Economic and Social Development

by

J. B. Condliffe, D.Sc.

Research Secretary, Institute of Pacific Relations, formerly Professor of Economics, Canterbury College, Christchurch, New Zealand; Sometime Sir Thomas Gresham Student, Gonville and Caius College, Cambridge

THE UNIVERSITY OF CHICAGO PRESS
CHICAGO, ILLINOIS

FIRST PUBLISHED IN THE U.S.A. IN 1930

PRINTED IN GREAT BRITAIN BY
UNWIN BROTHERS LTD., WOKING

TO

JAMES HIGHT, M.A., LITT.D.

PREFACE

So many friends have given generous assistance in the preparation of this book that it has almost become a co-operative work. My heaviest debt is expressed in the dedication to Dr. James Hight, Rector of Canterbury College, who first started me on the preparation of the research material more than fifteen years ago, and whose critical scholarship and unique knowledge of New Zealand economics and history have been freely placed at my disposal ever since. My former chief and colleague, Mr. Malcolm Fraser, and Mr. J. W. Butcher, of the Census and Statistics Office, have safeguarded me from many statistical errors; Sir Apirana Ngata, Dr. P. H. Buck, and Mr. F. M. Keesing have supplied materials without which the second chapter on the Maoris could never have been written; and Mr. W. Stewart, Commissioner of Crown Lands for the Canterbury District, kindly checked my references to land legislation.

I owe special thanks also to Mr. J. L. Martin, of the Lands and Survey Department, Christchurch, for patiently assembling the scattered information and drawing the excellent maps on which for the first time, as far as I am aware, the quality and tenurial distribution of New Zealand lands are clearly shown. Mr. George Lawn, of Canterbury College, rendered a similar service in bringing up to date and drawing the diagrams of trade and of public works expenditure.

I have drawn freely not only upon my own previously published work, but also upon the research dissertations prepared by students under my direction at Canterbury College. As far as I am aware, all specific obligations are acknowledged in the notes and references appended to the book; but I must acknowledge also the help which I received over many years from discussion of New Zealand economic problems with my colleagues of the New Zealand University Colleges, as well as in the classroom discussions, both within Canterbury College and in the Workers' Educational Association tutorial classes. The close contact maintained since 1924 between my department and the Canterbury Chamber of Commerce has, I hope, resulted in a greater degree of reality in the treatment of controversial problems. It is a great pleasure to have this opportunity of expressing gratitude for the co-operation of the Chamber, and especially of Mr. Norton Francis, who has from the beginning acted as chairman of the joint Economic Committee.

While I have drawn thus heavily upon the help and criticism of so many friends, the opinions expressed, especially in the later controversial chapters of the book, are entirely my own. I have, I hope, weighed with due care the critical opinions of those by whom the manuscript has been read; but the responsibility for the statements made is entirely mine.

J. B. C.

HONOLULU,
July 1929

CONTENTS

LIST OF MAPS AND DIAGRAMS

NEW ZEALAND IN THE MAKING

CHAPTER I

THE MAIN PERIODS OF DEVELOPMENT

THE EARLIEST TRADERS, 1792–1840 (1)

New Zealand at the present time has a population of slightly less than a million and a half. Of these the Maoris number only 64,817. This small community, situated almost at the antipodes of Great Britain, is hardly a century old. Effective settlement did not begin till 1840. Since that date such rapid progress has been made that to-day New Zealand claims the largest overseas trade per head of any country in the world and has a very high standard of economic welfare. It has a worldwide reputation also for experimental legislation and especially for measures of social improvement. There are few other lands where human life and welfare enter so consciously into political consideration.

Yet it is less than a century and a half since its name was a synonym for savage barbarism. Macaulay, straining for epigram, perched a New Zealander upon the ruins of London Bridge; but could hardly have anticipated that the most famous scientific chair of his university would come to be held by a New Zealander together with a fellowship in his own college.

Governor Philip, reflecting in 1787 upon the difficulty of maintaining discipline in the convict settlement which was to be planted at Botany Bay, reserved New Zealand as the ultimate punishment for criminals too vicious to be restrained by fear of death. In the same way, a contemporary observer of the industrial slums of Manchester in the early years of the nineteenth century could find no more dramatic emphasis than the statement that he would as soon trust himself to the aborigines of New Zealand as to children brought up in such surroundings.

Such statements as these are not surprising in view of the fierce hostility with which the Maoris took "utu" (payment) for any injuries or breaches of etiquette committed by the rare visitors to their shores. The experience of Tasman, who lost a boat's crew on the first recorded visit of any European to New Zealand, was many times repeated. Cook, the next visitor, a century and a half later, had to exercise continual caution, and three years after his visit the French explorer, Marion du Fresne, paid a terrible price for the ruthless actions of his predecessor, de Surville.

Whaling, sealing, and the timber trade, as well as the over-estimated possibilities of the New Zealand flax, continued, however, to tempt adventurous traders. In 1792 a sealing-party camped for several months at Dusky Sound. In 1795 the first shipload of timber was taken from the Thames. Whaling commenced on a great scale in the first decade of the nineteenth century, despite the monopoly of the South Sea Company. Within the first two decades of the nineteenth century the deep-sea whaling industry and the sealing on the New Zealand coast and the adjacent islands were practically destroyed, as much by wanton destruction as by exploitation.

The advent of the bay whalers in the twenties reinforced the settlements of "beachcombers" that had begun to spring up on the shores of the beautiful harbours of the northern peninsula. These settlements became a byword for lawlessness and crime. Maori outrages increased in ferocity, and the advent of the white traders enlarged the possibilities of tribal warfare on a grand scale. Marsden had opened the first mission station in 1814, but had not found any clergyman willing to face these terrible conditions till Henry Williams came in 1823. It was not till 1832 that the occasional visits of a British man-of-war were supplemented by the appointment of a British Resident, who, however, was given no means of enforcing his authority except the suggestion in his instructions that he should use "moral suasion". With the exception of this futile gesture and the growing influence of the missionaries, there was nothing to check the ferocity of Maori warfare and outrages, or the criminality of the settlements. The British Government was still loth to add to its responsibilities and categorically denied any intention of governing New Zealand. Not till colonists had actually left Britain was any effective Governmental action taken.

Beyond the bringing of New Zealand into the sphere of British influence and, ultimately, government, this earliest period of New Zealand's history has little importance for the economic historian. The missionary farms which so impressed Darwin in 1835 were designed primarily for Maori education, but Maori agriculture was strangled in its infancy. The earliest trade in whale-oil, seal-skins, timber, and flax, contributed only negatively to future development.(2) The later farming enterprises of certain bay whalers and pioneer settlers were of more importance, but were quickly merged in the economic progress that resulted from systematic colonisation. There are few other lands where beginnings can so definitely be dated. For all practical purposes the economic history of New Zealand begins with the arrival of the first Wellington settlers in 1840.

The Geography of Development

Giving evidence in 1836 before the House of Commons Select Committee on the methods of disposing of lands in the Colonies, Edward Gibbon Wakefield drew attention to the possibilities of New Zealand.

"Very near to Australia", he said, "there is a country which all testimony concurs in describing as the fittest country in the world for colonisation, as the most beautiful country, with the finest climate and the most productive soil; I mean New Zealand."

This was the first public indication that Wakefield's thoughts had turned to the land which was in the next decade to provide him with the field for his greatest experiments in systematic colonisation. Later on in his evidence he pointed out the inevitability that New Zealand would be colonised, and pleaded for forethought and planning in its development.

"We are, I think, going to colonise New Zealand," he went on, "though we be doing so in a most slovenly and scrambling and disgraceful manner."

The success which attended his efforts to substitute orderly and well-prepared plans of group settlement for the slovenly, scrambling, and disgraceful methods of individual adventurous enterprise is probably his greatest title to fame. The mistakes which he made were due, on the other hand, primarily to the pioneer character of his work, and in no small degree to the fact that he necessarily lacked sufficient knowledge of the geographical conditions which were to control the economic development of the new colony.

Three-quarters of a century after Wakefield gave his evidence, a shrewd and penetrating summary was made by a French economist, André Siegfried, of "Geographical Conditions and their Influence on the Evolution of New Zealand". The first characteristic of the islands which attracted his attention was "their more than insular character, their enormous distance from anywhere, their complete isolation". Here was an obstacle to economic progress of which Wakefield could not well have been unaware, but the controlling importance of which he obviously underestimated.

When he took settlers to the islands and planted them there to work out their economic salvation they were forced in their isolation to make an attempt at self-sufficiency. Transport and communication were so slow and uncertain that they had to provide for themselves the materials of economic and social organisation. It is true that, more than in most new colonies, they brought with them and continued to import large stocks of material capital; but there was no ready means by which they could export any means of payment. They were therefore forced back to primitive and even rudimentary scales of living until they discovered the prospects of raising sheep upon the open plains of the south island, and so were enabled to export wool in large quantities.

The necessities of external transport in fact divide the economic development of New Zealand into three well-marked periods: the first ten years or so of self-sufficient agricultural farming, the pastoral age which followed, and the development of more diversified and smaller scale farming once again after the practical success of refrigerated transport in 1882 opened up a wider external market.

The testimony upon which Wakefield based his glowing estimate of New Zealand's possibilities has proved to be right in the long run; but it must have ignored almost all the practical difficulties, not only of external transport, but of internal transport also. New Zealand has, as Siegfried notes, a well-indented coastline; but it "is a narrow land, whose mountains rise to heaven in mighty piles, and are touched at their bases by inlets of the sea".

When the first settlers arrived, therefore, they found themselves isolated, not only from all other lands, but almost equally from each other. With remarkable prescience Wakefield chose as the first region of settlement the central region on either side of Cook Strait, and planted colonies at Wellington, Wanganui, New Plymouth, and Nelson. With the exception of Nelson, these settlements, once their initial difficulties were overcome, proved to be admirably located. They had access to some of the richest plains in the country and have since developed into closely settled regions of small-scale farming.

In their first years, however, their progress was hampered by many factors which Wakefield could hardly have foreseen. The central region of the north island was then, and for many years continued to be, unexplored territory. Access to it was blocked by mountain ranges, which, though lower than the great mountain system of the south, were rugged and confused, offering almost insuperable obstacles to transport until the colony gathered sufficient capital resources to build roads and railways.

The coastal plains of the west, moreover, were covered with the characteristic dense New Zealand rain-forest. A glance at the rainfall map will show that all the western sections of the north island have a consistently heavy rainfall, not as great, indeed, as the narrow coastal strip on the west coast of the south island, but quite adequate to account for the growth of heavy forests. The prevailing warm westerly winds gather moisture in their passage over the Tasman Sea, and deposit most of it on the western shores of New Zealand. At a later stage of development, when the forests had been cleared, these regions of the north island offered, as Wakefield had foreseen, the largest scope for intensive agricultural development. Their greatest asset is the combination of regular and abundant warm rains with plenty of sunshine, making possible the grasslands which support a high degree of dairying and mixed farming production. Such advantages, however, remained latent until the settlement of Maori troubles in the seventies and eighties, combined with the new demands opened up in the external markets by refrigerated transport, encouraged the settlers in the eighties and nineties to take up again the heavy task of felling and clearing the bush.

This task, the first which the New Zealand pioneers set themselves to undertake, was interrupted for a quarter of a century, between 1850 and 1873, by the greater immediate advantages of extensive sheep-raising on the more open plains of the east coast of the south island, and to some extent of the north island also. It was not till the twentieth century that settlement was pushed into the central districts of the north island. After the Maori troubles ceased to be effective barriers to progress, the limiting factor has always been transport. As roads and then railways open up the country, settlement passes through fairly well-defined stages, from the rough and ready use of natural pastures for the grazing of sheep and store cattle to more highly organised mixed farming and, in specially favourable areas, intensive dairying.

The settlement which was diverted into the south island has always been governed by the dominant influence of the mountain chain which runs the length of the island. At its narrowest, in the centre of the island, this mountain system is about sixty miles wide. In the south-west, and again in the north, it spreads more widely. Within it there are no less than two hundred and twenty-eight named peaks over 7,000 feet in height, as against three in the whole north island. In the south these peaks run right to the water's edge in the fiord country. A narrow plain, with an annual rainfall of 70 to 100 inches, extends along the west coast in the middle of the island, narrowing still further towards the north. This plain, like the river valleys in Otago on the eastern side of the mountains, was proved in the sixties to contain rich alluvial gold-fields, the rush to which put New Zealand on its feet at a critical stage in its history. Later, in the seventies, the valuable coal-fields on the west coast were developed, and in more recent years still, dairying has made some progress there.

The most important development of the south island, however, has come from the utilisation of its eastern plains and foothills for pastoral purposes. When progress was checked in the north island, pioneers began to follow the example of Australian squatters, some of whom, in fact, led the new development, by pushing out over these plains and depasturing flocks upon land which was both readily accessible and available upon easy terms under the pastoral leasehold system.

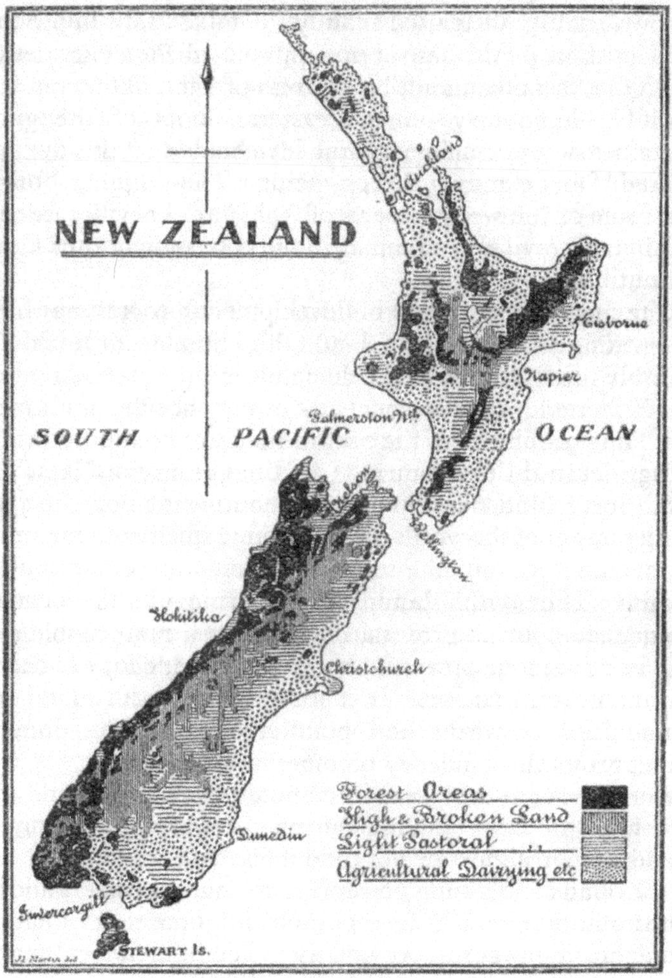

LAND UTILISATION IN NEW ZEALAND

By this time the last of the Wakefield settlements had been planted at Dunedin and Christchurch. Around these centres there were compact areas of small agricultural farms, but outside those areas large-scale sheep-runs were built up.

A comparison of the maps which show the character of the land and the tenures under which it is now held indicates very clearly the nature of subsequent progress. All the good and accessible land on the coastal plains has passed into freehold ownership and is used mainly for mixed farming. Some small portion of this has been repurchased for closer settlement. On the other hand, large areas of the lighter and less accessible hill-country on the eastern slopes of the great mountain system remain pastoral leaseholds to this day, and are used for extensive sheep-grazing. The higher, broken areas, some of the western parts of which are heavily forested, remain, and are likely to remain, in the possession of the Crown and unutilised.

In the most recent period of development, progress has been most striking in the north island, the climate of which has admirably fitted it to meet the demands of the external market for refrigerated produce such as butter, cheese, and frozen meat. The possibilities of the south island are bound up rather with agricultural development. It is the granary of New Zealand. North island development is contingent upon the purchasing power of the world's market being sufficient to maintain the demand for animal products, which are comparatively expensive. The south island, while sharing in the northern dependence upon the external market, has a more stable element in its economic prospect because of its tendency to depend more upon local markets. It exports to the north island such commodities as wheat and potatoes, and as the domestic market grows this tendency becomes more important.

Water-power is fairly well distributed over both islands and is perhaps the chief manufacturing asset, compensating in some degree for high costs of production and transport of coal. New Zealand's isolation, however, its small market, and the decentralisation which is geographically necessary, hamper manufacturing progress very greatly. The limited local market is further broken up, not only by the difficulty of concentration to give the economies of large-scale production, but by high transport costs from point to point. It is often cheaper and easier to import goods from overseas than to ship them from one place to another in New Zealand.

There are few lands, therefore, where dominant geographical

considerations so obviously determine economic organisation. The whole history of New Zealand has been shaped by its isolation, its forests, and its mountains. Its present organisation, a decentralised rural democracy dependent in an uncommon degree upon an external market at the other side of the world, is equally determined by its geographical resources and situation. There is as much dissimilarity between Australia and New Zealand in this respect as Siegfried noted in their geography. The economic development of New Zealand has radiated from many centres, mostly ports. There is a striking absence of urban concentration and a comparatively weak development of manufacturing industry. These facts colour the whole political outlook of the Dominion, in imperial as well as local politics. They are implicit in the geographical structure of the country.

The Period of Settlement, 1840–50

The first ten years of organised settlement were years of economic struggle and disappointment. From the arrival of the first settlers at Wellington on January 22, 1840, to that of the first four ships of the Canterbury Association, last off-shoot of the New Zealand Company, on December 16, 1850, the economic circumstances both of the Company and of its settlers were very difficult. There is fortunately no need even to sketch the history of that heroic Elizabethan enterprise, the New Zealand Company, or of its founder and champion, Edward Gibbon Wakefield. Recent historical research, delving in the mass of Parliamentary and other official records, newspaper controversies, private diaries and papers, to say nothing of the voluminous mass of secondary literature, has provided a reasonably clear picture of the tangled relations between the Company, the missionary societies, and the Colonial Office in England and their representatives, the Governor, the missionaries, and the settlers in New Zealand. There can be no better illustration of the traditional muddle out of which the Empire has grown. (3)

For the most part these very complicated and heated disputes centred round the welfare of the Maoris and the disposal of the native lands. The narrative story of the period does not need to be retold, and the present economic significance of its related problems is discussed in succeeding chapters. There is no need, therefore, at this point to do more than summarise in broadest outline the economic progress achieved in the first decade.

By 1850 there were settlements in Wellington, Taranaki, Nelson, Wanganui, Otago, and Canterbury, all of the Wakefield model, compact, and restricted by the policy of selling land at a uniform and sufficient price per acre. The only other considerable centre of population was the official missionary settlement at Auckland. In addition there were scattered settlers in other areas and, in particular, pioneers were building up the pastoral industry by grazing their flocks on lands leased cheaply from the Crown in areas outside the Wakefield settlement boundaries. These early pastoralists were men of substantial capital, either squatters from Australia or the wealthier immigrants from the agricultural settlements. They led the way to New Zealand's pastoral age.

The six Wakefield colonies were isolated from one another and from Auckland, and in consequence developed a considerable amount of separatism, the influence of which can be traced even at the present time in a healthy provincialism, which prevents any one centre from dominating New Zealand. There are many striking resemblances between these settlements and the first American colonies. Isolated groups developed in comparative independence and soon began to display strong community spirit, in many instances reinforced by deep religious sentiment. The level of ability and character among the settlers was uncommonly high and was displayed to full advantage in meeting the hardships of the first years of settlement, as well as in the political invention displayed in the struggle towards self-government. Both in New England and in New Zealand the settlers were harassed by warlike native tribes, and in both cases they were forced back to the primitive necessity of wringing subsistence from a virgin soil. Later immigration has for a time overlain the austere idealism of the pioneers, but in New Zealand there are some indications that their spirit may reconquer the later generations. What the Pilgrim Fathers have meant and mean to New England, the pioneer settlers are beginning to mean to New Zealand.

In 1851 (Sir) William Fox was in England as the representative of the colonies in their agitation for a charter of self-government. He published in that year a small descriptive book entitled significantly *The Six Colonies of New Zealand*. In it he gives a vivid picture of the isolation of each of the settlements and the great difficulties of communication between them. His scathing criticism of the official settlement at Auckland is typical of the colonists' resentment against the restrictions imposed by the Colonial Office and the Governor upon their economic expansion.

It is not difficult to understand their resentment. The whole basis upon which the New Zealand Company had been organised was the sale of land at a "uniform and sufficient price" to intending settlers. Much land had been sold in England, even before the Company's agents had bought any from the Maoris. To arrive in New Zealand and find the Company's purchases invalidated by the Governor, in consequence of a treaty hastily entered into with the natives, was a bitter experience. Neither the Governor nor the Company officials had appreciated the complexity of the customary land tenures to which the Maoris clung so tenaciously. Before allowing any land sales to be validated the Governor awaited the report of a commission, and as the work of this commission dragged through the years the settlers and the Company were forced into economic distress.

Wherever hasty action was taken to occupy or even survey land which had been bought by the settlers in good faith before leaving England, the watchful and suspicious Maoris resorted to war. At Wairau, in the Hutt Valley, on the Wanganui, as well as in the northern peninsula, there were outbreaks of sudden reprisals, "utu" taken by the natives in resentment of "Pakeha" (white) encroachment on their rights. In these years, too, were sown the seeds of future trouble in Taranaki, and throughout Maoridom generally there spread alarm and resentment against Pakeha methods.

Besides these administrative and native difficulties the infant settlements struggled under the handicap of their situation. Edward Gibbon Wakefield and his fellow theorists had correctly foreseen the central importance of the Cook Strait region. But they did not appreciate the practical difficulties of settlement and had sent settlers to four points, Wellington, New

Plymouth, Wanganui, and Nelson, none of which was suitable for rapid development at this stage. Besides the active resentment of numerous and hostile native tribes, the settlers had in each case to contend with mountainous and densely wooded hinterlands. The only fertile open valleys were already in Maori possession and cultivation, and it is significant that to this day the Maoris date their hostility to the Pakehas from the time when the first Wellington settlers attempted to eject the Maori occupants of lands which the Company claimed to have bought in the Hutt Valley.

Economic development would in any case have been slow in this period before the most profitable avenues of future progress had been discovered. The first settlers had visions of founding self-sufficient communities. Some of them brought machinery with which to establish such manufactures as rope-walks. Only through hard experience could they learn that division of labour is governed by the extent of the market. Inevitably they were forced back upon cultivation of the land; but access to the land was denied them. In any case their only considerable market, Great Britain, was half-way round the world and means of communication were slow and precarious.

It is little wonder, therefore, that the infant settlements quickly became scenes of unemployment and distress. Matters were not improved by Governor Fitzroy's experiments in 1845 with inconvertible debentures.(4) The best commentary upon the economic state of the colony six years after its foundation is to be found in the laconic report of the directors of the Union Bank of Australia in July 1846 that "the branches in New Zealand have been greatly reduced during the half-year, and may now be regarded rather as small exchange agencies than as Branch Banks. The Inspector has expressed his determination not to allow them to be increased until he is fully satisfied of the security and prosperity of those colonies." Rates of interest ranging to 15 per cent. gave a further practical indication of the estimate bankers placed upon the risks involved in colonial enterprises.

This was, however, the lowest depth. In 1844 the first considerable beginning had been made in the pastoral industry. A new governor, afterwards to become famous as Sir George Grey, arrived in 1845 and effected drastic reforms in the public finances. He had more liberal support financially from the Home Government, and was able to bring the Maori wars to a quick close and thereafter to buy large areas of Maori land. The New Zealand Company also received a new lease of life by its compact with the Colonial Office in 1846. Its finances were considerably relieved by Governmental advances, and Wakefield embarked upon his last colonial ventures, settling Otago in 1848 and Canterbury in 1850. Both these colonies were planted in the more open south island, the bulk of which had been bought from the Maoris in 1848. The circumstances under which they were founded were more favourable also, and they escaped the worst of the tribulations of the four earlier settlements.

The Period of the Gold Discoveries, 1851–69

By 1850, therefore, the main stream of economic development was fairly clear. Wherever the settlers were able to obtain access to the land, they were pushing out beyond the restricted boundaries of the high-priced Company lands in order to graze sheep upon land which they could obtain from the Government upon pastoral licence. The land-purchase policies by which the Government bought large areas from the Maoris will be treated in Chapter II, the problem of tenure which arose as the land was alienated to private ownership in Chapter III, and the economic development of the pastoral industry in Chapter IV. It is sufficient here to point out that wherever the Government was able to buy land, as in the Wairarapa district outside of Wellington and in the south island, sheep-farmers took out pastoral licences for large runs and grazed their flocks over the unfenced, unimproved native pastures. The first considerable flocks had been imported by Bidwill in 1843 and (Sir) Charles Clifford in 1844. Three years later Clifford and his partner, Weld, drove sheep from Port Underwood to the plains north of Canterbury, and by 1850 they had 11,000 sheep on their station at Flaxbourne.

At this time wool was the main item of export. Some by-products could be obtained at the end of a sheep's career. There were "boiling-down" works at which skins, tallow, fertiliser, and similar products were produced; but until the advent of refrigeration in the eighties, wool remained the great staple product of the pastoral industry. Flocks were allowed to multiply and some deterioration set in. By 1851 there were almost a quarter of a million sheep in the country, by 1861 there were two and three quarter millions, in 1871 there were almost ten millions. The export of wool in 1853, the first year in which trade statistics were recorded for the whole colony, was valued at £67,000; ten years later it had grown to £830,000, and by 1873 it was £2,702,000. New Zealand had discovered the golden fleece.

Until direct and regular steamer communication was opened up with England in the seventies, the great bulk of New Zealand trade went through Sydney. It was natural, therefore, that the colony should participate directly in the gain that resulted from the Australian gold discoveries in the early fifties. Temporarily the new demands created by these discoveries placed the New Zealand farming industries upon a much sounder basis. The disturbance of agriculture in Australia by the rush to the gold-fields, the new demands created by the great rush of immigration and by the increased purchasing power made available, all reacted in the most favourable manner upon New Zealand trade. The rise in the general price-level, which was to become worldwide, was marked and even extravagant in markets where men used gold-dust and small nuggets as current coin.

> The chief effect of such an immediate rise in prices [says Saunders] was to beneficially direct the settlers to agricultural pursuits, and to make such pursuits profitable for many years, as still higher prices were quoted in 1855 and 1859. All wages rose, all accessible good land was in great demand, the dealers in produce found the advantage of prices rising in the article as it passed through their hands, live stock increased in value, shipping was profitably employed, and the general prosperity added not a little to the reputation of the Government and the Governor under whom it had occurred. (5)

One of the most important aspects of this beneficent revolution lay in the fact that it affected the agricultural farmers of the Wakefield settlements more immediately and more favourably than the sheep-farmers of the outside areas. The economic situation of the country was precarious as long as wool was almost the only considerable export. The political power thrown into the hands of the great sheep-owners under such circumstances was to prove intolerable at a later period. In the fifties, however, while wool participated in the general rise of prices, it was the demand for flour, live stock, grain, potatoes, and other food-stuffs which was mainly responsible for the general prosperity of New Zealand.

In 1857 gold was discovered in the Nelson Province, but no large rush occurred until in 1861 Gabriel Read discovered the field that was to bear his name, Gabriel's Gully, near Tuapeka, in the Otago Province. The Australian alluvial fields were petering out and a great rush set in. Pyke has described the result.

> The excitement became intense. Thousands were bitten by the gold-fever and abandoned their ordinary pursuits to try their luck at the diggings. The contagion spread to the adjacent provinces, to the north island, and finally to Australia and the Australian colonies. Then commenced one of those startling revolutions which, under the direction of an all-wise Providence, are everywhere wrought by the discovery of gold. In a few months Otago was elevated from the position of a comparatively unknown settlement to the foremost rank among the provinces of New Zealand. In 1860 only sixty-nine vessels were entered inwards. In the following year 256 vessels, many of them of large tonnage, arrived at the port. The population, computed in December 1860 at 12,691, had increased by December 1861 to 30,269 souls. The revenue [provincial] advanced from £83,046, the figure for the financial year ending September 30, 1861, to £280,097 in 1862.(6)

Rush succeeded rush as new fields were opened up not only in Otago but in Westland, which at that time formed a part of the Canterbury Province. For a time Hokitika was the foremost port of the colony and a great population rapidly covered the west coast of the south island.

The boom of the gold-rushes, however, was comparatively short-lived. The richest deposits of alluvial gold were worked out within a decade, and by 1869 depression and unemployment were worse in Dunedin than they had been since the settlement was founded in 1848. Few of the gold-diggers were permanently enriched: many of them perished from the hardships of winter on the exposed uplands, many were drowned crossing the treacherous rivers of the west coast, most endured privations and toil for which their rewards were inadequate. The cost of living was exorbitantly high. Even in Dunedin, in the early sixties, flour was £44 to £52 a ton; butter, 2s. 6d.

per lb.; meat 10d. to 13d. per lb. At Tuapeka prices were much higher, if only because of the costs of transport.

The gain which New Zealand received from the gold-rushes was the influx of new immigrants and the capital they brought in with them, rather than the actual value of the gold they produced. Between 1861 and 1870 the population grew from 99,021 to 248,400, the greatest gain being in 1863, when more than 35,000 new immigrants entered the country. These were men in the prime of life, adventurous and hardy, industrious and on the whole law-abiding. Their industry enriched the country immediately. In 1860 the total exports had been half a million pounds, in 1863, the year in which the gold production and export reached its peak, exports had increased to four and a half million pounds. This increase, however, is dwarfed by the great amounts of capital which accompanied the influx of immigrants. Imports in the same period rose from one and a half to seven million pounds in value.

There were other incidental benefits also, and particularly the abounding revenue which flowed in to the provincial treasuries from the sale of land as well as from gold duties. It was in this period that Canterbury and Otago, the chief beneficiaries in this respect, consolidated their economic leadership. The north island provinces were harassed by the long-drawn-out and costly Maori wars, which broke out in 1860 and continued spasmodically until 1872. The almost complete cessation of land sales, and the psychological check to development added to the actual destruction, almost destroyed the prosperity of the north island. Meanwhile Otago and Canterbury were building roads and even railways, and undertaking great public works. The first railway line was opened from Christchurch in 1863, and a tunnel was shortly afterwards put through the Port Hills to Lyttelton. The dominance of these two south island provinces is one of the important facts to remember in the ensuing period. Not until 1901 did the population of the north island again surpass that of the south.

It is important also to emphasise again that one of the chief effects of the gold-rushes both in Australia and in New Zealand itself was to stimulate the demand for the products of agricultural farming in the Wakefield settlements. When that demand began to fall off towards the end of the sixties the precarious economic situation of the colony began to be revealed. There had been hints of that situation as early as 1861, at the very beginning of the gold-rushes. In that year a petition signed by 1,010 unemployed in Dunedin was presented to the Otago Provincial Council, demanding in no uncertain terms to be provided with livelihood, or at least the means of obtaining it. Their truculent manifesto demanded that the Council provide money for public works to give employment.

This was precisely the kind of situation of which the older colonists had been fearful; but they were powerless to avert it. The newer immigrants were in the majority, and as the production of gold fell off after 1865, the demand for Governmental action became more and more insistent. Imports fell steadily from their peak £7,024,674 in 1863 to £4,078,193 in 1871, while exports increased slowly at about the same rate as the population. By 1870, imports and exports were approximately equal again, the boom of the gold-rushes was over, and New Zealand was facing the painful necessity of producing a surplus of exports to pay interest on its debts.

Borrowing, Boom, and Depression, 1870–95

The patient endurance of difficult economic situations of this character seems almost impossible to a democracy. The necessity of rigid economy, both public and private, a steady pressure of taxation, and the seemingly inevitable unemployment and social distress, are very irksome, particularly in young countries like New Zealand, which have large resources awaiting development.

Against the warnings of the more conservative leaders of the older colonists, a policy substantially following the lines proposed by the unemployed petition in Dunedin in 1861 was proposed to the General Assembly by Julius Vogel, who had come to Dunedin as a journalist in the early sixties, was elected Member for Dunedin in 1863, and became Colonial Treasurer in 1879. His proposal, which followed previous schemes outlined by Domett, Reader Wood, and Fitzherbert,(7) simply was to use the credit of the whole colony to borrow substantial sums to be used for the encouragement of immigration and the building of public works. There was no inherent economic fallacy in this policy, and all that can be said against it and its proponent was that it came at an unfortunate time and was carried to lengths beyond economic defence. Borrowing for development is perfectly legitimate and economically sound policy in a young country provided the loans are floated conservatively at opportune moments and the expenditure from them is carefully controlled.

It so happened that the years 1870 and 1873 were the last good years of rising prices before the fall in the price-level set in which was to continue till 1894. The trade boom following the Franco-Prussian War accentuated that rise in prices. After the lean years of the late sixties the unwonted prosperity, further enhanced by the expenditure within New Zealand of the first borrowed money, went like new wine to the heads of the political leaders of the day. Conservative warnings passed unheeded as jeremiads. Members of all parties and from all districts joined in the scramble. Canterbury and Otago, having the greatest populations and the most members, got the lion's share of the money, which was spent "politically rather than wisely". The most extravagant schemes of development were entertained, railways were built which have never paid interest on their capital expenditure from that day to this, land speculation went to unprecedented lengths. A setback in prices in 1874, which might have served as a warning, went unheeded, and in 1878 the boom reached its height. The crash came in the following year, and the whole of the next decade was a gloomy period of depression and retrenchment.

The political history of this period has been the subject of much recrimination. Vogel, at one time the idol of New Zealand, was and still is subjected to the harshest criticism and even abuse.(8) Neither his financial ability nor the purity of his motives is, however, of especial interest to the economic historian, who is primarily concerned with the effect of the policies he initiated upon the economic prosperity of the country. It has been urged, with some justice, that the worst of the speculative aspects of the boom came after he was no longer at the Treasury. It is also true that many of the safeguards he urged were swept away by the House. In particular his original proposals provided for the setting aside of six million acres of land, in the area to be opened up by the projected public works, as an endowment for the repayment of the loans. This sound provision was swept away by the opposition of the Provincialists, who would brook no interference with the right of the provincial legislatures to control the waste lands in their areas. In 1876 Vogel took drastic revenge by destroying these legislatures. The abolition was perhaps inevitable, but the failure to develop in their place a satisfactory system of local government is profoundly regretted now by most students of New Zealand history. It may be conceded that the responsibility for the borrowing boom was shared in by most of the politicians of the day and by the electorate; but it is not likely that Vogel's name will ever be dissociated from it as its originator and chief exponent.

It is often argued that the policy needs no defence, that on balance it was productive of economic benefit to the colony. In particular it is urged, by no less an authority than Mr. Reeves, that most of the evils of this period were due to private speculation, and that it is "due chiefly to the much-criticised public-works policy that New Zealand is now a pleasant and civilised country".(9) But it must be stated that it was the Government's borrowing policy that provided both the incentive to and the means of indulging in the land-gambling which caused the private debts. There could have been no speculative mania nor reckless importation if the large Government loans had not provided a fund for such improvidence. Nor is it possible for an economist to admit that New Zealand could not have become "a pleasant and civilised land" without first impoverishing herself by reckless expenditure.

The actual amounts borrowed were considerable. In 1870 the population of the colony was 248,400, in 1880 it had grown to 484,864. In those ten years the public debt grew from £7,841,891 to £28,583,231. In the same period there were many notable developments. (10) Vogel had real political imagination. To his lasting credit he has the first forest conservation policies, the establishment of the Public Trust Office, and the Government Life Insurance Department. Under his regime a steam shipping service was started to San Francisco in 1870, and a cable connection made with Australia in 1876.

The New Zealand Shipping Company was founded in 1873 and the Union Steam Shipping Company in 1875.

In the four years from 1873–7, 907 miles of railway were completed; in the ten years following, 701 miles were built; in the next ten years 304 miles, and in the ten years ending March 3, 1908, only 416 miles were completed, not because the colony had all the needed railways, nor because none of the projected lines was likely to pay, but chiefly because of the inability of the Government to borrow adequate sums, and this may be traced chiefly to the unprofitable character of the lines already built.(11)

Roads and public works also opened up the country-side and made possible the development of the large-scale wheat-farming which was characteristic of the early eighties, besides preparing the way for the great increase of production which followed the successful experiment in refrigeration in 1882. Banking and commercial organisation, secondary industries and mining, all show substantial development. The national system of education, including the establishment of a federal university, also dates from this period. These are substantial developments in a brief space of time; but the test of their economic validity is to be found in their effect upon productivity. In the absence of adequate domestic statistics the best, and indeed the only possible, test of productivity and of economic prosperity generally is to be found in the statistics of external trade. Domestic production at this period was very small. There were, it is true, some small beginnings of urban industry. Indeed, it is one of the chief criticisms of Vogel's immigration policy that immigrants were badly selected, came out to find land values prohibitive, and remained in the towns to produce unemployment, sweated labour conditions, and finally a demand both for Labour legislation and for tariff protection. Even in 1885, however, the number of workers in the secondary industries was less than 3 per cent. of the population, so that their labours were not a considerable offset to the decline in the country's external trade.

That decline was masked during the boom by the swollen import returns due to the expenditure of borrowed money. The crude returns show large but fluctuating imports rising to a peak of £8¾ millions in the year 1878. The exports meantime increased steadily but more slowly than the increase in population. If the trade returns are corrected for population and for changes in the price-level so as to show the quantitative volume of exports per head, it becomes clear that between 1871 and 1881 productivity declined in the proportion of 120:100. In other words, the boom period witnessed a loss in trading efficiency of approximately 16 per cent.(12)

Nor is this the whole story. It has been emphasised that the one product of overwhelming importance at this stage of New Zealand's development was wool. There were a few years in the early eighties when it appeared probable that large "bonanza" wheat-farms might develop.(13) In 1883 the export of grain reached a peak of £1,287,000; but the rapid development of refrigeration after 1882 encouraged mixed farming, and wheat became again a commodity mainly of domestic consumption. After the success of refrigeration was assured, exports increased rapidly; but even this real and substantial progress was not sufficient to avert the consequences of the borrowing boom. It took until 1888 to reach again the volume of exports per head that had been attained in 1871.

During the eighties, indeed, and after the great development of refrigeration was well under way, the costs of the boom became evident and had to be met. There is a great deal of evidence concerning the depression of domestic industry, but the best quantitative measure of the rigid economy that was necessary is to be found in the decline of imports. Despite increasing production and exports, New Zealand was able to purchase less and less in the markets of the world. The imports fell off absolutely and still more *per capita*, until in the depth of the depression, which was reached in 1888, the volume of imports per head was only 60 per cent. of what it had been in the boom year 1878 and 20 per cent. less than it had been when the boom started in 1870.

These are heavy costs for any community to pay, and it is little wonder that social conditions became steadily worse, until in the years 1889–90 there was a veritable "exodus" from the country, an excess of emigration over immigration. The labour conditions of this period and the financial troubles that culminated in the reconstruction of the Bank of New Zealand will be discussed in subsequent chapters.

Prosperity and Rising Prices, 1895–1921

The economic problems which are discussed in detail in the remainder of this book arose in the most recent period of prosperity which followed the turn of prices in 1895. The financial and economic strains of the previous period had gathered together all the forces of discontent in a massed attack upon the Conservatives, who held political power and were commonly regarded as representative of the "landowning oligarchy". Trade-unionism, the movement for women's suffrage, the temperance movement, were reinforced in their radical demands by the advocates of tariff protection, theoretical Socialism, and above all by the increasing numbers of people with a real land-hunger. The eighties were a period of intense political agitation. The culmination of the long depression in the labour troubles and the financial crash that ushered in the last decade of the century gave point and purpose to the agitation. The election of 1890 placed the Liberal-Labour Party in power, and their sweeping victory three years later confirmed their mandate. The remainder of the century was occupied in placing most of their programme of experimental legislation on the statute-books. Factory Acts leading to a complete labour code, drastic land legislation, compulsory industrial arbitration, old-age pensions, and many other novel measures followed each other in rapid succession. The attention of social scientists all over the world was attracted to these experiments, and most of the books descriptive of New Zealand economic problems were written under their shadow, thus giving the country a reputation for socialistic tendencies, which is strangely at variance with its true character.

The fact is that this legislation was really the accumulated result of many years of struggle and resentment against a privileged landowning class in a time of intense depression and economic distress. Not unnaturally the discontent came to a head just when the depression reached its lowest depth. Before the Radical Party could get its legislative programme translated into effective administration the economic circumstances had greatly improved, so that the experiments in State Socialism were carried through into the period of prosperity.

It is quite understandable, also, that the new Government should have claimed and received a good deal of credit for the onset of prosperity, though to an economist this seems to have been due only in slight degree, if at all, to political causes.

The chief cause, indeed, is very clearly the upward turn of the price-level in 1895 and the steady rise in prices thereafter, with only one major setback in 1907, until the post-war boom broke in 1921. Minor depressions occurred after the South African War, and again in 1904 and in 1913. Each of these, as well as the great crisis of 1907, reacted upon New Zealand's prosperity; but they were only temporary checks, and the rising tide of prices carried New Zealand along with buoyant prosperity.

These more favourable price conditions enabled the Dominion to exploit the new industries made possible by the refrigerating processes, now well established scientifically and thoroughly organised commercially. There was a subtle but very important change-over from sheep-farming for wool to more mixed farming in which frozen meat, butter, and cheese assumed greater and greater importance. The farmers supplemented their wool cheques by the sale of fat lambs, breeders paid more attention to the carcass as well as to the fleece of the sheep, and the revolution went right down into such technical matters as the improvement of pastures. Moreover, a great new industry was made possible by the fact that butter, cheese, and other milk products could now be transported half-way round the world to the great European markets. The rapid expansion of dairying has been one of the most important characteristics of New Zealand economic development in the last forty years. It has meant not only that the range of production has been broadened and made more stable, but also that more intensive farming has been possible. Closer settlement, better cultivation, the use of more machine-power, better organisation, and more concentrated labour have meant a substantial increase in productivity.

The prosperity of New Zealand in the pre-war period was based securely upon a genuine increase in productivity, aided and intensified by more favourable prices. Not only were prices rising, but the relative shortage of animal products in the markets of the world placed New Zealand in an especially favourable position. It is not to be wondered at, therefore, that the pastoral industries assumed a more and more dominating position in the economic life of the Dominion. There was some revival of gold exports in the years round about 1900, owing to the opening of the deep-level quartz-mines in the north island, and the use of improved technical processes in the extraction of the gold. During the South African War, also, there was a temporary spurt in the production of grain; but these were relatively minor incidents, and it is broadly true to say that there has been a marked tendency, continuing till the present time, for New Zealand to concentrate more and more on pastoral production, and particularly upon the dairying industry.

There is one aspect of this development which deserves passing notice. The land legislation of the early nineties was the outcome mainly of land monopoly, which was blocking the progress of the south island. There has been a good deal of closer settlement in the south island provinces since that time; but the great increases of production that have occurred have been mainly due to the opening up of the north island. Vigorous land-purchase policies and confiscation after the Maori wars, road building and railway development, but above all, the encouragement to dairying caused by refrigeration and higher prices, began a steady drift from south to north just before the end of the century. In 1901, for the first time in more than forty years, the population of the north island exceeded that of the south. In the last census—1926—61·87 per cent. of the population was shown as resident in the north island.

The year 1906 is memorable in New Zealand politics. By a curious coincidence the great chief of the Liberal-Labour Party, Seddon, died in that year when economic conditions had arrived at the point where they began to undermine his policies. The next six years till 1912, when the Reform Party came into power backed mainly by the small farmers of the north island, are years of political interregnum. In 1906 the index of land values rose again to the level which had been reached in the boom year 1878. It was more than a coincidence, therefore, that this year should have seen the winding up of the Assets Realisation Board, which had taken over the mortgaged lands of the Bank of New Zealand. Rising prices had at last wiped out the burden of the great depression. By this time, also, the first impetus of the State Socialist experiments was obviously spent, the trade unions broke away from their former allies and organised the Labour Party; in their industrial affairs, also, they challenged the control of the Arbitration Court and began the first of a series of bitter strikes.

The years following 1906, therefore, were years of political compromise. The land legislation was overhauled and on the whole weakened in 1907. Amendments to the arbitration system were made, and kites were flown by influential ministers suggesting further amendments, without, however, appeasing the growing Labour opposition to the Court.(14) In 1912 the change of political fortunes was complete, and the new Government lost no time in taking up the Labour challenge and also in reversing the trend of land legislation away from leasehold and back to the freehold. Before the Great War began, prosperity had undermined the support of the so-called experimental legislation, which had been fashioned in a time of economic distress. The pathological necessity for such legislation had passed away and the true conservative temper of New Zealand stood revealed. A nation of prosperous farmers seldom evinces radical tendencies and New Zealand had proved no exception to the rule.

The advent of the Great War in 1914 found New Zealand a contented, prosperous country, whose wealth was based mainly upon the increasing productivity of the pastoral industries. There is some evidence that productivity was not increasing after about 1910 in anything like the proportion which had been evident for the previous two decades.(15) With prosperity had come slackening of effort. There was an increasing drift to the towns, the urban industries were growing relatively faster than the primary rural industries, the professional and commercial occupations increased disproportionately, and there was a disturbing tendency towards excessive public borrowing.

These facts were masked by the constantly rising level of prices, which brought greater and greater wealth to the

Dominion. Judged by any monetary test, the pre-war period was one of great prosperity. Savings-bank returns, insurances, overseas trade, land values, income-tax returns—all the recognised tests of prosperity tell the same story. Most convincing of all is the steady and rapid increase of the population, both by natural increase and by immigration. For the forty years preceding 1921 the population of New Zealand was increasing at the steady cumulative rate of 12·11 per cent. every five years, which is a faster rate than that recorded in the same period for any other country in the world.(16)

While there was naturally some unsettlement and uneasiness at the outbreak of the war, and while New Zealand took her full share both by the provision of fighting men and by shouldering a heavy deadweight burden of debt, yet it is probably true that on balance she received some economic gain from war conditions. The war demands for raw materials and food-stuffs, together with the further steep rise in the price-level, contributed materially to her enrichment. At the end of the war, therefore, her economic position was enviably sound.

It was probably inevitable that the post-war inflation of prices, and the consequential boom, which was worldwide, should have affected New Zealand. Economic and financial fluctuations of this character are inevitably transmitted to the Dominion from Great Britain by reason of the banking and monetary system, by which the New Zealand currency is, within narrow limits, pegged to the pound sterling.(17) It will be argued in a later chapter, however, that the post-war boom in New Zealand was greatly aggravated by unsound public finance, and particularly by lavish borrowing for public works and for the purchase of lands upon which to carry out a costly policy of repatriating the returning soldiers.

Whatever the causes, the speculative boom in land values and all the related hectic manifestations of fictitious prosperity reached unprecedented heights in 1920. Butter-fat was selling at 2s. 6d. per lb., and dairying land was being sold for prices that now seem fantastic. This was the exaggerated culmination of a quarter of a century of prosperity built upon a price-level which had been rising so long that it was expected not only to keep on rising, but to rise ever faster and faster.

The Strain of Falling Prices, 1921

The denouement came suddenly in a collapse of export prices in the season 1920–1. To the farmers sitting in dismayed silence in the galleries listening to the wool-buyers bidding dispiritedly for odd lots, the new level of prices spelt difficulty if not bankruptcy. Those who had bought land at high values, based upon the high prices of the years immediately preceding, found their returns quite inadequate to meet their heavy obligations. The fall in dairy prices, as always, lagged by a year, but when it came was even more disastrous, since speculation had been worse in the dairying industry. Prices revived in the years 1923–5, but slumped again heavily in 1926 and 1927. Through the revivals and slumps of this whole period there runs a definite downward drag of the price-level, and in consequence there are strains and stresses through the whole economic structure of the Dominion.

It has become clearer than ever that under cover of the pre-war prosperity there had been a loosening of efficiency and a general tendency to demand higher standards of living for less effort and output. There has been an elaboration of commercial and Governmental services which may prove to be greater than the community can support; labour conditions have greatly improved, and standards of living, in such matters as housing and motor-cars, have risen sharply. There was in the period of prosperity, also, some tendency to less efficient farming under easier conditions. It resulted naturally from the speculative attitude adopted by farmers in times of rising prices. If one eye is firmly fixed on the property market, preparation for the produce market is apt to suffer.

In a rising market, also, the tendency is for the speculative value of land to keep well ahead of its actual productive value, and the opportunity is always present for successful speculators to retire early from actual production and form a leisured class, living in the towns upon receipts of interest from mortgage and investment.(18)

The truth of the matter seems to be that the forces of unsettlement due to land speculation, lavish public borrowing, and private extravagance were sufficient just before and during the war and post-war boom to check the gain in production from natural advantages in dairying. The high prices of the boom period served to cover up an increasing relative decline in productivity. What were merely hidden weaknesses in a time of prosperity become serious drains in adversity, and New Zealand is facing the necessity of extensive readjustments in almost every department of her economic life.

The most fundamental difficulty has been and still is the reduction of farming costs (including mortgage interest) to levels comparable with the new levels of export prices.(19) Despite the fluctuating and at times very high prices of some recent years, the farming industries as a whole have suffered heavily. There have been and must still be reductions in land values: some land has gone out of cultivation, a great deal more has not been adequately worked for lack of adequate capital, and generally there has been a marked economic weakness in the rural industries which has been reflected in a drastic curtailment of rural employment.

This in turn has concentrated unemployment in the towns and so raised problems of wages and of poor relief. The immigration policies of the Government have been strongly attacked and temporarily restricted. The arbitration system, caught between economic stringency and high costs of living, has not escaped drastic and sustained criticism.

The urban industries, and some of the rural industries, notably wheat-farming (which has become dependent upon the local market), have gone to the Government for assistance, mainly in the form of tariff protection. The rural industries, generally, have used their political power to push through experimental measures of agrarian Socialism such as legislation establishing various pools, and the payment of subsidies upon such subsidiary exports as fruit, eggs, and honey. Their agitation for increased rural credit facilities has as yet been less successful, though a beginning has been made on sound conservative lines and experiments in the reorganisation of long-term mortgages are now being carried out.

The public finances have not escaped some measure of disorganisation. The burden of deadweight debt was greatly increased by the war, and taxation remains high. In a time of high taxation and economic stringency inequities become manifest, and these have been the subject of much critical discussion in recent years.

Such are the economic problems which have been revealed by the recent fall in prices. The remaining chapters of this book are devoted to a more detailed examination of some of the more important of them. Such an examination is easier and more profitable in a time like the present, when a sudden change of fortune has bared weaknesses which might not be so apparent in times of easier prosperity. But it would be quite false to conclude therefrom that New Zealand is in a state of economic distress and social disorganisation. There has been a sharp descent from the heights of fictitious prosperity achieved in the boom period, and the fall has been cruelly hard on certain sections of the population. But it still remains true that New Zealand is in a very enviable position compared with other lands. Population still increases very fast and immigrants are still attracted by the better conditions obtainable there. The rate of infant mortality, test *par excellence* of social prosperity, is the lowest in the world, and still falling. In her volume of overseas trade New Zealand surpasses any other country. Her wealth per head is surpassed only by the United States of America. It would be difficult to find any other country where wealth is more evenly shared, and this fact in itself is sufficient to lend interest to the problems of economic and social organisation discussed below.

The Influence of the External Market

The main periods of economic development indicated in the preceding sections tend to precede and foreshadow political events. From the political and constitutional point of view the important events of New Zealand history are the appointment of the first Governor in 1840, the inauguration of responsible government in 1852, the abolition of the provincial legislatures in 1876, the advent to power of the Liberal-Labour Party in 1891, and the triumph of their opponents in 1912. The interaction of political and economic events is very clear in a new country, but the economic historian naturally finds somewhat different landmarks from those which attract the attention of the political theorist.

It will be obvious that the division of the economic history of New Zealand into five periods, beginning in 1840, 1851, 1870, 1895, and 1921, corresponds roughly with similar periods marking fluctuations in the long-term trend of the world-level of prices. New Zealand was founded at a time when prices had been falling for many years. The first ten years of settlement, from 1840 to 1850, were rendered more difficult by the depressing effects of falling prices. The discoveries of gold in California and Australia were partly responsible for causing the price-level to rise in the fifties and sixties, and this undoubtedly was a main cause of the first period of prosperity during the gold-rush period. The adoption of a gold-standard currency by Germany after the Franco-Prussian War was the chief proximate cause of that trend being reversed. From 1874 prices fell steadily, and as they fell, New Zealand lapsed into deeper and deeper depression. The gold discoveries in the Transvaal marked another turning-point in the value of gold in relation to goods in general, and prices moved upwards after 1895. This rising tendency of prices was in evidence with few checks until 1921, and prosperity was general in New Zealand during this time. Since 1921 violent fluctuations have been followed by a downward drag of the price-level, and the strain so caused has laid bare many latent weaknesses in the economic organisation of the Dominion.

To state this coincidence of New Zealand development with the movements of the general level of world-prices is to do no more than draw attention to the fact that progress in New Zealand is largely dependent upon economic conditions in the outside world, and especially in her chief market, Great Britain. This does not mean that the historian can neglect significant happenings within New Zealand itself, such, for example, as the outbreak of Maori wars, which drove settlement into the southern provinces; the subsequent development of the north island, which in a later period reversed the whole political and economic outlook of the country; the creation of new industries by such inventions as refrigeration, and the growth of domestic industry in general. Political policies also, such as the abolition of the provincial system, have not been without important economic reactions. But it remains broadly true that probably the most significant factor affecting the fluctuations of prosperity in the Dominion is the influence of the external market for her products. The organisation of her economic life, therefore, is most conveniently and profitably studied in the setting provided by her place in a world-economy.

The fluctuations of the price-level are important to any country which like New Zealand is necessarily both a primary producer and a borrower. In a time of rising prices her exports, mainly raw materials and food-stuffs handled in bulk wholesale markets, are sold for prices which catch the upward tendency of the market at least a year before the consequential imports—manufactured goods for the most part—can filter through the retail markets and put up costs in the Dominion. When the rising tendency is continued year after year, as it was from 1895 to 1921, certain fixed costs of production, notably interest on capital borrowed from abroad at a fixed rate for long periods, become less burdensome. With the greatest overseas trade per head of any country in the world, and a very large overseas indebtedness both public and private, New Zealand is affected more than most countries by price movements, or as modern economists phrase it, by variations in the "real terms of international trade". Her domestic development is as yet too small to provide a very effective counterpoise to fluctuations in external conditions. Moreover, the great bulk of her produce is exported to the London market, which itself is peculiarly sensitive to international influences. Broadly speaking, therefore, it may be said that a rising price-level brings prosperity, and a price-level which tends to fall brings economic stringency.

There is a larger sense also, in which the whole economic development of New Zealand may be regarded as part of the process of the industrialisation of Great Britain. During the nineteenth century a new economic world has been called into existence to redress the balance of the old. An urbanised and industrialised Europe has needed new sources of food-stuffs and raw materials, and the opening up of new markets and avenues for investment. The rapid economic progress of New Zealand affords an excellent illustration of the impact of these needs upon a virgin undeveloped land.

There is some temptation to forget that from the beginning of British colonisation a native question has existed in New Zealand. At the present time the Maoris are so outnumbered that they tend to be regarded merely as romantic survivors of an interesting but passing race. Yet New Zealand affords a classic illustration of "economic imperialism". There are few better examples of the interaction of trading enterprise with missionary endeavour and colonising initiative. It is to be remembered that the period in which New Zealand was settled was one of the most aggressive periods of British overseas expansion. That great up-welling of national vitality which followed the increased command over natural resources which we now call the Industrial Revolution found vent both in vigorous trading and in missionary activity, as well as in colonisation.

It is more than a coincidence that the same year, 1840, which saw the first arrival of colonists in New Zealand was the year in which Britain fought the war which first opened up the ports of China to European commerce. Both events proceeded from the same economic situation in Great Britain. The coincidence, moreover, provokes the reflection that the economic forces which awoke these widely separated regions to new life have eventually brought them into contact with each other as well as with Europe. The economic history of New Zealand is an episode in the creation of a new world in which the Pacific Ocean is destined to play an increasingly important part.

CHAPTER II

THE ECONOMIC STATUS OF THE MAORIS

THE RACIAL HERITAGE

The Maoris have provided an element of romance and colour in the history of New Zealand of which full advantage has been taken by many writers.(1) Their feats of seamanship and exploration, the savage outrages and cannibal feasts in the first period of contact with Europeans, the murderous tribal warfare that followed the introduction of firearms, and the gallant struggle made to preserve their lands from Pakeha aggression—these have often been described. In the attention paid to such picturesque episodes, however, something less than justice has been done to the less romantic but more important aspects of Maori life and character which emerge from a study of their economic problems. The day of the warrior is long past. The Maori at the present time faces baffling problems of social and economic reorganisation. He must adjust himself to a civilisation centuries removed from that in which his neolithic ancestors lived only a few short generations ago. As a leading chief has recently put it, he must start out again on a new voyage of discovery, to discover and settle in the realities of his new world.

It is important, therefore, to emphasise the fact that the Maori life of pre-European days was laborious and highly organised. It was not a continual round of tribal wars and cannibal feasts governed by complicated ritualistic "tapus". The worst of these features of savage life occurred after and not before contact with the different and more variable ethics of white civilisation. The normal run of life was far too dependent upon systematic and laborious cultivation with primitive implements for anything like continuous indulgence in the luxury of fighting. It was in fact a highly disciplined existence that was led by the old Maori.

This is the reason why Maori leaders of the present day appeal so confidently to past tradition as a sure guide to the solution of modern economic problems. Their appeal is not merely to a somewhat idealised pride of race. They speak in definite terms of heredity. Knowing the family history of their people in great wealth of detail as far back in some cases as twenty-five generations, they speak with assurance, not only of the industry and ability possessed by Maoris generally, but of the particular combinations of personal qualities inherited by individuals from their ancestors. When the dairying experiment mentioned in a later section of this chapter was being urged upon the Ngati Porou tribe by certain younger men of modern education and outlook, the elders to whom they took their appeal delivered judgment in these significant words:

> We understand that the matter under debate relates to the production of food. This is a Pakeha method of producing food, butter, to send to London, where the people of England may buy and eat it. Very good. Your ancestors cultivated taro and kumara with great care, patience, and knowledge. It is true that in some seasons the crops were plentiful, and in others they were poor. But they went on cultivating because it was necessary to their life. We sent you to school and out among the Pakeha to learn his way of doing old and new things, and to bring the knowledge back to your villages. You are now called upon to use it. The rest you have in you from your forefathers. Therefore we say—go ahead.

There is ample justification in their history for this superb confidence. After adventurous voyages of discovery and exploration the Maoris came to New Zealand, stopping at many Pacific islands by the way, in thoroughly planned and carefully executed colonising expeditions. The outline of these voyages is known, but their epic story has still to be written. It will need to be written by a member of the Maori race who can piece together the fragments of old songs, shadowy myths, genealogical trees, and exploits of heroes, till definite personalities take shape against the dim background of their homeland, Hawaiki. The story grows clearer and fuller as they journey from island to island and finally catch Maui's last and greatest fish, Te Ika a Maui, the north island of New Zealand.

Having conquered the distances of the Pacific Ocean they had still to achieve the conquest of their new and more exacting environment. Their settlement and colonisation of New Zealand involved adaptation to a more rigorous climate and experimentation with new types of food, implements, clothing, and shelter. When the first European explorers came to the islands this adaptation had been accomplished. From the materials and craftsmanship they brought with them, the Maoris had worked out characteristic arts and crafts of a highly conventionalised type, but displaying both industry and artistic skill. By this time they were not only the most numerous, but the most vigorous, branch of the Polynesian race, with carefully elaborated social and economic organisation. It is the province of the anthropologist rather than the economic historian to describe their life at this stage; but the qualities of character revealed even in a cursory analysis are of profound economic significance to-day. Sir Apirana Ngata has stated this fact in words that cannot be bettered. Describing an "ohu" or working bee as he saw it even as recently as forty years ago, he writes:

> The spirit of the old usages prevails—leadership, co-operation, communal discipline. May not this same spirit still prevail in these later days, now that the spur of necessity is once more applied, now that the mist is lifting from before the eyes of the youth of the race and they see that what was achieved by their neolithic ancestors is possible in the present with all civilisation to help, if only the spirit of the intrepid Polynesian navigators, of the patient, orderly, and disciplined agriculturists, of the expert nature-taught fowlers and fishermen, of the ingenious boat-builders, carvers, and artists, were revived in their descendants.

An economic historian is bound to state also that Maori industry has not been confined to the cultivation of food-supplies for their own people. The technical organisation of ancient Maori agriculture had little to contribute to civilisation, though it should not be forgotten that in the earliest stages of colonisation the Maori farmers, profiting by missionary instruction, supplied the European settlers with large quantities of food-stuffs. Thomson, writing in 1859, gives statistics of canoes arriving at Auckland with foods valued at £16,180 in 1854. This included 3,715 bushels of wheat.(2) It will be argued later in this chapter also that in combining communal landownership and tribal organisation with modern methods of rural co-operation and modern technique the Maori has within the last two decades been making a contribution of considerable economic significance. In technique, however, the Maori was still in the Stone Age. He had little capital and has had to depend largely upon the Pakeha for that necessity of modern production. His land tenures, and the tenacity with which he fought to preserve them, were a considerable obstacle to economic progress for many decades. But there is one respect, the supply of labour, in which he made an immediate contribution of the utmost importance to the economic development of New Zealand.

There has grown up a tendency to underestimate the place of Maori labour in the economic life of the young colony. It is true that at the present time the Maoris are so heavily outnumbered that their labour supply is a relatively minor factor. In earlier days, however, from the time when visiting sea captains impressed Maori sailors to fill vacancies in their crews, Maori labour was a factor of considerable importance. Much of the real drudgery involved in "carving homes out of the wilderness" has been the work of Maori hands. The pioneer work of bush-felling, scrub-clearing, fencing, still draws heavily upon Maori labour. Nor is this the whole story. Road-making, sheep-shearing, coal-mining, gum-digging, even railway construction, have in certain areas depended a great deal upon the Maoris. It was not to be expected that technical occupations would be open to them in earlier days, but at the present time the service cars of many motor-omnibus routes in the north island are driven by Maori mechanics, and there are not wanting examples of skilled workmen in other occupations. Agriculture, however, remains their primary concern, though in any occupation of manual dexterity, particularly if it can be performed by teamwork involving some measure of communal co-operation, the Maori worker is second to none. No one who served in the New Zealand Expeditionary Force is likely to forget the speed and skill with which the Pioneer Battalion, composed wholly of Maoris, built roads and dug trenches.

Despite the vicissitudes through which they have passed, therefore, and their reputation among certain Pakehas who have only known them in the difficult days of transition, there is no reason either to underestimate the economic contribution they have made to New Zealand in the past or to doubt their capacity under proper conditions for sustained and exacting labour, skilled craftsmanship, and patient agriculture.

British "Imperialism" in New Zealand

The melancholy story of declining population begins with the advent of the white traders.(3) There seems little evidence that any previous decline had set in from causes peculiar to the native organisation. On the other hand, there are clear records and traditions of the introduction of disease by the whalers and other early visitors. At a later stage infectious epidemic diseases swept the country and inspired great terror among the natives, leaving behind memories that are still potent. The Maoris can hardly be blamed if they regard such terrible visitations as akin to the dreaded "makutu", the black magic of the tohunga.

It is clear that the resistance of the Maoris to disease was lowered by psychological causes of this kind. The consequences of abandoning their old industrious habits of life were even more serious. In some districts they came down from their hill fortifications to lower ground, and avoided the drudgery of cultivation by trading with the Pakeha, which did not tend to improve either their moral or their physical stamina. In this, however, as in most other respects, the history of every tribe is different. There are some which had very little contact with the Pakeha, and others where a good deal of understanding and respect for ancient customs was quickly swept away.

The white man also introduced alcohol to a race that had not previously used fermented beverages and, still worse, introduced and encouraged the use of firearms. The incessant murderous wars that occupied the first thirty years of the nineteenth century, and the outrages perpetrated in the same period upon white communities as "utu" or revenge for injuries, constitute one of the worst blots upon the record of the contact of European civilisation with native races.

These destructive forces of civilisation preceded the constructive work of missions, Government, and schools by at least a generation. Trade began to increase in the last decade of the eighteenth century. The first missionary visit of Samuel Marsden was not made till 1814, lay workers were stationed at the Bay of Islands from that year; but the Wesleyan Mission dates from 1822, and Henry Williams did not begin work in New Zealand till 1823. There are few mission fields that have rendered a greater harvest both of direct conversions and of indirect influence. To this day the "mana" (prestige) of the early missionaries is very powerful, and their influence on Maori development is gratefully recognised as wholesome and constructive by almost every leader of the race. But they were sadly hindered by the lawlessness of the white trading communities and the lack of organised government. They were not unnaturally associated in the Maori mind with their fellow Pakehas, whose manner of life was hardly Christian. The bitter sectarian controversies, intensified by the appearance of Roman Catholic missionaries, were also a cause of stumbling to the Maoris, if only because they entered so readily and with such zest into the rivalries thus created.

Both the missionaries in the field and the officials of missionary societies in London were opposed for some time to the proposals made by Edward Gibbon Wakefield to colonise New Zealand with British settlers. The steady opposition maintained by the Colonial Office to the schemes of the New Zealand Company was in accord with the *laissez-faire* philosophy of the time; but it was encouraged by the fears expressed in mission circles concerning the effects of colonisation upon the welfare of the Maoris. Historians are now generally agreed that the worst abuses of the period before organised settlement were due to the lack of Governmental control. Mr. Reeves, in a famous passage, has placed the responsibility squarely upon the Colonial Office.(4) It has, however, required a century of development to evolve the sense of trusteeship for native races which is embodied in the mandatory system of the League of Nations. In the early nineteenth century such a constructive idea was hardly conceivable, and the thought of missionaries and Government officials hardly went beyond the negative conception of keeping hands off the native races, whose welfare is now regarded as "a sacred trust of civilisation".

Recent historical research has stressed the solicitude of the Colonial Office for Maori welfare as the chief reason for the official opposition to colonising schemes.(5) There was no indecent haste on the part of the British Government, but on the contrary the utmost reluctance to add New Zealand to its responsibilities. It seems obvious now that a far-sighted statesmanship might have conserved Maori welfare at the same time as it promoted settlement. The Maoris suffered badly from the failure of British officials to envisage this possibility; but at least those officials are free from the charge of disregarding native welfare in an effort to extend imperial boundaries.

When it became evident that the islands would be colonised by other Powers if not by Britain, the attitude of both missionaries and officials began to change. Formal Governmental action was forced in 1839 by the dispatch of colonists under the aegis of the New Zealand Company. A governor was appointed immediately, with instructions to treat with the natives for the cession of their lands. The settlers arrived at Wellington on January 22, 1840, the Governor reached the Bay of Islands a week later. Thenceforward the efforts of the Governor and of the missionaries were directed towards safeguarding the interests of the natives not only against the Company's settlers, but against the horde of land-sharks who had descended upon the islands as soon as it became evident that organised government could not long be delayed.

The main step taken was the negotiation early in 1840 of the Treaty of Waitangi, by which leading chiefs acknowledged the sovereignty of Queen Victoria and were confirmed in the ownership of their lands. (6) In the negotiations for this Treaty, Governor Hobson had the advice and assistance of Henry Williams and, along with other missionaries, Henry Williams travelled the country securing the signatures of those chiefs who were not present at the Waitangi meeting. Hobson followed up the Treaty with a proclamation suspending all land sales until their validity could be investigated by a commissioner appointed for that purpose. In this way the Crown established its right of pre-emption over all the land of New Zealand, and saved the natives from being despoiled of their heritage at the very outset of their contact with the colonists.

The policy embodied in the Treaty ended the activities of the land-sharks who had swarmed into the colony. It was a sore blow also to the Wakefield settlers in the Cook Strait region and the prime cause of their distress in the first decade of colonisation. Its consequences involved the New Zealand Company in financial troubles that finally wrecked it. Of more importance still, the paralysing controversy between the Colonial Office and the Company in London was extended to include the Governor and the settlers in New Zealand. It was not lessened in bitterness by the hasty and unfortunate steps which the Company had taken in attempting to purchase Maori lands, in sending out immigrants before land was securely in its possession, in negotiating with a German syndicate for the settlement of the Chatham Islands, and in drawing up a code of regulations which eminent counsel ruled to be an infringement of the sovereignty of the Crown.

On their part the settlers had reason to complain not only of the lack of imagination displayed by the Colonial Office, but of the irritating delays and positive blunders involved in the official policy. There is no reason to regard Wakefield and his associates as mercenary land-grabbers nor to underestimate their high motives. The published statements of the Company always laid stress upon the setting aside of adequate native reserves. Nor were the settlers invariably hostile to the natives. Many of them, like Fox and Featherston, were champions of the Maori cause in later years. There is no doubt, however, that the controversy rushed both the Government and the settlers into precipitate action. The intricate complexity of Maori customary land tenure and the delicacy of Maori etiquette presented baffling problems out of which arose misunderstanding and ultimately conflict. It was perhaps inevitable that the officials of the Government should gradually be forced into defending Maori rights against the settlers' desire for land, and that the settlers should become impatient and embittered against both officials and Maoris.

The Maoris themselves had rather welcomed the advent of the useful white man. They were especially keen on getting supplies of firearms for their new methods of warfare. But they were quick to recognise the consequences of organised settlement. They realised that if it continued they would need to conform to its ways instead of using it for their own purposes. Their suspicions were aroused by the haste with which the settlers sought lands for cultivation and by their lack of understanding of Maori usages. In some parts of the country leading chiefs had refused even to sign the Treaty of Waitangi, so little did they trust the white man and his fair promises. In other districts the first trust quickly passed into disillusionment and hostility. Incidents occurred in the Hutt Valley, at Wairau in the Nelson Settlement, on the Wanganui River, and in the far north at Hokianga, where leading chiefs took their disputes with the settlers to the arbitrament of war.

By 1850, therefore, there were all the elements of trouble. It was well for the future of New Zealand that at this stage the main stream of colonisation was diverted to the south island, where the Maoris were fewer and less aggressive. During the fifties, and still more after the discovery of gold in the sixties, the progress of the south island provinces provided a solid basis for the growth of the colony. The ease with which the land was purchased both in Otago and later in Canterbury removed what continued to be the greatest cause of unsettlement and economic depression in the north.

A Struggle for Existence

The second series of Maori wars, which began in Taranaki in 1860 and was not finally ended till 1872, has always been a disconcerting theme for New Zealand historians.(7) The first series of local outbreaks, beginning with Hone Heke's war in 1843, was ended quickly by Sir George Grey's effective military measures(8); but more by the fact that he won the confidence of Maori leaders, who were once again persuaded to sell land and to treat with the Government on a basis of confidence. It is not easy to explain away the fact that, despite the Treaty of Waitangi and the scrupulous care with which it was observed by the first governors, and despite the renewed confidence which the Maoris placed in Sir George Grey, the second series of Maori wars can only be regarded as a desperate struggle by the natives to preserve their interests in the face of what they regarded as Pakeha aggression. The fact is unpalatable but inescapable. By 1860 the Maoris in almost every district where they had come into close contact with the settlers were convinced that they had no alternative but to defend their land by war.

The causes of the wars go far back beyond the somewhat trivial incidents which precipitated hostilities. There is a Maori proverb that war is waged for land and women. The complexity of Maori land tenure is proof also of the importance attached to landownership. After their first experiences with organised settlement, however, Maori leaders began to realise that land was what the Pakeha wanted. Many of them saw that the goods offered in purchase of their lands, however tempting, were inadequate.

> The things you give us [they said] are nothing like the value of the land. That lasts for ever, but what will become of our blankets? They will become sick or dead. What becomes of your tomahawks? They will be sick or dead. Glass and iron are brittle. You are going to steal our land from us; your payment must be good to us. There is this tree. If one branch falls there will come another. It will remain to your children, but what will become of our children when these things are worn out?

The Company's settlements caused the first real clash of interests. Earlier purchases of waste lands or small areas were in practice not very different from Maori tenure. There were no fences, merely a right of occupation and use, with certain spots, such as the storehouse and sleeping-rooms, "tapu" (sacred). Trouble came with the fence and the sign "Keep Out".

It is not surprising, therefore, to find that as early as 1848 and in the Wellington district, where the first colonists had settled, there was a definite movement for the formation of a Land League to sell no more land to the Pakehas. The leader of this movement, Wiremu Kingi, soon afterwards migrated to his ancestral lands at Waitara, and in 1857 organised the Land League on a definite basis. The Maoris have always regarded it as significant that the very land on which he was living should have been the cause of the Taranaki War. A brief glance at the circumstances is illuminating. The Taranaki tribes had had a chequered history. Their strength had been drained by the migration of many of their numbers with Te Rauparaha to Wellington. In their weakened condition they were beaten by their neighbours to the north, the various tribes of the Waikato district. Many of them were enslaved, others were driven into exile, taking refuge with their fellow-tribesmen in the Wellington district, and even in the Chatham Islands. All of these retained in Maori custom their rights to the land of their forefathers, since there remained members of their family who "kept the fires alight" on their ancestral lands. The agent of the New Zealand Company treated with the natives whom he found in occupation of the land and bought from them the lands on which the Taranaki colonists settled, including the

Waitara block. This purchase was declared valid by the commissioner who investigated land claims after the Treaty of Waitangi was signed. One result of the coming of the Pakeha, however, was to facilitate the return of the Taranaki people. Slaves were set free under the influence of Christianity, and exiles returned when the Pakeha Government established peace. Under Maori custom these returned members of the tribe had valid rights to the usage of the land. Governor Fitzroy in 1843 reversed the commissioner's decision and declared the Company's purchase of the disputed lands to be invalid. Wiremu Kingi, who had migrated from Waikanae in 1848, had been living on the block and cultivating it for more than ten years when another chief of subordinate rank, named Teira, sold it to the agent of the Government in 1859. The Governor of the day, who lives in Maori memory as "a stiff soldier", or more graphically still, "Angry Belly", accepted the contention of the purchasing official that Teira was the rightful owner of the land. Wiremu Kingi passively resisted all attempts to occupy the land, and out of the feeling thus created hostilities naturally developed.

The Maoris felt, and still feel, that their case was absolutely valid and that the aggression was on the part of the Government, egged on by the settlers who were so urgently in need of land for expansion. This Maori contention was upheld at the time by such men as Bishop Selwyn and Sir William Martin; it was admitted after enquiry by Sir George Grey when he was recalled to take control of the situation in 1861, and it is now generally recognised to be true. The Royal Commission set up to enquire into Maori land confiscations in 1927 definitely accepted the Maori case as proven.

There were many other elements which entered into the conflict, but land difficulties of the type just mentioned were the chief. Beneath them all was the deepening suspicion of the Maori tribes that the Pakeha meant at all costs to have their lands, and the fear of what the future might hold if once they parted with the land on which was based the only way of life they knew. There is no doubt that to the settlers they appeared merely obstructive or insolent; but they were fighting a losing battle for the retention of their old customs and culture. The tribes have never at any time presented a united front, and during all the period of hostilities there was never anything more than sporadic fighting in one district after another.

Even in the western districts, where feeling was strongest and where the King movement seemed to unite three powerful tribes under the leadership of the so-called Maori King and his able adviser, Wiremu Tamihana, there was great diversity of opinion. Disaffection was rife from Taranaki to Auckland, among all the Maoris who felt the pressure of settlement from north and south. The east coast and Urewera tribes were sheltered behind their mountain frontiers from the first impact of Pakeha land-hunger.

The Government failed to distinguish, within the King movement, between the constructive efforts of the moderate party headed by Tamihana, which sought by peaceful and orderly means to redress the genuine grievances of their people, and the defiant words and actions of the war party headed by Rewi Maniapoto. The Government failed also to appreciate the effect which Pakeha law had had in undermining the tribal authority of the chiefs without substituting therefor any adequate means of social discipline. So great was this failure to appreciate the inner significance of the situation that Gorst, probably the most detached and impartial observer of the King movement, came to the definite conclusion that the only hope for the Maoris was to remove the administration of native affairs from the control of the colonial legislature, into which it had passed at an early stage in the war, and vest it once more in officials appointed by the Colonial Office.

As the misunderstandings grew deeper and hostilities spread, the Maori "rebels" in their chagrin and disappointment tended to regress to the worst aspects of their pre-European savage life. Modern psychology helps one to glimpse the repressions and disappointments and hatreds that found vent in barbaric rituals and atrocities. The fantastic Hau-Hau religion, described by Sir William Fox as "a large infusion of Judaism, some leading features of Mormonism, a little mesmerism, a touch of spiritualism, occasional ventriloquism, and a large amount of cannibalism", shocked and revolted not only the Pakehas but also the friendly Maoris. It was difficult at the time to realise that behind these manifestations of a savage spirit was the real psychological injury resulting from unredressed grievances and a sense of hopelessness, futility, and frustration. It was even more difficult to appreciate the very real religious feeling behind them and to realise that even the fanatical Hau-Hauism with all its barbarity was, as a modern Maori leader has recently written of a later cult (the Ringatu movement introduced by Te Kooti):

> a system, built up entirely by Maori leaders, which in its simplicity, in its ritual, in its methods of government is more within the comprehension of the Maori mind, and appeals more to his heart than any religious organisation imposed on the people and governed from without. Its lure may be its simplicity, or it may be that it is deemed to be the refuge of those who revolt against the complexities of modern religious systems, or even difficult moral standards. But with all its faults it has deep lessons at this day for the would-be workers among the Maoris.

The long-continued wars and their accompanying unsettlement paralysed the progress of the white communities in the north island; but their effects were far worse on the Maori tribes concerned. As the war proceeded and plunged the colonial Government further into debt a demand arose for confiscation of the lands of the tribes engaged in the conflict. There was violent controversy at the time concerning the proposal. The Governor was instructed by the Colonial Office that he might sanction confiscation as a measure of punishment but not as a measure of financial relief to the colonial Government. The general commanding the regular army in New Zealand openly accused the ministers of using imperial troops to rob the natives of their land.

As a measure of financial relief to the Government the receipts from the confiscations, which totalled £26,738, were insignificant. The area confiscated ran into millions of acres, but some of it was afterwards returned and some was purchased by the Government.(9) Lands which were declared forfeit in some districts were reoccupied by their former owners and allowed to remain in their possession. In other districts the most actively hostile tribes escaped comparatively lightly, while tribes that were far less culpable had their best lands taken from them. The Maori of the present day bitterly remembers that where injustices of this kind were perpetrated the net result always was that the best land for Pakeha purposes was lost to the Maoris, whether they were clearly guilty or not.

Not only was there injustice among the tribes who were leagued against the Government, but even friendly Maoris were involved. The complexity of land tenure is such that these groups within the disaffected areas who were either passive or active allies of the Government had rights of ownership over much of the confiscated land. Moreover, the rewards of friendship were far from justly distributed. Families and individuals who had given loyal service waited vainly for recognition and reward, too proud to present their claims. Others less scrupulous in such matters were better treated.

The legacy of the wars in all these respects was a psychological situation far more important in its ultimate results than the immediate economic consequences of either the war or the confiscations. It is difficult and perhaps impossible to disentangle its effects from those of the subsequent land-purchase policies described in the next section; but it is important to remember that over a large part of Maoridom there was this feeling of utter despair of justice at the hands of the Pakeha.

The feeling was strongest in tribes which had from the beginning distrusted the Pakeha and had even refused to sign the Treaty of Waitangi. It took different forms, according to the leadership of the tribe. In some cases the tribe was welded more closely together than ever and in face of discouragement and economic difficulty fought a successful battle for survival while refusing to accept Pakeha co-operation except in the most limited and necessary degree. In other tribes the loss of their land, which they had defended vainly in what they believed to be a fair fight for a just cause, resulted in the apathy of frustration and contributed quickly to the rapid spread of disease and depopulation.

Generally speaking there was a loss of faith in the Pakeha's justice, and consequently suspicion of every action of the Government as well as of the settlers. The results of the land-purchase policies confirmed this suspicion. The Maori seemed to lose at every turn. The natural consequence was a refusal to follow out a policy of co-operation with the constructive Governmental agencies. Government efforts in a later period to provide schools and medical assistance, as well as more complicated measures looking towards redress of grievances and economic reconstruction, have been met with sullen passive resistance. The tribes so affected lost at least a generation and a half of reconstruction, and in that loss was involved impoverishment, which now hampers them at every turn. The recent renaissance of the Maori people began significantly enough in tribes which were protected by their remote isolation from the brunt of early contact with the white man and his devouring civilisation. They are blazing a possible way for other tribes to follow, but it is not easy in a short time to cast off the effects of a generation or two of resentment, suspicion, and distrust. Nor is it easy to recover the necessary means of development. In the present stirring of new life throughout the Maori tribes it is broadly true to say that those who have so far lagged behind have done so mainly because of the fact that they suffered most in the transition period by reason of the situation of their lands. Every tribe has a different story, and it is impossible to generalise; but all the stories are combinations of the elements described above, together with the even more disastrous results of land sales sketched in the following section. In them all the psychological consequences of the experiences through which they have passed form an extremely significant group of factors.

The Peace of the Pakeha

One of the chief causes of friction in the period prior to the wars was the lack of adequate Governmental machinery to determine the ownership of native land and complete its purchase upon an equitable basis. Most of the conflicts which arose trace back to the fact that sale or lease was allowed to become effective before full enquiry into native ownership had been completed.

By the Treaty of Waitangi (1840) it had been rendered illegal for private individuals to purchase land directly from the Maoris. The Crown had established its right of pre-emption. This right was waived temporarily in favour of the New Zealand Company, which was allowed to retain possession of a proportion of the lands which it claimed to have bought. Certain of the purchases made prior to the Treaty by private individuals were allowed also, and much of the land surrendered by the Maoris but not allowed to the purchasers was created Crown land. This is the foundation of the problem of "surplus lands" in the North Auckland peninsula, where the Maoris have never been able to appreciate the justice of the Crown's action in seizing on land resumed from private purchasers. The New Zealand Company was further allowed to purchase land in the south island on behalf of its related project, the Otago Association. In 1844 also, Governor Fitzroy, in a desperate effort to promote settlement, had issued proclamations waiving the right of pre-emption generally. His proclamations were disallowed, he was recalled, and only a small proportion of the claims made under the proclamations were validated. In 1846 the Colonial Office sent out a projected constitution and land regulations which virtually repudiated the Treaty of Waitangi by acknowledging Maori ownership only over those lands in actual cultivation. These regulations were, however, blocked by the courage of Sir George Grey, and were withdrawn.

From 1840 to 1862, therefore, the purchase of Maori lands, which might be thrown open to settlement either by sale or lease, was one of the most important functions of the governors. Sir George Grey especially was very successful in persuading the Maoris to sell land to the Crown, especially in the south island, where over thirty million acres were sold for a small cash price and promises which were only partially fulfilled.

Governor Hobson had created the office of Protector of the Aborigines shortly after his arrival in 1840. Sir George Grey replaced this official by a Native Secretary in each of the two divisions, New Ulster and New Munster, into which New Zealand was divided by the constitution of 1846. In 1852 these officials gave way to a Native Department, which still remained, however, under the control of the Governor. Even after the passing of the Constitution Act of 1852 the control of native affairs was expressly reserved for the Governor acting under instructions from the Colonial Office. This remained the constitutional position until Sir George Grey on February 26, 1863, acting upon instructions from London, formally handed over control to a Minister of Native Affairs responsible to the colonial legislature.(10)

There had naturally been increasing pressure upon the officers of the Native Department from settlers who wanted land, and the tendency was for control to pass into the hands of Parliament even before formal action was taken. When the change did take place it was mainly because of the impossible friction created in time of war by divided control. The Governor, the officer commanding the imperial troops, and the colonial ministers, conducted a triangular controversy of singular bitterness. This controversy was aggravated by accusations and counter-accusations concerning the proposals to confiscate "rebel" lands; but it involved the whole policy of native administration, and particularly of land purchase.

The Native Land Act of 1862, passed by the colonial Parliament and assented to by the Crown, marked the beginning of a new era.(11) It provided certain safeguards which were obviously necessary in view of past experience, and in particular forbade the completion of sale or lease of lands before ownership had been determined. Having provided these safeguards, however, the Crown waived its right of pre-emption and thus ushered in a period of free trade in Maori land. Pre-emption was not resumed till 1892, and in the thirty years intervening the Maoris lost the greater part of their ancestral heritage, including most of the best situated and most fertile lands.

In 1865 the Native Land Court was created as a permanent tribunal charged with the investigation and settlement of native land titles. For more than sixty years this Court has functioned steadily and, within its limits, successfully. One of the chief purposes of its creation was to secure sound titles for land which had been or would be bought. In quieting titles and apportioning the purchase-moneys equitably between the Maori owners it has been invaluable. Throughout its history, however, it has been a means of facilitating the separation of the Maori from his land as equitably and painlessly as possible. In this way it has been the chief mechanism in the breaking-up of Maori economy and the destruction of tribal organisation and discipline.

At first the Court was bound by statute not to recognise more than ten individuals as owners of any piece of land, the intention of this unfortunate provision apparently being to force the natives to work through a small enough number of representatives to enable the Court to reach agreement quickly. Two years later an amendment went some distance towards recognising other beneficiaries, but the chief tendency of the colonial legislation concerning Maori lands is summed up in the official statement concerning the last measure of first-rate importance, the Native Land Act of 1909, which according to the Under-Secretary of Native Affairs, writing in the New Zealand Official Year Book of 1910, "widens the avenues and facilitates the alienation and settlement of native lands".

This Act, based on the recommendations of a Royal Commission consisting of Sir Robert Stout and (Sir) Apirana Ngata, aimed deliberately at throwing the possessors of more advanced land titles on their own resources, with greater freedom of action and concomitant realisation of the responsibilities of landownership. The Act also introduced for the first time the policy of consolidation of interests which was so greatly developed later. The pronouncement of the Under-Secretary concerning it is therefore of considerable interest, as showing the official point of view somewhat in conflict with legislative intention and subsequent experience.

Various safeguards have been enacted from time to time, but the main drift of native land legislation has been to separate the Maoris from their lands. This is especially true of the period after 1873, when an Act was passed establishing the principle of individualising the titles to land, a principle which was described by the Royal Commission of 1891 as having been "the foundation and source of all the difficulties which have since arisen not only in the transfer of land from natives to Europeans, but in the settlement of the north island of New Zealand".

No better summary of the effects of this free trade in native lands has ever been made than the extract from the report of the 1891 Commission, which was quoted again by the Royal Commission of 1907–9:

> The tendency in the Act to individualise native tenure was too strong to admit of any prudential check. The desire to purchase native estates overruled all other considerations. The alienation of native land under this law took its very worst form and its most disastrous tendency. It was obtained from a helpless people. The crowds of owners in a memorial of ownership were like a flock of sheep without a shepherd, a watch-dog, or a leader. Mostly ignorant barbarians, they became suddenly possessed of a title to land which was a marketable commodity. The right to occupy and cultivate possessed by their fathers became in their hands an estate which could be sold. The strength which lies in union was taken from them. The authority

of their natural leaders was destroyed. They were surrounded by temptations. Eager for money wherewith to buy food, clothes, and rum, they welcomed the paid agents, who plied them always with cash, and often with spirits. Such alienations were generally against the public interest so far as regards settlement of the people upon the land. In most of the leases and purchases effected the land was obtained in large areas by capitalists. The possession of wealth, or that credit which obtained it from financial institutions, was absolutely necessary to provide for native agents, interpreters, and lawyers, as well as to distribute money broadcast among the native proprietary. Not only was this contrary to public policy, it was very often done in defiance of the law.

Of all the purchase money paid for the millions of acres sold by the Maoris not one sixpence is left. Their remaining lands are rapidly passing away. A few more years of the Native Land Court under the present system, and a few amended laws for free trade in native lands, and the Maoris will be a landless people.

But it was not only in the alienation of their lands that the Maoris suffered. In its occupation also they found themselves in a galling and anomalous position. As every single person in a list of owners comprising perhaps over a hundred names had as much right to occupy as anyone else, personal occupation for improvement or tillage was encompassed with uncertainty. If a man sowed a crop, others might allege an equal right to the produce. If a few fenced in a paddock or small run for sheep or cattle, their co-owners were sure to turn their stock or horses into the pasture. The apprehension of results which paralyses industry cast its shadow over the whole Maori people. In the old days the influence of the chiefs and the common customs of the tribe afforded a sufficient guarantee to the thrifty and provident; but when our law enforced upon them a new state of things, then the lazy, the careless, and prodigal not only wasted their own substance, but fed upon the labours of their more industrious kinsmen.

The pernicious consequences of native land legislation have not been confined to the natives, nor to the Europeans more immediately concerned in dealing with them for land. The disputes then arising have compelled the attention of the public at large; they have filled the courts of the colony with litigation, they have flooded Parliament with petitions, given rise to continual debates of very great bitterness, engrossed the time of committees, and, while entailing very heavy annual expenses upon the colony, have invariably produced an uneasy public feeling.

The disposal of native land was checked for a time by the effort between 1884 and 1886 to establish a paternalistic control by the Government over land sales by the resumption of the Crown's right of pre-emption in certain areas. The Maoris, however, objected to being totally deprived of all authority and management of their ancestral lands, and therefore they refused to bring those lands under the Act, which had left this action optional on their part. Free trade in native land was revived in 1888, and in the urge for closer settlement that was the principal feature of Liberal-Labour policy in the last decade of the nineteenth century, the sale of native land was accelerated. Consequent upon the report of the 1891 Royal Commission, pre-emption was resumed in the following year. An abortive effort was made in 1900 to restore the paternal principles of the legislation of 1884–6, but this merely resulted in a deadlock, so that in 1905 the Government reverted to its policy of freer trade both in native land sales and in leasing native lands. The Royal Commission of 1907–9 recommended that "the purchase of native lands by the Crown under the present system be discontinued", and that alienation by direct negotiation between the owners and private individuals be prohibited so that further alienation should be made only through native land boards. The Act of 1909 gave effect to these recommendations, but the sale of Maori lands continued with these safeguards until at the present time the total area remaining to the Maoris is less than four and a half million acres, of which by far the greater part is not of the best quality or readily accessible.

The Rating Amendment Act of 1910 brought certain Maori lands within the scheme of taxation provided by the Rating Act of 1908, a measure which has always been resented by the Maoris and has proved difficult of administration. In recent years local body expenditures upon roads and similar utilities have greatly increased, and the Maori owners in many districts have opposed passive resistance to the effort made to collect rates for services they did not want upon land which was not in effective use. Moreover, communal ownership has made it difficult to fix responsibility for such charges. The result has been in many districts as confusing and irritating both to Maoris and to Pakehas as the baffling intricacy of native land legislation generally. From both situations the Maori has felt that the ultimate result was likely to be a further loosening of his hold upon the land.

As a result of sixty years of colonial legislation and administration, therefore, the Maoris have lost the greater part of the land. It is true that they retain something over four million acres; but this is very unevenly distributed among the tribes, and much of it is poor land which the Pakeha did not want. There are tribes which have very little land left, and that of the poorest quality. In one district the areas are so small that ownership is counted by rows of kumaras, or potatoes, instead of by acres. In others resort has to be had to intensive market- and even flower-gardening. In most some form of labour for the Pakehas is necessary for the youth of the tribe. In very few areas have the Maoris retained their best lands. In recent years, however, the necessity of conserving what remains has been forced upon them, and some tribes have even begun the re-purchase of lands formerly sold to the Pakehas.

Maori leaders realise that their birthright has been lost, most of it sold for a trifling consideration. There is, not unnaturally, considerable feeling that the more astute Pakeha has in the past taken advantage of Maori weakness and ignorance. It is not only that land has been lost as a result of war and confiscation. The more subtle processes of land purchase have been far more potent. "Flour and sugar" policies have kept peace and contentment while the land was slipping from beneath Maori feet. The individualising of titles and free sale of the lands so acquired has allowed many tribes to live for a time in idleness and ostentation and worse, the price being the loss for all time of their patrimony. Moreover, the squandering of easy money received from the sale of land has reacted to the detriment of the Maoris by hastening their physical and moral deterioration and by lowering their reputation in the eyes of their Pakeha neighbours. It was in this period that they came to be regarded as shiftless, improvident, and incapable of sustained industry. Only the stoutest courage and the most profound faith in the hereditary qualities of the race could enable their leaders to face the task of restoring "the spirit of the old usages, leadership, co-operation, and communal discipline".

Another trap is afforded by the complexity of Pakeha administration. Taxation of many kinds, the expenditure of public moneys, the baffling ways of the law in general, leave the Maori in only too many cases suspicious and resentful. There are disputes over timber royalties and the purchase of timber lands, over excessive legal fees and inadequate legal protection, over unpaid rates and needed services. The Maori is caught in a tangle of circumstances that he only dimly comprehends. He knows that in the past the main result of such things has been that he lost more land and he fears for the future. "The peace of the Pakeha", he says, "is more to be dreaded than his war."

Tardy Justice

In pleasant contrast with the depressing facts outlined above, it must be recorded that in recent years there has been a distinct effort on the part of the Government to co-operate with and assist in the regeneration of the Maoris. The four native members of the House of Representatives, whose conduct even a generation ago was severely criticised, have more recently captured the sympathy and respect of their colleagues. An ex-governor of New Zealand has suggested that their presence is perhaps a disadvantage, since Maori affairs are left so much to their leadership instead of being a general responsibility of the whole House(12); but this view seems unduly flattering to the imagination and understanding of the ordinary Pakeha member, preoccupied as he is with the claims of his electorate upon the public purse.

The most recent legislative developments owe their success primarily to the fact that, unlike the legislation of 1884 and 1900, they are not paternalistic but co-operative, working with and through Maori leadership instead of depriving the Maoris of control. The most important features of the policy have been the creation of various trusts upon the east coast and elsewhere which under Pakeha, or mixed Maori and Pakeha, management have served to some extent as models of farming enterprises; the creation in 1920 of the Office of Native Trustee as a department separate from the Public Trust Office; and the active administrative sympathy towards, and where necessary legislative support of, the movement towards consolidation and incorporation of native lands.

The essential feature of this new legislation has been the emergence of Maori leadership competent to solve native problems along lines combining Maori tradition and European legal and economic experience. One of the most important aspects of this Maori leadership lies in the fact that it is now possible for such Governmental activities as administration and education in matters of health to be entrusted to experienced

Maori leaders in so far as their own people are concerned. The constructive work being done in this department is of the utmost value and promise, and is going far to develop an attitude of co-operation and understanding even among tribes which have long cherished a sullen resentment and suspicion of all Pakeha activities.

In the same way and under the same leadership progress is being made in the examination of outstanding grievances. In 1921 a Royal Commission was appointed to examine certain claims that promises made in connection with land purchases, mainly in the south island, had never been fulfilled. When in 1848 all that part of the south island lying between Nelson and Otago and bounded on the west by the Southern Alps, thirty million acres in all, was bought for £2,000, the Government promised to provide schools and hospitals and also to set aside land for Maori use. In 1877 the Maoris formed a committee to press for the fulfilment of these engagements. The Commission of 1921 reported the justice of the Maori claims and honourably, though tardily, recommended that the Government make recompense by calculating the payment due at compound interest and taking steps through the Native Land Court to establish the claims of present-day Maoris to share in the benefits of the substantial sum—£354,000—so computed. It is open to some doubt whether the Treasury will accept the basis of the computation, but some substantial recompense will be made.

This is not the only case where recent Governments, backed by general support from the whole House and guided by the knowledge and insight of the Maori members and officials of the Native Affairs Department, have made genuine efforts to seek out long-standing Maori grievances with a view to their settlement. Another notable example, not quite in the category of grievances, has been the creation, after due enquiry, of the Arawa Trust Board. The Arawa tribe, located mainly in the tourist region around Rotorua, found its ownership, involving valuable fishing and other rights in the central lakes and rivers, disputed by the Crown. It had vainly been trying to get some form of monetary recognition of its claim at least since 1908. It is significant of the new spirit animating the modern Maoris that long-standing jealousies were at last set aside, plans were worked out for tribal rather than individual compensation, and legislation accepted which placed the resources provided by the Government in the hands of a board representing all the parties concerned. What this means, not only in material advancement in such matters as hygiene, education, and acquisition of land for farming, but also in promoting constructive co-operation within the tribe, may be judged from the fact that one of the first acts of the board was the repurchase of Maketu, the ancestral landing-place of the tribe. Following this compensation another trust was set up separately for the Taupo Lake—the Tuwharetoa Trust Board. The principle of monetary compensation laid down in the Arawa settlement and followed in the Taupo Lake dispute is important as setting a precedent likely to be followed in the vexatious grievances arising from the confiscations of land after the Maori wars.

Examples might be multipled. Perhaps more significant, however, than the redress of more or less isolated grievances of this nature has been the appointment, gazetted in October 1926, of a Royal Commission to enquire into grievances arising from the confiscations that followed the wars of the sixties. During 1927 this Commission, one of whose three members was a half-caste Maori, sat in many districts of the north island. For the first time in nearly three-quarters of a century a competent tribunal considered the issues raised by the wars which began in 1860, and particularly the justice of the various confiscations.

The problems involved are extremely complicated. Counsel for the Maoris occupied the attention of the Commission for a week in making his opening statement of the Maori case during the first sitting at Waitara, where the wars originated. The position in every district demanded separate consideration. The confiscations have been overlain by more than sixty years of subsequent land-selling. In some cases the previous owners of the confiscated lands were tacitly allowed to reoccupy them, in other cases land was returned formally and vested in a trust. The existence of such a trust as the West Coast Trust, in which much Taranaki land was vested, did not, however, debar the owners from selling their holdings, and it is extremely difficult at this time to disentangle the consequences of confiscation from those of improvident land-selling.

The important fact, however, is that the Government, as representing the dominant Pakeha community, has recognised that injustices have been done and has taken steps to make generous if tardy atonement for the injury. The past cannot be undone, nothing can restore the sadly thinned ranks of the tribes concerned; but the constructive efforts of future promise can be assisted. The amounts of compensation recommended by the Commission are a compromise, or rather a series of compromises, but they will go far towards removing the sense of grievance and will also provide much needed means for stimulating constructive educational and economic movements of the type illustrated by the pioneer experiments described later in this chapter.

It is true that the Commission had to interpret its order of reference concerning the justice of the confiscations in a somewhat narrow legal sense. It is also true that the suspicion of Governmental motives ground into the mentality of certain tribes by many decades of unfortunate experiences has not been wholly removed. The Commission did not receive wholehearted co-operation in every district. On the other hand, its coming was hailed by many tribes with the greatest expectations, and omens were observed that have aroused high hopes that a new era has dawned, an era of hope and effort, stimulated by the Pakeha's long-delayed but generous compensation for past injuries and injustices.(13)

As the long-delayed settlement of the south island grievances indicates, the task of securing agreement between the Government and the tribes concerned is a laborious and lengthy procedure. The Government which set up the Confiscations Commission was defeated in a General Election and resigned early in December 1928. Before resigning, the Prime Minister (who was also Minister of Native Affairs) left a general statement expressing the sympathy of his party towards any scheme for the settlement of the confiscation grievances. He was fortunately succeeded as Native Minister by Sir Apirana Ngata, whose knowledge of these matters is unequalled, who was privy to all the steps hitherto taken, and whose skill in negotiation of such delicate affairs along constructive lines is quite without peer in the Dominion. Negotiations therefore moved forward in much the same hands as before without any check.

In the middle of January a series of meetings was commenced with the various tribes concerned in the confiscations. These meetings extended over several months. With the exception of Waikato, where an epidemic unfortunately caused the Department of Native Health to place an embargo on all Maori assemblies in that district after only one preliminary meeting had been held, all the tribes have agreed to accept monetary compensation instead of compensation in land.

The latter was urged by the older men, who insisted that only the return of part of the confiscated area would remedy the injustice. The younger men were, however, persuaded that wider and more varied issues were involved than the land problem, and that these could be met only by the possession of a tribal fund. The dominance of the younger men in these negotiations, and the reluctant submission of the elders to their opinions, is the most recent victory of the new spirit permeating Maoridom. Everywhere, most notably at Waitara, it was clear that behind the attenuated ranks of the older men who had once sat at the feet of Tawhiao (the Waikato King), Te Whiti and Tohu (the priests of Taranaki), and Te Kooti (the east coast "rebel" leader and the founder of the Ringatu Cult), the younger people had their minds set on education, health reforms, farming, and other things that interest the youth of the race in other parts. Latest news from Ngaruwahia confirmed the views expressed after the March meeting that the Waikato people are prepared to fall in line with other tribes, thus completing the psychological conversion of Maoridom, a memorable victory for the forces of conciliation.

The Revival of Maori Agriculture

The investigation and redress of grievances is important both psychologically and economically, but of even greater importance are the experiments in land tenure and rural co-operation which lie behind the recent revival of Maori agriculture. Stress has been laid in the previous section upon the trend of native land legislation being almost wholly in the direction of facilitating the sale of land to the Pakehas and upon the evil effects that followed the individualising of land titles. It is not easy to appreciate the full results of these measures in destroying the economic life of the Maoris by breaking down tribal organisation and encouraging habits of extravagance, instability, and lack of industry.

Broadly speaking, the days of easy money from the sale of land have passed by. Much of the best land is sold. Where tribes retain good land in fair quantities, policies of conservation are being pursued. The Native Land Court and Maori Land Boards in the different districts still function in the administration of native land matters, but the halcyon days of large sales and ready money are a matter of memory, and mostly bitter memory.

It is all but impossible to generalise concerning the economic position of the Maoris at the present time. A complete account would need to take into review all the varied geographical, historical, and psychological as well as economic factors, district by district and tribe by tribe.

The total area of land remaining in native occupation—4,422,046 acres—seems at first sight a large area for a people that, including those of mixed native-white descent, numbers only 64,817 men, women, and children. But it would be quite wrong to deduce from these crude figures visions of a wealthy landowning native race. In the first place the land that is left to the Maoris is seldom of the best quality. Much of it lies in such districts as the pumice region of the middle of the north island, and the gum-lands of the peninsula north of Auckland. Other large areas, particularly along the north-east coast of the north island, are potentially more valuable but are more or less inaccessible. The country is heavily forested, the confused and rugged mountain ranges make railways and even roads difficult to construct, and there is a lack of good harbours from which access might be gained by sea.

Where the Maoris still retain large areas in accessible regions the Pakeha settlers have only too often "spotted" the country, or in colonial parlance "picked the eyes out of it", leaving the less desirable stretches to the Maori. It is true that there is a considerable area leased to Pakeha farmers by the natives either directly or through the Native Trustee and the Maori Land Boards. From these lands a steady revenue is derived by the Maoris concerned. There are, however, many areas where the conditions are reversed and Maoris are having to lease or buy back from the Pakehas at enormously higher prices than their ancestors received for it.

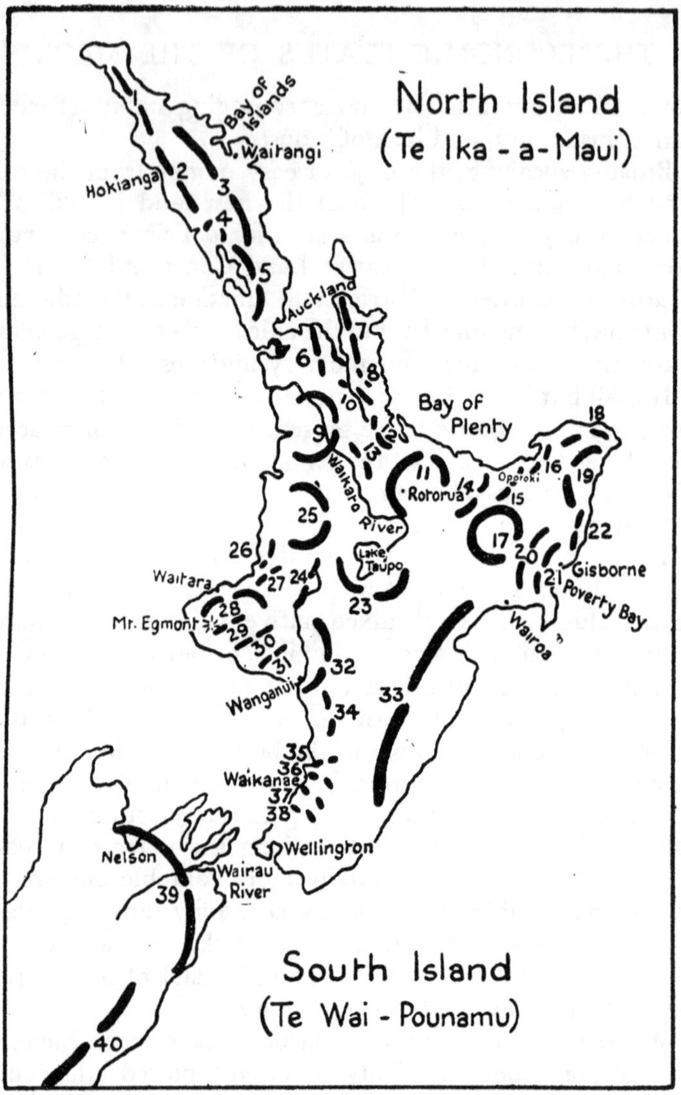

PRINCIPAL MAORI TRIBES OF TO-DAY

1. Te Aupouri; 2. Te Rarawa; 3. Ngapuhi; 4. Uriohau; 5. Ngati-whatua; 6. Ngati-paoa; 7. Ngati-whanaunga; 8. Ngati-maru; 9. Waikato; 10. Ngati-tamatera; 11. Te Arawa; 12. Ngatierangi; 13. Ngati-haua; 14. Ngati-awa; 15. Whakatohea; 16. Ngaitai; 17. Urewera; 18. Whanau-a-apanui; 19. Ngati-porou; 20. Rongo-whakata; 21. Aitanga-a-mahaki; 22. Hauiti; 23. Ngati-tuwhare-toa; 24. Ngati-hau; 25. Ngati-maniapoto; 26. Ngati-tama; 27. Ngati-mutunga; 28. Taranaki; 29. Te Atiawa; 30. Ngati-ruanui; 31. Ngarauru; 32. Whanganui; 33. Ngati-kahungunu; 34. Ngati-apa; 35. Muaupoko; 36. Ngati-raukawa; 37. Ngati-toa; 38. Ngati-awa; 39. Ngati-awa, Ngati-kuia, Ngati-rarua, Ngai-Tahu; 40. Ngati-Tahu (scattered through the south island).

[After Keesing, *The Changing Maori.*]

The situation is complicated by the fact that in recent years, particularly after the legislation of 1909, many Maori tribes, having gained experience, proved to be very astute negotiators of land sales. They knew their own land and were careful to sell only the poorer sections of it to the Crown. Their ingenuity was sometimes too much for the State purchasers, as when a powerful tribe sold hill-country but ceased to sell when the more accessible and fertile valleys were reached, and later had the satisfaction of watching the white settlers use their political power to obtain roads which necessarily opened up Maori lands also. The most recent land sales, under controlled conditions and with more experienced Maori bargaining, have probably been for the benefit of the tribes concerned. Moneys have been placed in trust where they are available to finance the working of the land that remains in Maori ownership or to assist in such economic developments as butter-factories. These facts illustrate again the impossibility of generalisation regarding Maori affairs. Some fortunate tribes have been able to make good use of their heritage.

Those tribes which bore the brunt of the first contact with the white man are generally speaking the worst off. In the peninsula north of Auckland there is a state of comparative poverty. The tribal community, apparently never as strong in this region as in others, has all but vanished. Individualisation has proceeded to great lengths. By dint of hard work with unpromising resources the tribes are winning through, but are disposed to imitate European ways of life rather than build anew their old Maori customs. In February 1928 they accepted a scheme of land consolidation, the details of which are now being worked out. There is good recent evidence that the tribes in this district have a much more optimistic outlook than appears on the surface. The Maori Land Board is rendering assistance to a large number of small-holders. Closer organisation and supervision will do much to knit these people together into a progressive and fairly comfortable community. Their poverty makes them satisfied with a lower standard of housing and living generally, and more easy to fit into the pressing economic conditions of the day in New Zealand. It should be emphasised that the population is increasing in greater proportion in the north than in other parts of Maoridom except, possibly, the east coast.

In the districts behind Wellington every mile is reminiscent of the history of Maori contacts with the first settlers; but depopulation has been almost complete. A few scattered people live in modernised villages here and there, but the land has passed from them and they form a mere remnant of once powerful tribes. In their effort to survive they are forced to day-labour and to experiments in small-scale farming, and even market-gardening.

In Taranaki, where the wars broke out in 1860, the situation is more complicated. The survivors are rather more in number, but still a pitiful proportion of a once thriving population, though it is probable that the population is now not much less than it was after pressure from the north drove back the Taranaki tribes in the thirties. Most of the best land near the coast has been lost, but south of the mountain (Egmont) and further north above Waitara there is to be found a large area of native land, most of it leased to Europeans, but some in Maori cultivation. The existence of this scattering of Maori dairy-farmers working on an individualistic basis and competing successfully with their Pakeha neighbours is a matter of great importance and good omen.

The West Coast Trust, which was formed after the confiscations, has not retained all the land entrusted to it, but the Taranaki Maoris are, on the whole, favourably situated economically. The main barriers to progress are psychological, the heritage of war and confiscation. The findings and compensation of the recent Commission should do much to bring a new era of effort and co-operation.

Without doubt the heaviest sufferer from the war and attendant confiscations was the Waikato tribe. Between it and its neighbour of the rugged King country, the Maniapoto tribe, which also acknowledged the authority of the Maori King, the Government failed sufficiently to discriminate. The military campaign stopped at the Puniu River on the bounds of the Maniapoto Territory. The rich valley of the Waikato was confiscated; but the real leader of the war movement among the King party—Rewi, a high chief of the Maniapoto—was left with territory and prestige almost untouched. The Waikatos, whose great leader, Tamihana, had opposed the war movement till hostilities were inevitable, and even then had fought relatively on the defensive, lost their lands and retain a bitter memory of injustice.

A chief of the Maniapoto has recently compared his people to a spectator sitting in the front stalls watching other people engaged in a drama and getting more emotional about it than the actors had time to be. Where the Waikato were inclined to be sullen and aloof, the Maniapoto assumed a defiant pose, tinged with an attitude of scepticism for anything Pakeha. The cessation of hostilities on their borders was interpreted as an admission by the Government, represented in their minds by the military authorities, of their (Maniapoto) superiority. To some extent, no doubt, this interpretation was correct, as the prospect of continuing hostilities in such uninviting country could not have been alluring. Maniapoto scepticism has, however, reacted adversely against them in their land transactions, their distrust of Government agencies rendering them an easy prey to land-sharks. Only recently has the Maniapoto tribe relaxed its hostility to the Government and allowed settlement and modern communications to penetrate the "Rohe Potae". In April 1928 a definite forward move was made by the acceptance of a scheme for land consolidation and the settlement of some outstanding grievances over rates.

The grievances of the Waikato are not yet salved, despite the reconciliation between Seddon and King Mahuta many years ago. In this particular case tribal unity is still very pronounced. The bluest blood in Maoridom flows in the veins of its leaders, and unlike other tribes in such dire circumstances there has been no giving in. The men have worked as labourers in agricultural and mining occupations, and the tribe, while resolutely maintaining its policy of non-co-operation with the Government, has increased in numbers and has preserved its pride of race.

Within recent months, however, there has been the notable recognition of the constructive efforts of the "Princess" Te Puea Herangi in leading her tribe to ways of co-operation and friendship. Her noble work, especially her efforts to care for the children in her orphanage, has captured the imagination of both Maori and Pakeha. The Governor-General has visited her, and her return visit to Wellington showed the high regard in which she is held. The very timely recommendations of the Royal Commission awarding compensation to the Waikato for their just grievances will go far to encourage and support such leadership as she has shown.

So the story goes on, with different combinations of factors and different emphasis in every tribe. The Taupo tribes, after long litigation concerning inequitable timber leases and even timber robberies, are beginning to work their own valuable forests. The Arawa and Tuwharetoa Trust Boards in the same region have already been mentioned.

In different localities in the Bay of Plenty economic conditions are bad. Confiscations were heavy and land sales were even more disastrous. Some of the people also felt implicated in some of the worst incidents of the latter stages of the war and therefore unable to protest as vigorously as they might have done against what they regarded as arbitrary treatment.

In Hawke's Bay, after an era of improvidence in land-selling, the tribal leaders are facing steadily towards a policy of education and building for the next generation. In the wilder and less accessible parts of the north island, on the upper reaches of the Wanganui River, in the mountainous Urewera country, and in the extreme north-east above Gisborne, more land remains in Maori possession and more remains also of the tribal organisation and Maori ways of life.

It is worth noting that the Urewera people, reputably the most backward portion of Maoridom, were the first to follow the Ngati-Porou with a scheme of land consolidation, completed as early as 1922. Unfortunately the area of land suitable for farming is very limited.

While there is a general stirring of new life all over Maoridom at the present time, the chief manifestations of enterprise and experiment are therefore to be found in the regions which were fortunate enough to be saved from the first rough contacts with civilisation.

The tribes in the thermal regions, fishing districts, and similar tourist resorts are turning the tourist traffic to good account. Others supply skilled shearing gangs in pastoral districts or maintain sheep-farms. Maori chauffeurs, saw-millers, workers in State forest plantations, labour with the Pakeha; while others work out experiments in rabbit-trapping, commercial fishing, and truck-farming. The Wairoa people accepted and pushed through a contract for twenty-six miles of railroad construction in record time. There are even more important experiments in dairying, competing successfully with the Pakeha farmers, notably in North Auckland, Taranaki, and the Bay of Plenty. A co-operative dairy factory with a large number of Maori suppliers is at work at Ruatoki in the North Urewera country. Another at Nuhaka in Hawke's Bay has worked successfully for many years and was one of the stimuli leading to the Ngati-Porou experiments described below. All along the east coast dairying is beginning to flourish, around Poverty Bay, Wairoa, and east of Opotiki among the Whanau-a-Apanui. Everywhere there is "the spur of necessity" driving the young men of Maoridom to find a way of economic salvation for their people, and everywhere there is a growing realisation that the first step on the road must be to take advantage of the Pakeha's education.

Not all the Maoris are agriculturists or rural workers. An increasing number of educated youths find their way into city offices, the Civil Service, medicine, engineering, accountancy, nursing, law, and the Church. In these occupations also they are proving their ability to compete with the Pakehas.

It is, however, among the Ngati-Porou in what is generally termed the east coast region of the north island that the most significant progress has so far been made. Their isolation, which in earlier days earned them the derisive title of "Nati" (country cousins), has been due to the lack of good harbours, a mountainous hinterland, and very difficult approaches by land. For at least three generations—that is, practically ever since the policy of free trade in Maori land has been followed—their tribal leaders have stood firm against selling any but the unoccupied mountain hinterlands of their fertile valleys. At the time of the Maori wars they were led by Major Ropata Wahawaha, "one of the very few captains on either side who went through the wars without anything that could be called a defeat". After his death the leadership of the tribe passed to his kinsman, Paratene Ngata, and thence to the latter's son, (Sir) Apirana Turupa Ngata. It is of more than passing interest to note that this accepted leadership is not a matter of ceremonial inherited by right of birth. The mana* of hereditary chieftainship lies elsewhere. The mana of business has become identified with the sword of Major Ropata, which on his deathbed he gave to Paratene Ngata, who thereupon returned it to the tribal leaders in council. The elders of the tribe bestowed the emblem of leadership, together with their individual mana, upon Paratene Ngata, and after his death upon his son, who had become the acknowledged leader of the tribe in all matters of business organisation. As their Member of Parliament and Minister of Native Affairs, as well as the inspirer and leader of economic social movements, Sir Apirana Ngata occupies a unique position among his own tribe.

Under such leadership the retention of the best tribal land became "the persistent and thought-out policy" of the Ngati-Porou; but the genius of Sir Apirana Ngata has added the constructive elements of policy necessary to enable positive use to be made of these lands. The first expedient worked out was an interesting adjustment between the extremes of land Communism and individual property rights. The several owners of a tract of land were incorporated by the processes of Pakeha law, and from their number a committee of management was elected which was able to supervise the management of farming operations and to arrange for adequate funds. This development of incorporation was already in progress and is the chief element of Maori policy which is referred to by the Royal Commission of 1907–9 in their statement that the reopening of free trade in Maori lands in 1905 had forced the Maoris to contemplate the possibility of using their lands in the Pakeha way.

In 1911 a further important development occurred when the first effort was made to consolidate the scattered holdings of individual Maoris or family groups into compact farms. It is difficult to convey in brief outline even a dim realisation of the almost infinite patience, industry, and knowledge necessary to carry out this process of consolidation. Communal rights of landownership in such a country as England were probably never as complex as among the Maoris, and were greatly simpli-

* Mana, a Maori word meaning power, prestige, authority, honour, has passed into general usage in New Zealand.

fied at the time of the Norman Conquest by the individualising tendencies of the Norman-French lawyers. The processes of consolidating the scattered strips of the feudal tenants and the enclosure movements which grew out of these processes occupy the chief place in English agricultural history from the fourteenth to the nineteenth century. In the course of these movements the English peasantry lost both their individual holdings and their rights in the common land. With these facts in mind the Pakeha historian has nothing but unqualified respect and admiration for the way in which Maori leadership has worked out methods of consolidation within a brief period of time, and methods, moreover, which safeguard the rights of every holder of the land.

The first basis adopted was "a system of exchange of interests laboriously worked out, involving endless meetings, conferences, groupings, and re-groupings, the breaking down of long-standing ties and overcoming of sentimental opposition—all calling for supreme patience and tact, together with confidence in the essential rightness of the solution offered".

Even to-day, when experience has provided a simpler basis for the exchange of interests by the acceptance of the Government valuation of the land concerned, the process of consolidation is involved and difficult; but its success among the Ngati-Porou has been so striking and the essential soundness of its principles so obviously demonstrated that in a number of north island districts to-day consolidation schemes are putting new life into Maori landownership.

The effective utilisation of the land so consolidated and incorporated respresents a still further and very successful stage in the economic and social rehabilitation of the Maoris. Even twenty years ago a competent and not unsympathetic economic historian laid great stress upon the weaknesses and failures of Maori farming. (14) There are some districts where his discouraging description may still be taken as approximately correct but exaggerated. In the twenty years that have intervened the promising Ngati-Porou experiments to which he makes reference have been proven by experience, and it can no longer be said that they affect only a small proportion of the Maori population. Their influence and example is bearing fruit both directly and indirectly in many other districts.

Moreover, these experiments have an interest that transcends their importance in the regeneration of Maori agriculture. Even a quarter of a century ago the possibility of the Maoris contributing any significant ideas to the organisation of rural industries hardly entered the minds even of their best friends. The apologists for the Maori have until recent times tended to claim that his contribution to the common life of New Zealand would be made in the intellectual and spiritual sphere rather than in the sphere of material development. Yet work has already been done which justifies the claim that the Maori tribes on the east coast of the north island have profited by the experience of European civilisation and have evolved a combination of individual initiative with communal landholding and profit-sharing and of both with tribal organisation and a revival of racial pride that is likely to save their people from the fate that has overtaken the original owners of most agricultural land.

The first experiments, now a quarter of a century old, were made in sheep-farming, which already had been a communal pursuit of the tribe for some decades. The committee of management of an incorporated tract of land appointed managers who in turn engaged their labour from among the owners of the land. Unlike most communistic experiments, these ventures of the Maoris have shown the discipline and organising ability necessary for commercial success. They have not been afraid to use and give authority to Pakeha managers, nor have they been lacking in the confidence of ultimate success necessary before the owners could be brought to mortgage their lands so as to obtain adequate capital to finance their undertakings. The Pakeha managers are being steadily replaced by trained Maori agriculturists, and the financial situation is well in hand and sounder than many Pakeha farming enterprises. The landowners, even though they be high chiefs by lineage, receive as labourers just as much or as little as they earn, and as owners of the land participate in the profit according to their share. The mana of business is kept entirely distinct from the mana of hereditary descent. The importance of this statement needs some emphasis. It is the key to the success of the Ngati-Porou and the slogan for the most recent movements in Maoridom. The Ngati-Kahungunu of Wairoa have, after a generation of aloofness from the example of the Ngati-Porou, satisfied themselves that the secret must be laboriously learned. Their fellow-tribesmen of Hawke's Bay made it the chief subject of debate at a meeting at Omahu early in May 1929. The lesson needs to be learned by other tribes. At the same time the most zealous care must be taken, as in the case of the Ngati-Porou, that the mana of hereditary descent is not invaded in any way in the sphere of ceremonial.

In 1923 certain younger members of the tribe urged that dairying, involving not only the arduous labour of feeding and milking cows, but also the organisation and scientific conduct of a butter-factory, was the only solution to the increasing pressure of population on the tribal lands. In the four seasons of its operation this dairy factory, co-operatively owned, and therefore reflecting the welfare of its suppliers, has shown increasing success, despite the troubled course of the dairy industry in New Zealand generally. In bold irony it took as its trade-mark the term of contempt, "Nati", which had formerly been applied to the tribe, and it has had the satisfaction of placing that term among the leading brands receiving top prices on the London market. The balance-sheet of its second year showed 76 suppliers producing nearly 300,000 lbs. of butter, which were sold for £19,601. At the end of its third season it had 107 suppliers and produced 462,560 lbs. of butter. For the season now ending (1928–9), 136 suppliers produced 285 tons of butter.

Of even greater significance is the continued success of the co-operative trading venture established in close connection with these productive enterprises. The Waiapu Farmers' Co-operative Company has completed sixteen successful years of trading and is sufficient evidence in itself of the ability of Maori leadership to handle commercial as well as productive organisation. It may justly be claimed, therefore, that where so many idealistic experiments in economic Communism and co-operation have failed, the Maoris, by reason of tribal discipline and enlightened leadership, have succeeded. The English in which the review of the first sixteen years of co-operative trading was presented to the Maori shareholders is sufficient contrast with the business English of most Pakeha companies to indicate that leadership of uncommon ability is present.

It is true that these particular experiments in the management of land are confined largely to a few sections of the Maori people. It is also true that in the case of the Ngati-Porou descendants of an old missionary family (the Williams) rendered much needed financial and technical help at the first critical stages. It is a fact also that the Ngati-Porou and other tribes which have experimented in this fashion have used Pakeha management and have depended a good deal upon financial advances from banks and from Government departments. But these facts do not detract from the importance of the experiments.

It is, moreover, abundantly clear that the success of some tribes and numbers of individuals is blazing a path for the other members of their race to follow. It may be taken as a proven fact that the Maori, given a fair opportunity, is able not only to adapt himself to the necessities of modern economic organisation, but to make his own distinctive contribution towards its improvement.

The Maori Renaissance

The background both of the economic experiments so lightly sketched in the previous section and of the more sympathetic Pakeha attitude of recent years is a real renaissance movement of the greatest interest and promise. This renaissance has political, economic, religious, and literary aspects; but its great driving-force is an intense racial consciousness and pride of ancestry. Many of its leading figures have European blood in their veins, and it is arguable that the vigour of the movement is at least partly due to this fact. The present generation of Maoris is being largely recruited from sections of the race which have escaped the worst of the transition period, and there is a much larger mixture of white blood than is generally realised.(15) It is, however, significant that they should turn with such pride to an appreciation of their Maori ancestry, an appreciation which seems to be deeper and more intense in the degree to which they have received Pakeha education and training.

This revival of race pride and confidence is all the more remarkable when one considers the psychological environment in which the present generation was brought up.(16) The political and economic aspects of the difficult transition period that followed the wars, together with the ravages of disease, have already been mentioned. It may be readily understood that the middle generation of Maoris tended to lose heart. Defeated in the struggle to drive the Pakeha out, overwhelmed by the rush of settlement, caught in the confusing intricacy of land legislation from which they seldom emerged without losing their lands—baffled, thwarted, and unable fully to comprehend what was happening to them, they might well lament the passing of their race.

The most important consequence was an attitude of passive resistance that followed upon convinced distrust of Pakeha intentions. The mental attitude of suspicion was in itself a barrier to progress and mental growth; but the policy of non-co-operation, by which certain families and settlements refused to take advantage of Government schools or health measures, was even more disastrous. In many of these cases it must be said, too, that there were genuine economic as well as psychological reasons behind the refusal. Wherever the lands had been confiscated or sold without due precautions for the future, many Maoris were not able to send their children, even if they so wished, to school and college for education beyond that provided in the State primary schools. It is little wonder, therefore, that this difficult period has aptly been named a cultural Slough of Despond. Caught in it, some of the tribes went down numerically and in tribal solidarity; others drew together the more closely.

Few Pakehas have caught even a glimpse of this tragic situation. Yet it does not need expert psycho-analytic knowledge to divine something of the burning resentments and hatreds and thwarted self-expression that found vent in the atrocities that sometimes accompanied Maori warfare. It is significant that in the case of the worst outrages—those which followed the escape of Te Kooti from the Chatham Islands—there was a definite background of arbitrary Governmental action (deportation) which was resented as unjust. Te Kooti, according to very good authority, was innocent, but was herded with others who were deported to the Chatham Islands without trial.

Nor can the Pakeha, after the exploits in recent years of

what are commonly regarded as more developed civilisations, be unduly critical of such war hatreds, or of the religious developments which often accompanied them. The courage and uprightness of the lives of the early missionaries made a profound impression upon the Maori mind, which readily accepted the Christian teaching. Missionary effort gained some of its greatest rewards in early New Zealand. But who can blame the Maori for regression when one remembers the bitter sectarianism to which they were so quickly introduced and the very evident disparity between missionary teaching and general Pakeha practice?

Such incidents as the capture of an important "pa" one Sunday morning when its defenders were engaged in Christian worship were apt to be disconcerting. That this was not a mere accident quickly became apparent. "The missionaries", said a Maori chief, "taught us to look up to Heaven, and while we were looking, the land slipped away from under our feet."

One can understand, therefore, why from time to time quasi-religious movements sweep across Maoridom, incorporating large elements of ancient magic with the teachings of the Christian religion. They remind us that the transition to modernity is still far from complete; but the credulity of the twentieth century in regard to the very similar pseudo-psychologies, new religions, and mob movements generally, leave the Pakeha little room to scoff at the Maori, who has decades of European civilisation behind him where the Pakeha has centuries. The strangeness of such movements should not blind us to the rapid progress of the Maori race, nor to the very real spiritual values often sought in them.

Maori progress in its latest phase can be traced fairly definitely to the association of students of Te Aute College, which in the nineties became known as the Young Maori Party. The actual party organisation was never very rigid, and has now passed into memory. The band of leaders whose discussions crystallised the principles of the renaissance have, each in his own way, rendered devoted practical service to their people. As statesmen, doctors, nurses, teachers, ministers, lawyers, business men, and not least as practical farmers, they led the way to the new order. Leadership came in greatest degree, naturally enough, from those more fortunate tribes, notably from the east coast, who had retained much of their lands and had not banked up a heritage of suspicion and enmity against the Pakeha. They had the wealth and the willingness, even eagerness, to send their young men and women in increasing numbers to receive Pakeha training. Other tribes also threw up notable leaders in sufficient numbers to prove that capacity is widely distributed over Maoridom.

There are signs that the hereditary leaders of the race are beginning to appreciate the fact that they must fit themselves for leadership under modern conditions just as their forefathers had to in the days when prowess in war, mental superiority, and efficiency in diplomacy had to be harnessed to rank to maintain their position. It is wonderful and very full of hope to note how readily sections of a tribe will fall into line behind any scion of a rangatira family who shows his fitness to lead them in the modern ways. The greatest leaders of the race to-day, like Sir Maui Pomare and Sir Apirana Ngata, are continually on the lookout for this material in order to encourage individuals of high rank to step into their proper and natural place in the renaissance of the tribes.

In the last few years there have been unmistakable stirrings of new life. Old resentments die hard and suspicions are too deep-rooted to be easily allayed; but youth meets youth in sport and on the common ground of racial problems and interests transcending tribal jealousies. The economic achievements of the Ngati-Porou are impressing all Maoridom, and their great leader, Sir Apirana Ngata, entirely without self-seeking, is rapidly becoming a national figure acclaimed alike by Maori and Pakeha.

It would indeed be a simple and grateful task to catalogue the many achievements of the Maoris in the life of New Zealand. To do so would, however, take more space than is available here. The names mentioned below are only those of a few outstanding figures. It is one of the best features of the Maori situation that for every leader of the present day there may be counted numbers of promising youthful successors. The greatest name of all is that of Sir Apirana Ngata, M.P., M.A., LL.B., scholar, poet, statesman, leader of his people in every constructive endeavour. A Maori half-caste, Sir James Carroll, now deceased, acted as Premier of the Dominion and as Minister of the Crown in various capacities. Sir Maui Pomare, a graduate in medicine of the University of Chicago, has been Minister for Health and minister in charge of the Cook and other islands. A Maori clergyman, the Rev. F. A. Bennett, has been appointed suffragan to the Bishop of Waiapu, with the title of Bishop of Aotearoa. A Maori anthropologist, Dr. P. H. Buck, is recording with careful skill and unrivalled insight the material culture not only of New Zealand but of the other Pacific islands. He is the first gift of a reinvigorated Maoridom to the international world of scientific investigation. These are a few of the outstanding examples of success achieved in open competition with the Pakeha.

The native land problem of New Zealand, therefore, is not a question of transferring land as justly as possible from an inferior native race to the superior white settlers. It is rather a problem of the survival of a people with a remarkable history and heritage. In less than a century and a half they have bridged the gap between a neolithic culture and modern civilisation. Their experience has been a bitter one. The Maori to-day is disillusioned and rather resentful as he reflects on the consequences to his people of the lack of imagination and understanding, sometimes even of justice, on the part of the Pakeha. But he is conscious also that he is on the road to survival and that leaders are emerging once again to guide their people on the most difficult voyage of all their history.

His leaders are increasingly confident that the race will not only re-establish itself, but that the Maori farmer will solve many difficulties which confront land settlement in New Zealand to-day. They see clearly that the Maori is not trained or mentally equipped for intensive farming and cannot contribute much to the closer settlement of improved lands. But he will fill the rôle heretofore played by the pioneer, and should be at least moderately successful in the lower quality and less accessible lands of the Dominion, where a lower standard of living is acceptable, with less efficient farming methods and a lower rate of profit.

The Maori has found his niche. His feet are on solid ground again, and he has hope for the future. The ancient watch-cry of the sentry on guard above the sleeping pa begins to have new meaning:

> The night is dark and long,
> The young sleep and dream their dreams,
> In the minds of the old is doubt, trouble, and fear,
> Long and dark is the night, but its hour draws to a close,
> Behold it is dawn, it is dawn, it is day.

CHAPTER III

THE ALIENATION OF THE LAND

The First Land Claims

The first sale of land recorded in New Zealand was a purchase made on February 24, 1815, by Samuel Marsden, on behalf of the Church Missionary Society.(1) Approximately two hundred acres were bought, the purchase price being twelve axes. The deed was signed by the drawing of the facial "moko" (tattoo) pattern of the chief concerned, a precedent that was followed at Waitangi. Marsden's chief reason for purchasing land is given in a footnote to a letter written on August 7, 1830, to an official at Church Missionary House, as the necessity for providing neutral territory on which Maori youths could take sanctuary under missionary protection from tribal feuds.(2) His policy was evidently followed vigorously, as a large missionary purchase of fifteen thousand acres in the Bay of Islands as early as 1821 was reported in the evidence proffered to Mr. J. T. Bigge, who had been commissioned by the British Government to enquire into the atrocities which were making New Zealand infamous at that time.(3) In 1822 the adventurer de Thierry claimed to have acquired land by purchase, and in 1825 the first New Zealand Company was formed. The settlers it sent out in 1862 refused to carry on, but individuals remained at Hokianga and the Company's land claims proved very costly of settlement to the later and more important company founded by Edward Gibbon Wakefield in 1838.(4)

These early purchases by direct negotiation with the natives are typical of many made by genuine settlers like F. E. Maning, the author of *Old New Zealand*, by whalers and Pakeha Maoris who later added farming to their activities, by pioneer settlers such as (Sir) John Logan Campbell in Auckland, and by more speculative buyers of various types. As the approach of British governance became more obvious, the speculative purchases of native land reached extraordinary proportions. The claims for land so purchased as submitted to the Land Commission appointed by the first Governor aggregated 56,654,000 acres.(5) The great bulk of this area was claimed as a result of purchases made in 1839 and 1840, and there were the most ludicrous documents submitted in support of some of the transactions. Even highly placed public men like the Australian explorer and statesman Wentworth joined in the scramble.

The traffic in Maori lands which centred in Sydney was virtually stopped by a proclamation of Governor Gipps of New South Wales, on January 14, 1840, that no land title would be acknowledged as valid unless authorised through, or confirmed by, a grant from the Crown. Wentworth, who subsequently claimed to have bought about twenty million acres in the south island, led a bitter fight against Gipps's proposal that the New South Wales Legislative Council should appoint land commissioners to investigate all purchases. The Governor, however, carried the day, and the commissioners were appointed.

Hobson, as Lieutenant-Governor of New Zealand, issued a similar proclamation to that of his chief, on January 30, 1840, and the separation of New Zealand from the colony of New South Wales in November 1840 placed in Hobson's hands the sole responsibility for the settlement of the land claims. His instructions were very clear.(6) They were based upon the principles laid down by Lord John Russell to the Land and Emigration Commissioners, appointed in 1839 to deal with waste lands in the Colonies. In following them out Hobson issued, on June 9, 1841, a Land Claims Ordinance (No. 1) terminating the New South Wales commission and taking power to appoint a similar commission under New Zealand authority.(7) The important clause of this Ordinance is the second: "All titles to land in New Zealand absolutely null and void unless allowed by Her Majesty."

The result of these measures is greatly to the credit of the British Government of the day and its representatives in New South Wales and New Zealand. As the hearing of claims progressed, the purchases of the speculative land-sharks were reduced almost to vanishing-point. The Ordinance mentioned above prescribed purchase prices on a sliding scale according to the time when the purchase was made, ranging from 6d. per acre for land bought between 1815 and 1824 to 8s. for land bought in 1839. No purchases after the proclamations of January 1840 were considered. In earlier purchases the goods paid were estimated at three times their selling price in Sydney at the time of purchase and an acreage allowed according to the schedule of purchase prices laid down. Grants even then were limited to 2,560 acres, except in special cases.

The Land Purchases of the New Zealand Company

Governor Hobson had a comparatively easy task in withstanding the exaggerated claims of land-sharks and protecting the natives from their depredations. He successfully established the constitutional principle that in British territory all claims to land rest upon grants from the Crown. In disposing of the almost fraudulent early claims and reducing genuine purchases to areas comparable with the prices paid he rendered a signal service both to the Maoris and to later settlers. Moreover, by negotiating the Treaty of Waitangi he made any further land purchase impossible except through the Crown.

He was faced, however, with a much more complicated and difficult task in settling the status of the land purchases which had been made by the agents of the New Zealand Company. The Company was a powerful group with a large vested interest and possessing many important channels of influence in London. Its purchases were hastily executed and open to grave criticism; but settlers had bought the land in good faith before leaving England, and would have been placed in an intolerable position by the strict observance of the Governor's instructions. Some immediate action was necessary, and in September 1841 Hobson waived the Crown's right of preemption over certain lands at Wellington, Porirua, the Hutt, Manawatu, and Taranaki. This afforded temporary relief, but no real solution of the deadlock of policies could be arrived at until the Land Commission settled the area to be finally awarded the Company. The Commissioner did not arrive until Christmas Eve, 1841, and his first court was not opened for another four months. His duties dragged out over several years, and were only terminated in 1846 by the new agreement entered into between the Colonial Office and the Company. In the meantime the company officials in New Zealand contested very bitterly the view which he took of his powers and questioned the legality of the Treaty of Waitangi, and even of the Government which had been set up. The Commissioner, however, persevered in his court and reduced very considerably indeed the twenty million acres that the Company claimed to have purchased. (8)

His interim awards were sufficient for the immediate necessities of the settlers, but the Company itself would have fared badly if the matter had ended there. In 1846, however, while Wakefield was ill, other leaders arrived at an agreement with the Colonial Office by which the British Government granted a loan of £100,000, and in 1847 passed an Act giving the Company "the entire and exclusive disposal of all Crown lands; and the exercise of the Crown's right of pre-emption of lands belonging to the natives in the southern government of New Zealand". (9)

This arrangement, together with the cancellation of debts due to the Government, the further loan of £136,000 within the three years following, and Governmental recognition of a charge of £268,370 for land awarded previously to the Company, gave it a new lease of life. By this time it was becoming frankly commercialised, and Wakefield repudiated the agreement in scathing terms. Its existence was not prolonged, however, and in 1850 it surrendered its charter. It took a further seven years before the colonists in New Zealand could be brought to shoulder the liability assumed on their behalf by the Colonial Office; but the debt was finally paid in 1857 out of a loan from the British Government. (10)

Before this conclusion was reached, the most successful of the Wakefield experiments were launched by the Settlement of Otago in 1848 and Canterbury in 1850. The 400,000 acres of the Otago block and the 1,000,000 acres (afterwards increased to 2,400,000) of the Canterbury Settlement were granted without the complications of the earlier north island purchases. The natives were fewer and less aggressive, so that the Government agents had no difficulty in purchasing the Otago lands or the much larger areas comprising almost the whole of the south island from which the Canterbury grant was selected. The settlers, therefore, came to land of which the native titles had been extinguished, so that no conflicts were possible.

By Section 72 of the Constitution Act of 1852, giving New

Zealand responsible government, control of the waste lands passed to the colonial legislature. The New Zealand Company had surrendered its charter in 1850 and the Canterbury Association transferred its functions to the colonists of Canterbury after the passing of the Constitution Act, which also took power out of the hands of the Otago Association.

The stormy career of the New Zealand Company (paralleled by the controversies within its related associations in Otago and Canterbury) still affords ample scope for the political and constitutional historians. It is hardly adequate to consider its achievements from a purely economic standpoint. In essence it was an idealistic venture of imperial scope and purpose. Its great protagonist, Edward Gibbon Wakefield, in his vigorous repudiation of the agreement of 1846, wrote that it "was founded by men with great souls and little pockets and fell into the hands of men with great pockets and little souls". That agreement clearly rescued the shareholders of the Company from the risk of imminent bankruptcy, and eventually enabled them to conclude operations without great loss, if with little profit to themselves. It is not on this level, however, that the work of the Company was commenced, and its importance can hardly be judged by such statements. It is, to say the least, very doubtful whether New Zealand to-day would be a self-governing dominion of the British Empire if the New Zealand Company had not acted as it did in 1839.

It is not to be expected that any New Zealander will place a low estimate upon the importance of his country's development as an integral part of the British Empire. The value to the world in general of this remote and even yet small community of British settlers, almost completely homogeneous racially, must be judged in the light of the social characteristics which should be revealed in the analysis of its problems essayed in this book.

To Great Britain and the British Empire its economic value has already considerably exceeded the cost of its plantation, most of which in any case became a charge upon its own later revenues. As a source of raw materials and food-stuffs and the most valuable market in proportion to its population that Great Britain possesses, it has considerably enriched the Motherland. This value is enhanced by its reception of steady streams of immigration and capital, by the opportunities it adds to the financial, shipping, and commercial services which Britain provides, and by an increasing return flow of individuals seeking larger fields of leadership.

In one other respect the operations of the New Zealand Company afford material of great interest to modern economists. They form an outstanding experiment in the economics of group settlement. In appraising this experiment it is to be remembered that it was undertaken almost a century ago. Its mistakes and weaknesses were those of a pioneer venture. Moreover, there was clear progress from Wakefield's first venture in South Australia to the last venture he inspired in the Settlement of Canterbury. It is easy after the event to point out the weaknesses and rigidities of his conception, the essentially aristocratic conception of society which lay behind it, and the economic difficulties into which adherence to his "uniform and sufficient" price for land plunged even Canterbury at the last. A truer test would be to compare the results of his theories with the promiscuous and unorganised emigration which settled Canada, the convict shipments which blighted Australia's earliest decades, or the Uitlander problem which arose in South Africa. New Zealand escaped many real dangers, such as those of convict settlements; its land problems were greatly reduced; and the character of its first settlers was kept extraordinarily high, largely by reason of Wakefield's activities. These are not unimportant consequences even from a narrow economic viewpoint. After three-quarters of a century of settlement such positive values loom far larger than the points of criticism with which Wakefield's contemporaries were naturally preoccupied.

The Disposal of Waste Lands to 1852

Apart from the settlement of the first land claims, and in particular of the relations of the Company with its settlers and the Maoris, the history of land alienation in the first phase of New Zealand history has two main aspects. The first of these is the task which was placed upon the Governors of purchasing land from the Maoris and extinguishing native titles. The complications of this task have been sketched in the previous chapter dealing with the economic status of the

Maoris. It remains to consider the obverse policy of disposing of the land once purchased.

Disposal of the waste lands in colonies and possessions was a fruitful theme for controversy, but New Zealand gained enormously from the experience of earlier difficulties in Canada and more particularly in Australia. By the time Hobson received his first instructions the principles advocated by Edward Gibbon Wakefield had so far gained the day that free grants of land were frowned upon and the principle of selling land at a uniform price was established. There were subsequent periods in New Zealand history when free grants were lavishly made; but for the most part the Crown estate has been sold.

The first sales in New Zealand, as in South Australia and other colonies, were of town sections, for which speculative prices were paid. The revenue derived from land sales in 1841, indeed, though relatively small (£28,540), was more than the total received from sales for the eight years following. After 1842, sales were negligible until they began slowly to pick up in 1848. At the lowest depth of the economic difficulties of the first decade, in 1845, the revenue from this source was only £155. It is to be remembered that land was obtainable also from the Company in its various settlements, but even so, the areas taken up must have been small. In 1852 the total area fenced was only 40,625 acres and the area under crop 29,140 acres.(11)

Governor Fitzroy in 1844 made desperate efforts to promote land sales even at the cost of revenue by waiving the Crown right of pre-emption and permitting purchases to be made direct from the Maoris. His first proclamation on the subject was issued in March 1844, and stipulated for a grant fee of 10s. per acre and for one-tenth of the area to be conveyed to the Crown for native reserves. A following proclamation in October 1844 reduced the grant fee from 10s. to 1d. per acre.

These proclamations, however, were in conflict with the Australasian Land Sales Act of 1842, which fixed £1 per acre as the minimum upset price at which Crown land was to be sold, instead of, as in the former instructions to Hobson, the uniform price. Fitzroy's ordinances were disallowed and he was recalled. His successor, Sir George Grey, investigated claims made under the ordinances and incidentally provoked a serious conflict with the veteran missionaries by referring in scathing terms to claims made by them. The whole extent of land claimed under these proclamations, very little of which was validated, was less than 100,000 acres.

In 1846 Sir George Grey received from the Colonial Office, along with the draft of a constitution which he courageously suspended, detailed instructions for the disposal of waste lands. These were in support of an Act of the Imperial Parliament, which ended the application to New Zealand of the Australasian Land Sales Act of 1842; but in practice they carried on the main features of that Act and particularly the sale of lands by auction at an upset price of £1 per acre. The Act of 1846 also divided the colony into two Governmental areas, New Ulster and New Munster, a division which was to have little practical importance beyond creating a few Government offices. The control of administration, including the disposal of waste lands, remained in the hands of the Governor. The subsequent legislation of this period made no significant alterations in policy except in the matter of pastoral licences, which is considered below.

As far as land sales were concerned, therefore, in this period before self-government, the areas disposed of were small. Both in the Company lands and the Crown lands outside the Company areas, the principle was adhered to of sale at a price not below £1 per acre. No statistics exist which make possible any accurate estimate of the area so alienated.

The Australasian Land Sales Act of 1842 had, however, permitted two departures from the policy of sale at a sufficient upset price, and both of these exceptions were to have important results in New Zealand. Free grants were allowed to military and naval settlers, a precedent which became important in New Zealand during the second series of Maori wars in the sixties, when volunteers were encouraged by hopes of free grants of land, which were to be made possible by confiscations from the "rebel" Maoris. But in the period now under consideration such grants were not important.

Much more significant were the pastoral licences designed to regulate the growing tendency for pastoralists to take up large areas outside the limits of the Wakefield settlements. New Zealand fortunately escaped almost completely the squatting era through which Australia passed in the thirties. The term "squatter" is now by a strange irony used loosely to designate any wealthy sheep-owner; but it was originally applied to the adventurous pioneers who forced their way into the interior plains of Australia and squatted without title upon land as the dispossessed small-holders of the late eighteenth century had squatted upon the village greens in England. The pastoral industry did not emerge in New Zealand until after the system of pastoral licences had been fashioned out of Australian experience. The Act of 1842 made these licences annual upon payment of a small fee. The Crown Lands Amendment and Extension Ordinance, 1851, followed in New Zealand the precedent set by the Imperial Orders-in-Council of 1847 by creating pastoral leases with a currency of fourteen years. The annual fee was £5 plus £1 for each 1,000 sheep above the first 5,000. In this way a new and most important tenure was suddenly created which was to be of great and continuing importance. "In a moment a vested interest was created, to protect which powerful influences have ever since struggled, quite naturally, but to the infinite harm of progress."(12)

The next section will deal with the advantages which this new form of leasehold tenure that had sprung from the pastoral licence system gave to the wealthy sheep-owners in the struggle to take advantage of the free sales of Crown land which were inaugurated by Sir George Grey in 1853. Most of the land troubles of the colony in the ensuing period sprung from the situation thus created. When the control of the waste lands was handed over to the colonial legislatures by the Constitution Act of 1852, comparatively little had been alienated. Statistics are unfortunately not available, but the speech of Dr. Featherston, the newly elected Superintendent of the Wellington Province, at the opening of the first session of the provincial assembly in 1853 may be taken as typical of the situation in other provinces. He gave the area of his province as 10,500,000 acres, of which 2,000,000 had been purchased from the natives, but only 235,000 had been sold.(13) Outside the area of close settlement, however, and notably in Hawke's

Bay, large areas were held upon pastoral lease, and very significantly he added the statement that further blocks amounting to 1,250,000 acres of land would be available shortly in Hawke's Bay and the Wairarapa, for selection under the regulations issued by Sir George Grey.

The situation differed from province to province merely in the amount of land purchased from the Maoris.(14) In Taranaki and Auckland very little was available; in the south island provinces, on the other hand, the native titles had been completely extinguished. Very little of the land thus available had, however, been sold, and it does not need much imagination to realise how strategically placed were the holders of pastoral leases to gain the first all-important advantage in the scramble which inevitably set in as soon as restrictions upon the sale of land were modified.

Provincial Land Policies, 1853–76

The Constitution Act left in the hands of the Governor a great deal of discretionary power in regard to the machinery for putting the new powers of self-government into effect. Sir George Grey, before he left New Zealand in 1853, took two decisions of great importance to the future development of the colony, both of which had a special bearing upon land policy. He proclaimed the provincial boundaries and convened the provincial legislatures, leaving his successor to call together the colonial legislature. In this way the provincial bodies were well organised and received a flying start before Parliament could be convened. The influence of these provincial councils, backed by a strong Provincialist Party in Parliament, threw a great deal more power into the hands of the councils than was reasonable. Most of the political controversies of the next twenty years ranged about this question. The extraordinary contrast between the struggles of the north island provinces and the abounding prosperity of those in the south island, especially in the sixties, after the outbreak of war in the north and the discovery of gold in the south, lent a great deal of bitterness to the controversies. Both the north island councils and the General Assembly were in continuous financial difficulties, while Otago and Canterbury had abundant revenues.(15)

The real cause of this peculiar situation lay in Grey's action. By the time the Central Parliament met, the Provincialists were strong enough to force through the so-called "Compact of 1856", by which the disposal of waste lands was recognised as a function of the provincial councils. This Compact lies behind the economic history of the whole period. Canterbury and Otago were the richest provinces to begin with. Their abundant revenues from land sales enabled them to keep on building public works and attracting immigrants, so that their domination continually increased, and the Central Government was powerless to reverse the agreement into which it had entered.

The second important decision made by Grey was the promulgation on March 4, 1853, of general land regulations, reducing the price of rural lands to 10s. per acre, or where certified by the Commissioner of Crown Lands, to 5s. per acre. These regulations were in force in the Province of Wellington (including Hawke's Bay), where Grey had bought large areas from the Maoris in the later years of his tenure of office; but Grey's proclamation extended their validity to all provinces with the exception only of certain lands belonging to the Otago and Canterbury Associations. (16)

There was an immediate rush to take advantage of this new opportunity. Unfortunately official statistics do not begin to show the details of land sales year by year until 1856. By this date, however, there was a marked increase in the amount of land alienated which totalled considerably over three million acres.

Grey's inspired biographer has defended the regulations vigorously and quotes Grey's own account in later life of his motives. (17) His action was a deliberate attempt to break the Wakefield system, to destroy the possibility of building up large endowments for an established church, and to allow free access to the land by men of small capital. Moreover, he claimed that the evil results which followed his regulations were due to the fact that their intent was altered by subsequent legislation and that the land-tax which he proposed as a safeguard against aggregation was never brought into being.

> As soon as Sir George Grey's back was turned his intentions were frustrated and his wishes neglected. The Hundreds Ordinance was never brought into existence by proclamation; the Regulations were altered; the

General Assembly gave over the control of the waste lands to the provincial bodies; and the provincial bodies framed such ordinances and regulations as enabled those in power to possess themselves of large portions of the public estate in different places. Dr. Featherston did indeed propose a land-tax to the Wellington Provincial Council, but it was not pushed.(18)

In view of these facts Grey always vehemently disclaimed the responsibility for setting in motion the processes of land aggregation which he was to fight so bitterly at a later date. He claimed credit, on the contrary, for settling small farmers in the Wairarapa and parts of Hawke's Bay. Wherever the responsibility may lie, the important fact is that land aggregation dates from these regulations and the provincial legislation which was largely based upon them.

The legality of Grey's action in issuing the regulations was impugned by a court decision, but the Waste Lands Act (1854) of the General Assembly confirmed them.(19) In the same year a provincial Waste Lands Act was passed delegating the power of disposal of the waste lands to the provincial assemblies. This Act was reserved for the Queen's assent, and a similar Act in 1856 was disallowed on the ground that the General Assembly had no authority to delegate its powers.(20) The "Compact of 1856", however, achieved the object of the Provincialists, and the various provinces continued to pass and act upon ordinances and regulations by which large areas of Crown land passed into private ownership. These were validated by the Waste Lands Act passed by the General Assembly in 1858. It is significant that there was no portfolio of lands in the Central Parliament until the passing of this Act in 1858, and that in 1864 the portfolio was again dropped until 1872. The real control of land policy lay in the provincial councils. "The Waste Lands Act of 1858 laid down the general conditions on which Crown lands could be dealt with by the provinces, and the virtual control of the lands then passed into the hands of the Provincial Councils, subject to the approval of the Governor."(21)

The only other important Land Act of the central legislature in this period was the New Zealand Settlements Act, 1863, the primary purpose of which was to provide free grants for military settlers in districts where the Maoris were disaffected and threatening.(22)

It is difficult in a brief summary to follow the ramifications of land legislation and regulations in the ten provinces between 1858 and 1876. These are set out admirably in Jourdain's *History of Land Legislation and Settlement in New Zealand.*(23) The broad principles underlying them and their economic consequences are, however, important. This is the period during which the great bulk of the best land of the south island and the open parts of the north island was taken up, much of it in large areas. The great object of all the provincial legislation was to sell the land and induce settlers to come into the country. Conditions of sale were made as easy as possible in most of the provinces. As early as 1856, Auckland had initiated sales on liberal credit terms, and in 1871 Wellington began sales on deferred payment, a system which was copied by Hawke's Bay, Auckland, and Otago. In 1870 Auckland adopted a homestead system of free grants, and in the Auckland and Taranaki Provinces free grants to naval and military settlers totalled 349,112 acres.(24) It was Auckland also which initiated in 1855 the system of free grants to immigrants and in 1858 a further system enabling schoolteachers to select country lands up to eighty acres. Various special settlements were also encouraged by land grants in the north island provinces.

The policy in Canterbury and Otago was in striking contrast. Within the areas granted to the original associations, sales proceeded steadily at the uniform and sufficient price of £2 per acre in Canterbury and £1 per acre in Otago. The gold discoveries helped these provinces along, and their freedom from native difficulties, as well as their accessibility, was very attractive to new settlers. Outside the areas originally granted to the Associations the sales of land were more dubiously economical. Many of the great estates of "squattocracy" were built up from pastoral leaseholds by devious methods in the back-country of the south island provinces, as well as in the more open areas of the north island in Hawke's Bay and parts of Wellington.

The net result of all this provincial legislation was that between 1856 and 1876 a total of 8,131,862 acres was sold for £7,638,731, while 2,246,806 acres were given away under various systems of free grants.(25) The methods by which these large areas were bought are not less important than the fact that the national estate was sold. By a strange irony it was in the southern provinces, Otago and Canterbury, where Wakefield's system was best demonstrated, that most of the evils of aggregation occurred at this time. Within the limited area owned originally by the Otago and Canterbury Associations, the sale of land at the fixed price of £1 and £2 per acre brought in a steady revenue and kept the settlements compact. Outside these areas, however, especially in Otago, the holders of pastoral leases used the most ingenious devices to take advantage of the policy of free selection at low prices, which was inaugurated by Grey's regulations of 1853, and continued by the Waste Lands Act of 1858. The small man with little capital had few chances of combating their devices. They used the various pre-emptive rights contained in their pastoral leases, 50 acres for each shepherd's hut and for every 38½ chains of wire-fencing, to pre-empt all the desirable areas in their runs. Fences were run up all the watered valleys, shepherds' huts were put up and occupied by "dummies", sections were "gridironed" so as to enclose areas which could be used by the runholder, the most desirable portions of an area were "spotted", and gradually, as was most convenient, the large runholder achieved the ownership of his great holding on the easiest possible terms. (26)

Moreover, the boom conditions engendered by the spending of borrowed money in prosecution of the "immigration and public works policy" initiated by Vogel in 1870 raised land speculation to such a height that the "uniform and sufficient price" was, in fact, adhered to long after its usefulness had passed. As Mr. Reeves has pointed out in a well-known passage:

> After twenty years, indeed, the system broke down in Canterbury. In the seventies, railway lines were suddenly rushed through the province; there was an inrush of population; and the 40s. per acre was no longer a sufficient price. The people very foolishly neither raised this price nor imposed settlement conditions upon purchases. A fever as hot as that in Adelaide in 1837 raged in Canterbury between 1872 and 1878. During it the whole of the agricultural land in that part of New Zealand passed away from the State; and the ruinous collapse which followed may be regarded as the end of the completest trial of selling land at a high uniform price without settlement conditions. The history of the experiment began with a land-fever in Adelaide and ended with a land-fever in Canterbury. (27)

The Abolition of the Provincial System

The anomalous situation created by the "Compact of 1856" could not have been expected to endure. The provincial councils occupied a far more important place in the politics of New Zealand than the central assembly, and some of them were much better off financially than the central body. Their finances varied widely, however, and provincial loans were at a heavy discount in the early seventies. The variety of their land legislation was very confusing, and the mere cost of supporting eleven legislatures in a colony of less than 300,000 inhabitants was excessive. Within the provinces themselves there had been secession movements, creating new provincial assemblies, and functional devolution had also transferred many of the powers of the councils to such bodies as harbour boards.(28)

It was the land policies of the provincial legislatures which in the end proved their undoing. As long as the Maori wars preoccupied the attention of the north island provinces and of Parliament, they were relatively immune from attack. In 1868 (Sir) Edward Stafford, the recognised leader of the Centralist Party, and at that time Premier of New Zealand, launched a vigorous attack upon the parochial policies of the provincial councils; but it was not until Vogel announced his borrowing policy in 1870 that the conflict became really acute.

There can be no reasonable doubt that in the very real conflict of authority and jurisdiction provoked by Vogel's measures, the Provincialists followed a shortsighted and unfortunate policy. The paramount authority of the central legislature was never in doubt. The "Compact of 1856" handing over control of land sales and revenue to the provinces had been an act of grace which at the time had been seriously criticised by the Colonial Office. That compact had not hitherto been challenged because there had not been any constructive central policy to be crossed by the Provincialists' grip of the colony's waste lands. Vogel's policy supplied such a cause of conflict. It was an integral part of his plans that the borrowing which he proposed for "immigration and public works" should be accompanied by the reservation of approximately six million acres of lands in the areas to be opened up by railway development. Such reservation would not only have prevented much of the speculative boom which ensued; it would also have provided a revolving fund for the continuation of his policies of development.(29)

The proposal to vest control of these lands in the Central Government was fiercely assailed by the Provincialists, who had a majority in Parliament, and was therefore thrown out. With this safeguard deleted, the borrowing policy was a plain incitement to the worst form of land-gambling. The Ministry, under Vogel's guidance, made a cardinal blunder in giving way at this point; but it must be conceded that popular pressure was almost irresistible. The alienation of waste lands, which had been proceeding rapidly enough before, was greatly accelerated and indeed rose to a feverish boom. Its economic effects were disastrous. The construction of public works was made far more costly, new borrowings were necessary to keep the boom going, land passed into speculative ownership in large holdings, and the immigrants who had been brought to the colony by fair promises found themselves cooped up in the towns with little possibility of taking up land. Instead of productivity increasing, it fell off, and the burden of the debt incurred soon became a major contributing cause of the financial depression induced by falling prices.

As early as 1872, Vogel, who had rapidly become an almost unchallenged dictator, had indicated his dissatisfaction with the power of checkmate exercised by the provinces in their control over waste lands. New borrowings by the Central Government were handicapped also because of the discount at which provincial loans were standing. When in 1874 the Provincialists threw out a Forest Conservation Bill on the ground that it interfered with their control of land policy, it became obvious that some measure of readjustment was necessary.

Vogel acted with characteristic energy and decision. He had formerly been one of the leaders of the Provincialist Party, but he now determined to overthrow the whole system. There was ample reason for reviewing the legislative and financial relations of the provincial and central legislatures, but the drastic step of abolition was one of doubtful wisdom. Vogel, however, did not hesitate once his mind was made up. He received the support of the House to a resolution introduced in the Session of 1874; and during his temporary absence in London, but with his consent, despite the bitterest opposition headed by Sir George Grey, who emerged from his retirement when danger threatened the provincial institutions which were largely his creation, the Abolition Bill was carried in 1875, to take effect from November 1, 1876. An election supervened and confirmed the decision, so that the whole provincial system was swept away. In place of the provincial councils a series of local institutions was set up. The lands of the colony came under the control of land boards, which have functioned as purely administrative bodies under the general legislative and administrative policies laid down by Parliament and the Department of Lands. From 1877, therefore, the land policy of the colony was again centralised. The damage, however, was done. Under provincial rule, especially in the later stages when abolition was clearly imminent, waste lands had been sold recklessly. There was no effective check to this policy until 1890, and by that time most of the colony's best land was freehold. The later battles of leasehold and freehold tenure concerned land of far less area and value than that which was disposed of so freely by the provinces.

The First Attempts at Land Conservation, 1877–90

A revulsion of popular feeling carried Sir Julius Vogel out of office in 1877. Sir George Grey thereupon came into power as Premier in the colony which he had twice governed. He was surrounded by a group of young men of ability and promise, many of whom were to leave their mark on the history of the Dominion. Of these the two outstanding examples were John Ballance, who afterwards led the Liberal-Labour Party to victory in 1890, and (Sir) Robert Stout, whose long lifetime of devoted and able service has spread over at least two generations. As Liberal statesman, educationalist, Chief Justice, and in many other capacities, he has touched New Zealand development at almost every point since he first rose to important office in Grey's Ministry.

Grey commanded widespread popular support. He enunciated an alluring if somewhat vague programme of radical legislation. Electoral reform and land taxation loomed large in this programme; but unfortunately Grey's great gifts did not include those of Parliamentary leadership. After a brief and stormy career the Liberal movement was broken into pieces, and after Grey's defeat in 1879 it did not again come into power as a definitely organised party until 1890.(30)

One of the first necessary pieces of legislation to which its hand was put was the preparation of a Lands Act to consolidate and bring some order into the chaos of provincial legislation.(31) This Act repealed fifty-six statutes and laid the foundation of centralised administrative policy. Its chief innovations, other than the setting up of administrative machinery, were the introduction of auction sales for pastoral leases, and the adoption of the system of deferred payments in the sale of waste lands. This system had been in force in some provinces, but was now made national in its scope. Under it no less than 7,687 settlers took up over a million acres of land between 1877 and 1892.(32)

Grey's Ministry also was responsible for the first land-tax enacted in the colony. The idea of a land-tax had been suggested by Grey when as Governor he promulgated his land regulations in 1853, and he lost no time in bringing the measure forward, though the actual drafting of the Bill was largely the work of Stout and Ballance. It was a mild measure imposing a flat rate of a half-penny in the pound on all land exceeding £500 in value; but taken with a reduction in Customs duties, it was significant as an attempt to alter the distribution of taxation. It was not destined, however, to become effective. Grey was out of office in 1879, and one of the first measures of his opponents was the repeal of this Act and the substitution therefor of a property-tax. In making this change (Sir) Harry Atkinson bluntly stated that the main need of the colony was to encourage settlement, and that it was unwise to place any obstacles in the way of land being taken up, even if there were the possibility of a few individuals acquiring large estates.

This argument was typical of the attitude of the party which was destined to remain in power, with one brief interval, until 1890. Atkinson himself was in office from 1879 to 1884, and Premier from 1887 to 1891. His support came largely from the landowners, who in this period wielded an extraordinary degree of political power, reflecting the economic dominance of the grazing industry.(33) The alienation of the land, therefore, continued apace until it was checked by the Liberal-Labour victory in 1890. The remaining legislation of the period is mainly concerned with administrative machinery and with relatively minor projects of small settlement. The efforts at conservation which were attempted met an unfriendly legislature and were turned into mechanisms for further alienation.

This applies particularly to the measures introduced by Rolleston in 1882 and 1884.(34) Rolleston had been Superintendent of Canterbury and was much impressed with the necessity of conserving the remaining lands of the Crown. His Land Act of 1882 is chiefly remarkable for its introduction of the so-called "perpetual lease".(35) This tenure provided land at a low rental for tenants who thereafter were to be subject to revaluation of their leases at thirty-year intervals. The whole intent of the measure was defeated by the insertion of a clause giving tenants the right of purchase at prairie values. With this possibility added, the lease naturally became very popular, so that by 1892, 4,525 holders had taken up 1,327,632 acres.(36)

From 1884–7 John Ballance was Minister for Lands in the short-lived Stout-Vogel Government, and in that capacity he initiated a series of measures that foreshadow the later Liberal-Labour efforts to encourage closer settlement. In the Land Act of 1885 a new tenure, known as the small grazing-run lease, was initiated.(37) Land not exceeding 5,000 acres could be taken up for terms of twenty-one years with the right of renewal. The leases were auctioned at an upset price of 2½ per cent. on the capital value fixed by the land board of the district. The tenure quickly became popular and still remains so, nearly 2,750,000 acres being so held at March 31, 1927.(38)

In the same Act, Ballance took power to set land aside for "special settlements", to be taken up by associations of purchasers, mainly on the deferred-payment system. While the area so disposed of was comparatively small (98,018 acres by 1892), nearly 1,000 settlers were involved, and the experiment was of some importance in the north island. The regulations were amended in favour of the small settlers by the first Lands Act of the Liberal-Labour Party in 1892 and became more important thereafter. (39)

Ballance's remaining experiment, the "village-homestead special-settlement" system, proved to be less important, except that these tenures were later used in disposing of areas repurchased under the Lands for Settlements Acts. (40) It traces back to experiments made by Reid in Otago and by Rolleston, when Superintendent of Canterbury, as early as 1874, and incorporated in the Land Act of 1879. The areas taken up were small and the selectors were involved in the economic depression of the late eighties. In 1892 there remained 895 selectors holding 23,535 acres, on which they had paid rent and interest amounting to £8,350, while £2,127 was in arrears. (41) This tenure also gained a renewed impetus when the Liberal-Labour Party came into power, but the village-homestead idea, on which it was based, has never been really suitable to the individualistic temper of colonial farming. It did not fit New Zealand conditions in its attempt to provide workers' homes and small farms producing for a limited local market commodities such as fruit and vegetables, which were perishable and liable to gluts of overproduction.

In 1889 a Settlers' Revaluation Act was passed, which is important for the indication it gives of general economic conditions rather than for its intrinsic interest. (42) It provided for downward revisions of rents and valuations in substantial proportions, and indicates something of the stress through which the farming industries were passing. Prices had been falling steadily since the wild land boom of 1878 had burst and caused the acute crisis of 1879. The colony had only the one substantial export—wool—and sheep-raising was essentially a large-scale enterprise. The interesting effort to organise wheat-growing in Canterbury in the early eighties was also large-scale organisation. In 1882 the refrigerating processes had been proven successful; but it took time to organise them commercially, and the first gains naturally accrued to the large landholders who had the capital to invest. The small settlers were therefore badly handicapped at every point. Moreover, the land was locked up in large holdings, many of which had changed hands at high prices in the boom period. As prices fell, these holdings tended to revert to the financial institutions (many of them absentee owners) which had advanced the mortgage-money by which their sale had been financed. The difficult economic situation thus produced and the measures taken to combat it will be considered in more detail in Chapter V.

The Era of Alienation

Meantime it is essential to realise that by 1892 the great bulk of the best lands of New Zealand had become freehold. Large areas remained and still remain in the ownership of the Government; but these with few exceptions are not good quality lands. For the twenty years from 1892 to 1912 a policy of conservation and repurchase was pursued, vigorously at first, and then mildly as rising prices brought prosperity. Since 1912 the freehold policy has again triumphed. But these oscillations of policy after all affect only the fringe of the land problem of New Zealand. The bulk of the good land passed into private ownership before 1893, and comparatively little was repurchased (1,997,870 acres in all up to March 31, 1927).(43) Since the policy of conservation was reversed in 1912, successive Acts have made available to freehold purchasers every class of Crown leasehold, but the transferences resulting have not compared in area with the great quantities which passed into private ownership before 1892. Moreover, the great bulk of native land was purchased from the Maoris, mainly in large holdings, in the period between 1873, when the individualising of native titles commenced, and 1892, when pre-emption was resumed. In the latter year nearly eleven million acres remained in Maori ownership, over fifty-six millions having been sold either to the Crown or to private purchasers.(44) In the remaining quarter of a century another six millions have passed from Maori hands; but the greatest evil was wrought before 1892.

Accurate statistics of alienation are unfortunately difficult to obtain. There are many returns scattered through Parliamentary papers, official year-books, statistical volumes, special reports, departmental returns, and private documents. Inevitably the information found in these various sources is contradictory and confusing. The earlier surveys, particularly of the provincial governments, were inaccurate, so that even the total area of the colony was not finally determined for some years. The returns available are made for different purposes and group holdings in different ways, so that it is difficult to attain consistency. Moreover, the tenures have been changed frequently by legislation, and many of them give opportunities for tenants to convert their holdings to freehold. Some of the holdings are given up or allowed to lapse in time of economic difficulty, and this adds a possibility of error in making historical comparisons.

Probably the best summary of the alienations made up to 1892 is contained in an appendix to the first Official Year Book (1892), which includes the following table:

	Million Acres.
Freehold	13·6
Held by lease and with right of purchase	1·7
Held on lease from the Crown	12·5*
Reserved for public purposes	6·6
Crown lands	8·4
Midland Railway Company	4·0†
Native lands	10·8
Barren, lakes, etc.	9·0
	66·7

It is difficult to compare these figures with the latest returns, since tenures and grouping have changed so much in the meantime. One figure, however, is significant. The Crown lands sold for cash between 1856 and 1891 totalled 10·7 million acres. To this total should be added the area sold before 1856, approximately 3 million acres. In 1927 the total area made freehold by sale amounted to 17½ million acres,(45) so that in the twenty-six years from 1891–1927 less than 4 million acres were sold in all the various ways in which sale was possible. Sales of Crown land, which in the five years 1873–7 averaged 607,000 acres annually, have dropped in the five years 1923–7 to 20,000 acres annually, supplemented by leases of various kinds (which may later be turned into free-

* Of this area, 11·8 million acres were held on pastoral lease; the leasehold policy of the Liberal-Labour Party is of later date.

† Later resumed by the Crown because of failure to fulfil contract.

hold) to the annual extent of 105,000 acres.(46) Very little of the land now being disposed of can be compared either in quality or in accessibility with the land sold in earlier periods. It is to be remembered also that very large areas, totalling five million acres in 1892, were disposed of by free grants in the earlier period, a system that has entirely ceased since the policy of conservation was introduced.

It is of considerable importance to bear these facts in mind when considering the experimental land legislation of the most recent period of New Zealand. With the exception of the land-tax and the repurchase policy, that legislation has been confined to the poorer lands remaining to the Crown. There is no need to depreciate the importance of the problems involved; but a sense of proportion can be maintained only when it is remembered that the overwhelming bulk of the best land of New Zealand had passed into private ownership before 1892.(47) The only way in which the Liberal-Labour programme and its subsequent reversal affected these lands was by making them subject to a land-tax, the effects of which will be shown to be mainly illusory, and for a few years to the possibility of forced purchase at a Government valuation.

CHAPTER IV

THE RISE OF THE PASTORAL INDUSTRY

Natural Industries

The outstanding feature of New Zealand's economic development is the dominating importance of the pastoral industries, an importance which strengthens as these industries become more diversified and work out characteristic methods suitable to their new habitat. These are the "natural industries" of the Dominion, and in their organisation the practical empirical genius of the colonists is seen at its best. The ability of these antipodean farmers to compete successfully in world markets is reflected not only in good wages and a comparatively high standard of comfort, but also in land values, which seem preposterously high to many visitors from older and more densely populated lands. Such high costs of production would prove an impossible handicap if it were not for two main reasons.

In the first place, New Zealand has unparalleled natural advantages, which are often summarised in the statement that New Zealand has an ideal climate for pastoral pursuits. These, however, would be insufficient if they were not exploited by efficient organisation in the various phases of the primary pastoral industries. It is the high degree of technical skill which has been evolved in animal breeding, in the development of pastures, economy of labour costs, and careful attention to quality and mass-production in the manufacturing of food products, which make possible the volume of production that alone could support the high standard of living demanded in New Zealand. There are many respects in which efficiency is lower than it ought to be, and others in which abuse of the natural powers of the soil has led to deterioration. Some of these will be discussed later. It is important that they should be recognised, and if possible remedied; but the fact remains that there is a high degree of efficiency, different, indeed, from intensive farming methods in other lands, but suited to the extensive type of farming in New Zealand, and that upon this efficiency rests the prosperity of the Dominion. Wages and profits depend upon production, and if New Zealand enjoys high standards of comfort it is because managerial skill of a high order has maximised production. Shearing-sheds, where highly trained workers make individual tallies paralleled only in the sister Dominion, Australia; meat-works, where all the advantages of mass-production are achieved; and butter-factories of a size which opens wide the eyes even of expert overseas observers, supplement the more elusive but even more important skill involved in the primary farming processes.

It is obvious, therefore, that a clear statement of the events which led to New Zealand specialising in such economic activities is fundamental to any understanding of her problems. Any such statement involves a recognition of the empirical, trial and error methods by which specialisation was finally achieved. New Zealand did not become a pastoral country without many efforts to develop other supplementary industries and to discover the best methods of organisation. The remaining sections of this chapter attempt to outline the main features of the first stages of this double line of experiment.

The Exploitation of Natural Resources

The whaling and sealing carried on in New Zealand waters in the first thirty years of the nineteenth century is a classic illustration of the wanton destruction of an important national asset by unscientific and unrestrained exploitation.(1) This picturesque episode is of some importance in the political history of the Dominion, since it led to the first settlements and involved the British Government in the necessity of taking steps to regulate the intercourse of the visiting sailors with the native race. Economically, however, the importance of the period is greater to Australia and to the eastern ports of the United States of America than to New Zealand. The south seas fisheries, which included the coastal waters of New Zealand and its adjacent islands, seem originally to have been concentrated in Bass Strait. Their exploitation was directed by merchants whose bases of operation were Hobart, Sydney, and New Bedford and Salem, then thriving ports of Massachusetts. Accurate statistics do not exist, but there is ample evidence to show that large quantities of whale-oil, whalebone, and seal-skins were taken from New Zealand waters. The China fur trade was glutted, and the Greenland whaling industry also suffered heavily. It is difficult at the present day, when as far as New Zealand is concerned the sealing industry has completely passed out of existence and whaling is restricted to one small shore station and an occasional ship, to realise the magnitude of the industry a hundred years ago. The number of American ships (which were said to control nine-tenths of the trade) was estimated in 1840 as between 600 and 700 vessels, employing more than 18,000 seamen. The value of their catch was estimated in 1845 as £1,400,000.

Apart from the destruction of what might have been a national asset of considerable value, the sole importance of this booming activity to present-day New Zealand is to be found in the settlement of bay whalers in the late thirties. The earlier sealers landed shore parties for a few months at a time, but left no permanent settlements. It was not till the late thirties that whaling stations on the southern coasts began to develop farming of a rough extensive type. In one or two cases they tided the colonists over their first difficult year or two by supplying them with sources of food-stuffs, but their farming enterprises were not highly developed, and the main reason for their existence—whaling—passed quickly into the category of forgotten episodes.

Two other lines of early trade warrant more attention. The whalers had been directed to New Zealand by the mention of their quarry in Captain Cook's writings. Cook also mentioned the possibilities of the tall timber of the north island and of the native flax. The latter provided one of the arguments advanced for the settlement of Botany Bay as a convict station, and early governors of New South Wales displayed a good deal of interest in obtaining supplies of flax and securing Maori workers to handle it. Rather cavalierly they spoke of securing "a flax-dresser or two", and actually kidnapped chiefs on one occasion to do what the latter regarded as the work of women and slaves.(2)

The export of flax prepared by native labour came to be an important trade after the return of Hongi from his visit to England in 1820. The armament race, which he began by pawning all his presents in Sydney and turning the proceeds into muskets and gunpowder, was sufficient inducement to cause the natives to undergo the laborious task of preparing quite large quantities of the fibre for sale in Sydney. The Maoris well understood the value of the plant, which they used extensively for their own purposes; but the preparation of large quantities for export by crude methods entailed upon them a vast amount of labour. The export rose rapidly, however, from the first commercial shipment to Sydney in 1818 to a peak of over 10,000 tons in 1831. By this time there was considerable interest in the fibre in Britain, and a Captain Harris, R.N., C.B., Member of the House of Commons for Grimsby, had set up a factory for its manufacture, which was honoured by the patronage of King George IV. (3)

Despite these auspicious beginnings the trade languished after the boom of 1830 and 1831. Unscrupulous traders sold badly prepared fibre at boom prices and gave the trade a bad reputation from which it did not recover for many years. The Maoris were disgusted with the slump in prices which followed and their production fell off. The export trade did not recover until the Civil War period in America led to prices in that market which stimulated another boom in the early seventies. New machines were introduced, but little success has to this day attended the efforts to devise satisfactory methods of preparation. The fibre has gradually taken its place as a secondary substitute or complementary fibre to Manila and similar hemps. It has had its booms, notably in the period of scarcity at the close of the Great War, and has contributed steadily in more recent years to the wealth of New Zealand, but it has never fulfilled the high expectations of the pioneer days, and is now a relatively unimportant item in the economic life of the Dominion. (4)

The forest history of New Zealand is a more depressing story. Few countries have had such a magnificent heritage of forest wealth and sacrificed it for so little gain. Expert opinion is that before the arrival of the Maoris, possibly a thousand years ago, practically the whole area of the islands was forested. "By the year 1840, however, 34,000 square miles, or 35·8 per cent., of the forest lands had been converted into permanent open plains, rolling downs, and uplands." (5) The chief agent of destruction had, of course, been fire, an element introduced by the Maoris, but rendered vastly more destructive by the first white settlers. Most of this early destruction, however, occurred in the more open drier regions, particularly of the eastern plains of the south island, which had but light forest covering at any time. The valuable commercial forests upon the wetter western coast and in the north island were protected by natural conditions until the settlers made a concerted attack upon them at a later period.

There was a growing export of New Zealand timber to Australia (which still remains the chief market) from the last decade of the eighteenth century. This trade began naturally in the manner described in the college doggerel:

> One summer morn in eighteen one
> A ship her anchor cast,
> Stole a piece of kauri from the Maori,
> And used it for a mast.

The actual date of the first cargo of timber of which record exists is 1795, when the *Fancy* brought a cargo of spars varying from 60 to 140 feet in length from the River Thames, where Captain Cook had reported the excellent timber "growing close to the water's edge, and of size and quality superior to any hitherto known", mention of which appears again and again in colonising schemes and prospectuses.(6) The extent of this earliest timber export was not very great. What statistics there are give the quantities in "loads, spars, rickers", and similar units that defy tabulation; but the value seems to have reached about £10,000 annually in the late twenties and to have declined somewhat in the thirties.(7)

The first settlers found the forests a profitable source of income and established timber-mills in practically every province, so that after 1840 the export values grew rapidly, till by 1853, the first year in which trade statistics were collected in detail for the colony as a whole, timber was the leading export, valued at £93,000. With such an apparent wealth of resources there was naturally a good deal of destruction involved in timber-getting, and Hobson as early as 1841 gazetted forest regulations to check the wasteful destruction of the kauri forests.

As the statistics of forest resources plainly show, however, it was the extension of settlement in the north island after 1880 that was responsible for the worst destruction. Between 1840 and 1880 the forest area decreased from 62,000 to 52,000 square miles, over half of this decrease occurring in the decade 1870–80. In the next ten years another 6,000 square miles were cleared, and between 1890 and 1900 no less than 14,000 square miles suffered the same fate. So the process has gone on, necessarily with diminishing rapidity, until to-day the forest area of the Dominion is approximately 19,000 square miles, less than a third of what it was in 1840. Of this area rather more than half is classified by the State Forest Service as unprofitable or inaccessible.

A good deal of this destruction was deliberate and returned only indirect benefits.

> The vital energies of the pioneer were concentrated on deforestation. Before axe and fire the virgin forests melted away. Decade after decade this process went on, for ingrained in the settler from childhood was the tradition that the forest was his enemy, to be destroyed before the soil would yield its riches. Indeed, in time it came to pass that the forests were driven back to the uplands, to the mountainous hinterlands, to the cold morainal bogs; but the unreasoning habit of bush destruction had become a sort of religion—fire was now the master instead of the servant. In the eyes of many the indigenous forest was so much garbage, to be swept out of existence.(8)

From time to time there were discussions of conservation, and even spasmodic and limited attempts at legislation and administration. Parliamentary discussions date back at least as far as 1860. In 1869 the six provincial superintendents reported to Parliament upon the state of the forests in their areas, and the geologist Hector warned the country of the ultimate consequences of the policy of destruction. In 1870 Vogel pleaded for an effective forest policy, and in 1874 passed the New Zealand Forests Act. The first Conservator appointed had a rather hopeless task, and remained only twelve months. The extraordinary progress of destruction in the eighties led to further half-hearted measures, which for the first time recognised the necessity of proclaiming forest reserves for their timber, as distinct from their climatic and scenic, value. Forest officers were appointed under the Department of Lands and worked out a policy on sound lines, but the pressure for settlement was too strong for them, and in 1888 an economy campaign practically killed their activities. No effective measures of conservation were taken thereafter until the timber famine of the war period forced the problem again to the front. Following a masterly report by Sir David Hutchins, a State Forest Service was created in 1920 and has had considerable success in safeguarding the remaining indigenous forest resources of the Dominion.

That this action was overdue is clear, not only from the rapid rate of destruction and the comparatively small resources remaining, but also from the growing danger from floods and erosion in certain areas. It is somewhat alarming to realise that "New Zealand possesses two and a half million acres of desert wilderness which is being added to at the rate of a hundred thousand acres per year, producing nothing of value to man or beast, but valuable for the production of forest crops".(9)

It is for this reason, as well as to check denudation and floods, that the State Forest Service has carried on a vigorous campaign for the dedication of forest areas, for the combating of pests like rabbits and deer,(10) the regulation of timber-getting, and for reafforestation. As a result of rather more than six years' operations, over seven and a half million acres have been dedicated to forest purposes, and a comprehensive programme of survey, research, and education is being carried out.

The other aspect of forest policy, reafforestation by the planting mainly of exotic trees, dates back to the arrival of the first settlers on the Canterbury Plains. Local bodies began afforestation as early as the seventies, again in the open lands of Canterbury and Otago, and some of these plantations, notably those controlled by the Selwyn Plantation Board and the Ashburton County Council, are now very useful illustrations of the deferred but highly profitable returns from timber-planting on suitable lands.(11)

The Governmental attempts at afforestation date back to 1896 and have been connected with the employment of good-conduct prisoners in healthful open-air occupations. The advent of the State Forest Service has, however, given a great impetus to tree-planting, which has increased steadily until there are now a hundred thousand acres of plantations, which are being added to at an increasing rate which in 1927 had reached twenty thousand acres annually. Commercial ventures in afforestation in the same year planted more than 50,000 acres.(12) There is some ground for criticism concerning the operation of some syndicates engaged in this business, and the profit will probably go in greater part to the promoters than to the shareholders in many cases; but the ultimate returns of the soundly organised companies, though likely to be less than prospectuses suggest, will be worth while. Of the soundness of forestry as a Governmental venture there can be little doubt, and New Zealand seems to be grappling with its problem successfully, though rather late in the day.(13)

The Beginnings of Agriculture

It is a clear step forward from the exploitation and destruction of wasting assets like timber, flax, whales, and seals, to the first efforts at permanent agriculture. It is obvious enough that with properly regulated conservation even the whaling and sealing industries might have become organised on a permanent basis. The flax and timber trades have at length been brought to this point; but neither has provided the main line of economic progress. Between these early trades and the establishment of the now dominant pastoral industries there are two or three experimental stages which demand brief notice.

The first of these is the possibility foreseen by the early navigators from Captain Cook onwards, that the Maoris might develop agriculture along European lines. There is a picturesque legend that the wild pigs that provide sport in many districts of New Zealand to-day are descended from pigs set free by Cook; but historical research lends little support to that theory.(14) The Maoris had memories of the Polynesian pig; but the name "poaka" (porker), given to the modern pig, indicates a different origin. There is no evidence to show that the pigs liberated by Captain Cook survived any better than the cattle he landed. There is plenty of evidence, however, of pigs being landed by succeeding visitors. Of all the gifts made by visiting officials and seamen the pig and the potato seem to have been most appreciated by the Maori, probably because of their similarity to the pig of Polynesian tradition and to the kumara, which was still cultivated assiduously. By the twenties of last century there was quite an active export in both articles, and the first Governor of New Zealand, Hobson, wrote officially in 1841 that "the natives raise a considerable quantity of pork, potatoes, and maize which, although it does not contribute much as a return for imports received from New South Wales and Van Diemen's Land, provides the colonists with an ample supply of food and, in fact, relieves them from the necessity of applying to their neighbours for articles of primary necessity".(15)

As Hobson's dispatch indicates, the early export trade was diverted after colonisation to supplying the wants of the settlers. Mention has been made in an earlier chapter of the large number of canoes arriving at Auckland with cargoes of food-stuffs. It is one of the tragedies of Maori history that this first adaptation to a new economic order should have been thwarted by the early outbreak of war and racial misunderstanding.

Missionary experiments in agriculture were closely connected with this Maori development. Samuel Marsden, the pioneer missionary, who planted the first mission station in 1814, brought with him on his first voyage "one entire horse, two mares, one bull, and two cows, with a few sheep, and poultry of various kinds". From time to time this first shipment was reinforced by others; but not all the missionaries shared Marsden's agricultural enthusiasm and ability.(16) He was reduced in 1821 to begging that "a pious farmer" might be sent out from England to care for his precious cattle.

Fourteen years later, however, Charles Darwin visited the mission station at Waimate in the Bay of Islands and wrote of it as "the one bright spot" of his visit:

> Fine crops of barley and wheat were standing in full ear; and in another part, fields of potatoes and clover. There were large gardens, with every fruit and vegetable which England produces; and many belonging to a warmer clime. I may instance asparagus, kidney beans, cucumbers, rhubarb, apples, pears, figs, peaches, apricots, grapes, olives, gooseberries, currants, hops, gorse for fences, and English oaks; also many kinds of flowers. Around the farmyard there were stables, a thrashing-barn with its winnowing machine, a blacksmith's forge, and on the ground ploughshares and other tools; in the middle was that happy mixture of pigs and poultry, lying comfortably together, as in every English farmyard.(17)

This pleasing picture leads Darwin to describe the flour-mill tended by a Maori and to remark upon the fact that Maori labour under missionary direction was responsible for the whole farm.(18)

It is clear that it was intensive mixed farming based upon English agricultural practice which the missionaries tried to introduce into New Zealand. The same desire is revealed by the following description of the pioneer settlement in Taranaki given in Vogel's *Handbook of New Zealand*.(19)

> The earth also yielded abundantly—wheat just chipped in with a mattock returned rich harvests of golden grain. Mills were erected, and quantities of fine flour exported. Grass also flourished: Dutch white clover sprang up in all directions; and butter soon became an article of export. Poultry became plentiful, and the bee produced great quantities of honey. The settler found comfort, and if his farm brought little cash to his pocket he was amply supplied by it with all the necessaries of life, and was cheered by seeing the daisy, primrose, and other British flowers, and all the fruits of his native land flourish in luxuriance round his humble cottage.

This is a pretty picture; but it masks much real distress. If the economic progress of the colony had depended upon the breaking in of land to intensive cultivation, it would have been a slow and heartrending business. The export of flour and wheat, even when supplemented by that of timber, flax, and potatoes, was quite insufficient to command the requisite quantity of imports to keep the settlements going.

It was some time, indeed, before the settlers discovered that sheep-raising was the easiest and most profitable industry to establish. The first pioneer farmers had stocked their runs with scrub cattle and there was some little export of live stock to Sydney in the forties. As early as 1839 also, the first experimental shipment of wool reached Hobart from one of the southern farms—a small shipment only, but "exceeding both in length and staple and firmness of texture any wool ever produced in New South Wales, the beautiful manner in which it was washed and sorted sufficiently explaining the superiority of the climate of New Zealand".(20)

After the Wakefield colonists landed at Wellington in 1840 the few small experiments in animal-farming were quite unable to supply the needs of the settlers. "Butter, beef, and mutton were almost unknown luxuries, there being few domestic animals in the country." An early colonist later was able to write of "the only cow then in Wellington".(21) The spreading out of pioneer settlers, particularly to the south island, is well illustrated by the arrival of John Deans in June 1843 at Port

Cooper (Lyttelton), bringing with him "three mares, 61 head of cattle and 43 sheep, and a supply of implements, wheat, barley, lucerne, potatoes, and oats" with which to begin farming the land he and his brother had taken up the previous year. (22)

In the same way Bidwill imported a flock of 300 Romneys in 1843, while Charles Clifford imported 400 merino ewes to Wellington in 1844 and drove them round the sea-coast to the Wairarapa Plains. Two years later Clifford and his partner Weld landed larger flocks in the Nelson Province and drove them overland to the plains north of Canterbury.

By this time there were altogether 36,352 sheep in the country, as well as 5,611 head of cattle, mostly in the plains above mentioned. (23) It was at this juncture that a depression and drought in Australia turned the attention of many of the squatters there to the opportunities offered by the newly opened lands in the south island of New Zealand.

The Discovery of the Golden Fleece

The diversion of organised settlement to the more open and less hostile plains of the south island came, therefore, at the time when the settlers were realising that sheep-raising was destined to be the most immediately profitable avenue of development. The settlement of Otago in 1848 and Canterbury in 1850 was, of course, influenced partly by this fact, though the Wakefield policies, which were based upon agricultural rather than pastoral organisation, remained unchanged in these last organised efforts. It was at this juncture that New Zealand profited most from the experience and difficulties of Australia.

In the years immediately preceding the discovery of alluvial gold in Australia there was severe economic depression. Prices had not yet responded to the stimulus of the Californian gold discoveries, and bad seasons in Australia accentuated the depressing effects of low prices. Station property and stock were at a discount. It was not uncommon for sheep stations to be sold "with all the sheep depasturing thereon at a price computed according to the number of sheep, valuing the latter at from fourpence to sixpence per head, and this aggregate sum included station buildings, boiling-down establishments, and all the appurtenances of a first-class station".

The natural result of such a depressing situation was that these experienced Australian sheep-farmers began to look elsewhere, and in the words of a Canterbury pioneer,

finding the Canterbury Plains eminently adapted for stock-grazing, and the climate of New Zealand promising an immunity from those periodic visitations of floods and droughts which were frequently so destructive to stock in Australia, they may be supposed to have summed up the prospective advantages somewhat in this wise: New and fertile pastures, more lambs, more wool, fewer casualties, and for some, perhaps many, years a good market for stock, dispensing with the boiling-down process. Favourable reports soon found their way into the Port Philip (Victoria) and New South Wales papers, particularly one written by Mr. Joseph Hawdon, a gentleman upon whose judgment and experience the greatest confidence was placed, and in consequence many of the squatters joined in the migration to Canterbury, and a brisk carrying trade of sheep, cattle, and horses to Lyttelton was the result.(24)

It was in Canterbury that this development mainly occurred. The open nature of the plains so well described a little later by Samuel Butler invited occupation.(25) Similar developments occurred, however, in the Wairarapa district after Sir George Grey opened them to selection by his cheap-land regulations of 1853, and in the Hawke's Bay district. Elsewhere the extension of pastoral industry was relatively slow. Even in Otago the number of sheep in 1856 was only 83,196.(26)

The rapid growth of the "extensive" type of sheep-farming in the ensuing period is shown by the rapid and cumulative increase in flocks, improvement in the weight of the fleece, and the improvement of pastures. The brief table on the opposite page, culled from census returns, shows between 1858 and 1881 an eightfold increase in flocks, the weight of wool per sheep almost doubled, and an increase in the area of land under cultivation (almost wholly sown grasses for pasture) from a hundred and forty thousand acres to over five millions.

The year 1881 is a convenient point of comparison for many reasons, chief of which is the revolution induced in the sheep-grazing industry by the first successful shipment of frozen meat in the following year. Another very important fact to be remembered is that by 1881 the pastoral industry in the south island had reached the peak of extension. The subsequent development both of sheep-raising and of dairy-farming has been predominantly in the north island. Between 1886 and

1926 the flocks of the south island fluctuated about ten millions and hardly increased at all; but the number of sheep in the north island grew from five and a quarter millions to almost fourteen millions. The economic problems of this latter period, therefore, are very different from those of the first "extensive" phase of pastoral farming. It is convenient, however, at this point to indicate the main trend of subsequent progress. As

SHEEP-FARMING IN NEW ZEALAND

NUMBER OF SHEEP, EXPORT OF WOOL, AND EXTENT OF CULTIVATED LAND AT CENSUS PERIODS 1858–1926

I. Year.	II. Number of Sheep.	III. Wool Exported.	IV. Value.	V. Column III divided by Column II.	VI. Land under Cultivation (mainly Sown Grasses).
	Millions.	Lbs. (millions).	£ (thousands).	Lbs.	Acres (millions).
1858	1·5	3·8	254	2·5	·1
1861	2·7	7·9	524	2·8	·2
1864	4·9	16·7	1·071	3·4	·4
1867	8·4	27·2	1·581	3·2	·7
1871	9·7	37·8	1·606	3·9	1·2
1874	11·7	46·8	2·835	4·0	1·9
1878	13·1	59·3	3·293	4·5	4·0
1881	12·2	59·4	2·910	4·8	5·2
1886	15·2	90·9	3·073	6·0	6·8
1891	17·9	106·2	4·130	6·0	8·9
1896	19·1	129·2	4·392	6·7	10·7
1901	20·2	146·8	3·699	7·0	12·7
1906	20·1	154·4	6·766	7·7	14·2
1911	24·0	169·4	6·491	7·0	16·3
1916	24·8	185·5	12·386	7·5	16·9
1921	23·3	158·7	5·221	6·9	18·2
1926	24·9	213·2	11·830	8·5	18·8

disclosed by the statistics, it may best be summarised in the statement that between 1881 and 1911 the flocks doubled in numbers with a very slight increasing tendency thereafter. The yield of wool per sheep has also shown a fairly steady tendency to increase, and is now at least three times as great as it was when New Zealand first began the pastoral industry.

This improvement is due to many reasons, among which must be reckoned the improvement of pastures, which now cover almost nineteen million acres, of which sixteen and three-quarter millions are in permanently sown pasture, and over a million in hay, green, and root crops, used for pasture purposes. This is in addition to the more than fourteen million acres of tussock and native grasses used for grazing purposes. (27)

Improvement of pastures was, however, a comparatively late development, and it belongs mainly to the economic re-organization induced by the more intensive farming of the period following refrigeration. The census returns of 1867 show nearly eight and a half million sheep and less than three-quarters of a million acres of improved pasture. It is at this point that progress begins to be greatly accelerated by the stimulus of the borrowing boom which began in 1870. Between 1871 and 1881 the area of improved pastures was more than quadrupled. This area was more than trebled in the thirty years following.

Of much greater importance in the early period was the effort to stem the threatened deterioration of flocks from indiscriminate breeding and failure to select the better stocks. The first sheep brought over to New Zealand were chiefly merinos, descended from the flocks introduced to Australia by Captain Macarthur in 1803. They were as well adapted to thrive on the hill-country of New Zealand as on the rather scanty feed of the interior plains of Australia, but they were an inferior breed compared with the merinos which hold their own to this day in the back-country. As the first pioneers brought over their flocks the number of breeds increased and a great deal of cross-breeding ensued. There was no market for meat, and as long as the native pastures were abundant, the flocks were allowed to multiply without culling as long as they could carry a fleece.

The inevitable tendency to deterioration was stayed in three main ways. By a process of trial and error, still incomplete, but now well advanced, sheep-farmers learned to suit their flocks to the widely differing conditions of the various localities. From the hardy merino on the back-country to the heavier breeds such as the Romney Marsh on more productive lands, all the various breeds of sheep were tried out.

As interbreeding went on, tending to reduce all flocks to a heterogeneous mixture of cross-breeds, efforts were made to develop stud flocks. The Canterbury Pastoral Association held its first show of sheep as early as 1859.(28) It is extremely difficult, if not impossible, to indicate all the pioneer experiments. Nor is this necessary in a general account of economic development, though there is room for a technical review of the progress of sheep-farming in New Zealand. It is sufficient here to point out that the effort to develop pure-bred stud flocks has met with increasing success, so that not only the stud flocks themselves, but the proportion of sheep of distinctive breed, is steadily increasing.(29) There is little indiscriminate breeding to-day.

The third and most interesting line of development besides the selection of breeds suitable to different localities and the raising of the general standard by controlled breeding is the definite establishment of a characteristic New Zealand breed, the Corriedale. Older breeds, notably the Romney and the merino, are still in the great majority, but in 1927 there were enumerated over 900,000 Corriedale sheep, of which nearly 50,000 were in stud flocks registered in the flock-book. It is mainly this dual-purpose sheep, producing both a heavy, lustrous, fine-wool fleece and an early maturing carcass, that has brought New Zealand into the position of exporting stud sheep to countries like South Africa, Argentine, Uruguay, and the United States.

The experiments which finally resulted in evolving this new breed began between 1866 and 1868 upon the Corriedale sheep station in North Otago.(30) The pioneer in these experiments was Mr. James Little, who inbred the half-bred progeny of Romneys and merinos. This first flock was dispersed, but other experiments followed by Mr. Little and by other breeders. The breed was finally stabilised in the seventies as a new type inbred from half-breds resulting from crossing merinos with long-woolled varieties. Though the first cross was with Romneys, the main foundation of the present flocks is a merino-Lincoln cross. There is also some English Leicester and Border Leicester blood in the breed. There are still some echoes of controversy concerning the stability of the new type, and it has by no means displaced the older varieties, which are more suitable for some conditions of soil and climate; but its establishment is an indication of the technique which has developed in the hands of skilled sheep-breeders.

A Developing Technique

It is not the purpose of this book to provide a scientific description of the technique of sheep-raising as it has been developed in New Zealand. Such a description would involve not only a great deal of historical research, but considerable technical equipment and knowledge. There is scattered information to be gleaned from such manuals as that which was published by Weld as early as 1851 under the title *Hints to Intending Sheep-Farmers in New Zealand*, and Fuller's *Five Years' Residence in New Zealand*, written in 1859, as well as from official publications. Adequate treatment would also involve the utilisation of the great store of practical knowledge which exists only in the experience of practical sheep-farmers.

Such a task, however, is one for the practical farmer or the biologist. All that is necessary for purposes of economic record is the establishment of the fact that this developing technique exists and is, indeed, the chief foundation of New Zealand's material prosperity. A hint has already been given of the importance of cultivation and the improvement of pastures. The importance of sheep-breeding has also been mentioned. These primary techniques calling for skill that is gained mainly by experience are still in process of development. In them the natural scientist, hitherto rather neglected in New Zealand, has much to offer. There are many problems which have remained unsolved or have actually been created by reliance upon purely empirical methods to the exclusion of scientific research. This question will be raised later in another connection. Meantime one may notice, in passing, the very healthy tendency in recent times to turn to the scientist for practical help. The biologist can help in breeding grasses as well as animals, the soil chemist in fertilising and cultivation, the entomologist in controlling plant diseases and introduced pests.(31)

It is the organisation of sheep-farming as a business, both in its primary and secondary processes, that offers the best illustration of the success of the practical farmer in devising technique to suit the new conditions in New Zealand. It is essential to realise that sheep-farming, especially in the earlier period with which this chapter is mainly concerned, is a large-scale industry. Even in the later period, when smaller scale mixed farming has grown to be more important, the advantages of large-scale methods are still obtained by co-operation and commercial organisation. All of the essential features of mass-production, usually credited only to the newer factories in America, are to be observed in a well-organised shearing-shed, and most of them anticipated and owe little to Henry Ford or the Fordisation of industry. The maximum use of mechanical power, highly specialised and skilled workers, and careful planning of processes result in maximum output and minimum labour costs.

A shearing-shed on a big station is indeed a lesson in economic organisation. The thousands of sheep gathered in from the outlying hill-slopes are massed about a long low shed. At daybreak the shearers begin on the sheep that have been driven indoors overnight so that their fleeces will not be damp with dew. The pens within the shed are kept full throughout the day. With a deft kick the shearer opens the low swing-door of the pen and drags his sheep on to the "board", where it is pinned helplessly by a firm pressure of the knee behind its shoulder. The machine shears hang just where the shearer can readily seize them, and with his long sweeping motions the fleece falls unbroken upon the floor in a minimum of time. "Fleece-ohs" gather up the wool and take it to the end of the shed, where it is thrown with one motion across the sorting-table. The stained and ragged pieces are skirted off and flung into separate piles, and the fleece is placed by the wool-classer in the bin appropriate to its quality and kind. Thence it is taken a few steps to the press, and within a few hours the bales, pressed, sewn, and marked, are ready for carting to the wool-store. Only by the most careful organisation could large flocks running into the tens of thousands be handled so expeditiously. The slightest fall of rain halts the work, for damp wool under pressure will cause fires by spontaneous combustion. The shearer, working by piece-wages, makes as great a tally as technical skill and sheer hard work render possible. The machines start at daybreak, rest-pauses, accompanied by "snacks" which to a town-dweller seem substantial meals, occur about every two hours, and as a result of labouring skill and effort, supplemented by equally careful organisation, production is maximised and labour costs minimised, even though the shearer rightly demands a substantial price for his labour.

It is this high organisation of the primary industries, rather than any measures of labour legislation, upon which the prosperity of New Zealand really rests. There is no need to underestimate the beneficial effects or the historical necessity for such legislation; but it is emphatically necessary to remember that without the volume of production made possible by the characteristic technique evolved in the primary industries, such regulation of labour conditions would be futile. Moreover, this technique is novel. It does not exist in the farming industries of older lands, where smaller units of production are the rule and labour is cheaper. It is the characteristic expression of the empirical, experimental, but thoroughly practical temper of the colonist, evolving new methods to suit the circumstances of a new and vastly different environment.

The manufacturing side of the wool industry lacks an adequate market in New Zealand, so that over 95 per cent. of the clip is exported overseas. (32) The commercial organisation of this large trade is practically an extension of the Yorkshire woollen industry and is again highly organised. The wool-bales are carefully inspected, by the sample method, by buyers whose practical experience enables them to estimate with extraordinary precision the extent of yolk in the wool, its probable loss of weight in the long voyage overseas, as well as its quality and spinning counts. With their catalogues marked with approximate prices in which these estimates have been summed up (largely by almost subconscious calculation), and with buying instructions on their desks, these experts meet in auction competition at the regular wool sales held in various centres. All the wool-using countries of the world are represented; but the Yorkshire dialect prevails in the bidding, and British financial enterprise provides the credit upon which the growers' cheques are drawn. The variant qualities of wool forbid the standardisation upon which speculative future markets are based. Competition is fiercely personal and based entirely upon individual judgments of qualities and values. The expert buying of wool, with its related operations of finance, shipping, and insurance, parallels in the commercial field the skilled technique of the wool-grower.

The Advent of Refrigeration

The essentially large-scale methods of organisation sketched in the preceding sections relate mainly to the production and sale of wool. As long as New Zealand's distance from her principal market remained an effective barrier to the transport of perishable products, wool was the dominating commodity, both of production and of export. Its importance is well illustrated by the following summary table showing the chief items of exports at ten yearly periods between 1853 and 1883.(33)

PRINCIPAL EXPORTS OF NEW ZEALAND, 1853–83

(000s *omitted*)

Export.	1853.	1863.	1873.	1883.
	£	£	£	£
Timber	93	18	44	125
Wool	67	830	2,702	3,014
Grain	19	—	136	1,287
Kauri gum	16	27	86	337
Gold	—	2,432	1,987	892
Tallow	—	—	67	234
Flax	—	—	144	37
Meat by-products	—	12	49	69
Flour	—	—	12	65
Butter	—	—	—	42
Rabbit-skins	—	—	—	101

This table, which includes all the commodities whose value reached £10,000 in any of the years recorded, is an epitome of the economic life of New Zealand in this period. The rise and decline of the alluvial gold-mining industry, the diminishing importance of the early trade in timber, flax, and kauri gum, and the dominating importance of wool, are already apparent. The large export of grain, which reached a peak in the year 1883, was due to the efforts made to develop large-scale wheat-farming by mechanical methods essentially similar to those described in connection with the shearing-shed.(34) The pictures of great wheat paddocks, with large numbers of harvesters following one another in succession, which sometimes occur still in books on New Zealand, really date from this period. The advent of refrigeration quickly turned attention from this experiment, and except for a brief spurt at the time of the South African War, grain-growing has for the past forty years been a domestic industry. The beginnings of export in tinned meats are also indicated in the table,(35) and the sudden appearance of rabbit-skins as an important item of export is a reminder of the rapid increase of this imported pest.(36) By the end of the seventies they had increased so greatly, especially in the back-country, that they had eaten the scanty grass from under the sheep. Their depredations were especially severe upon the pastoral leasehold lands where holdings were large—the rough country afforded more protection, and there was not the incentive of ownership to check their increase. Their destruction of the grass close to the roots, added to the effect of overstocking, reduced the value of large areas of land in Otago and Canterbury, and contributed not a little to the failure of these south island provinces to maintain their economic leadership in the next period of development. In certain areas the destruction of the scanty pasture on the hill-sides facilitated erosion and denudation in the same way as deforestation. In recent years the increased value of rabbit-skins and more effective methods of combating the pest, vigorously enforced by Rabbit Boards and the Department of Agriculture, have greatly reduced their depredations. In many areas the pastures have greatly improved in consequence.

The table of exports as a whole reveals clearly the overwhelming importance of wool and wheat among the primary industries, both of them large-scale types of farming. As the appearance of tinned meats among the exports indicates, attempts had already been made to find some more profitable outlet for the sheep's carcass than the boiling-down works. Successful experiments in refrigeration, however, altered the whole outlook of the industry at this juncture. Not the least important result of the new development was the possibility which it opened up to the small farmer of using more intensive methods of mixed farming. The ultimate results of refrigeration struck a heavy blow at the dominance of the wool-kings, but it was they who made the first experiments and reaped the first profits from the new process.

The development of the new methods of preserving meat so that it could be transported long distances and kept over long periods of time was not an accidental fortuitous discovery. It was made only after prolonged patient research and many false leads.(37) The economic situation obviously demanded it. In Britain, and to a less extent in other European lands, the food problem became more and more acute as the industrial revolution developed and concentrated a rapidly increasing population more and more in the manufacturing towns. The possibility of making some connection between the flocks and herds of South America and the Southern colonies, on the one hand, and the hungry British market on the other, was recognised early in the nineteenth century. It is a rather sad commentary upon the tendency of economists to generalise from local and temporary circumstances, that the foremost British economists in their zeal for free trade assured the British farmers that there could never be any reason for them to fear overseas competition. As late as 1842 J. R. McCulloch could argue that "no country is likely to send any stock to England, or, indeed, has any to send, with the exception of the countries round Hamburgh, and the imports thence cannot be considerable".(38)

Yet experiments in the preserving of meat from Australia go back at least to 1843, and meat tinning or canning dates back another thirty years still. Experiments which met with promising success in Australia in the late forties were checked by the discovery of gold in the fifties and sixties creating a local market and disorganising local organisation. In the late sixties, however, canning experiments were resumed, and in 1869 a New Zealand Meat Preserving Company established works in several places, mainly in the south island.(39) This was not a profitable venture, since it was not possible at that time to make use of the by-products, but, as the statistical table quoted above shows, it did develop a small export trade. In the meantime Australian pioneers, notably Mort and Harrison, were at work on more scientific lines. The latter used the first refrigerating machine in the world in a brewery at Bendigo in 1851, and ten years later Mort set up the first meat-freezing works at Sydney. At the same time, experiments in chilling processes for the shorter voyage from the United States to Britain were well under way, and it had become apparent that transport under low temperatures was destined to solve the problem. It was not till 1879 that the mechanical and commercial problems involved had so far been solved that a trial shipment on a commercial scale could be made. Both Mort and Harrison had met with failure in earlier attempts. The *Strathleven's* cargo, however, was landed in excellent condition at London on February 2, 1880. The first careful report upon the venture, made after personal inspection, was that made by the London representative of the New Zealand Loan and Mercantile Agency.(40)

The problem of the Australian sheep-farmers was, of course, almost identical with that of their fellows in New Zealand. By this time the economic depression following the Vogel boom had set in in real earnest. The year 1879 had seen a most disheartening fall in prices, and it was of the most immediate and pressing importance that the export of wool should be supplemented by that of its joint product, meat. One of the great financial companies, into whose control many large sheep stations had fallen and many more were destined to fall before the financial stringency worked itself out, authorised the preliminary expenditure necessary to fit up a ship for a trial voyage. Many were the problems to be solved. A mechanical failure caused the experiment to break down in its early stages, but another effort was made and, after an exciting and perilous voyage, was at last crowned with complete success. The *Dunedin* arrived in London on May 24, 1882, with its cargo of 4,460 sheep and 449 lamb carcasses in such excellent condition that they met a ready sale upon the Smithfield Market. The net returns were not large, but sufficient to indicate the possibilities of the trade, which was well launched by this courageous enterprise.(41)

The first successful shipment was indeed "a prodigious fact", as *The Times* called it, both for the producers in New Zealand and for the consuming public in Great Britain; but much remained to be done before the trade was firmly organised. The first technical problem had been solved, but there were a host of subsidiary problems. Improvement in methods has been continuous and is still continuing as the result of practical experience and scientific research. The first shipment had been frozen on board the *Dunedin*; but even before that ship sailed, the first frozen meat company was floated in Dunedin. This pioneer company, the New Zealand Refrigerating Company, was never on a very large scale, but upon its absorption in 1905 by the Christchurch Meat Company it gave its name to one of the largest existing enterprises in the Dominion. Other companies quickly followed: the Canterbury Frozen Meat Company in November 1881; the Gear Meat Company, of Wellington, almost exactly a year later, being earliest in the field. (42)

The meat-works operated by these and other companies are now such a familiar sight in almost every district of the Dominion that it is easy to forget the difficult steps by which they reached their present methods of large-scale efficiency. As economic enterprises they are excellently organised, producing a whole range of joint products, from the wool and pelt of the slaughtered sheep to the frozen carcass, kidneys, sweetbreads, potted tongues, concentrated extract, casings, and even blood and bone fertilisers. Nothing is wasted, and the most spotless cleanliness is maintained under detailed Governmental inspection and grading. The same system of high organisation, piece-wages, and skilled specialised labour obtains as in a shearing-shed, with the same result of mass-production at low cost.

This, however, is not the whole story. The meat had to be carried as well as frozen. Vogel's great programme of railway construction in the seventies had opened up the country-side effectively if somewhat expensively. By a process of experiment it was now necessary to evolve the refrigerated vans that are so common a sight upon the railways at the present time. Swift had built the first refrigerated car in the United States in 1875, and his effort was quickly copied in New Zealand when the need arose. (43) In the same way, the needs of the new bulk cargo revolutionised shipbuilding for the colonial trade. The New Zealand Shipping Company had begun operations in 1873. In 1883 it initiated a direct steamer service with Britain and fitted its steamers with refrigerating machinery. Other companies followed suit, until steamers now sail with the regularity of railway expresses, and rarely have any difficulties in landing their cargoes in first-class condition. The fitting of the ships, defects in the refrigerating machinery, and insufficient care in the preparation and freezing before shipment were responsible for a substantial proportion of failures in the first decades, but that proportion has declined almost to vanishing-point.(44)

In the same way insurance and commercial services have gradually been brought to a high pitch of efficiency, with a consequent steady lowering of transportation costs.(45) It is upon this commercial revolution, almost as much as upon the technical invention which it exploited, that the subsequent prosperity of the Dominion has rested. The reduction of costs lowered prices in the home market relatively, though in a time of generally rising prices not absolutely, and so stimulated demand. At the same time, it increased the proportion of the value of the product which reached the primary producer, and so contributed directly to the economic welfare of the colony. The problems involved in this great commercial development are by no means all solved yet, but the first most difficult bases of achievement were reached before the end of the century.

It will be obvious, from all that has been sketched in this section, that the whole development of meat-freezing was a large-scale enterprise promoted and financed by the great sheep-owners and their financial affiliations. Their constructive initiative in these matters is clear and needs no comment. It added enormously to the wealth of New Zealand. If the story had ended there, however, it is possible that the economic organisation of the Dominion might have taken the same shape as in the very similar situation produced in some of the competing South American countries. New Zealand might have been a country of great sheep and cattle stations, the operations of which were integrated closely with large-scale secondary manufacturing and financial enterprises, with a clearly marked division between the capitalist owners and the labourers.

It is essential, therefore, to turn next to a consideration of the forces which challenged and largely overthrew the entrenched power of "the landed oligarchy". Financial and economic power is not absent in New Zealand to-day, but there are few countries where wealth is so widely distributed, where the small- and medium-scale farming is so influential, and where labour is so capable of safeguarding its own interests. The next chapters are devoted, therefore, to a description of the movements, partly political, but more largely economic and social, that wrought this change.

CHAPTER V

THE ORIGINS OF STATE SOCIALISM

A STUDY IN ECONOMIC PATHOLOGY

Between the booming prosperity of New Zealand in the early seventies and the experimental legislation which made the colony famous in the nineties there is a long period during which the forces of discontent gathered themselves for an attack upon the land monopolists. Any analysis of these forces must take account of two sets of factors, unless, indeed, one is content with such an all-embracing theory as the materialist interpretation of history. No economist is likely to deny the influence of economic forces upon political change; but in addition to the facts of economic development, some account must be taken of the theories to which those facts gave rise. It is important, in other words, to know not only what happened in this period of discontent, but also what people thought about it. Whether the happenings produced the theories, or the theories influenced the facts, is a problem that may be left to the metaphysicians of social science.

In the following pages an attempt is made to outline the economic condition of New Zealand at the end of the Vogel boom, and to show how the efforts to remedy that condition became concentrated into the legislative programme of the Liberal-Labour Party. The story is not a simple one, nor is it possible to treat this or any period of economic history out of relation to preceding and following periods. The depression which ruled in New Zealand throughout the eighties was the result of complex causes which lead into many different aspects of economic, political, and social organisation. Part of the story has necessarily been anticipated in tracing the native land difficulties which diverted settlement into the south island provinces, in discussing the methods by which land was alienated to private ownership, and in sketching the large-scale organisation of the principal farming industries at this time.

The continuity of social development is further illustrated by the fact that the economic basis upon which the experimental legislation of the nineties was built was already being undermined by the transformation of the farming industries caused by the introduction of refrigeration. Some mention has been made of the frozen-meat industry and of the revolutionary changes in farming practice which it portended. The even more important growth of dairying, however, has yet to be sketched. It is treated more conveniently in a later chapter, both because it was slower to get under way and because it was connected so closely with the opening up of the north island.

It is essential, therefore, to remember that the economic stress of the period treated in this chapter was a passing episode due to a chance combination of factors, and that when the stress was at its worst, the beginnings of a new and more prosperous order might well have been clear to a prophetic eye. Neither the economic depression of the eighties, nor the legislative experiments to which it gave birth in the following decade, was truly characteristic of New Zealand. Rather were they the products of a pathological situation which yielded, in the ensuing period of prosperity, to such healing economic forces as a widening basis of industries, the opening up of new lands, and more favourable external markets, rather than to political regulation. It is, unfortunately, only too easy to approach economic history by way of politics. The constructive organisation of economic life is difficult to describe, but the records of political interference with it lie open to the most casual student or observer. Yet it is only in periods of economic difficulty that such political interference is really of first-rate importance, and obsession with this aspect of history tends inevitably to stress the pathology rather than the physiology of economic growth. In this respect, as in many others, that country (or that industry) is happiest which has least history.

The true and characteristic economic history of New Zealand is to be found in the progress of farming methods; the improvement of pastures; the breeding of sheep and cattle; the opening up of the country-side by public works; the organisation of transport, banking, commerce, and secondary industries; and above all, in the increase of numbers and the improvement of human welfare. When, as in the period now to be studied, there is a perceptible check to such progress, political and legislative measures become important; but that in itself indicates an abnormal situation. The New Zealand people, as a shrewd French observer has acutely remarked, are "practical and opportunist to the point of cynicism". In this they exemplify the Anglo-Saxon concern for results rather than principles, and

> are more intent upon achieving things than reasoning about them. They proceed empirically, without theory, without principles, without pretensions, one might almost say, always prepared to amend or even repeal a law they have passed, if experience should show that it does not produce the results they expected; and without the least concern for the results which it may possibly have in fifty or one hundred years. Such is the character of English politicians. They do not pique themselves on arriving at a final solution of problems; all they care for is to serve the needs of the moment, and they look no farther.(1)

With such facts as these in mind, we may pass to a consideration of the circumstances which temporarily led the New Zealand colonists to undertake extensive experiments in legislative interference with economic development. It will be clear that as their difficulties thickened in the eighties, they laid hold of expedients which for the most part were theoretical suggestions originating in other lands. These they translated into practical measures of immediate application without, however, following them to their logical theoretical conclusions. As economic pressure was relieved, whether by the success of such legislation or by extraneous economic developments, they again followed a characteristic Anglo-Saxon course in retaining the form of experimental legislation while subtly modifying its administrative effect. There were, indeed, certain institutional developments, notably in connection with the Arbitration Court, which took on a life of their own, somewhat different from the intentions of their authors. In other cases, as in the leasehold tenures, laws were frankly amended or repealed. Broadly speaking, however, as economic development emerged into easier circumtances, the importance of legislative controls was lessened, and these controls underwent considerable, if subtle, administrative change.

Barriers to Settlement

Perhaps the easiest way to approach an understanding of this episode in New Zealand's history is by a recapitulation of certain elementary but fundamental features of the economic organisation of the colony at this time. The first outstanding fact is the maintenance of what may be regarded as an artificial frontier or barrier to settlement by the locking up of the rich north island lands. Until the late eighties settlement was, broadly speaking, confined to the south island, and to certain more accessible areas such as the Wairarapa district and Hawke's Bay in the north island. The dominance of the southern provinces in politics, especially after the increase of immigration consequent upon the gold-rushes, enabled them also to get the lion's share of public works and immigration resulting from the expenditure of borrowed money in the Vogel boom of the seventies. This, in turn, increased their population and political influence. It was a New Zealand mainly concentrated in the south island which felt the strain of economic depression, and embarked upon heroic measures of legislative experiment in order to find a way out. The pushing back of this frontier of settlement by the cessation of native troubles, and the opening up of the north island, was the principal means of relieving congestion in the next generation, and the principal reason also for the administrative modification of much of the experimental legislation.

It is possible that this relief might have come earlier if it had not been for another obvious barrier to settlement—the system of land tenures, by which great landholders were enabled in the seventies and eighties to aggregate large areas of land. Evidence has already been adduced to prove that before 1890 the great bulk of the colony's most fertile and accessible land had already passed into private ownership. This evidence needs to be read with the description given of the large-scale methods of farming then in vogue. Land was held in large areas and farmed only by the most extensive methods. This is primarily true of the south island; but it applies also to those areas of native land in the north island which were purchased from the Maoris in the period between 1862 and 1892, when the Crown right of pre-emption was waived and private purchasers, "plying the natives with cash and often with rum", made haste to build up great estates. The very complexity of Maori titles, as has already been pointed out, played into the hands of the large landowners.

The free trade in Maori lands, especially in the period after the war settlement in 1872, and the legislation of 1873 for individualising land titles, was not only disastrous to the Maoris, but, as the Royal Commission of 1891 emphasised, was "against the public interest" also.

Some colour of necessity was given to this aggregation of land in large areas by the overwhelming importance of the wool industry in New Zealand economy at this time. Sheep-raising for wool is essentially a large-scale industry, calling for low labour costs and extensive, rather than intensive, methods. As long as wool remained the mainstay of the colony's exports, the economic dominance of the wool-growers was paralleled by their influence in the legislature. This barrier to settlement was considerably modified when the demonstrated success of refrigeration opened up profitable markets for other forms of pastoral produce. This was a development of the late eighties, which fortunately checked also the exploitation of virgin fertility by the continuous wheat-cropping which was being practised on a large scale in certain areas, especially in Canterbury.(2)

It was therefore into a New Zealand largely cooped up in the south island provinces, with its lands held in large areas by a comparatively few great landowners, and with only three products—wool, grain, and gold—of outstanding importance, that Vogel injected the forced development of his borrowing policy in 1870. The broad features of that policy have already been outlined, and the economics of borrowing for development will be considered in a later chapter. It is the effects of the expenditure of loan money upon industrial organisation which should be noticed at this point.

The first important effect was the incentive and opportunity which it provided for the further aggregation of great estates. The Vogel policy of borrowing for public works and assisted immigration might have survived criticism much more effectively if the safeguards against aggregation originally proposed by its author had not been swept aside. The borrowing was launched just at the time when "new colonial values were being created by the development of mechanical transport",(3) and when Britain needed new sources of supply. It was one of the earliest signs of that secondary "migration of capital" from which the structure of the modern British Empire has grown. (4)

Its almost inevitable weaknesses, arising from hastily considered and wasteful expenditure and from poor selection of immigrants and lack of adequate preparation for their reception, might have been much less obvious blemishes if the colonial legislature had not negatived the proposals for setting aside reservations of public lands. With these safeguards omitted, the expenditure of twenty millions of borrowed money within ten years, and the introduction of 100,000 immigrants in the same period, created a wild boom in land values. (5) In the scramble that followed, the large landowners held all the advantages. The ensuing depression only served to consolidate their grip of the land, which passed back from the hands of optimistic purchasers to the mortgagees and, in only too many cases, to finance companies, many of which were largely of absentee ownership. As the depression deepened in the eighties, the banks also found themselves burdened with real estate, so that their assets became "frozen" and credit for further development was almost unobtainable.

The net result on landholding, therefore, was to add a financial frontier to the existing geographical and tenurial barriers to settlements. The land was locked up in large stations that were unprofitable, even when organised as extensive wool-producing units, and were still more unprofitable when viewed in relation to the opportunities of the new mixed farming after refrigeration. Until their finance could be readjusted no progress was possible. Many stations were for sale, but at prices commensurate with the mortgages. Reductions of land values involved long, painful processes of liquidation; legislation directed against large holdings helped to break them up in the nineties, but it was not till after 1900 that a rising level of general prices floated land values back again to the level of 1878 and finally lifted the incubus. The effect of this financial situation is well stated by Reeves:

> Few extensive holdings were being worked to anything like the best advantage. Most of them were heavily mortgaged; many were in the grip of the financiers, and were carried on from year to year with the least possible outlay of capital. It was a commonplace that half the great estates were for sale; and so they were, at a price. The mortgagees would not sell

at a loss, and could seldom sell at a profit. They hung on to the land, watching one another and waiting for a rise in prices and for a brisk demand which naturally did not come. Prices could not rise until a good proportion of the land was cut up and settled. The owners could not afford to cut it up until prices rose. There was a deadlock. What, more than anything else, exasperated the public was that many parts of New Zealand are perhaps as well suited for fairly close settlement as any spots in the world. Rainfall, soil, and proximity to seaports combine to mark out the more fertile tracts as the small man's country. And, whilst the country was just fitted for working farmers, and lying empty and waiting for their hands, men in hundreds and thousands, farmers' sons and country labourers, were growing up and working on other men's land, albeit they had the skill, knowledge, and strength to manage holdings of their own. The cry for land in New Zealand in 1890 was no mere urban sentimentalism. It was no mere factitious outcome of the preaching of theorists, who imagined that by calling "Back to the Land!" loudly enough and long enough they could transplant superfluous men and women from the cities to the wilderness and keep them there. There was something of this, no doubt. But in the main it was a genuine hunger for land, coming from the landless amongst a rural population. Distress in the towns strengthened it, and an exodus to Australia in the years 1886–91 pointed the moral. A colony, when population is deserting it, is like a child that shrinks instead of growing. (6)

The Beginnings of Urban Industry

The secondary effects of such a situation extended far beyond the farming industries. The land-hunger itself was genuine and important, and found vent in the steadily increasing hostility to the "landowning oligarchy", which provided the drive behind the Liberal-Labour land legislation of the next decade. But it must also be viewed in its relation to the wholesale immigration of the seventies and to the industrial prospects held out to assisted immigrants. The prolonged depression of the local market, and the stringent finance caused by the locking up of capital in overvalued land, reacted detrimentally on these prospects and caused great bitterness.

The character of the inducements held out to immigrants is clearly revealed in the *Handbook of New Zealand*, printed in London in 1875 and edited by Vogel himself. This compendious little volume contains excellent descriptive articles by such eminent authorities as Fox, McLean, Gisborne, and Hector, and is supplemented by detailed accounts of the various provinces. The provincial accounts follow a uniform arrangement, stressing the opportunities for land settlement, the possibilities of new industries and public works under construction. There is a strong competitive note running through them, and a tendency to lay stress upon industrial prospects which have only too often proved illusory. Vogel himself tended to stress this feature, as the following passage from his Introduction will show.

> Success naturally induces imitation, and hence, perhaps, the existing industries may have become too deeply grooved. The fact that sheep and wheat have been so successful in the south does not make it a necessary consequence that they are the most suitable productions for the north. Amongst the benefits an influx of population will bestow on the colony may be anticipated that of an impetus being given to new industries, suitable to the circumstances of the several parts of the colony, but which in the early days were overlooked.(7)

This fairly careful and plausible statement was only too apt to be expanded into such an essay as that of E. J. Wakefield's in the following year, entitled "The Malvern Hills Guide; or Mines and Manufactures, cheap Coal and Building Materials, great helps to the colonization by Railway of a large Farming and Grazing District". It was equally likely to be translated into an ambitious programme of railway and road construction, which, in this case, was to "terminate in the immediate vicinity of the coal-fields and deposits of iron-ore".(8) Fifty years have passed since these statements were made and the railway was built. Brown coal has been mined in the district in small quantities; but no iron-ore has ever been worked, and the clay deposits, despite many efforts, have returned little profit. The railway, in consequence, has steadily contributed to the difficulties of the railway system as a whole.

This somewhat extreme example has been cited to emphasise the fact that the great bulk of assisted immigration in this period of boom consisted of town-dwellers who were led to expect employment in urban industries. They brought with them the urban outlook. Their numbers included many trade unionists and Radicals. Along with manufacturing industry, therefore, came the typical labour reaction to it, and this formed no inconsiderable factor in the fashioning of political ideas in the ensuing generation. It was not, however, and still is not, characteristic of the New Zealand people as a whole. As in Australia, "the city has been built up, and many of its industries are still carried on, by the immigration of the town-dwellers of the United Kingdom".(9) In New Zealand, however, unlike Australia, this phase passed with the depression of the eighties. The restored dominance of the country-side in the last generation is the fundamental reason for most of the marked differences between the two sister Dominions to-day.

As long as the expenditure of borrowed money carried New Zealand along prosperously in the seventies, local manufacturing industries found fairly easy lodgment. Mechanical industries had received their first impetus from the demands created by the gold-rushes. The best coal-deposits of New Zealand were opened up in the same period—the late sixties.(10) They lie on the west coast of the south island, just north of the gold-fields, which centred at Hokitika after 1865. Coal production and export were not recorded till 1878, but by that time the annual production was 162,000 tons. The development of large-scale wheat-farming further stimulated machine industries in the seventies, and evoked new types of agricultural implements suited to local conditions.

In the boom period also there was a considerable expansion of industries using raw materials of local production. The official catalogue of the international exhibition, held in Christchurch in 1882, refers to the range of exhibits in the following optimistic terms.

> Pottery, terra-cotta ware, ornamental glassware, furniture, upholstery, cabinet-work; doors, sashes, and other woodware; inlaid work, for which the adaptability of New Zealand woods is beautifully demonstrated; ranges, stoves, grates, and such ironwork; brushware; clothing, hats and caps of all kinds; woollen goods, wool rugs and mats, feather dressing; ropes, lines, and twines; leather and leather goods of all kinds, including boots, shoes, saddlery, and harness; jewellery and silversmiths' work; grain and wool produce, biscuits and various kinds of flour and farinaceous food, confectionery; bees, beehives, and honey, dairy produce, pickles, sauces, essences, jellies, jams, cordials, and liquors; coffee and spices; ales and beers; wines; garden and other seeds, flax and flax manufactures; oils, glues, manures; chemical and pharmaceutical preparations; soap, tallow, candles; printing, stationery, photography, electrotyping, and engraving; scientific apparatus, watchmakers' and jewellers' tools; Maori wares; all kinds of ladies' fancy and plain work; water-colour and oil paintings and drawings; machinery, tinware, brassware—all are displayed here in admirably arranged bays and glass cases, showing that in those industries suitable to the colony into which energy and capital has been thrown, New Zealand can well hold her own, and need not be ashamed to compete against any country in the world.(11)

The details of individual exhibits, however, indicate plainly that most of these industries were in an embryonic stage, and in the following period of falling prices and depression, their difficulties were greatly multiplied. Those that survived quite naturally demanded tariff protection, and this demand allied itself with and reinforced both the radical demands of the trade unionists and the land-hunger of the small farmers.

The actual growth of local industries was very slow. In 1887 the chief Government engineer, W. N. Blair, wrote very pertinently that "although the question of promoting colonial industries is a very old one, it has only risen into prominence during the last five or six years, and within the last three years the importance of the subject has literally been forced on the attention of the colony. The low price of wool, the falling off in the returns from the gold-fields, and the practical collapse of the grain trade has convinced the whole community that we must have more outlets for our energies."(12)

(Sir) Robert Stout, who was then Premier, wrote in 1886, with justifiable optimism, of the progress made by the colony since 1864, and showed the progression of wants from "the bush saw-pit and the blacksmith's forge" to "industries dependent on natural products, which are not easily obtainable from other countries", and thence to a wider range of manufactures. He was able to show that at least the beginnings had been made in a fairly considerable number of industries catering for the local market, even before tariff protection. The beginnings, however, were small indeed, and the figures he quoted from the census of 1881 showed that the only industries with total capital (value of land, buildings, machinery, and plant) greater than £200,000 were saw-milling, gas-works, breweries, grain-mills, printing establishments, and collieries. The woollen-mills in operation had less than £100,000 capital, and the boot-factories less than £50,000 between them; while the agricultural implement works producing "ploughs, chaff-cutters, grass-mowers, winnowing machines, disc-harrows, drills, reapers and binders, horse-powers (? mowers), corn-crushers, horse-hoes, scrub-cutters, grass-seed threshers, cream-separators, churns, etc.," had only £43,854 invested in the whole industry.(13)

Even in 1890 industrial development was still rudimentary, as the following summary table will show.(14)

NEW ZEALAND MANUFACTURES, 1890

Industry.	Number of Factories.	Hands Employed.	Wages Paid.	Value of Land, Buildings, Machinery, and Plant.	Total Value of Produce.
			£	£	£
Meat, preserving, freezing, and boiling-down works	43	1,568	138,459	476,151	1,464,659
Tanning, fellmongering ..	104	1,196	92,442	153,592	1,026,349
Grain-mills	129	499	52,384	391,828	991,812
Saw-mills	243	3,266	271,814	500,272	832,959
Boot and shoe factories ..	47	1,943	124,990	82,137	403,736
Printing establishments ..	142	2,569	214,185	341,683	354,559
Iron and brass foundries ..	68	1,727	152,687	262,042	390,943
Collieries	95	1,655	173,538	155,671	279,777
Woollen-mills	8	1,175	79,040	259,955	279,175
Gold and quartz-mining works	135	1,971	183,582	241,715	278,893
Flax-mills	177	3,204	116,168	146,792	234,266
Gasworks	27	249	31,700	730,490	178,947
Clothing factories	19	1,290	52,754	59,735	166,579
Soap and candle works ..	19	209	21,394	74,443	155,714
Cheese and butter factories	74	269	14,928	100,453	150,957
Machines, tools, and implements	43	556	46,887	76,783	148,364
Other industries	295	11,881	117,415	671,172	860,851

The Nemesis of Depression

The precarious economic situation of New Zealand at the end of the Vogel boom will be apparent from the foregoing analysis. It was recognised at a very early stage, not only by Vogel's political opponents, but by such former colleagues as the Hon. G. M. Waterhouse, who in 1873 resigned the Premiership of the Cabinet in which Vogel was Colonial Treasurer and leader of the Lower House.(15) Such protests, however, passed unheeded, and so did a sharp fall of prices in 1873–4. Not until the great fall in prices of 1878–9 was there any effective realisation of impending catastrophe.

The ramifications of the depression of the eighties extend into every department of economic life. There is little need to follow the complicated and rather debatable financial methods of Vogel and his successors upon the London Money

Market. These have been trenchantly and somewhat bitterly recorded in Carter's *An Historical Sketch of New Zealand Loans*, published in 1886.(16) Colonial borrowing was in its infancy, and the market had not at this time accumulated the fund of experience and laid the traditions which now safeguard both home investors and taxpayers in the borrowing Dominions. It is clear that the loans were in many cases expensively raised, and that the burden of interest was thereby made disproportionate to the benefits received from loan expenditures.

When this expenditure was halted after 1879, and imports began to fall heavily in value, the public finances were jeopardised. In the decade 1881–90 the Customs duties furnished 72 per cent. of the revenue raised by taxation. Imports fell heavily from the boom figures of the seventies and Customs revenue fell also. Territorial revenue derived from land sales and leases fell in a single year to 20 per cent. of its total in 1878. The financial state of the colony may be judged from the following summary table.(17)

PUBLIC FINANCE IN NEW ZEALAND, 1874–90
(000s *omitted*)

Year.	Revenue.	Expenditure.		Public Debt.	Population.
		Out of Revenue.	Out of Loan.		
	£	£	£	£	
1874	3,069	2,961	2,726	13,367	342
1875	2,814	3,432	3,108	17,400	376
1876	3,580	4,305	2,066	18,678	399
1877	3,916	3,822	1,827	20,691	409
1878	4,168	4,365	1,288	22,608	433
1879	3,135	3,845	1,973	23,958	464
1880	3,285	4,020	2,229	28,583	485
1881	3,757	3,676	1,070	29,659	501
1882	3,917	3,825	822	30,236	518
1883	3,871	3,924	1,192	31,385	541
1884	3,707	3,854*	1,566	32,861	564
1885	3,860	4,046*	1,179	35,790	575
1886	3,688	4,170*	1,584	37,588	589
1887	3,463	3,954*	1,573	38,226	603
1888	4,110	3,963*	825	38,326	607
1889	3,992	3,982*	515	38,483	616
1890	4,208	4,082*	399	38,802	626

* Exclusive of charges for sinking fund met by debentures issued to an equivalent amount.

The statistics of population in the last column of this table are eloquent evidence of the results of the financial situation disclosed. Despite a cumulative natural increase by excess of births over deaths, there was a perceptible slackening of the population returns, due to the fact that, in the five years 1886–90, the departures from New Zealand exceeded the number of new immigrants by 13,200. This "exodus" was a striking reversal of the immigration influx with which the borrowing boom started.(18)

The sharp fall in revenue in 1879 and 1880 was responsible not only for increased difficulties in raising loans,(19) but also for a drastic curtailment of Governmental expenditure. A Royal Commission was appointed to survey the management of the railway system, and another to investigate expenditure on civil services generally.(20) The report of the Commissions disclosed many instances of laxity and inefficiency, and their chief recommendations, especially the all-round reduction of 10 per cent. in salaries, were again in striking contrast with Vogel's action in raising salaries all round and creating new appointments. Such measures, however, almost invariably come too late, and when they come, add to an unemployment problem already acute.

The lavish expenditure of public money during the boom period of the seventies was, unfortunately, paralleled by an unsound banking policy pursued in New Zealand as well as in Australia. The early history of New Zealand banking is very chequered, despite the fact that few banks have operated, and those always under a Charter or an Act of Parliament. A State bank was urged upon the colony as early as 1846 by the Secretary of State for the Colonies, Lord Grey, and such a bank, with a monopoly of note-issue, was in actual operation between 1850 and 1856. At this period the only other bank was the Union Bank of Australia, which had been founded at Launceston in 1837 and had opened branches in New Zealand in 1840. A local bank, named the New Zealand Banking Corporation, had opened at Kororareka in 1839, and had extended operations to Auckland in 1841, but closed its doors in 1845. When the State bank experiment ended, the Oriental Bank, with head-quarters in Melbourne, opened branches in 1857, but its branches were taken over by the Bank of New

South Wales in 1861. In the same year, also, the Bank of New Zealand was formed and, as the only locally owned bank, it received the Government accounts and was successfully established.(21)

In the period of the gold-rushes there were other banks formed: the New Zealand Banking Corporation (1862–4) continued as "The Commercial Banking Co. of N.Z." (1864–6), the Bank of Otago (founded 1863 and absorbed by the Bank of New Zealand in 1874), and the Bank of Auckland (1864–6). The Bank of Australasia also extended its operations to New Zealand in 1864. The only other banks operating in New Zealand during the boom period of the seventies were the ill-fated Colonial Bank (founded 1874, absorbed by the Bank of New Zealand, 1895) and the National Bank of New Zealand (founded in 1872).

The enumeration of these banks will indicate the fact that they were all either Australian or New Zealand in origin and ownership. Not unnaturally they yielded unwisely to local pressure and pursued policies which were harshly criticised, particularly by the London *Economist,* as unsound banking. The local financial newspaper, the *Australasian Insurance and Banking Record,* met these criticisms spiritedly on the ground that the different local conditions in Australia and New Zealand demanded more liberal policies of advances upon real security, and that there was no question of crisis involving the liquidity of the real estate assets upon which loans were being advanced. The year 1878 saw this duel at its height; but this boom year was followed by a disastrous fall in prices, and the honours of the controversy lay obviously with the *Economist.*

A competent economic historian, writing almost half a century after the events recorded, has put the matter plainly. "The banks", wrote Dr. H. D. Bedford in his unpublished *History of Banking in New Zealand,* "greatly extended their credit beyond their immediately available resources. Their management betrayed in many cases utter recklessness. The commonly accepted checks were disregarded. The banks became largely Loan Mortgage Companies, advancing with the utmost liberality on fixed securities as though the need for liquid assets in banking had passed away."

A rough measure of the excessive credit advances made in this way is the disproportionate rise in bank assets (chiefly advances and discounts) as compared with deposits. Between 1870 and 1886 deposits rose from £3·1 millions to £10·6 millions, but assets rose in the same period from £6·3 millions to £19·0 millions.(22) The ensuing years were occupied in writing down assets that could not be realised, and it was not till 1903 that the figures of 1886 were again reached. Throughout the period of boom, and well into the period of depression, the banks paid high rates of dividend, and it was not until the Colonial Bank was in difficulties and the Bank of New Zealand stared bankruptcy in the face that dividends were curtailed. In the depth of the depression, in the years about 1890, this payment of profits out of capital or, if the banks had closed, out of deposits was open to the severest criticism.(23)

The only plea that can be urged in extenuation of such unsound banking methods, apart from the general atmosphere created by the expenditure of borrowed money and the public pressure which was thereby brought to bear upon the banks, lies in the competition of the loan companies which are characteristic of Australian and New Zealand finance. These companies, which go under various names, such as stock and station agencies, investment companies, etc., originated in the pastoral period, as their name, stock and station agency, implies. They are primarily commission dealers, not only in stock, but in farm requirements. In part their financial operations consist of various extensions of "dealers' credit".(24) A farmer is helped financially to buy and stock a farm and is carried on for some time by one of these agency firms, to which he becomes tied by his loans. It is a natural development, from the provision of credit in this way, to the acceptance of deposits and the gradual assumption of all the essential functions of deposit banking. These firms are subject to none of the safeguards exacted from the chartered banks, though in the last analysis they may be regarded as very imperfectly controlled extensions of the credit-issuing powers of the banks. In times of boom they may so far extend the issues of credit that when the boom bursts and they are forced to the banks for accommodation to cover advances to their clients, the extent of their commitments constitutes an extra, indeterminate and very embarrassing drain upon the banks' credit resources and reserves.

This development was very obvious in the depression of the eighties, and resulted especially in the constant expansion of the banks' commitments, as the loan companies had to be propped up. Where they failed, their frozen assets were taken over by the banks, which necessarily resulted in further restricting the supply of loanable credit. This consequence was somewhat unforeseen and largely beyond the control of the bank authorities. There is, however, little that can be said in extenuation of their entering into competition with the loan companies in the boom period, and less in defence of their attitude in continuing to pay dividends and so disguising the true credit situation until the risk of imminent failure forced public action on their behalf.

Unemployment and Sweating in Local Industries

The collapse of public expenditure, and the cumulative credit stringency of the eighties, naturally threw the local urban industries, which had been encouraged in the boom period, into most difficult straits. Unemployment was not new in New Zealand. Reference has already been made to the troubles of the early Wakefield settlements in this respect, and also to the demands of the unemployed in Dunedin in 1861, the first year of the gold-rushes. As the alluvial gold-fields began to peter out towards the end of the sixties, unemployment naturally reappeared. Meetings were held in Christchurch in 1868, and in 1870 it was reported that there were 3,000 miners out of work on the Thames gold-fields in the north island, and that half of them were so desperate that they would work for food alone.(25) In this year distress was widespread also in Great Britain, and when both the Canterbury and Otago Provincial Councils were forced to set up select committees to consider the matter in New Zealand, the attraction of Vogel's borrowing proposals was greatly reinforced.

Unemployment did not reappear in any considerable degree until the winter of 1877, and then the boom year following absorbed most of the difficulties. The final break of boom conditions in 1879, however, intensified a desperate situation, which was widespread over the colony but worst in Canterbury, where the boom had been wildest. In May 1879 meetings in Christchurch disclosed a very angry temper among the unemployed. It found vent partly in resentment against the immigration of Chinese, which was then threatening to become a serious menace to labour conditions, and in efforts to stop any further immigration from Britain. At the same time, the bitterest reproaches were heaped upon the head of the legislators and Vogel in particular. Palliative measures, such as the provision of relief depots and soup-kitchens, were of little avail, and in June 1880 a meeting of unemployed drew up a petition to the President of the United States, begging him to render assistance by which they might migrate to America. "If this petition fails in its object," they wrote, "it will at any rate be a standing record against legislators who have brought this colony into such a deplorable condition."

In 1883 Parliament was forced to appoint a Royal Commission to investigate the problem of unemployment, which continued to be most acute in Canterbury. The Commission reported that the towns had been overbuilt, that the cessation of Governmental expenditure upon public works, coupled with bad farming seasons and high overseas freights and high rates of interest, had crippled the farmers' purchasing power and had been reflected in the towns. No constructive measures of any great significance were suggested. The indifferent attitude of the Continuous Ministry was clearly responsible for the return to power of the Stout-Vogel Ministry in 1884. Vogel still had faith in his methods of borrowing for development, but loans were not so easily raised, and after three troubled years, during which the radical tendencies of subsequent years were foreshadowed and some sound administrative reforms were put through, the Continuous Ministry came into power again in 1887. Meantime the incidence of unemployment had shifted to Dunedin and Auckland. A meeting at Dunedin in 1885 petitioned the Government of Victoria to help transfer the surplus labour of New Zealand to that colony, where conditions were much easier and were, in fact, on the verge of a boom. In 1887 the Christchurch unemployed sent a resolution to the New Zealand Government in the following terms:

Resolved that, since the Government refuses to provide work and private persons have no work to give, the unemployed should petition His Excellency the Governor to memorialise Her Most Gracious Majesty to exercise her prerogative during the year of her Jubilee by sending relief to the starving people of New Zealand.

Such meetings and resolutions, however, were of little avail before the attitude of the Premier, Sir Harry Atkinson, who bluntly lectured the unemployed on the immutable laws of political economy, and told them of his personal hardships as an early settler. In face of such a hostile reception the only course for mobile labourers was to migrate to Victoria, by this time at the height of its banking boom.

The inevitable result of prolonged urban unemployment was aggravated by the exploitation of the labour of women and minors. This was naturally worst in the clothing trades, where a vicious system of subcontracting and homework had grown up. Generally speaking, wages were desperately low, hours were long and lengthening, and working conditions were very bad. Adult male labour had escaped the worst of such conditions by standards of hours set early in the colony's history, but the sweating of female and child labour undoubtedly tended to lower wages and accentuate male unemployment, if it did not materially worsen the conditions of labour. The trade unionists, therefore, felt a vital interest in the welfare of the unorganised workers in home industries.

Public interest was aroused in the situation by a series of outspoken sermons by the Rev. Rutherford Waddell, who ministered to the largest Presbyterian Church in Dunedin. These sermons, beginning with one on "The Sin of Cheapness", were published in the *Otago Daily Times* and became the centre of a vigorous controversy. The *Times* sent around a special investigator, whose articles reported conditions that awakened the public conscience. The *Lyttelton Times* took up the agitation in Christchurch, other newspapers joined in, and gradually the full extent of the problem was revealed.

It was partly a problem of depression, low wages, and falling prices; but largely, also, a problem of lack of Governmental regulation. Inadequate organisation of labour contributed by making possible the abuse of the apprenticeship system and the growth of subcontracting. As always in such cases, it was the homeworkers whose conditions were worst and whose competition brought down general standards. The chief need, therefore, was such Governmental regulation as would enable the more efficient employers to withstand the competition of their weaker and less scrupulous rivals.

A wave of public indignation created much public sympathy with the effort, made in Dunedin and copied in other centres, to form trade unions in these sweated industries. It also forced the unsympathetic Continuous Ministry to appoint a Royal Commission, whose report contains much detailed information concerning labour conditions at this time.(26) Though the majority of the members of this Commission found that no sweating existed in the technical meaning of that word, a minority produced a vigorous report in which the evil conditions were fully described. The chief recommendations of the Commission were in the direction of Governmental regulation. Following the Commission's report, a Factory Act was laid before the House in 1890; but it remained for the Liberal-Labour Government, which came into power in 1891, to pass the measure and, subsequently, to extend its operation considerably in the Act of 1894.

This was by no means the beginning of factory legislation in New Zealand, which goes back to 1873, when an Act was passed on the motion of J. B. Bradshaw.

In its few lines was embodied the principle that no woman or girl-child should work for more than eight hours a day in a workroom, and that the employment of a single person of the weaker sex in working on articles for trade or sale should be enough to bring a place within the definition of workroom.

At a single step the colony went as far, in principle, as any regulators of women's factory hours have dared to go since. The Act, indeed, expressly excluded piece-workers, and ignored the saleswomen in retail shops, and males of all sorts and conditions. But it prohibited factory work for females between two o'clock on Saturday afternoon and nine o'clock on Monday morning; enacted that the beginning of the regular day's work should not be earlier than nine in the morning or its end later than six in the evening; and secured four specified holidays in the year, as well as the Saturday half-holiday, all without loss of wages. One of its seven clauses dealt with sanitation, and was probably the briefest specimen of this difficult branch of legislation to be found in any statute-book. It ran: "All workrooms shall be properly ventilated."

During the next twelve years a series of small amending Acts were passed to cure the more obvious defects and supply the more patent omissions of the pioneer Act. Women on piece-work were put on the same footing as those on time-work. Children between the ages of ten and fourteen were put on half-time, and in 1881 the factory age was raised to twelve years. Females and persons under eighteen were to have extra pay when working overtime.(27)

Beyond this weak but promising beginning there was, before 1891, little protection for the workers. The only other measures of importance before 1891 were an Employers' Liability Act, 1882, and the Workmen's Wages Act, 1884, which extended and improved the Contractors' Debts Act of 1871, which was designed to protect the wages of workers whose employers got into difficulties. Both Acts proved difficult to administer under a subcontracting system.

If legal protection was weak, the collective power of the workers to organise themselves was also at an embryonic stage. Trade union activity occurs early in New Zealand history. It is recorded that both in Wellington and in Otago, trade unionists among the first settlers stood out for the principle of the eight-hour day. As early as 1841 there was a strike for this principle among the labourers constructing the road from Wellington to the Hutt, and an attempt by the provincial authorities of Otago to revert to a ten-hour day in 1848–9 led to prolonged labour difficulties in which the men won. The actual organisation of trade unions in New Zealand, however, proceeded slowly. Immigrant unionists often retained their membership in the societies in England; but the first local societies were formed in the period of the gold-rushes in the early sixties. None of these first unions seem to have survived.

There is a dearth of primary material on the early history of trade unionism. Records have not been kept, but it is apparent from newspaper files that the next period of activity was the boom period, 1872–5. There are records of ten unions being formed in Dunedin, a similar number in Canterbury, and six each in Wellington and Auckland. It was in this period also that the interest of the great pioneer of agricultural unionism in England, Joseph Arch, was enlisted in the Vogel immigration schemes. English agriculture was just then entering its long period of depression following the importation of cheap food-stuffs, and there was great need to find employment for agricultural labourers. In 1874 a representative of Joseph Arch's National Agricultural Labourers Union visited New Zealand, the first of a long succession of English labour leaders to visit and report upon the colony.

This early unionism was registered under the Friendly Societies Act, and had no clear legal status until in 1878, on the initiative of (Sir) Robert Stout, a Trade Union Act was passed on the English model. The chief importance of this Act, beyond the facilities it provided for the re-formation of unions in the early eighties, was in the alternative it gave the militant unions which seceded from the jurisdiction of the Arbitration Court after 1906. Unions were formed and re-formed in the eighties, some of them several times. They were strongest in Otago, which was then the largest and most industrially developed city of the colony. From 1881–6 the Otago Trades and Labour Council functioned with some vigour, and in 1885 sponsored an important Trade Union Congress, to which delegates came from all over New Zealand.(28) (Sir) Robert Stout, always a stanch friend of unionism in this industrial stage of its development, was Premier at the time, and was given a rousing reception by the delegates when he addressed them. His presence was indicative of the sympathy growing up between the Liberal political movement and the trade unions, a sympathy which was very similar to that existing between Gladstonian Liberalism and the English trade unionism of the time. A Trades and Labour Council existed in Wellington also between 1884 and 1885, and efforts at co-operation were made in other centres. The congress called at Auckland for 1886, however, revealed the poverty of the unions, which was too great to enable them even to provide travelling-expenses for delegates. The strong Otago Council went out of existence temporarily in 1886, and was not revived till 1889; its vicissitudes are indicative of the troubles of unionism everywhere in the depth of the depression.(29) By the end of the eighties the movement appears to have gathered a great deal of momentum, and active trades and labour councils were functioning again in each of the centres. The "new unionism" of the late eighties in England had hardly had time to furnish much inspiration to New Zealand unionism, but organisation was being extended to the unskilled workers, particularly the waterside workers, who in turn collected financial help for the dockers of Great Britain when they embarked on their famous strike in 1890.

Essentially the New Zealand unionism of this period was based on craft organisation, Liberal in its politics, and non-revolutionary in its aims. It is doubtful if it had much Socialist theory, and quite certain that any leanings in that direction were Fabian and State Socialist. Marx was practically unknown, and "scientific" class-conscious Socialism had not penetrated to New Zealand. The American secret society organisation of the Knights of Labour had established chapters in the New Zealand towns, but their membership was drawn mainly from the unions and they were only a passing fashion. The main stream of the movement was in the organisation of trade union opinion in the trades and labour councils. The councils in Christchurch and Dunedin were particularly active. They served as forums of political discussion, and in them was fashioned a great deal of the programme of experimental legislation with which the Liberal-Labour combination swept the electorate in 1891.

One other element in the industrial situation needs to be recorded. Throughout the eighties the first definitely organised movement for tariff protection of local industries gathered a great deal of strength. The beginnings of agitation go back to the seventies. The first pamphlet on the need for a tariff appeared in 1872, and about the same time a Colonists' Protection League Society was founded in Auckland.(30) An anonymous paper read before this Society in 1873 correctly anticipated that "the public works scheme carried out by means of borrowed money will in the end prove a curse to the country, unless means are taken for the future employment of the people".(31) It was not long before this prediction began to receive practical confirmation in the complaints of industrialists and labourers, who had been led to promote new industries in the expectation of the continuance of boom conditions.(32) Generally speaking, the ruling opinion of the colony was in favour of free trade, which was by this time almost an unchallenged dogma in Great Britain, whence the colonists derived the bulk of their opinions. When Grey's Government imposed the first land-tax in 1878 it also reduced the Customs tariff in an effort to shift the incidence of taxation. Both actions were in strict accord with Orthodox Liberal opinion in England and could be justified from the writings of John Stuart Mill. The report of the Royal Commission appointed in 1880 to investigate the demands for a higher tariff was uncompromisingly free trade in tone.(33) The beginnings of a new order were, however, foreshadowed by meetings in Christchurch and Dunedin, which passed resolutions urging the Government to foster the manufacture within New Zealand of all structural materials needed for Governmental undertakings.(34)

When the depression broke upon the colony in the eighties the protectionist agitation became linked with the trade union movement and also with the agitation against unemployment and sweating. The first political platform of the Otago Trades and Labour Council, published in 1881, contained planks advocating a protective tariff and the cessation of immigration. At the great congress of 1885 a Christchurch delegate, afterward prominently identified with the protectionist agitation, moved the following resolution, which was carried with only two dissentients:

> That with a view to encouraging local industries a system of protective duties of not less than 20 per cent. should be imposed.

The New Zealand Protection Association, formed in 1884, and re-formed in 1888, counted confidently and correctly upon support from the growing trade union movement. By the end of the eighties there were active leagues or associations in every centre, and the demands for tariff protection were pressed upon the Continuous Ministry. The Sweating Commission of 1890 drew attention to the importation of shoddy, causing depression in the clothing industries, and recommended an increase of Customs duties. When the exodus of workers commenced, the demand for protection became irresistible. To the workers and city people it appeared that the stubborn opposition came mainly from the great landowners, who were primarily interested in cheap labour. Popular indignation was aroused and, somewhat unexpectedly and to the dismay of his party, Sir Harry Atkinson yielded to the clamour. In the session of 1888 he introduced a tariff giving protection to "boot manufacturers, clothiers, machinery makers, and workers in brass and iron". This departure from free trade policy wrecked his party, and the tariff was only carried with the aid of Opposition votes. (35) It proved to be the last necessary blow to the prestige of the Conservatives and greatly helped the welding together of the Liberal Opposition. The stage was set for new policies of State interference in industrial matters generally.

The Theory and Practice of "State Socialism"

The preceding sections of this chapter have depicted a period of economic stress and social discontent. Financial and monetary deflation, which would in any case have been troublesome, had been rendered distressing by the necessity for paying off the cost of a wild land boom generated by the lavish expenditure of borrowed money. As the payment proceeded, obvious weaknesses of economic structure revealed themselves. An increasing population, many of whom had been attracted to the colony by glowing reports of economic opportunities awaiting them, found themselves hemmed in by land monopoly and other barriers to settlement. Manufacturing industries were difficult to establish, wages fell, unemployment increased, and conditions of labour worsened. The beckoning opportunities opened up by the refrigeration experiments were largely monopolised by the sheep-owners. What was to be done in such a desperate situation? Where was the way out of the impasse? What did the colonists think of their plight, of its causes and possible remedies?

The answer is superficially clear. They looked to the powers of the State and appealed to the Government for help. They agitated for, and finally got, legislation and taxation to break up the great landholdings, a protective tariff to assist local industry, labour laws to ensure reasonable working conditions, a tribunal to fix a fair level of wages, Government loans to establish small farmers on the land, State experiments to compete with trading monopolies, and Governmental relief of poverty in old age. This formidable programme of social legislation was put on the statute-book within a decade. New Zealand was in the forefront of Australasian legislative experiments. The attention of social students all over the world was directed to the study of her laws. Before the end of the nineteenth century she had gained a reputation for "radical Socialism" that still clings to her. (36) Moreover, there were many optimists within New Zealand, and more in other lands, who hailed these measures as but the beginning of even greater experiments, ushering in an era of Socialism or at least social democracy.

Rather less than thirty years after the initiation of the experiments, however, it is clear that such expectations were unfounded. No revolutionary changes have been made in the economic structure of New Zealand. Capitalism is still firmly entrenched, the land has not been nationalised, the single-tax is not in operation, the organised wage-earners are very definitely in minority opposition, and many of the legislative experiments, already restricted both by amendments and by administrative policies, are under severe criticism. New Zealand has long since yielded the initiative in socialistic endeavour to the Australian States, and her general policies are at the present time sharply contrasted with them on such important questions as the tariff, trade union organisation, and State enterprise. It is no longer possible for an economic historian to assume a general convergence of policies. The Australian Commonwealth, and more emphatically one or two of its component States, pursue policies which make New Zealand appear conservative by contrast.

The major reason for this divergence of policies has already been suggested by inference. Australia, despite its great area, remains hemmed in by its frontiers of settlement. Its problems retain to a large degree their urban character, though happily it has for many years escaped from the burden of economic depression which it shared with New Zealand in the eighties. Its population of six millions supports two great cities (one of which has well over, and the other little less than, a million inhabitants) and several others great in proportion to their surrounding population. From this situation New Zealand has escaped by the opening up of the north island. Her towns and town problems are relatively far less important than Australia's, and much less important than they were when her experimental legislation was introduced.

When this fact is borne in mind it is easier to appreciate

the characteristic qualities which were responsible for the use of the powers of the State in an emergency, and were equally responsible for the modification of those powers when the emergency had passed. Two factors are involved, the theoretical sources of the expedients introduced, and the social situation which facilitated their introduction. A survey of the literature of the period indicates very clearly that the ideas came mainly from theorists in other lands, while the opportunism which accepted them was characteristic of New Zealand.(37) This opportunism New Zealand shares with other British colonies and notably with Australia. When her economic circumstances marched with those of the Australian States, as in the period of depression, her legislation and administration was little different from theirs. Both Dominions have subsequently climbed out of the economic depression of the eighties and early nineties; but New Zealand's recent prosperity has been based primarily on closer settlement, and especially on dairying development, while Australia since federation has consciously pursued a policy of industrial progress. This divergence of economic development is clearly reflected in their political life.

The theorists from whom ideas were taken prove upon investigation to be very mildly socialistic, and the application of their ideas in New Zealand has stopped short even of their theories. In New Zealand, as in England, whence New Zealand opinion was and still is mainly derived, there was in the eighties a good deal of interest in Utopian Socialism. The social aspirations expressed in England by literary men such as George Meredith, Matthew Arnold, and John Ruskin, scientists like Alfred Russel Wallace, Socialists like H. M. Hyndman, and academic economists like Arnold Toynbee and Cliffe Leslie, to say nothing of the great master John Stuart Mill, were very influential in New Zealand.(38) Mill had founded the Land Tenure Reform Association in 1870; Henry George published *Progress and Poverty* in 1879, Bellamy's *Looking Backward* appeared in 1887, the *Fabian Essays in Socialism* in 1889. One might almost regard the articles published by Reeves in 1890 on *Communism and Socialism* as the philosophical manifesto of the social reform movement in New Zealand.(39) The closing paragraph of these articles is significant in view of the economic depression and the passive attitude towards it of the Government of the day.

> The Socialist may be wrong; may be deluded; may be a blind leader of the blind. But at least he has something to offer, something to suggest. He does not mock us by bidding us be content with a society with which no thinking man can be content. There lies his strength.

It is difficult to resist the feeling that as far as New Zealand is concerned, the source of social legislation might almost be found in John Stuart Mill. The great master of political economy was widely read in New Zealand and had many correspondents in the colony.(40) His "infant industry" argument for tariff protection was much used, and he wrote many letters to combat what he regarded as unwarranted applications of it. His views were sought on the functions of Government, loans for housing, immigration restriction, land nationalisation, electoral reform, protective labour legislation. It would be difficult to point out any of New Zealand's social experiments to which this economic oracle would not have returned a favourable answer.(41) Even mildly Conservative colonists took refuge in his authority. Gisborne's definition of the limits within which legislation for social improvement should be confined obviously re-echoes the treatise *On Liberty*, which Mill himself regarded as his supreme contribution to political thought.(42) Those limits have been fairly observed in New Zealand.

Every competent student of this legislation has stressed the lack of socialist drive behind it. It is not revolutionary, or international, or class-conscious. Its two outstanding elements have been the use of State machinery for special purposes and a steadily deepening humanitarian trend. It will be argued later that, despite Siegfried's somewhat ungallant description,(43) the women's vote in New Zealand has been a powerful factor in pressing on humanitarian measures. It may be recalled also that Mill in his autobiography attributes the socialistic trend of his *Principles of Political Economy* almost wholly to the influence of his wife.(44)

The widening of State functions is due primarily to colonial opportunism and freedom from theories. It has little to do with Socialism. Reeves's phrase, "colonial governmentalism", is a truer description of New Zealand practice than "State Socialism" or Metin's "socialisme sans doctrines". It is "étatisme" rather than Socialism. The most penetrating analysis yet made of this "perfect mania for appealing to the State" is Siegfried's.(45) His acute and sometimes acid analysis goes beyond the reasons usually put forward. It is true that the colonists learned early to rely upon the Company and then upon the Government which replaced it. Public ownership and disposal of land, later Governmental development and ownership of transport, the weakness of local bodies and equally of private organisation—all these threw action naturally into the hands of the Government. There were, moreover, few vested interests or other obstacles to overcome. State action had a comparatively clear field.

With such a history it is understandable that the advent of a greater measure of democracy should have coincided with an enlargement of State functions. Such an enlargement, Siegfried points out, appealed to colonial *naïveté* and contempt for theories. It created a feeling of self-satisfaction and distinction.

A people can advertise itself, just as a merchant or a manufacturer can. The New Zealanders are quite aware of it; and if their object has been to get talked about, they have not chosen the worst means, for, since the passing of such measures as those for compulsory arbitration and woman suffrage, everybody has heard of the little antipodean colony, of whose very existence people were once scarcely aware.

This method of carrying forward a people by appealing to its vanity, without letting it lose sight of the advantage of clever self-advertisement, is very efficacious. For more than ten years the New Zealanders have been won over to a policy which both serves their interests and flatters their pride. They are proud of their innovations and their trials of what has been tried nowhere else; they enjoy being able to smile at the timidity of old countries, and to believe that they are giving them lessons. Votes for Women? Why not? It is new: it is something to try. Is not New Zealand peculiarly fitted to undertake it? Is it a matter of old-age pensions, or some other reform of the sort? The same temptation is at hand, that of out-distancing others. And it is the same with all kinds of measures. For this strange rage for novelty lies at the inception of most of their laws.

Such are the motives on which the citizens of this too new country usually act—a country where the most advanced ideas do not meet with the necessary, though often galling, check of tradition and of the past. What the New Zealanders most need, in fact, is principles, convictions, reasoned beliefs. Parties are based much less on ideas than one might at first argue from their pretentious legislation, and much more on the interests of sections, classes, and groups. As for the influence of imagination and sentiment, it shows itself under the curious form of a patriotic vanity, which makes the New Zealanders believe that the world expects much of them, and that they must not be false to their destiny. This blend of a too practical outlook with a too exalted sense of apostleship will meet us over and over again in our study of New Zealand.(46)

Even at the time Siegfried wrote (1904), "the labour element seemed to be all-powerful". In his view the Liberal Party in 1890 "allied itself with the Labour Party" and "appropriated their programme". There is truth in this statement to the extent that the actual planks of the party platform were largely worked out in the discussions of the trades and labour councils. But the ideas go farther back and are essentially Liberal. Vogel after all was the father of State enterprise, having founded the Government Life Insurance Department in 1869 and the Public Trust Office in 1870, to say nothing of the construction of railways and public works by State enterprise. Stout advocated the leasehold system at least as early as 1875,(47) and with Ballance framed the first Land Tax Act in 1878. Moreover, Reeves, the theorist and programme-maker, and Seddon, the leader and driving-force of the Liberal-Labour Party, were both Liberals. The actual planning of the Liberal-Labour legislation was largely the work of Reeves's brain. He was in close touch with the trade unions, but was not "a leader of the Labour Party", which, in fact, had no separate existence in New Zealand until 1906.

In the period of "State Socialism", therefore, the opportunist use of State action is a characteristic New Zealand trend; but the theories upon which the various experiments were based, but which were not driven to their logical conclusion, are mainly imported. It so happened that in 1890 the economic circumstances were such as to cause ready acceptance of rather vague Utopian Socialist ideas. Political power was concentrated in the towns, where organised labour bodies were very active. Their programme of land taxation and land conservation, tariff protection, and labour legislation gained acceptance, and the powers of Government were used on its behalf. As Siegfried correctly foresaw, however, other sections of the community, temporarily in the political ascendant, could and would use the machinery of the State with equal readiness. In the nineties the land-hungry small farmers joined with the urban workers to attack the land monopolists, but such an unstable alliance could not long outlast the opening up of new opportunities for land settlement. It is the small farmers more than any other class who "like practical men have become almost Conservative, since, according to the classic phrase, they have been given something to conserve". Upon their conservatism, Socialist propaganda has about as much effect as the beating of the waves on the New Zealand coast.

CHAPTER VI

THE EXPERIMENTAL PERIOD

A Practical Programme

The Liberal-Labour Party came into power in 1891 and remained in power till 1912. In this long, unbroken term of office there were three distinct phases. In the first phase, described by Reeves as "the eight years' tussle", legislative experiments came thick and fast.(1) The second phase, from the passing of the Old Age Pension Act in 1898 to the death of Seddon in 1906, saw a perceptible slackening of the pace. This is a period of consolidation and settling down. Some extension of legislation took place, but there were no new departures of great significance. After Seddon's death there was an interregnum. Between 1906 and 1912 the Liberals, from whom the Labour Party had split in policy as early as 1906, though the Parliamentary Labour Party was not a real political force till 1914, remained in power under the leadership of Sir Joseph Ward; but their legislative policies were critically reconsidered and considerably amended. When the Conservative Party was reorganised under its new name of Reform and took office in 1912, it leaned rather upon the small farmers of the north island than upon the great landowners. It continued a good deal of the Liberal-Labour legislation, and even carried it further. But it soon became clear that the socialistic impulse had been lost, and the subsequent period has seen both legislative and administrative revision of the major experiments.

It is the first and second of these phases with which we are concerned in this chapter—the attempt, unusually successful, to place a whole legislative programme upon the statute-book within a brief space of time. Economically speaking, it is best to regard this period and this programme as belonging to the era of economic depression. It is true that the world-level of prices turned to rise in the years 1895–6, and that signs of returning prosperity were immediately manifest in New Zealand. It is also true that production was steadily increasing from the advent of refrigeration in 1882, and that this increase was greatly accelerated by the dairying developments of the early nineties. Moreover, the opening up of the north island lands to closer settlement proceeded rapidly in the last decade of the century. The favourable turn of the price-level, therefore, found New Zealand ready with all the essential preparations for rapid economic progress. This progress must, however, be regarded as the economic reason for the changed emphasis of legislative policy after 1906 rather than the basis of the experimental legislation of the nineties.

It was human and natural for the Liberal politicians, and even for the social scientists who investigated the experiments in the first flush of their success, to take a somewhat different point of view. Most of the social scientists in question held Liberal opinions themselves and were attracted to the study of New Zealand legislation by sympathetic interest in it. They tended to accept the view of the Governmental authorities in New Zealand that the returning prosperity was at least partly due to the political measures that had been taken. There was no other source from which they could get authoritative opinions, statements of purpose, accounts of progress, statistics, and even the photographic illustrations which are duplicated in so many of their writings. Such contemporary accounts are invaluable, but they lack the necessary material, and still more the detachment, for a critical estimate of the working of the experiments. The thesis that the prosperity which began to be so pleasantly in evidence by the end of the century was at least partly due to the Liberal-Labour administration is readily defensible. It is, however, easily apt to be overrated, and in particular to be generalised, by unwarranted application to the different economic conditions of other times and other lands. As the following sections of this chapter should show, it would be ungenerous and incorrect to deny or unduly to minimise the beneficial results of the legislative steps taken to break through the economic deadlock which existed in New Zealand in 1890. The Liberal-Labour programme of legislation was soundly based upon careful analysis of the needs of the colony at the time when it was introduced. It had strong popular backing, which increased as its first results became manifest. It had been the subject of widespread popular discussion and was thoroughly understood by the constituencies. Moreover, the actual legislative measures were carefully thought out and formed an integrated expression of a positive and definite political philosophy. The drafting of the Acts was very thorough, and great care was paid to their administration. The appropriate departments of Government were staffed with able men, so that, unlike many legislative experiments, the Liberal-Labour programme was rapidly and successfully translated into effective machinery producing practical results upon everyday economic life.

The greatest injury to the reputation of the statesmen who carried out this programme has come from the enthusiasm of those of their advocates who have viewed their work as the beginning of even greater and more revolutionary changes instead of as a very practical set of measures designed to meet a particular conjuncture of economic circumstances.(2) Such advocates imported into a practical situation much of their own theoretical attitude. The State Socialism of New Zealand was not designed to try out a theoretical conception of social organisation. Still less was it undertaken with any notion that it might lead the way to similar experiments in other lands. The absence of the international point of view was, indeed, very striking to a detached observer like Siegfried, who was used to Continental Socialist theories. The ready reconciliation of apparently socialistic measures with a perfervid patriotism amused him a good deal.

The experiments, therefore, must be viewed as merely practical expedients put into force at a critical time in the colony's history. The general effect, owing to sound administration in a small, easily governed, homogeneous community in general sympathy with the principles invoked, was immediate and striking. The same circumstances which made such success comparatively easy to obtain, also made it easy for subsequent administrations based upon different constituencies to shift the emphasis of policy very considerably. Much of the Liberal-Labour programme proved itself and passed into general and unquestioned acceptance. Its former opponents, when they came into office, took over and greatly extended the operation of many of the measures they had obstructed while in opposition. But they also took steps to reverse other legislation, particularly the leasehold tenures, and to change the spirit while retaining the form of such important experiments as

State trading enterprises, land taxation, and wage regulation. The economic and political history of New Zealand in the thirty years that have elapsed since the end of "the eight years' tussle" is a striking illustration of the way in which economic and geographical factors profoundly influence political conceptions.

The Political Background

The previous chapter has outlined the background of economic discontent focusing into resentment against the monopoly of the great landowners. The economic bases of the land and labour legislation are clear. The political organisation necessary to give legislative effect to measures designed to remedy this situation may also be readily summarised. It is apparent now that throughout the period of depression in the eighties there was proceeding a realignment of political parties and personalities upon economic rather than political lines.

Many observers have commented upon the high political themes discussed by New Zealand's first Parliaments and upon the eloquence and debating powers that were revealed. The earliest legislators were conscious of the fundamental and important character of their tasks. They were politically minded also above the average. Moreover, in that age of *laissez-faire*, economic problems had not begun to occupy the centre of the political stage. In New Zealand the chief economic problem of the early decades was the disposal and settlement of waste lands; but even when the granting of self-government in 1852 vested this power in the colonial legislature, it was not long before the "Compact of 1856" virtually delegated it to the provincial councils. Until 1876, therefore, it was at most an indirect cause of political controversy.

From the foundation of New Zealand in 1840 to the realignment of parties in the eighties, three great political issues occupied the Parliamentary stage. In the first decade the agitation for responsible government overshadowed everything else. When that right was conceded by the Constitution Act of 1852 it took some time for the Governmental machinery to be set up. The National Parliament did not meet till 1854, when its first stormy sessions were concerned almost wholly with the definition of the powers granted by the constitution.

A short session of one month in 1855 was followed by a four months' session the following year. The dominance of the Provincialists was clearly indicated, not only by the famous compact of this year, but also by the decision to convene biennially instead of annually. No sessions were held in 1857 or 1859.

The outbreak of the second series of Maori wars in 1860 provided the second of the great political issues. It also provided the occasion for complete settlement of the first. When the Colonial Office acquiesced in Weld's "self-reliant policy", and early in 1863 handed over formal control of native affairs, together with responsibility for the conduct of the war, the powers of self-government in domestic concerns were complete. With the exception of one brief controversy over the powers of the Governor in 1892, there has since been no challenge to the responsibility and competency of the Cabinet in matters of local concern.

The conduct of the war and native policy remained the outstanding cause of political divisions until in 1870 Vogel introduced economic elements by his policy of borrowing for immigration and public works. The new issues raised by this policy were very far reaching. Vogel has some claim to be considered "the father of State Socialism" in New Zealand. His bold extension of State functions by the creation of the Government Life Insurance Office, the Public Trust Office, the first forest conservation policies, and above all, the direct undertaking of great public works, at once created a new area of controversy.

The first result of his initiative, however, was to precipitate the third great political issue, the struggle between Provincialists and Centralists. This issue, which had steadily been rising into prominence as the Maori wars died down, was settled once and for all by the abolition of the provincial assemblies, which took effect in 1876. Thereafter the way was clear for new political divisions to emerge.

For more than a decade, however, the lines of party cleavage were very blurred. Except for two brief intervals the so-called Continuous Ministry, a shifting combination mainly of Conservatives, held office from 1870 to 1890. After the collapse of the borrowing boom much of the attention of successive

Parliaments was necessarily concentrated upon public finance and administrative economy. The Continuous Ministry held fast to the ideals of *laissez-faire* and put forward no constructive policies to remedy the economic depression which haunted New Zealand from 1879 to 1895. The legislative programme, upon which it sought the electors' support in 1890, well illustrates its negative *laissez-faire* character. "Strict but not parsimonious economy, combined with cheerfulness and a firm belief in the unbounded resources of the colony, further borrowing within the colony, the purchase of Maori lands, retention of the property tax, non-interference by the Government or Parliament with industrial disputes"(3)—these represent clearly the essentials of Conservatism remaining after a long series of groupings and re-groupings had eliminated discordant elements within the party. The mild measures of social amelioration proposed from time to time (such as Atkinson's suggestion for a contributory pension scheme) were quite in keeping with a Conservatism upon which Disraeli's "dishing of the Whigs" and Bismarck's social legislation may be conjectured to have exerted a mild and distant influence.

The welding of opposition elements into a coherent political party was greatly influenced by the economic depression. The first break in the Continuous Ministry's power came when from 1877 to 1879 the Provincialists, under Sir George Grey's leadership, held office for a short troubled period which was brought to a sudden end by the onset of the depression. Grey was a Gladstonian Liberal with an eloquent but vague belief in the march of humanity. His early adult experiences in Ireland had made him the convinced and bitter enemy of large landholders. His Ministry, coming into office immediately after the abolition of the provinces, was faced with the necessity of organising national services hitherto performed by the provincial councils. The Lands Act and Education Act of 1877 are notable landmarks in New Zealand's history. The land-tax and Trade Union Act of the following year foreshadow later policy also; but the Liberal Party at this time lacked the protectionist and State developmental features which were to be essential elements of its victory in 1890.

When the second break came in the Continuous Ministry's long lease of power, the very shuffling and rearrangement of political allegiances indicated that realignment was well under way. After an extraordinary series of attempts by various leaders to form a Ministry, the Stout-Vogel combination took office in 1884 and remained in power till 1887.(4) Stout had held office in Grey's Ministry and, though now estranged from Grey, remained Liberal in his outlook. Vogel was on the whole a Conservative.(5) Some years earlier he had sought election to the House of Commons as a Conservative, while still Agent-General for New Zealand. The chief feature he contributed to the regrouping was the identification henceforth of State enterprise with the Liberal rather than the Conservative Party.

As the depression deepened in the late eighties and the Continuous Ministry took up more and more definitely the attitude of passive endurance rather than constructive effort, the opposition elements both in Parliament and in the electorate drew together in a coherent, if loosely organised, party. Stout lost his seat in the election of 1887 largely owing to his disinclination to acknowledge Governmental responsibility for action in economic problems such as unemployment. His Liberalism, even Radicalism, was of the *laissez-faire* type, and the loss of his leadership at this juncture threw initiative into the hands of less philosophical and more opportunist politicians, among whom Seddon gradually emerged as a natural and forceful, if untrained and unpolished, leader. The Liberal Party in Parliament carried on under the loose guidance of a small committee, but the split in the Government Party over the tariff of 1888 gave them confidence, and in the following year Ballance, the senior member of the party in political experience, was chosen as leader. It was a wise choice. Ballance was a Liberal of mild views, very friendly, and tolerant. In essential characteristics he suggests the type of leadership which was later to be exerted by Campbell-Bannerman in the House of Commons. Ballance was able quickly to rally round his genuinely Liberal views practically all the so-called "progressive" movements which sought a way out of the economic impasse by Governmental action.(6)

The election year 1890 saw a conjuncture of events peculiarly favourable to such movements. The "sweating" revelations, which strengthened the demands for a protective tariff and protective labour legislation, the culmination of prolonged depression in an alarming exodus of population, and finally the rather unexpected and alarming outbreak of the Waterside Workers' Strike (7)—all made the Government's position very difficult.

Moreover, the electorate had been changed by the passing in 1889 of a Representation Act, to which Sir George Grey, as a private member, carried an amendment in committee abolishing plural voting.(8) The same Bill raised the "country quota", created in 1881, from 18 per cent. to 28 per cent.; but this did not militate against the Liberal-Labour Party's chances in 1890.

The development of this electoral principle of weighting the scales in favour of the country districts is worth at least passing mention. It appears to date from the Representation Act (No. 14) of 1881, which made provision for a redistribution of seats in the Lower House. The Act itself contained no mention of any discrimination between town and country; but in the course of the debate (Sir) John Hall explained that the new schedule of seats had been determined by making the numerical quota for country seats 25 per cent. less than that for the towns. Other speakers in the debate revealed the fact that it was really a device of the south island country representatives to checkmate the growing influence of the north island towns, which were just beginning to increase in population.

The next Representation Act (1887, No. 7) was introduced by (Sir) Robert Stout, who established the sound principle of appointing representation commissioners to settle electoral boundaries. In this way manipulation of boundaries in the interest of the party in power was frustrated. Stout pleaded the cause of the north island towns, but an amendment to his Bill was carried, making provision for special (i.e. country) districts to which a nominal addition of 18 per cent. was made to the number of the population. Seddon, himself a country member, voted for this amendment, a fact which supports the contention advanced above, that the country quota did not prejudice the electoral chances of the Liberals at this time.

In 1889 an Amendment Act (No. 6) was passed, raising the 18 per cent. addition to 28 per cent., "to be added to the population not contained in any city, borough, or town district which contains a population of over 2,000".

This country quota, further defined in 1914, and again in 1927, still stands at 28 per cent., which is added to the population of areas not "contained in a city or borough having a population of over 2,000, or contained in any area within five miles of the chief post offices of Auckland City, Christchurch, Dunedin, or Wellington City". Created originally in the era of southern ascendancy as a bulwark against the growing power of the north island towns, it has in recent years greatly accentuated the political power of the small farmers in the north island districts. From the point of view of the Liberal Party, Stout was right and Seddon was wrong in 1887. Once the alliance between the small farmers and Labour was broken, as it was in 1906, the country quota became an almost insuperable obstacle to the political progress of the urban Radicals. This simple electoral provision is no small part of the reason for the dominance of the country-side in New Zealand politics to this day.

These effects of the 1889 Act were, however, in the future. The election of 1890 was not influenced by them. Far more important were the results of the feminist movement, which was then at the height of its activity.

An agitation for female suffrage had begun as early as 1853, but had recently gained a new lease of life from the activities of the Women's Christian Temperance Union, which in 1886 created a "franchise department".(9) Supporters of the female franchise were to be found in both parties, and Sir John Hall, a former Conservative Premier, was perhaps the most influential among them. It is difficult to estimate how far this agitation and the connected temperance movement influenced the voters.(10) Both Ballance and his opponent, Sir John Hall, were strong advocates of woman suffrage; but in both parties there were determined opponents, and Seddon, who succeeded Ballance, was widely believed to be opposed both to the women's vote and to temperance legislation. It is probable, however, that both agitations contributed somewhat to the strength of the progressive movement, and it was Seddon's Ministry which in 1893 passed measures giving votes for women and granting local option in licensing the sale of liquor.

These were the chief confusing elements in the election of

1890; but the general economic background was such that the Liberal Party, strong in its alliance with organised labour, and backed also by the protectionist leagues, gained a majority of seven in the new House. Many of its victories had been gained by small majorities which might have been wiped out if plural voting had still existed. Among its successful candidates were six who were not only trade unionists, but were elected as Labour candidates.(11) None of these, however, attained ministerial rank, and the policy of the party was dictated by Liberal leadership, always in close touch with organised labour outside the House. The programme upon which the party had appealed to the electorate had been summarised by its historian as(12):

The stoppage of "dummyism" in land sales.
No more borrowing.
Self-reliance.
Thorough retrenchment.
The prevention of the acquisition of land in large holdings.
The resumption by the State of land urgently required for settlement, and vigorous settlement of the land.
The discouragement of absentee landlordism and of speculative land purchasers.
Better treatment of workers in factories.
The use of railways to develop the agricultural and pastoral industries rather than as a means of imposing taxation.
The establishment of scholarships from the primary schools to secondary schools, and to the mining and agricultural schools.
The establishment of technical schools.
Reform of the legislative council.
Measures to improve the condition of the workers.
The repeal of the property-tax and the introduction of a land- and income-tax.

The remaining sections of this chapter deal with the translation of this programme into effective legislation and administration. This translation was at first met with a constitutional difficulty of some interest.(13) Though the Continuous Ministry had been defeated at the polls, Sir Harry Atkinson did not resign for some months until Parliament had assembled and recorded a vote upon the election of the Speaker, which Atkinson took to be one of no-confidence. In the meantime he had persuaded the Governor to make a number of new appointments to the Legislative Council, the nominated members of which held office for life. When the Liberal-Labour Ministry finally took office, therefore, it was faced with an overwhelmingly Conservative Upper House, which dealt summarily with measures embodying important planks of the Liberal-Labour platform. For some time the Governor of the day stood firm against the Ministry's request to nominate new councillors. In the constitutional deadlock thus created, Ballance appealed to the Secretary of State for the Colonies, who instructed the Governor to act upon the advice of his Ministers.

The first sessions of the Liberal-Labour regime were, therefore, a period of apprenticeship. Some measures found their way on to the statute-book shorn of their most novel and characteristic features; new departments, notably of labour and of agriculture, were created, the officers of which worked out details of further legislation, and many measures were tried out in debate. In the meantime Ballance died suddenly and unexpectedly. There was a short period of doubt concerning the next Premier. Stout, whose long experience and great gifts marked him out as a natural leader, happened not to be a member of the House at the time. The post was offered to Seddon, who was encouraged by Sir George Grey to accept it.

The new leader's mandate was strikingly confirmed by the constituencies in the election of 1893, which gave him a pledged following of fifty-six in a House of seventy-four Members. With such a mandate from the country, and with the Legislative Council tamed by twelve new appointments and the prospect of more if necessary, the way was clear for the Liberal-Labour experimental programme to be passed into law. The following year, 1894, is the *annus mirabilis* of New Zealand legislation. The Compulsory Arbitration Act, Lands for Settlement Act, Shops Act, and Advances to Settlers Act were all passed in one famous session.

The Incidence of Taxation

It is not without significance that the first important measure passed by the Liberal-Labour Party upon its accession to power was the Land and Income Tax Act, 1891.(14) This measure had many claims to popular favour; but the chief was that it broadened the basis of revenue, opened the way to equitably devised and graduated direct taxation, and rendered possible the repeal of the inequitable and inelastic Property Tax. The property-tax first imposed in 1879 consisted of a flat rate of a penny in the pound on all assessed real and personal property, with an exemption of £500. It was regressive in its incidence and highly inelastic, but until 1891 it constituted an important source of revenue, together with customs and excise duties, registration fees, and stamp duties. All of these, with the exception of the death duties, were largely regressive in character.

Under the Liberal-Labour administration the distribution of taxation was somewhat altered. It is impossible at this date to make any quantitative measurement of the change, but the main tendencies are clear and easily stated.

No alteration in the Customs tariff was attempted until 1895, but in that year a thorough revision was made. The mild measures of protection granted in 1888 were considerably extended, the tariff level was raised, the schedules made more comprehensive and minute. The immediate result was an increase in revenue, which was sustained by the trade recovery that followed the turn of prices in 1895. At the same time there appeared the first movement towards "a free breakfast-table", duties being reduced or removed from food-stuffs and articles of common consumption. The next tariff revision in 1900 continued and extended both the protective duties and the remissions of duties on articles of common use, such as kerosene, which were not readily producible within the colony.

In 1903 the Preferential and Reciprocal Trade Act followed the Canadian lead by imposing additional duties upon a comparatively few items of goods of foreign origin, thus introducing an imperialist purpose. In 1907 this so-called preference was greatly extended in the last of the Liberal tariffs. In that year a complete revision of the tariff schedules was made, the major trend being the removal of duties upon such articles as sugars, dried fruits, mustard, spices, cereal foods, nuts, household chemicals, infants' food, children's boots, and sheetings. The net effect of such changes, therefore, was considerably to lighten the burden of indirect taxation upon household necessities.

While the Customs tariff, somewhat amended in the interests of the workers, remained the most important source of revenue, the land and income taxes, which replaced the property-tax in 1891, were both more equitable and more elastic. In the first effective year of their operation the receipts were approximately equal to what had been the proceeds of the property-tax; but within ten years the income-tax receipts increased from £67,000 (in 1892–3) to £179,397 (in 1901–2).

These measures of direct taxation were hotly debated; but upon examination they do not appear to have been very drastic. The rates of land-tax were low, and so were the rates of income-tax, while the graduation was not steep. Moreover, these taxes were mutually exclusive. A landowner who paid upon the unimproved value of his land did not pay income-tax upon the receipts from working it. It is difficult, therefore, to see how the land-tax could be regarded as a penal imposition. It was paid by the farmer out of income, and differed from income-tax merely in being calculated on the basis of land value rather than income. The only circumstances under which it could become penal were when the valuations proved excessive compared with income received (as in a year of low prices or in the case of land held for speculative purposes), when the rates of tax were inequitably high compared with the rates of income-tax, or where, as in the case of urban lands upon which shops and factories operated, there was what amounted to concurrent imposition of both land and income taxes. An inspection of the revenue derived from these taxes, and a comparison of the rates, will prove that on the average the rural producers have not been subject to heavy taxation as compared with the urban industrial or professional classes.(15)

The real significance of the Land and Income Tax Act of 1891 was the introduction of the progressive principle. The problematical effect of the graduated tax in the bursting up of great estates will be discussed later. From the point of view of the incidence of taxation it is clear that, while the substitution of land and income taxes for the property-tax did not greatly shift the burden as between economic groups, within those groups it made the burden more equitable and thus was in line with the Government's policy in the Customs tariff.

This change was not, however, very drastic. Nor were any

steps taken to stiffen up the death duties, which had been introduced into New Zealand in 1881. These duties were on a graduated scale, which had been somewhat steepened in 1885, but was not made any more effective until 1909.(16)

Graduated Tax on Unimproved Land Value

Stress has been laid in a previous chapter on the fact that the overwhelming bulk of the best land of New Zealand had become freehold before 1891. The locking up of much of this land in large overvalued and underworked holdings has also been described. Attention has further been directed to the genuine land-hunger that existed and became clamant when the economic opportunities opened up by the success of refrigeration were made manifest. The Liberal-Labour Party drew much of its support from the small farmers and farming aspirants. It came into power pledged to take steps to break through the economic deadlock created by land monopoly. A large part of its legislative programme was, in consequence, directed towards the encouragement of closer settlement. In this policy it used the powers of the State freely. Graduated land taxation, compulsory repurchase, the provision of technical experts, and loans to settlers were all novel extensions of Governmental activity. In none of them, however, was there a great deal of Socialism, except in the vaguest sense of that vague term. Single-tax arguments were used and land nationalisation was discussed, but never at any time were these really practical issues.(17)

The character of the Minister responsible for most of the land legislation clearly explains the practical, non-theoretical policies that were followed. John McKenzie had the Scottish crofter's passion for land. Closer settlement was his obsession. The small farmers whom he helped to place upon the land quickly rang the knell of any lingering hopes of land nationalisation.

The first measure of land legislation passed by the new Government was the Land and Income Tax Act of 1891. Its fiscal importance has already been discussed. When it was passed, however, it attracted more attention as a measure of land reform than as a sound piece of public finance. It was heralded as an instrument to break up the great estates an does appear to have had some immediate psychological results in that direction.

Of these the best known is the purchase of the Cheviot Estate, described by every writer on this period of New Zealand history.(18) The taxing Act of 1891 was based on self-assessment with the shrewd device of making Government purchase at the tax value an effective check on the owner's assessment. The owners of the Cheviot Estate challenged the Government and tried to bluff McKenzie into accepting the lower valuation. McKenzie, however, called the bluff and took over the estate. The transaction proved profitable to the Government and still more profitable to the leaseholders who were placed on the land. It was an effective lesson. Landowners thereafter discovered that the tax was not unduly burdensome, but that it would be enforced.

The theoretical basis of land taxation is to be found in the conception of economic rent as a surplus reward accruing to the fortunate landowner in proportion to the differential value of his land over the poorest land which is worth cultivating. This conception appears to the modern economist to be unduly simplified. It does not consider that this surplus may also be regarded as a price, the estimate which the market places upon the advantages of the land in question in relation to the whole price system. Nor does it recognise that similar surpluses exist in the profits of industry, even in wages; that the rent of land is, in other words, merely the "leading species of a large genus". Moreover, land has competing uses with different margins of cultivation, so that the surpluses are more complex in composition than this theory allows. It is true that the estimation of the market sums up these surpluses for any particular piece of land; but it is equally true that attempts to tax the "unearned increment" may materially influence the owner's choice among competing uses for his land and so disturb the price equilibria that have been worked out.

Modern economic theory, therefore, by no means gives emphatic endorsement of land-taxes as the most scientific or even the only scientific forms of taxation. Economic analysis has proceeded a long way from the simple and even naïve treatment which both John Stuart Mill and Henry George inherited from Ricardo.

The chief interest of the land-tax, indeed, lies in the disturbances and dislocations it produces in the economic organisation. As a rough-and-ready method of attack on the land monopolist it is perhaps justifiable; as a factor influencing the choice among competing uses for land and as affecting equitable distribution of wealth between town and country industries it is at least interesting.

The form in which the New Zealand taxes were imposed, at least till the rates were drastically increased in 1907, was such as to be broadly equitable as between town and country. There is no evidence to show that the returns from a given amount of capital invested in land were more heavily taxed than the returns from a similar amount invested in other forms of industry. Rather may it be argued that the rapid increase of land values (relatively to the appreciation of other forms of invested capital) proved that in the estimation of purchasers the returns from land were, on the whole, greater.

It seems obvious, however, that the bare fact of taxation upon a graduated scale favoured those uses of land, notably dairying, for which small rather than large holdings were most suitable. This is a fact of considerable importance. It is probably the principal way in which the tax helped to break up large holdings. It is to be remembered that very shortly after the tax was imposed New Zealand entered upon a prolonged period of continuously rising prices which were naturally reflected in a steady appreciation of land values. Indeed, once confidence was restored after the depression, the inevitable tendency was for market prices to leap ahead of productive values. Buyers discounted future increases. It is probable that after 1895 the actual sale prices for land were always in excess of what could reasonably have been calculated as giving a return upon investments comparable with that received in other industries. Farmers normally expected that a large part of the reward of their enterprise would come to them in an appreciation of the value of their land.

For this reason the land-tax was not as burdensome as it might have been if land values had been stable or falling. It did not unduly penalise rural, compared with urban, investment, and its mild rates were toned down further by the lag of valuations in a rising market. Early efforts at taxation by self-assessment and by triennial valuations were replaced in 1896 by the creation of a Valuation Department, which entered upon a continuous process of appraisal of land values. The definitions of value, of its improved and unimproved components and similar conceptions, were steadily clarified as the department improved in technique. The chief criticism to be made seems almost inescapable in any system of valuation. It is that much so-called "improvement" is intangible and is apt to be regarded as community created "unimproved value". The farmer who spends long hours straightening a creek, planning rotations, planting trees in odd corners, finds it very difficult to assess the benefit his land receives from such action. He has a resentful feeling, however, that it is he rather than the community that is responsible for the increased value of his farm.

This factor apart, valuations in New Zealand in a time of rising prices were accepted as practical, equitable, and not unduly severe. The land-tax based upon them, therefore, was not burdensome. The farmer may have grumbled, but he paid it out of a rising income or, more commonly, recouped himself at the end of his ownership by sale at an appreciated figure.

The real importance of the land-tax, therefore, lies in the fact that it was a sound measure of public finance admirably fitted to the circumstances of the times. For the property-tax with its regressive character, it substituted a new impost which fell lightly, if at all, upon the small farmer and placed the chief burden upon the large landowner. In other words, it was successful mainly because it worked with and through the economic forces which were already operating to encourage farming industries like dairying, where land value was a relatively small item of cost compared with labour and capital.

It is indeed doubtful whether, apart from these forces, it would have had a great deal of effect. With low rates and comparatively slight graduation, lagging valuations in a time of rising prices, and the coincidental imposition of at least equally heavy graduated income-taxes, the large landowners might well have grumbled and paid while retaining their lands. In the early stages of the law, until the consolidating measures of 1907, there were also a good many loopholes for evasion.(19) Statistics have often been used to show that the increase in the number of large holdings was mainly in the lower medium range. These figures must, however, not be exaggerated nor ascribed wholly to the influence of the land-tax. There is considerable evidence of evasion, of formal rather than real subdivision, and of much legal ingenuity expended in avoiding the appearance while retaining the reality of large-scale landownership. Moreover, other countries which had no land-tax show a similar tendency to closer settlement in this period. The same economic forces were at work in them as those which were operating in New Zealand.

These facts, however, do not detract from the soundness of the New Zealand tax at the time and, under the circumstances, of its imposition. They characterise it as a soundly conceived element in the tax system, admirably adapted to give a further impetus to constructive forces already at work. Its effect has undoubtedly been exaggerated both by its supporters and by its opponents. Its soundness, as subsequent discussions will show, is much more open to question in a time of falling prices and a time, moreover, of heavy income taxation. It shows no signs in New Zealand of supplanting all other forms of taxation, or even becoming the major element in the tax system, still less of leading to nationalisation of the land. These, indeed, were not its objects. It should be regarded as a measure designed to meet existing conditions at a particular time. As such it was successful if somewhat unimportant. It fitted into the economic trend of the day and played a minor part in encouraging closer settlement and breaking up the large landholdings.

The Battle of Tenures

When John McKenzie took office as Minister of Lands in 1891 the great bulk of the best land of New Zealand was already freehold. Apart, therefore, from the rather mild effects of the graduated tax upon unimproved value and the compulsory repurchase system described below, the battle of tenures which raged so fiercely in New Zealand politics was waged rather over the remains than over the body of the land system. The best land was already freehold, and there was never at any time the prospect of resuming any considerable proportion of it. In essentials the system of freehold based upon the Torrens system of land registration was very little modified.

It is in the land legislation, more than any other feature of the Liberal-Labour programme, that political opportunism and practical expediency is manifest. McKenzie had a practical problem of land-hunger to grapple with. He took vigorous and, on the whole, effective steps towards its solution. When he left office in 1900 the problem was largely solved for the time being, in some degree because of his legislation and still more his vigorous administration; but mainly by the working of normal economic forces. The more revolutionary of his measures were much less vigorously administered after 1900. It might almost be said that the return of prosperity based on rising prices took away the necessity of following his experiments through to a logical and definite conclusion.

The main features of his land legislation were embodied in two Acts, the Lands Act of 1892, and the Lands for Settlement Act of 1894.(20) The first was an important consolidating measure which, despite later consolidations, still remains the basis of the land system of New Zealand. Before this Act was passed, the Crown lands were disposed of in the following main ways: By sales for cash; by sales on deferred payment; by a system of perpetual lease, renewable with revaluations every twenty-one years and carrying with it the right of purchase; by various special tenures designed to suit small-holders; by pastoral leases in large areas; and by small grazing-run leases designed for closer settlement of pastoral country. Under these various tenures settlement proceeded steadily throughout the depression of the eighties. As the table below shows very clearly, a sympathetic administrator might use these tenures as Ballance did in the three years 1884–7, to settle large numbers of small-holders on the land. The number of new settlers in 1887 was considerably more than the number settled in any year of the Liberal-Labour regime. This was due, however, to Ballance's vigorous prosecution of his village-settlement schemes, and is not strictly comparable with McKenzie's results.

For the system of deferred payments McKenzie in 1892 substituted a new tenure, known as "occupation with the right of purchase". Under this tenure a settler obtained a licence to occupy the land for a term of twenty-five years at an annual rental of 5 per cent. on the capital value. After ten years' occupation under settlement conditions he could exercise his option to take up the freehold or a perpetual lease, or to continue until the end of the term. This was clearly a very favourable bargain for the tenant.

As a substitute for Rolleston's system of perpetual leases McKenzie rather reluctantly agreed to a curious and much criticised compromise tenure, known as the "lease-in-perpetuity". This tenure was inserted in his Bill in the committee stage and accepted by him. It gave the tenants a lease for 999 years at 4 per cent. of the capital value, with freedom from revaluation, but subject to graduated land-tax. In his exposition of the New Zealand land system in the Official Year Book of 1894 (21) the permanent head of the Lands Department claimed for this tenure, as against a freehold system, the great advantage of leaving the farmers' capital available for improvements. As a measure to encourage settlement the tenure was defensible, but it was a bad bargain for the State and did not have a long existence or exert a very great influence on New Zealand development. When it was repealed in 1907, less than two and a half million acres had been taken up under it by rather more than five thousand tenants. The total number of Crown tenants was much greater, being swollen by the great number of holdings smaller than the average. Owing to the large areas of the pastoral leaseholds, the area of Crown land also was superficially great; but this does not disprove the fact that the bulk of the most productive and best-situated lands was held in farms of medium size upon freehold tenure. The freehold has always been, and still remains, the most important tenure in New Zealand. The leasehold tenures at their most important period functioned at the extremes of settlement, the great areas of the pastoral leases at one end of the scale and the large numbers of small leaseholds, such as village homesteads, at the other, combining to give an impression of greater economic substance than was there in reality.

The following table shows clearly the increase in the number of settlers upon leasehold tenures which resulted from McKenzie's efforts. The area settled is probably a truer indication in this table than the actual number of settlers, which in the first decade is unduly swollen by the large number of small settlers upon Ballance's village settlements. The figures cannot be totalled, since some holdings were given up, but the rapid creation of a Crown tenantry has been tabulated officially elsewhere. By the end of the century the number of holdings from the Crown on various forms of tenure ranging from leases to incompleted purchases on the deferred-payment system was over 17,000. By 1919 there were 25,204 such tenants as compared with 45,000 rural freeholders.

NUMBER OF HOLDINGS TAKEN UP UNDER SETTLEMENT CONDITIONS IN NEW ZEALAND FROM 1883 TO 1902 (22)

Year.	Number.	Area.	Average Size.
		Acres.	Acres.
1883	644	90,000	140
1884	841	161,000	190
1885	872	103,000	120
1886	1,009	114,000	113
1887	2,423	287,000	118
1888	1,577	318,000	200
1889	1,636	444,000	270
1890	1,332	348,000	260
1891	1,221	412,000	337
1892	1,372	489,000	356
1893	1,951	507,000	260
1894	1,954	633,000	324
1895	1,573	360,000	228
1896	2,012	335,000	167
1897	1,343	280,000	208
1898	1,265	362,000	286
1899	1,398	357,000	255
1900	1,306	439,000	336
1901	1,371	501,000	365
1902	1,151	379,000	330

This summary table must not be misinterpreted. There is danger in lumping together the various types of holdings and the various qualities of land involved. The only conclusion that can safely be drawn from the last column of the table is that the years in which the greatest number of settlers went on to the land were the years when the average size of holdings was lowered greatly by so many of the settlers taking up small farms. The stimulus given to settlement immediately after the passage of the 1892 Act, and again when the legislation of 1894 became operative in the financial year 1895–6, is most marked.

It is significant also that after this year, the year in which returning prosperity first became manifest, the number of new settlers who chose to use these leasehold tenures rather than buy in the commercial market dropped to something like a normal figure.

This table, supplemented by details showing the advantage taken of each form of tenure, offers conclusive evidence of the attractiveness of McKenzie's tenures to the new settler. The figures are swollen by the results of his repurchase policies, since the land so repurchased was offered mainly upon lease-in-perpetuity and was never in any case sold outright to the small settlers. The first legislation for repurchasing lands was embodied in the Lands for Settlements Act of 1892,(23) but this Act contained no provisions for compulsion and provided only £50,000 annually for repurchasing. The Act of 1894 gave the Government permission to borrow up to £250,000 in any year for this purpose and gave powers of compulsory purchase at prices fixed by a board of civil servants, plus compensation for disturbance.

While McKenzie was in office the provisions of this Act were used vigorously and, on the whole, effectively. The first voluntary purchases under the 1892 Act did not turn out well, but the later purchases under the 1894 Act were economically successful. By the end of the financial year 1900–1 eighty-one estates had been purchased containing 331,128 acres at a cost of £1,798,614. The number of tenants settled upon these estates was 1,789.

It is important to remember that compulsion was very sparingly used indeed. McKenzie himself used the compulsory provisions of his Act only twice in the six years of his administration of it. The reserve of power provided by these compulsory provisions was probably of some importance as a bargaining factor on the Government's side, and as a variety of "eminent domain" in the case of a recalcitrant owner. Broadly speaking, however, it is obvious that the repurchase activities of the Government could not have been unwelcome to the landowners. The Government always had more estates offered to it than it could handle, and as Siegfried has pointed out, the State was a wonderful customer. Moreover, it must be remembered that the State was buying land in a rising market. There is a different tale to tell of land purchases after the war for the settlement of returned soldiers.

When all these qualifications are allowed for, the fact remains that at a time of acute land-hunger and commercial depression McKenzie's land policies, and still more his vigorous administration of them, broke through an economic deadlock. His programme was consistent and coherent. It was not motivated by doctrinaire devotion to land nationalisation, the single-tax, or any other theoretical conception. From his childhood in the Scottish Highlands he had brought one burning conviction: the right of a farming peasantry to have access to the soil. Closer settlement was his aim, and no statesman was ever more single-minded than he was in pursuing it. The graduated land-tax, the overhaul of the tenurial system, and the use of State powers to purchase and redistribute the land had but the one object in view: closer settlement. The same purpose lay behind the legislative restrictions he imposed on the area which any holder could henceforth obtain from the Crown, and the improvement provisions which he made a *sine qua non* of possession.(24) He was the unwearying and unrelenting foe of dummyism in all its forms. It was the genuine working farmer who was the object of his concern. Thousands of successful farmers, who later clamoured for the right to purchase the freehold of their farms, owed their start to the leasehold system. With little or no capital they were enabled to take up land at the very beginning of a period of rising prices and land values. It may be conceded that economic circumstances favoured them and the legislation which gave them their start. It is arguable whether that legislation was as necessary or wise when the economic depression had become a thing of the past. But there can be little doubt that it was the chief factor which broke through the deadlock of land monopoly and over-valuation in the early nineties.

The positive side of the Liberal-Labour land legislation ought not to be forgotten. Events have proved that it is the more permanent and valuable aspect of the experimental programme. Constructive help was offered to the small farmers in the two directions where they most needed it. Advances of capital borrowed cheaply upon the credit of the whole community, and expert guidance and instruction provided by the

Department of Agriculture have established themselves as Governmental functions of almost unchallenged usefulness. It is competent for critics to point out that the repurchase policies involved some cost to the community for the benefit of one class—the small farmers.(25) This, while an argument of some weight in normal times, seems to be quite adequately met, as far as the early nineties are concerned, by the fact that the abnormal situation of land monopoly demanded unusual treatment.

The State loans to settlers and the provision of expert advice have a much stronger case even in normal times. Their justification lies in the fact that the whole community benefits by the economic gains accruing from lowering the cost and increasing the volume of rural production. Moreover, the case is equally clear for similar services to other forms of production whenever and wherever it can be shown that private enterprise has failed to provide adequate and cheap organisation of essential services.

This was clearly the position in regard to loans upon rural lands, and to this day it remains a fact that the loaning of long-term credit upon real estate security is a badly organised and expensive part of the financial system. The market has not been systematised in such a way as to bring large numbers of borrowers and lenders into such competition as would stabilise and lower costs. The farmer gets his credit in almost a haphazard fashion from private lenders, whose costs are necessarily high. When Sir Joseph Ward carried the Advances to Settlers Act in 1894, and the State began to use the credit of the whole community to float cheap loans abroad and lend the proceeds upon approved security to small farmers, it was entering an unorganised economic field. If only because the principle of definitely calculated repayment or amortisation was introduced, the Advances to Settlers legislation would have justified itself. That it provided cheaper credit is proved by the fact that over 60 per cent. of the loans applied for in the early years were for the purpose of paying off obligations contracted at a higher rate of interest.

The great qualification that has to be made in respect of this legislation concerns its limitations. It has been conservatively administered. Loans are made only upon first mortgage with ample margins of security. As amortisation proceeds, these margins are steadily widened. There has, therefore, been no direct loss to the State, but instead, the rates of interest have been fixed to return a slight margin of profit. The system has been of undoubted assistance to farmers of substantial resources, but it has left unsolved all the really difficult problems of rural credit. The small farmer who needs a large amount of credit in relation to the value of his holding must raise the last difficult amounts by second, third, or even later mortgages from private sources. The problems that so arise, together with the whole question of speculation in land values, are more conveniently treated in a later chapter.

The establishment of a Department of Agriculture, as distinct from the department charged with the control of Crown lands, was the work of McKenzie in 1892.(26) The work of this department is primarily educational; but it is charged, also, with certain duties of inspection and grading of produce and, especially in recent years, has paid increasing attention to scientific research. By fields instructors who visit the farms and get into personal touch with the farmers, by demonstration model farms, by laboratory tests, by the promotion of discussions, exhibitions, correspondence—in innumerable ways the services of the experts of the department, and even more important, the pooled experience of the farmers themselves, is made generally available. The rapid and sound development of rural co-operative organisation, especially in the dairying industry, owes a great deal to the practical advice of departmental experts.

It is fair to say that by the end of the nineteenth century the power of land monopoly had been broken in New Zealand. State intervention in the various ways described in this section had created a numerous State tenantry and had provided not only the leaseholders, but the small freeholders also, with the necessary assistance to get a start. Rising prices and prosperity did the rest. It was not long before these State tenants turned to rend the party which first gave them their start; but whatever the merits of the leasehold and freehold controversy at a later date, it is at least clear that the leasehold system and its related State activities performed a useful service to the Dominion at a time when it was badly needed.

The Evolution of a Labour Code

The Liberal-Labour Party came into power pledged also to improve labour conditions. The election of 1890 was held in the midst of a period of unemployment and social distress, of trade union activity, strikes, and agitation. The Liberal candidates capitalised the sweating revelations, openly courted the trade union vote, supported the trade unionists who stood for election, and generally identified themselves completely with labour aspirations. It is not surprising, therefore, to discover in the next decade the emergence of a code of labour legislation probably more complete and effective than exists in any other country.(27)

It would, however, be wrong to credit the labour leaders themselves with the detail of this programme. It is quite clear that while their general sympathy and support of the Government's policy was essential to success, the actual framing of the legislative measures was due to two singularly able men, the Hon. W. Pember Reeves, first Minister of Labour, and the first secretary of the newly created Labour Department, Mr. Edward Tregear. Reeves was elected to the House in 1887. He was, therefore, comparatively inexperienced when he took office as Minister of Education in 1890 and shortly afterwards took charge of the Labour Department. Both he and his departmental head, however, were keen students of social problems and their collaboration was very fruitful. Without his Gaelic temper and stubborn forcefulness Reeves yet occupied in labour matters a position almost comparable with McKenzie's in land legislation. His interests were wider, and he contributed more to general policy. In debate his polished irony was subtler but not less effective than McKenzie's fire. Beneath his urbanity, moreover, was a determination as fixed as McKenzie's own. Within five years he had placed upon the statute-books a complete code of labour legislation, including the much discussed Industrial Conciliation and Arbitration Act. In doing so he had not accepted a single hostile amendment of major importance. The careful drafting and comprehensive planning of his measures has brought singular success. In all essentials they form New Zealand's labour code to-day. Consolidation and extension have taken place, but the only major addition of recent years has been the substitution of workmen's compensation for employers' liability. The effective legislative planning and administrative organisation that built up this labour code was done so quietly and effectively, and has been so much overshadowed by the later developments of the arbitration system, that it has not received the attention it deserves.

A mere list of the measures passed is impressive. They are summarised in successive issues of the official year-books, and, beginning with a modest reprint in 1894, in successive editions of *The Labour Laws of New Zealand*, which has now grown into a substantial volume.(28)

The first, and in many ways the most important, Act is the Factories Act, passed in 1891 and amended in 1892, 1894, and 1896, before codification in 1907 and again in 1908 and 1921–2. The chief interest of this measure lies in its wide definitions. A factory includes every workshop employing two, and in some cases one, hand. The minimum age of employment is fixed at fourteen years; holidays, hours, overtime, the working week, factory conditions, are all carefully prescribed. Effective sections regulate the system of giving out work and so prevent any possibility of a recurrence of sweating. The whole Act depends upon vigilant administration, and therefore inspectors with wide powers are provided for, so that the Act has become thoroughly effective.

The Shops and Shop Assistants Act of 1892 is the foundation of a similar series of precautions regarding the work of women and young people in shops and offices. It was also consolidated in 1908 and 1921–2.

The wages of workmen are protected by several Acts which make effective the early legislation described in the previous chapter. The Truck Act of 1891, Workmen's Wages Act, 1893, Contractors and Workmen's Liens Act, 1892, Wages Attachment Act, 1895, Threshing-Machine Owners' Liens Act, 1895, and Wages Protection Act, 1899, have all been consolidated by the Wages Protection and Contractors' Liens Act of 1908. Reinforced by amended sections in the Bankruptcy Act, Companies Act, and Public Contracts and Local Bodies Contractors Act, they give as complete protection to the wage-earner as may be desired.

The conditions of employment in various occupations

presenting special problems have given rise to such measures as the various Coal Mines Acts, and sections in the general Mining Act, the Servants' Registry Offices Acts, the Shipping and Seamen Acts, the Kauri Gum Industry Act, the Shearers and Agricultural Labourers' Accommodation Act, Inspection of Machinery Act, Scaffolding Inspection Act, and Licensing Act.

The inclusion among the labour laws of the Accident Insurance Companies Act, and sections of the Judicature Act, is evidence of the importance attached to social welfare. In the same way, the Workers' Compensation Act, 1908 (consolidated 1922 and 1926), and the Death by Accident Compensation Act, 1908, supersede the Acts designed to make the employer liable for injuries due to negligence or default. Accidents are now recognised as a legitimate charge upon industry, to be safeguarded like other risks by means of insurance.

The legal status and privileges of trade unions are assured by registration under the Industrial Conciliation and Arbitration Act, but in addition, the Trade Union Act of 1878 was amended in 1896 and consolidated in 1908. The Crimes Act, 1908, brings together the amendments to the Conspiracy Law, 1894, and to the Criminal Code Act, 1893, by which trade unionists are protected from conspiracy charges and the responsibilities of masters towards their apprentices are defined.

Sections in the Banking Act define holidays, and these are reinforced by the Labour Department and Labour Day Act and the Legislature Act, creating additional statutory holidays, to which the Arbitration Court may add by its awards. Finally there are included the Workers' Dwelling Act and sections of the Lands for Settlements Act, giving power to purchase land for workers' dwellings.

The creation of a well-organised department whose duty it is to administer these laws and to report on labour conditions took place earlier in New Zealand than in other lands. There is some complaint from time to time that the ever-increasing complexity of regulations is harassing to industry; but there is little of the bitter and almost incredulous criticism with which such regulation was at first greeted. Generally speaking, the labour laws and their regulations have been administered with common sense. There can be no reasonable doubt that they are adequate to safeguard the high standards of working conditions demanded in New Zealand.

The well-known Industrial Conciliation and Arbitration Act is discussed in a later chapter. The Immigration Restriction Acts, which begin at an early period in New Zealand history, are more important in another connection also; but they should be mentioned at this point as owing their origin mainly to labour agitation in defence of the accepted standard of living.

The Extension of State Enterprise

It has been argued that the chief feature of the experiments in land and labour legislation was a readiness to use the machinery of Government for economic purposes that are usually left to the normal working of economic forces. Such readiness is natural in new countries where there are neither traditions of *laissez-faire* nor vested interests to combat and where, moreover, the functions of the State have already been stretched to include the provision of public utilities and services which in older lands spring from private initiative. The experimental land and labour laws were naturally supplemented by, and in turn encouraged, an extension of State enterprise in trading and even production. There was some tendency among Radical groups to regard this enlargement of State functions as a good thing to be desired for itself, if only as a necessary stage in the progress towards Socialism. This, however, is a conception that has never really commanded the effective support of the New Zealand people. The very freedom from theoretical preconceptions which makes it easy for them to acquiesce in measures of State Socialism safeguards them also from driving these experiments to the logical conclusion.

There is more general support of the idea of conservation of common resources, especially when monopoly exploitation is threatened. In more recent years, for example, the Government monopoly of water-power and ambitious programmes of hydro-electric development have commanded general approval for social rather than economic reasons. The several strands in this conception will be discussed in a later chapter. One of the most important for our purpose at this point is the theory that

State enterprises are undertaken more for what an economist would call the "social net product" than for profit in the ordinary commercial sense of the term. The repurchase policies are judged by their success in promoting settlement rather than as a commercial venture in land-broking; the railways and other public services are constantly under pressure to provide non-economical services; the insurance departments were justified as breaking through a monopoly organisation; the State coal-mines shared a similar justification and were also defended as a necessary subsidiary enterprise of the railway system.

Much, therefore, depends upon the character of the administration of these enterprises. When a Government believes in the wisdom and necessity of State Socialism as the Liberal-Labour Government did, the railways will be used to promote settlement, freight rates and fares will be fixed so as to cater for the small farmers and for the workers. This administration of the railway and similar services, with a definitely rural bias, sharply differentiates the New Zealand enterprises from those of the Australian States. There is no network of lines leading to dominating centres; but rather construction has been directed and freights fixed to cater for the smaller towns whose growth has been such a marked feature of New Zealand in the twentieth century. (29)

The extensions of State trading enterprise, which were authorised by the Liberal-Labour Government, were not revolutionary. Reeves has summed the matter up neatly.

There was [he writes] nothing novel in the notion of extending the functions of the State in the hope of benefiting the community or the less fortunate classes of it. Already in 1890 the State was the largest landowner and receiver of rents, and the largest employer of labour. It owned nearly all the railways and all the telegraphs, and was establishing a State system of telephones. It entirely controlled and supported the hospitals and lunatic asylums, which it managed humanely and well. It also, by means of local boards and institutions, controlled the whole charitable aid of the country —a system of outdoor relief more needed then than now. It was the largest trustee, managed the largest life insurance business, and educated more than nine-tenths of the children. Nearly all the sales and leasing of land went through its Land Transfer Offices.

It will thus be seen that the large number of interesting experiments sanctioned by the New Zealand Parliament after 1890, though they involved new departures, involved no startling changes of principles. The constitution was democratic; it was simply made more democratic. The functions of the State were wide; they were made yet wider. The uncommon feature of the eight years 1890–8 was not so much the nature as the number and degree of the changes effected and the trials made by the Liberal-Labour fusion.

It might be added that nothing was attempted by the Liberal-Labour Government that could not be paralleled in the municipal Socialism of England and Continental countries. It was in the use of the State rather than municipal bodies that the New Zealand experiments were novel, but the New Zealand Parliament has less than twenty per cent. of the number of members of the London County Council, and served in 1890 a constituency of even smaller proportion.

Some of the problems involved in the conduct of economic enterprises by the State will be considered in a later chapter. In the meantime it is essential again to emphasise the importance of administrative policy. Two outstanding illustrations occur in the experimental period.

The first is to be found in the Government's attitude towards the banking legislation of 1895, to be later described. The bank came to the Government in its extremity. It accepted and even sought legislation which made the Government a large shareholder and placed in the hands of Government nominees the balance of power on the bank directorate. There was, and is, no obstacle in the way of using that power to make the bank into a central bank of issue or even into a State bank in the more Radical sense of the term. A really Radical Government might have used its power to dictate interest rates, exchange charges, and the direction of loan policies. The ever-present demand for rural credit and for State borrowings might have been met by a deflection of commercial banking policy. Instead of these developments we find that even the Liberal-Labour Government, and still more their successors, have been content to see the bank follow commercial policy, to act in co-operation with and even as the leader of the close association of banks. With the return of prosperity has come an increasing volume of profits which have largely been capitalised by transactions for which legislative permission has readily been granted. The Government has viewed itself as a fortunate shareholder, and has taken its attitude with other shareholders rather than with the theorists who have contended that accumulated profits justified reductions in the margins of various charges for the benefit of customers. Whatever the merits or demerits of such an attitude it is at least clear that successive Governments have been in possession of unusual power over the most important financial institution of the country, but have preferred not to use that power in any revolutionary way.

The second illustration shows the opportunism of the experimentalists in another light. As soon as the Government was definitely assured of power by the election of 1893 it embarked vigorously upon direct prosecution of public works construction and direct control of the railways. Seddon himself was Minister for Public Works before he became Prime Minister, and to his vigour is largely due the co-operative contracting system of constructing public works.(30) New Zealand is a difficult engineering country, and the Government's experience with private contractors had not been altogether happy. The system by which Government experts plan the construction, provide materials and plant, and then let the actual labour of construction by contract to gangs of workmen, has proved profitable and efficient. With workmen of the intelligence and integrity common in New Zealand, such a system calls forth extraordinarily good results. With capable guidance from skilled engineers in the public service there can be no reasonable doubt that it has greatly cheapened the cost of constructing essential public works, while at the same time giving employment at better wages under much more favourable and more dignified conditions. There are opportunities doubtless for petty graft, but the level of administrative honesty is high in New Zealand, and there have never been any really serious charges of corrupt practices. Moreover, the letting of large contracts, and of subcontracts thereto, opens much wider avenues for corrupt practices if such were sought.

The Liberal-Labour Government not only cut out the contracting middleman, it also terminated the appointment of the Railway Commission in 1894 and took over the contract of the Midland Railway Company in the following year. The Midland contract was a legacy from the borrowing boom of the eighties. The line was begun in 1886 and only finished in

1924, when a great electrified tunnel through the Southern Alps was opened for traffic.(31) The termination of its contract was regarded by the directors as harsh and unjust; but the position into which the contract had drifted was almost impossible, and it was quite in accord with the Government's policy to take over the construction of this line instead of allowing it to drift on under private ownership.

There was less general approval of the abolition of the independent railway commission that had been set up in 1887. Awkward problems of political patronage, log-rolling, and a Civil Service vote are involved in direct Governmental administration. Charges of petty corruption were freely bandied about and gave a sinister background of hinted meaning and innuendo to the term "Seddonism", coined to express the Government's policy. No evidence has ever been forthcoming, however, despite a Royal Commission on the police system, and similar incidents. The most truth that can be found in such gossip is that there was some tendency among certain classes to lean upon the Government for jobs and to look upon the local Members of Parliament as employment agents. This is rather curiously illustrated by a printed card of test questions in English, supplied officially to inspectors of primary schools in 1906, one of the exercises set being: "Write a letter to the Member of Parliament for your district, applying for a position on the railways."

This and similar problems connected with the conduct of State enterprises will be discussed later. The point to be emphasised here is that the principal extensions of State Socialism made in this period were in the administrative policy of existing State enterprises. There were no large attempts at nationalisation of industry. An accident branch was added to the Government Life Insurance Department in 1899, State coal-mines were developed, largely as an adjunct to the railway system, in 1901, and a State Fire Insurance Office was begun in 1903. These were the only new measures of State trading beyond those already discussed.

The Humanitarian Trend

With the exception of one American territory, New Zealand was the first country to give votes to women.(32) From the passing of the Education Act, 1877, women had participated in the elections for school committees at a time when they were much more important bodies than the centralising tendencies of later Governments allowed them to be. It is significant that their first use of the suffrage and the first participation in administration should have been in the educational field. From the middle eighties also, women ratepayers exercised the municipal franchise. When in 1893 they were granted full suffrage rights, there was much speculation as to the results. Seddon thought that Parliament had leaped into "an abyss of unknown depth". Stout very acutely prophesied that the woman's vote would be thrown on the side of State Socialism. There were dire prophecies of "domestic discord, children forgotten, husbands uncared for, dress and appearance neglected, divided skirts, smoking cigarettes, scorn of marriage, a general unsexing of women".(33) On the other hand, the immediate carrying of national prohibition was only one of many high hopes that was doomed to disappointment.

There is some tendency to disparage altogether the results of woman's suffrage, to regard the face of politics as having been completely unchanged.(34) On broad party questions and strictly economic and political issues, this view is fairly near the truth. But the addition to the electorate of the adult women created a new and powerful element of public opinion, to which politicians soon began to give heed. Even Reeves, whose writings have tended to minimise the importance of the women's vote, has written in recognition of this fact.(35)

> There were some [he admits] who connected the appearance of women in the political arena with the passing of an Infants' Life Protection Act, the raising of the age of consent, the admission of women to the Bar, the appointment of female inspectors to lunatic asylums, factories, and other institutions, improvements in the laws dealing with adoption of children and industrial schools, a severe law against the keepers of houses of ill-fame, and with the Liquor laws and the Prohibitionist movement, which is so prominent a feature of New Zealand public life.

It is difficult at first glance to assess the results of the agitations of women's societies, precisely because they are interested in and satisfied with what men are apt to regard as rather petty and minor details of legal and social reform. Rarely do they press for large measures except in the vaguest propaganda; but they do exercise continuous and well-organised pressure for specific reforms, the cumulative effect of which is very considerable. The full results of this pressure did not become obvious for some time and are best treated in a later chapter. (36) It should, however, be apparent that the new electorate was predisposed to humanitarian measures. When Seddon took the plunge and suddenly introduced his Old Age Pensions Bill, just before the election of 1896, Liberalism was getting a little shaky. The main programme of land and labour legislation was already on the statute-books. Seddon, one of the greatest tacticians that ever ruled a Parliament and an electorate, correctly interpreted the trend of public sentiment. His "crowning achievement", the passing of the Old Age Pensions Act of 1898, marked the end of the first era of State Socialism and ushered in the humanitarian trend which has subsequently proved to be the most characteristic expression of New Zealand public opinion.

The Breaking of the Liberal-Labour Alliance

The legislation of the early nineties forms a coherent whole, evolved from the necessities of the economic depression. It was a constructive, carefully thought out programme, in which several lines of action were interdependent. Reform of the fiscal system, the taxation of land values, higher protective duties, the conservation and repurchase of Crown lands, State loans to small farmers, protective labour legislation, and judicial fixation of wages, were all part of a consistent programme which also included an increased degree of direct Governmental activity in the construction of public works and in humanitarian activities. The whole programme must be viewed as an early illustration of an enfranchised democracy using political power to attempt economic reconstruction. As long as the composite majority of small farmers and town workers found a common focus of interest and point of attack in the monopoly power of the great landowners, the programme held together. As soon as a shift of economic circumstances and the first successful legislation broke the landowners' power, discordant elements were revealed. Democratic use of the franchise for economic ends results easily in using the powers of the State for sectional advantage. When this means, as it did in New Zealand in the early nineties, the advantage of an overwhelming majority of the population as against a comparatively few, the results may well be striking. As soon as returning prosperity divides the majority into factions with variant interests, the use of the machinery of the State to achieve sectional advantages becomes a more disputable policy. This has been very clear in New Zealand in the twentieth century as the interests and policies of the small farmers diverged from those of the town workers. The natural result was to slow up the pace of experiment, to shift the emphasis of administrative policies, and to cause a significant revision of legislation. In the sequel it will be seen that the State experiments which have proved themselves in fullest measure are those humanitarian policies which are broadly based upon popular approval transcending sectional boundaries.

In other words, the economic struggle in the nineties resulted from an obviously horizontal class division. It was largely a contest between the wealthy landowners and the less fortunate small farmers and town workers. In that struggle the majority won. After their victory, vertical class divisions appeared. There are those who would still maintain that the main class divisions are horizontal, that the interests of town workers and small farmers are broadly allied against employers. But the main cleavages in New Zealand politics since the beginning of the century have been vertical, and the small farmers remain stubbornly convinced that they have now little to gain and much to lose from alliance with the Labour Party.

This fact is the key to an understanding of the revision of the experiments in State Socialism. It arises from and must be studied in connection with the economic development which forms the theme of the next chapter.

CHAPTER VII

AN ECONOMIC TRANSFORMATION

An Economic Revolution

The political innovations summarised in the preceding chapter have received a great deal of attention. They have even been described as a political revolution. Early accounts of them ran to such chapter headings as "The Land for the People", "A Country without Strikes", "And then We Smashed the Money Ring". The supporting text might contain qualifying paragraphs, and even explicit statements of the limitations of the experimental laws; but the general impression, exaggerating both their scope and their influence, was apt to remain. The reputation of the Liberal-Labour statesmen has suffered a good deal by reason of such optimistic estimates of early progress. The more sober (and more accurate) conception of their legislation, as consisting of an effective set of practical measures designed to break through a particular situation of economic difficulty, places them in a more reasonable and more favourable light.

If the politico-economic experiments of New Zealand have been somewhat exaggerated and overemphasised, its recent economic development has not yet received the attention it deserves. The conquest of the soil has been a remarkable achievement. The best energies and most characteristic qualities of the colonists have found their outlet in the agricultural rather than the political sphere. Particularly after the favourable turn of prices in 1895 economic progress was rapid and solid.

It was almost as if the colony, after a troubled childhood, followed by a period of rather wild and unregulated growth and expansion of interests, had passed through a sobering period of self-examination and mistrust, and had only gradually emerged into the broader and more stable possibilities of adult life. Like an adolescent youth, New Zealand in the boom period of the seventies attempted too much, and tried out its powers prematurely in many directions. After this period of overconfidence the colony was gradually forced to realise and then to put forth strenuous efforts to overcome its deficiencies and limitations. It was in the salutary period of depression in the eighties that economic organisation broadened and became more efficient. Adversity served at least to deflate the over-optimism and inefficiency of the earlier boom. It was in the eighties and early nineties, therefore, that the foundations were laid of the rapid economic progress which brought prosperity in the twentieth century.

While these facts are generally known, the precise nature and extent of the economic transformation of New Zealand in the last forty years has not been fully worked out. It is no exaggeration to say that the New Zealand of 1928 is a vastly different country in geographical distribution, economic occupation, and political creed from the New Zealand of 1888. To discuss modern economic and political problems without fully recognising this change would be equivalent to considering the economic and political problems of the United States as if there had never been the great westward expansion, the influx of immigration, and the recent revolution in mechanical production.

The last forty years in New Zealand have seen a marked drift of population to the north island, a far-reaching shift of rural occupations and reorganisation of agricultural methods, and, more important than either, a markedly favourable widening of the external market, together with a rising trend in the price-level which has brought cumulative gains to the primary producers.

In the census of 1891 more than 55 per cent. of the population was shown to be living in the south island.(1) Dunedin and Christchurch were approximately equal in size to Auckland and considerably larger than Wellington. The census of 1926 showed only 38 per cent. of the population in the south, and Auckland practically as large as Dunedin and Christchurch put together, while Wellington from the fourth had become the second city in the Dominion. This remarkable shift of population from south to north has proceeded, and is still proceeding, very rapidly and cumulatively. It denotes the lifting of the geographical barrier to settlement described in earlier chapters.

Moreover, it is definitely connected with a fundamental change in the relative importance of the main industries of the country. In 1891 the exports of dairy produce were rather less than 2½ per cent. of the total; in 1926, despite a great increase in other exports, they accounted for over 32 per cent. In these thirty-five years the annual export of butter jumped from less than 2,000 to almost 68,000 tons, while cheese exports increased from 2,000 to 75,000 tons. The significance of these figures is heightened when it is remembered that there was a not less significant and parallel development in the sheep-farming industry. The quantity of frozen meat exported was trebled between 1891 and 1926, while the export of by-products increased in much greater degree. These changes reflected a revolution in farming practice that affected the size of holdings, the tenurial controversy, and went down into breeding, cultivation, and other forms of qualitative as well as quantitive improvements.

Underlying and reinforcing the whole development was the favourable trend in the price-level from 1895 onwards. The index of wholesale prices stood in 1891 at 99, and reached its lowest point (92) in 1895. In 1926 it stood at 162, having in the meantime (1920) gone as high as 218. The index-number of export prices shows somewhat different ranges and trends, the importance of which will be discussed later in this chapter. The most recent (post-war) range of the export-price index is narrower than the fluctuations of the general price-level for reasons of some importance in the economic life of New Zealand. Broadly interpreted, this variation of the indices discloses the attempt to build up in New Zealand a sheltered and protected standard of living.

This attempt, and the related growth of secondary manufactures and commercial and professional services, was, however, made possible only by the increased prosperity of the primary industries. Increasing production and the switch to the more profitable small- and medium-scale dairy and mixed farming were helped along greatly by rising prices. Moreover, in the early years of the twentieth century, and in fact right up to the artificial post-war boom, the prices of New Zealand exports rose more than the average. There is a rhythmical fluctuation in the export index-number, but on the average it keeps above the index of general prices.

In other words, New Zealand was producing from virgin land continually increasing quantities of products, which found a market that not only shared in the general rise of the price-level, but gained a further rise from the fact that animal products were in relatively short supply in the world's markets. The conjuncture of these favourable circumstances brought such rapid progress and such widely diffused prosperity that it might well be called an economic revolution. An economist may perhaps be pardoned for considering such factors as far more influential for economic welfare than any political programme, however well contrived to fit into and work with the economic trend of the times. The chief merit of the Liberal-Labour legislation (a very great merit indeed) is that it cleared the way for, and gave impetus to, the economic forces that were transforming New Zealand in this period. It worked with, not against, the current. At a later stage it spread itself and floated on the current, somewhat checking the rate of flow; but this is a natural development always to be expected in a world where man has "become parasitic upon his environment", and nowhere more markedly so than in the political sphere.

The Drift to the North

The "drift of population to the north" is probably the most important change that has taken place in New Zealand during the last half-century. Earlier chapters of this book have described the first efforts at settlement in the north island. The small Wakefield colonies in Wellington, Taranaki, and Wanganui, and the official settlement at Auckland increased in the first forty years but slowly in comparison with the progress made in the south island provinces. Wherever access to the land was made possible, particularly in the district behind Napier, which formed the Hawke's Bay Province and the valley of the Wairarapa, there was an extension of settlement. It will be noticed that these extensions were on the drier and therefore more open east side of the north island. In these districts the sheep-raising industry was even more dominant, and the aggregation of land in large areas at least as great as in the Provinces of Otago, Canterbury, Marlborough, and Nelson, in the south island.

The wetter, richer lands of the north island, notably the Taranaki and Waikato Plains and the hinterlands of Wanganui,

Wairarapa, and Wellington, were in the possession of powerful Maori tribes, were heavily forested, and presented great obstacles to communication, being separated from the ports by difficult mountain regions. What first-class land still awaits opening up for closer settlement in the north island is subject to the same hindrances to settlement at the present time.

The census of 1881 was the first to disclose any weakening of the south island dominance, and this date gives us the clue to the causes of the northward drift. Settlement of the Maori troubles and extensive land purchases after 1873, the end of the first phase of the borrowing boom, which was mainly a south island affair, and, more important than either, the first beginnings of the widening basis of rural industry, are the developments to be noted. It is significant that the first dairy factory was begun in the Taranaki Province in the late sixties.

The drift was at first a very slow and hardly perceptible change, though its pace increased rapidly. It was twenty years before the census of 1901 showed for the first time in forty years a slight preponderance of population in the north island. In the twentieth century the movement was rapidly accelerated, until in the last census (1926) more than sixty per cent. of the people lived in the north island, and the Auckland Province alone accounted for more than half of these.

While most attention has to be paid to the south island in the early stages of economic development, the great transformation of the last forty years is mainly in the north island. Moreover, in this geographical shift, New Zealand has returned to what the first long-visioned pioneers saw to be the true centre of economic development. It must be emphasised again that the bottling up of the people in the south island provinces during the boom and consequent depression of the seventies and eighties resulted in an economic situation and in economic policies which are not truly characteristic of the genius of the colonists. The removal of the barriers to settlement, which resulted in the population moving northward, restored the economic balance, and gave expression once again to the normal processes of economic development. Without in any way minimising or discrediting the effect of what might almost be regarded as a series of legislative "operations" in the nineties, it is apparent that the physiological processes of normal growth represented in the opening up of the north island were vastly more important than the "pathological" problems which the Liberal-Labour legislation was designed to cut through.

The settlement of native difficulties after the close of the wars in 1872, and the healing work of Sir Donald McLean in the years immediately following, have already been discussed, and will not be further treated here. Between 1873 and 1892 large areas of land passed from native ownership, mostly in the north island. After the legislation individualising Maori titles and allowing free sale by the natives, there remained no real check to settlement beyond the fact that large land-owners had great advantages in buying from the natives.

While such sales facilitated the growth of the sheep-raising industry, it was not until a definite attempt was made to promote public works opening up the north island back-country that closer settlement became possible. Such public works, again, depended upon the demand of pioneer settlers, who were lured by the possibilities of the new type of farming made profitable by refrigeration to face the hardships and isolation involved in taking up bush farms. In the last analysis, therefore, the present prosperity of New Zealand rests upon the courage and endurance of the men, and still more the women, who in the nineties left the more settled and comfortable south island provinces to take up sections of virgin bush in the north. A New Zealand Horace Greeley would have given the slogan, "Go north, young man, go north!" to any ambitious young farmer or tradesman or professional man who sought his advice at this time. Going north involved many inconveniences. The men and women on the land had first to turn their cattle into the bush (which in New Zealand means dense forest thick with undergrowth), and as opportunity offered, fell the timber, scatter grass-seed between the blackened stumps, run sheep on the first rough crops which sprang readily from the virgin soil, enriched as it was with potash from the burning of the bush, and gradually clear and cultivate the land. The labour entailed was paralleled only by the isolation, the remoteness from schools and hospitals, to say nothing of entertainment, and by the primitive and even harsh conditions of housing. This was as truly a pioneer period, with hardships as real and rewards as great as those which attended the first settlement of the colony a half-century earlier. It was in fact the logical completion of that earlier period of settlement so rudely interrupted by the Maori wars.

The change in farming technique consequent upon the development of dairying production and the growing importance of the fat-lamb market is discussed in the following section. While this revolution in the farming industry was general throughout New Zealand, except on the back-country sheep-runs, it was mainly in the north island that its full effects were seen. The agricultural statistics of 1894 were already beginning to show the trend.(2) The two southern provinces Canterbury and Otago (including Southland) then, as now, virtually monopolised the production of grain and pulse crops, the area devoted to these crops being much greater at that time. The same provinces were much more intensively farmed, the area in root crops being far greater in each of them than in all the north island provinces put together. In the area of sown grasses after the land had been broken up and cultivated, these provinces were equally far in the lead; but in the extent of surface-sown land not previously ploughed, the north island provinces gave evidence of the development that was later to be expected. There were 3,782,000 acres roughly cultivated in this way as against 892,000 acres in the south island. These figures leave no room for doubt as to where the new land for settlement was being taken up.

There were naturally somewhat definite stages in this development. The most accessible land was used first. Up to the completion of the north island main trunk line in 1908, probably the largest development occurred in the Wellington Province, which had been opened up on the Wairarapa side of the main range by the Government line to Napier, and on the coastal side by the private Wellington and Manawatu line, continued by the Government line to Wanganui and New Plymouth. The Manawatu line was completed in 1886 and incorporated in the main trunk system in 1908. Before this railway development was completed, the new settlement flowed mainly into those parts of the Wellington and Taranaki Provinces around Palmerston North, Wanganui, and New Plymouth. It is only in the last twenty years that the Auckland Province has really got into its stride, and progress is bound to continue there with the further opening up of the country.

There are many statistical series available by which the relative progress of the various parts of the Dominion may be compared in this most recent period. The shift of population referred to earlier in this section is one of the clearest indications of economic progress in a country like New Zealand, where the population is so mobile. The evidence of the population returns is borne out also by the statistics of land values and of exports. In the thirty-five years between 1891 and 1926 both the unimproved and the capital value of land in the north island increased six and a half times, while the increase in the south island was rather less than threefold. As a result the valuation of the north island rose from 47 to 67 per cent. of the total valuation of New Zealand.

In the same period there was a remarkable shift of overseas trade reflecting chiefly the production of the great bulk commodities of overseas export. In the seventies the shipping companies founded by the merchants of Dunedin and Christchurch made those ports their main shipping centres, because they were the ports from which the great bulk cargoes were to be picked up. The shift of export trade, direct shipping services, and import distribution to the north island ports is a very significant development of the twentieth century. By 1900 the change was well under way. Wellington had already displaced Dunedin as the great importing centre, and Auckland also had outstripped its southern rival. Trade was fairly evenly distributed, however, between the main ports both in imports and in exports. The latest statistics show that all the south island ports combined barely equal either Wellington or Auckland in imports or exports. The north island ports in 1926 handled more than 70 per cent. of the overseas trade of the Dominion.

A remarkable feature of the export trade which reflects the productive organisation of the Dominion is the growth of the secondary ports in both islands. This growth indicates a dispersion of population and decentralisation of economic (though unfortunately not of political) life which is of the utmost importance and value. The census of 1926 showed that 25 per cent. of the population were living in the 4 main cities, a further 14 per cent. lived in 12 towns with a population between 10,000 and 25,000, another 12½ per cent. in 34 smaller towns with population ranging from 2,500 to 10,000, and still another 10 per cent. in 138 boroughs and town districts with a smaller population than 2,500. The remainder of the people, over 500,000, lived either on farms or in centres not incorporated as town districts, though small hamlets of 500 people may be so incorporated.(3)

It is in keeping with this remarkable decentralisation of population that the smaller ports should retain quite a respectable proportion of the export trade. Outside of the four main ports there were in 1926 six other ports exporting more than a million pounds' worth of produce. These figures indicate a spread of trade which is very healthy in a young and growing country. There is perhaps some tendency for the smaller ports to over-capitalise their harbour contruction works, and handling might conceivably be cheapened by a little more concentration; but New Zealand is building for the future rather consciously.

If further proof be needed of the marked preponderance of north island development in the last thirty-five years, it may be found in the statistics of pastoral and dairying production. It has already been pointed out (Chapter IV) that between 1886 and 1926 the flocks of the south island fluctuated about ten millions, and hardly increased at all, while the number of sheep in the north island grew from five and a quarter millions to almost fourteen millions. About half of this increase came mainly in an extension of large holdings in the first ten years; but there has been a later tendency for small flocks to be run on mixed farms partly for the sake of the soil, but largely for the fat-lamb market. The south island farmers have shared in the transformation of technique resulting from refrigeration, but most of the actual extension even in sheep-farming has been in the north.

This is even truer of the dairy industry. In the export season 1926–7 two-thirds of the butter and 15 per cent. of the cheese came from the Auckland Province, while the other north island districts brought the proportions up to 90 per cent. of the butter and 78 per cent. of the cheese. The only part of the south island which has a really significant share in the dairy industry is Southland, which like the north island dairy districts was originally covered with heavy bush.(4)

IMPROVEMENT OF FARMING PRACTICE

The changes of farming practice induced in New Zealand by the success of refrigeration were very far reaching.(5) The beginnings of the frozen-meat industry have already been sketched. By the end of the century this new and promising industry was well on its feet and soundly organised in its primary manufacturing and commercial aspects. It owed a good deal to the enterprise and initiative of the large landowners and financial institutions, and might well have remained a large-scale industry with a sharp class division between a few great landowners and their subordinate workers. That this possibility was averted is due partly to the vigour with which the Liberal-Labour Government pushed its schemes for closer settlement; but much more to the changed technique which followed, and in turn encouraged the development of dairying, and to the appreciation of land values induced thereby.

The large sheep-owner remains in New Zealand. There are parts of the country where the soil is so thin and the natural pasture so scanty that extensive methods involving large-scale ownership are economical. There are other districts to which the pressure for closer settlement has not yet reached. But this pressure steadily encroaches on the large-scale sheep stations, driving up the price of land to levels where sheep-farming, pure and simple, is not profitable. When this point is reached, the land tends to be cut up into smaller areas where a more intensive "mixed farming" is practised.

Many causes have contributed to the multiplication of flocks. The average number of sheep to a flock in the years 1891 to 1926 remained fictitiously steady at about 1,000, but this is due to the fact that the reduction of the number of sheep in very large flocks and the multiplication of small flocks have counteracted a tendency to the growth of the middle-sized flocks. In these thirty-five years the number of flocks of 10,000 sheep and over has fallen from 408 to 139. The number of flocks numbering more than 20,000 in 1926 was only 19, compared with 169 in 1891. At the other end of the scale, the flocks under 500 sheep belonging to farmers pursuing mixed farming on small farms, the number has increased from 8,272 to 12,332, while the flocks numbering from 500 to 1,000 increased from 169 to 5,732. If this were the whole story, there should have been a considerable reduction in the average number of sheep per flock; but at the same time the middle-sized flocks between 1,000 and 5,000 sheep jumped from 1,636 to 6,310, and the flocks between 5,000 and 10,000 increased from 287 to 532. There are obviously two trends which cancel each other in the average—the tendency for medium-sized flocks to grow larger, and an opposite tendency towards a breaking up of the large flocks and a multiplication of the small flocks.(6)

The fact is that two types of farming are involved. Sheep-farming as a business in itself is evolving towards two fairly well marked "most economical sizes". There has been no detailed investigation of all the numerous factors involved in determining these sizes; but the industry is evidently trending towards flocks of 1,000 to 2,500, with another secondary trend just under the 10,000 mark.

At the same time as the sheep-raising industry is developing these types (due to the difference between the carrying capacities of hill-country and plain), there is a steady growth of mixed farming, in which the small flock is regarded mainly as a source of revenue from the fat-lamb market.

In both these tendencies, but particularly in the latter, there is a steady pressure for better cultivation, particularly towards the production of fodder crops such as roots, as well as the improvement of pastures. The use of fodder crops is a marked improvement on the way from extensive to intensive farming practice. It involves more scientific farming in the use of fertilisers and rotation methods and brings with it an increasing labour cost. That this cost, in a country where wages are relatively high, has not checked the tendency towards intensive farming, but on the contrary has allowed of a progressive increase in land values, is due to certain advantages of climate and of virgin fertility and equally great advantages of organisation.

The mild New Zealand climate produces a grass crop which has comparatively little seasonal variation either from summer drought or from winter frost. Carrying capacity is therefore increased. It is further maximised by the practice that has developed of "exploiting the maternity of live stock". Flocks and herds are culled so that the male animals are sent to the freezing-works in summer. In this way the winter count of live stock is about two-thirds the summer count when grass is more plentiful, most of the winter stock being female animals. This is the practical method by which the New Zealand farmers have kept their live stock proportionate to the seasonal variations in the carrying capacity of the grasslands. Nowhere in New Zealand need stock be housed during the winter, so that the costs of attendance are minimised. Moreover, farming operations can be spread over the seasons more than in most countries. To these advantages must be added the virgin fertility of the soil, greatly reducing the cost of fertilisation.

Such natural advantages are supplemented by the economies gained from operation on a comparatively large scale. The larger units of production enable machinery to be used a great deal. The latest official returns (1927) disclose the use in farm production of engines of 85,970 nominal horse-power, together with milking-machines, cream-separators, churning-machines, wool-presses, tractors, reapers, threshers, chaff-cutters, etc., in ever-increasing numbers.

In this adaptation of the sheep-raising industry to the demands of the new market opened up by refrigeration there was necessarily involved a change of breeding methods. The early maturing lambs with carcases suitable for the London market have occupied a more and more important place in the breeders' calculations. The technique of fattening these lambs on specially cultivated fodder crops has been brought to a fine art. The main gains in productivity have come, therefore, from the increased carrying capacity of the land, from preservation of the female stock so as to maximise breeding, and from improvements in the quality of the rams used.

The chief avenue for future progress lies not so much in the improvement of the practical technique of cultivation and handling the stock as in levelling up the general average to the best practice in breeding. The application of scientific research to the problems involved in the production and dispersion of suitable grasses and roots, in fertilisation, and perhaps, more important still, in agricultural organisation, is the *sine qua non* of further progress. The practical farmer, ingenious and successful to a degree in the empirical solution of practical problems, has failed to visualise the possibilities of help from the scientific approach to his larger problems. In particular, the study of rural economics is sadly neglected in New Zealand. Even a complete soil survey is as yet lacking, and farm management surveys on the sample method are still very few in number. (7)

In a favourable period of rising prices and expanding markets the farmers have with great ingenuity and skilful labour reaped a rich harvest from exploiting the stored-up virgin fertility of a rich soil. In this they have been aided by a unique climate. They have made haste to capitalise the sunshine and the showers, as well as the reservoir of plant-food left in soil that has never before been cultivated. In the period of less favourable prices and diminishing fertility ahead of them they will need not only their hard work and good practical methods, but all the knowledge that modern scientific analysis can give them. (8)

The Growth of Dairying

Even more remarkable than the great increase of production in the sheep-raising industry has been the development of dairying, which ranges from an adjunct of the older industry on the medium-scale farms to specialised production of butter and cheese on smaller farms. To the sheepmen, refrigeration meant the effective utilisation of joint products with wool, an extension of income which sustained and greatly increased the values in the industry, these increases crystallising in higher prices for sheep and above all in greatly increased land values. Refrigeration rendered an even greater service to New Zealand, however, in virtually creating a whole new export industry, the importance of which may be judged from the summary table on the opposite page.

Despite changes in prices, this table is quite adequate to indicate not only the great increase in the production of wealth, but also the shift of relative importance in the main industries. If we except the temporary spurt in gold production occasioned by the application of new methods of extraction from quartz by cyanide processes, it is the remarkable expansion of dairying that is the dominant feature of recent economic development. Moreover, the forces which made possible this dairying expansion still remain as powerful as ever. As railways are pushed through newly opened lands in the north island it is the smaller farmers relying mainly on dairying who settle the surrounding country. The statistics of production grow larger and larger year by year.

PRINCIPAL EXPORTS OF NEW ZEALAND, 1883–1926 (9)

(000s *omitted*)

Export.	1883.	1893.	1903.	1913.	1923.	1926.	1928.
	£	£	£	£	£	£	£
Wool	3,014	3,775	4,041	8,058	10,905	11,830	16,679
Frozen meat	118	1,085	3,197	4,450	9,013	8,656	10,079
Butter	42	255	1,318	2,062	10,689	8,695	11,303
Cheese	7	100	195	1,770	6,870	5,939	6,694
Tallow	234	184	518	663	785	741	804
Gold	892	916	2,038	1,495	699	516	240
Grain	1,287	583	534	130	79	6	—

The industry is not only comparatively new. It has many features of great economic interest. Essentially it is a small-scale industry as far as the primary productive processes are concerned. As in sheep-farming, local and individual circumstances cause considerable variation in the size of farms, but there appears to be a tendency for a most economical type of specialised dairy-farm to appear in the most closely settled districts.(10) Its area is determined largely by the amount of land that can conveniently be worked by the labour unit, the family. On the most productive lands the average dairy-holding would appear to be less than 100 acres; but there are many larger farms of a specialised nature, and dairying has an important place on many mixed farms.

Despite the relatively small scale of the farming, the size and efficiency of the dairy factories evoke surprise and admiration from visiting experts. In the secondary manufacturing processes, and to a great degree in the commercial marketing organisation, dairying must be ranked as an efficient large-scale industry, using all the internal and external economies possible to massive production in large units. The New Zealand dairy factories are the largest in the world. Over 55,000 suppliers use 580 factories, turning out 67,887 tons of butter and 75,365 tons of cheese. These figures, however, include some dual-purpose, non-specialised factories, and if these are disregarded the annual export production averages 275 tons per butter-factory, and 282 tons for every cheese-factory. The point may be stressed in another way by pointing out that New Zealand butter-factories have about four times the average production of Wisconsin factories, while cheese-factories are three times larger than those in America.(11) Within these large, highly mechanised factories, the quality of the product is kept high and uniform by the use of the most modern scientific tests. Moreover, the factory influence extends down into the farm methods, which also become mechanised and scientific in the effort to maintain supplies of raw material of the highest quality.

The link between the individualistic labour of the small-farm owner and these great factories and marketing organisations is to be found in a thoroughly well-organised system of rural co-operation.(12) The essential difference between the dairying industry and its older rival, the sheep-raising industry, lies in this co-operative development.

While the origins of butter and cheese production in New Zealand are a little uncertain, there is no difficulty in dating and accounting for the rather sudden development of the industry in recent years. The factory production of butter depends ultimately upon three inventions: the separation of cream by centrifugal force, the refrigerating processes, and the Babcock test for butter-fat content in milk. The first cream-separators began to be used about 1879, the first frozen butter was sent from New Zealand to England in 1882, and Professor Babcock invented his test in 1890. The latter provided a reliable means by which suppliers could be paid for the actual qualitative value as distinct from the quantity of the milk they supplied. Until these three applications of scientific method were available, the dairy factory possessed few advantages over farm methods of production; but after their use was possible, the factories could standardise and progressively improve not only the manufacturing methods, but also the farm practice.

The co-operative factories, indeed, have proved to be a potent instrument of technical education. Scientific checks kept on the careless or ignorant farmer quickly had the result of reducing his remuneration. They brought down upon him also the powerful force of public opinion. His fellow-farmers were not likely to tolerate practices which resulted in lowering the general average quality of the factory product. If occasion demanded, they would refuse to accept his milk at the factory and so bring most effective pressure to bear upon him. Competition between factories has become increasingly keen. The Governmental system of grading all export produce exacts high standards, but in addition the hundreds of factories concerned in the industry have evolved a managerial class which is keenly conscious of competing standards. The factory manager, therefore, will keep his suppliers up to the mark, and make his factory a model of cleanliness and efficiency as much from sheer professional pride and in emulation of his fellow-managers as from any other motive.

It is probable that this educative value of the co-operative dairying organisation is its greatest service to New Zealand. The factory is a centre of adult education which has real scientific and social value. Farm production is maximised thereby and the life of the farmer (though not of his wife) humanised. Moreover, the co-operative organisation gets for the farmer an astonishingly large proportion of the wealth he produces. Half-way round the world from his chief market, the New Zealand dairyman receives on the farm approximately 81 per cent. of the wholesale price for his butter in London. Cheese, a bulkier product, returns him over 70 per cent. An American expert has pointed out that the Wisconsin dairy-farmers, ten times nearer their market, get smaller proportions than these of the wholesale price of their produce.(13)

One of the most important ways in which the State has helped farmers in New Zealand is by insisting upon high standards of quality when the Government inspectors are grading produce for export. This service was particularly important in the early stages of the dairy industry's development. Every box of butter and cheese is graded by the department's inspectors. So well established is the practice that all dairy produce is marketed on the basis of grades without reference to or inspection of the produce. The efficient uniform and high standard of grading maintained has been a very important factor in the price of New Zealand's dairy produce on the London market.

An economist, weighing the effects of Liberal-Labour administration and legislation, is almost inclined to rate the encouragement and fostering of co-operative methods in dairying as the most valuable of all the services provided by Government departments. Like so many other extensions of State activity, this preceded the actual Liberal-Labour experiments, but was galvanised into new life by McKenzie. An agricultural branch of the Land Department was created in 1886 by the Stout-Vogel Ministry, in which Ballance was Minister of Lands.(14) Dairy instructors were appointed and were transferred in 1892 to the new Department of Agriculture. It was a cardinal feature of McKenzie's administrative policy to encourage closer settlement by the constructive method of providing the small farmers with expert advice and assistance. In the upshot this has proved to be the most valuable of all assistance. Great credit must be given to the unrecognised work of unnamed civil servants who directed the attention of the New Zealand dairy-farmers to methods of rural co-operation. They were not content with generalisation, but prepared practical, simple, detailed forms of organisation. In so doing they gave a bias to New Zealand rural development that will last. The growing point of the Dominion's social and economic organisation is the closer settlement of dairy lands. In that growth the co-operative factory is the most potent instrument of education.

The more recent efforts to extend the co-operative principle in the marketing field involve controversial material that is best handled in another setting. Except for the unfortunate experiment in dairy control from 1927 to 1928, the broad principle has been that co-operative effort stopped in the wholesale market. In great degree the financial and commercial organisation of the industry was provided by the London Money Market. Many factories sell their whole season's output in advance to representatives of London houses, others prefer to sell in London, still others maintain their own selling agency in London.

A number of the New Zealand co-operative dairy factories have set up an effective marketing board in conjunction with the Co-operative Wholesale Society of Great Britain, the combination being registered as the New Zealand Producers' Association. This board, consisting of equal numbers of representatives of the Co-operative Wholesale Society and the New Zealand factories concerned, has handled over three-quarters of a million sterling of New Zealand butter and cheese per annum, the amount for 1928 being approximately £1,500,000. The organisation has evidently passed through the experimental stage and marks a distinct advance in voluntary co-operation for marketing, and the successful linking up of co-operative manufacturers and retailers of Great Britain with some of the co-operative producers' concerns in New Zealand is likely to lead to important future developments involving more direct exchange of goods between producers and consumers overseas.

Occupational statistics may be quoted to sum up the change in New Zealand farming brought about by the rapid extension of dairying. Between 1901 and 1916 the number of workers engaged in dairying multiplied more than tenfold from 6,074 to 63,794. There is some difficulty in getting comparable figures after that date because of the differentiation into mixed farming; but the indications are for a falling off rather than an increase in numbers. The great increase in dairying production since that time has been due to greater productivity per worker rather than to a greater number of workers.

With the exception of the various types of civil servant, the dairy-farmers are the biggest single occupational group in the Dominion to-day. They are responsible for producing a third of the Dominion's purchasing power in overseas markets. There can be no doubt that the future of the Dominion lies largely in their hands. The stability of the industry, its steady remuneration all the year round, the little capital required, the small farms requiring mainly family labour, make it very attractive to settlers. Its growth has been the most remarkable feature of New Zealand's economic transformation in the last forty years and bids fair to increase rather than lose its importance in this regard.

The Gains from Rising Prices

The increase in productivity in the older sheep-raising industry and the rapid development of dairying have been stressed in the previous sections. They are the real foundation of New Zealand's recent prosperity. It is necessary to point out, however, that they have been greatly enhanced by favourable price movements, and that it was not until the favourable turn of prices in 1895 that progress was very obvious. It might even be argued that the scientific inventions which made possible the extensions of farming in New Zealand were themselves due to the pressure of demands reflected in the price system of the time. Without stressing this point it is at least clear that from 1895 to 1921 the course of prices was such as to bring great gains to New Zealand.(15)

The first and most important of these gains was derived from the long-term upward drift of prices after 1895. It is hardly possible to make a cumulative estimate of the extent to which the rising price-level assisted New Zealand development. Statistics showing what exports would be valued at if prices had remained at a certain level do not measure the actual gains, since they do not recognise the increase in costs of production.

The first effect of rising prices which should be noticed is the differential advantage it offers to the farming producers as against other members of the community. Prices of farm products rise in quick response to changing conditions in world markets. The export market is the determining factor of New Zealand economic life. When, as after 1895, the exports were subject to rising prices which were sometimes anticipated in speculative markets the farmers found their incomes enhanced before their costs were increased.

The chief cost which a New Zealand farmer has to meet is interest on his mortgages, and when these are fixed for even such a short term as three or five years this main item of costs becomes less burdensome in relation to the income he receives. In any case, the rise in the rate of interest lags jerkily behind the rising price-level. There is a decided lag also in wages, in taxation, in freight rates, though perhaps not so obviously in commercial charges, which are usually on a commission basis.

It is evident that when prices are rising, the balance of economic advantage is inclined to the rural and away from the urban occupations.

If this were the whole truth there would long before now have been much more acute economic division between town and country than actually exists. If the New Zealand farmer has an advantage over the town-dweller, he has an even greater advantage which the town-dweller shares with him over the customers for his export products. New Zealand exports are bulky products sold in sensitive wholesale markets, which catch the first impulse of rising prices. The imported commodities which are bought with the funds built up by the sale of exports are for the most part articles of retail consumption. New Zealand merchants in a time of rising prices are constantly finding that they can buy cotton goods or woollen goods at this year's prices, while wool is selling at substantially higher prices which will not be reflected in the prices of woollen goods for at least a year. This rather subtle variation between the course of export and import prices is obscured by a tendency for cyclical movements to reverse the situation from time to time. It is broadly true, however, that import prices lag substantially, and that this lag in a time of rising prices has materially promoted the economic prosperity of New Zealand.

The importation of overseas capital provides a special case of this kind, which is of very great importance. Much of the prosperity of New Zealand since 1895 has rested upon the expenditure of cheap borrowed capital. It will be more convenient to defer till a later chapter any discussion of the limits within which such borrowing was sound public policy in the long run. Unfortunately also, owing to the absence of anything like accurate statistics of the importations of private capital and to the extreme difficulty of arriving at even approximate measurement of the balance of trade, it is not possible even to estimate the extent to which capital flowed into New Zealand in this period. The statistics of public borrowing are of course available. Between 1891 and 1920 the gross public debt increased from £38·8 millions to £201·2 millions. Of the latter total rather less than half (£99·1 millions) was domiciled abroad, while practically the whole amount in 1891 was overseas debt. To this must be added the £7·8 millions of local body debt domiciled abroad in 1920 as against £5·0 millions in 1891. In addition to these public borrowings there was an indeterminable amount of private capital invested in New Zealand. In the absence of reliable statistics it is possible only to make the general statement that during the period of prosperity from 1895 onwards the net inflow of overseas capital was stimulated. Not only the construction of public works by the Central Government and local bodies, but banking and commercial services and private industry have been helped by overseas capital. Probably the most significant, if most elusive, portion of this capital is the short-term floating credit used to shift New Zealand overseas trade. The value of this trade has grown from fifteen to almost a hundred millions annually, and the circulating capital necessary to ensure that the dairy-farmer and all other producers shall receive payment immediately for goods which will not reach the final consumer till months afterwards comes from the London Money Market.

In the provision of all this capital—long-term loans for the Government and local bodies, debenture and share issues for private companies, and advances to rural producers—there was in the period of rising prices a fortuitous element of gain to New Zealand. No small part of her prosperity in the last forty years is due to the cheap overseas capital upon which fixed rates of interest were paid for long terms, while the prices of exports kept on steadily rising.

Moreover, there is some evidence to show that export prices rose more than import prices during this period. After a dragging start in the nineties the index-number of exports kept ahead of the general level right up to the war period. This is in conformity with the fact that animal products which supply the overwhelming bulk of New Zealand exports were in short supply in the world's markets.(16)

The only summary that can be made of the effects of rising prices upon New Zealand prosperity is that in these several ways the producers gained a quasi-rent from the fact that the prices of their products kept ahead of the general average and therefore well ahead of their costs. This meant that farming industries were favoured more than others, but that their welfare was so important to the Dominion that it was better for the others to suffer this less favoured position in a time of increased purchasing power rather than a more favourable trend at a time when purchasing power was generally restricted owing to the misfortunes of the primary producers. Rising prices are generally identified in New Zealand with prosperity, and falling prices with adversity and depression.

It must be said also that the more favourable position of the farming community gave rise to a greatly increased volume of speculation in land values. The gains from rising prices were heavily discounted in advance, and the values of land rose more steeply than the prices of the produce to be taken from the land. The paradoxical position was thereby created that at any particular moment the economic position of the farmers was unstable and unsound, while the upward sweep of the price-level kept on salving the farmers who had bought at higher than productive values. In so doing it provided the occasion to repeat the instability at higher values, and so the process went on until the check to the price-level in 1921 brought a drastic readjustment. The reactions of this speculation in land values and of the connection of borrowing therewith must be deferred for later discussion.

The Extension of Secondary Industries

The great gains in productivity resulting from the expansion of the sheep industry and the creation of the dairy industry were accompanied by considerable gains in the subsidiary industries. Some readjustments were necessary, the chief being the change in grain-growing from the export to the domestic market. This, however, is the principal exception to the general rule that the prosperity of the main industries carried with it opportunities of expansion in many minor and contributing industries also. The margin of profits was widened considerably, not only by extra production, but also by higher prices. The extra gains, therefore, made possible a considerable extension of services—Governmental, professional, and commercial—as well as the growth of many local industries which were not firmly rooted in economic necessity.

Probably the best measurement of these trends is to be found in the census statistics of occupation. The following table summarises the figures at successive censuses between 1891 and 1926.(17)

PERCENTAGES OF EMPLOYED POPULATION IN MAIN INDUSTRIAL GROUPS

Group.	1896.	1901.	1906.	1911.	1916.	1921.	1926.
Primary production ..	38·49	34·35	32·39	31·17	30·96	28·52	25·30
Industrial	23·61	26·81	27·04	25·89	23·25	22·32	23·86
Commerce and finance ..	12·36	12·45	14·04	15·42	15·24	14·85	14·92
Public administration and professional	6·57	6·85	6·59	7·00	9·03	9·74	10·37
Transport and communication	6·14	6·67	7·73	8·46	9·54	10·38	10·46
Indefinite	2·38	2·31	2·40	2·46	2·94	6·37	7·17

In this table the primary industries are taken to include fishing, mining, and saw-milling, as well as farm production. The only industry within this broad classification which has made a relative gain as far as the percentage of employment is concerned is dairying. Certain other qualifying facts must be stated briefly. The increase in the commercial group is due almost wholly to an eightfold increase in the number of women employed. The transport and communication group is greatly swollen by the inclusion of the Government railways, post and telegraph services.

It is apparent, therefore, that the really significant drift in this period has been the expansion of employment in the Government services. The problems involved in this expansion will be treated later in connection with the State enterprises.

It is apparent, also, that the secondary manufacturing industries have increased rather faster than the primary occupations, though not as fast as Governmental or commercial services. It is in this period, indeed, that secondary production first became really important. The extent of its development may be judged from the summary table on the opposite page showing the gross value of the production in the main manufacturing groups.

It will be obvious from this table that the chief increases in manufacturing have been in the industries which utilise and put into marketable form the chief export products. It must be remembered that the growing population constitutes a domestic market of increasing importance. Of the chief primary commodities practically all the flour, oatmeal, potatoes, 97½ per cent. of the bacon, 83 per cent. of the pork, 79 per cent. of the beef, 46 per cent. of the mutton, and 21 per cent. of the butter are consumed locally. (18) The proportions in such commodities as wool and cheese are much smaller, but practically the whole range of the secondary industries, properly so-called, produces for the local market with little or no export.

GROSS VALUE OF FACTORY PRODUCTION, 1891–1926 (19)

(*In millions*)

Industry.	1891.	1901.	1911.	1921.	1925–26.
	£	£	£	£	£
Meat-freezing ..	1·5	3·7	7·3	13·7	14·7
Butter	0·1	1·2	2·7	11·3	12·6
Cheese	0·1	0·3	1·2	6·3	6·3
Grain-mills	1·0	0·7	1·2	3·4	3·1
Ham and bacon ..	0·1	0·2	0·4	0·6	1·1
Biscuits and confectionery	0·1	0·3	0·4	1·3	1·6
Breweries	0·3	0·6	0·6	1·5	1·3
Clothing	0·2	0·4	0·5	2·9	2·5
Boots and shoes ..	0·4	0·5	0·6	1·5	1·2
Saw-milling	0·8	1·3	2·7	4·7	5·7
Gasworks	0·2	0·3	0·6	1·4	1·6
Electric light and power	—	—	0·1	0·9	2·2
Engineering	0·4	0·4	0·8	1·8	2·0
Printing	0·4	0·7	1·4	3·4	4·4
Motors and cycles ..	—	0·1	0·1	1·0	1·4
Tanning	1·0	1·9	2·0	3·4	2·8
Furniture	0·1	0·2	0·5	1·2	1·4
Woollens	0·3	0·4	0·4	1·3	1·2
Total of all industries	7·3	12·2	30·2	79·1	84·8

It is natural that with prosperity a wide variety of secondary manufactures should have sprung up to cater for local needs in this way. There is a great range of demands in engineering, printing, and similar industries which can best and most economically be met by local production. Some of the most characteristic manufactures have been successfully established with little or no tariff protection. A notable case is the agricultural implement industry. There has also been a noticeable tendency in the post-war period for branch establishments, such as large works for the assembling of automobiles, to be established close to the market. The chief gain from this departure has been a saving in freight.

The protective tariffs since 1895, together with the widening of profit margins in the primary industries, have made it possible for the secondary industries to increase somewhat faster than primary production. Upon examination it will be found that the tariff still in force in New Zealand is moderate compared with the tariffs of such countries as Australia, Japan, and the United States. While the addition of preferential duties against foreign products has had the effect of increasing protection in certain industries the general tariff level remains moderate and there is a large free list. The highest rates of duty (with the exception of those upon alcoholic liquors and tobaccos) are lower than many to be found in higher tariff countries. When the imports are taken by classes, the proportion of duty collected to the value of the imports ranges from 0·02 per cent. on live animals and 0·11 per cent. on unmanufactured metals up to 25·72 per cent. on apparel. The following table, compiled for the years preceding and following major tariff revisions, indicates the nature of the New Zealand protection.

NEW ZEALAND TARIFF RATES(20)

(*Percentages*)

	1894.	1896.	1906.	1908.	1925.
Merchandise—					
Free	31·25	32·17	38·29	50·20	44·76
Dutiable	79·00	78·00	62·00	50·00	55·00
Duty rate—					
On dutiable goods ..	38·00	37·00	33·00	34·00	38·00
On all imports ..	26·00	25·00	20·00	17·00	17·00

The highest rate of *ad valorem* duty in the tariff schedule is 60 per cent. In 1926, 45 per cent. of the imports came in free, one-tenth paid duty at 10 per cent., one-eighth at 20 per cent., a similar proportion at 25 per cent.; while duties of 35 per cent. and upwards were charged only on 6 per cent. of imports. The specific rates charged on 13 per cent. of the imports include the tobacco duties (averaging 83 per cent.) and the heavy duties on alcoholic liquors (averaging 124 per cent.); but otherwise conform broadly to the *ad valorem* rates.

It cannot be said, therefore, that New Zealand has extremely high protection. The stability of her tariffs and the infrequency of revisions are also in contrast with the flexible protection afforded by the Australian Tariff Board. There has been some widening of local production under the shelter of protective duties, but the political power of the small farmers has been consciously exerted against undue development of this tendency. It may well be argued that such widening as there has been may be more burdensome to the primary industries in a time of falling prices than it has been in the period of prosperity, but broadly considered the tariff and industrial statistics bear out the conclusion which has been emphasised before in various connections, that the characteristic trend of New Zealand economic development has been towards rural and mainly dairying expansion both relatively and absolutely.

A Check to Productivity

The natural result of the progress outlined above was an extraordinary increase in the value of production. Official estimates are available from 1900 onwards, and show that in the first twenty-five years of the twentieth century the total value of New Zealand production increased almost fourfold. The greatest gain was shown in the dairying group of industries and in fisheries. An abbreviation of the official table is shown (p. 230) for comparative purposes, together with a rough estimate for 1890–1 interpolated on the basis of other comparable figures such as exports and factory statistics.

Before the information contained in this table can be of any great scientific value, allowance must be made for the rapid increase of population and the rise of general prices which occurred in this period. Such a correction has been made in the second table.

It is to be remembered that the mere attraction of population is generally an economic gain in a country at New Zealand's stage of development. During this period the Dominion grew in numbers faster than any other country for which records are available.(21) Moreover, the rate was

VALUE OF PRODUCTION, 1890–1 TO 1925–6(22)

(*In millions*)

Year.	Group I. Agricultural.	Group II. Pastoral.	Group III. Dairying.	Group IV. Mining.	Group V. Factories.	Group VI. Fisheries.	Group VII. Forests.	Group VIII. Builders.	Total.
	£	£	£	£	£	£	£	£	£
1890–1	3·9	8·1	0·6	1·5	3·0	0·1	1·5	2·4	21·1
1900–1	4·1	11·0	2·8	2·7	5·3	0·1	2·1	3·9	32·0
1910–11	4·0	20·2	6·4	3·8	8·1	0·2	3·5	5·8	51·9
1920–1	9·0	27·5	25·7	3·4	19·1	0·4	5·6	9·2	100·0
1925–6	8·4	36·4	26·4	3·1	22·3	0·6	6·7	12·1	116·0

steady, and this in itself showed that the absorptive capacity of the country was not being unduly taxed. It is not immigration which has lowered the productive capacity of New Zealand. On the contrary the most noticeable falling off of the index of productivity per head has taken place in the war period, when immigration slackened off, while the most recent

INDEX-NUMBERS OF RELATIVE PRODUCTIVE ACTIVITY(23)

1910–11—Base, 100

Year.	Value of Total Production.	Population.	Index of *Per Capita* Production.	Wholesale Price-Index.	Index of Productivity.
	£ (millions).	Millions.			
1890–1	21·1	·67	64	97	66
1900–1	32·0	·81	80	93	85
1910–11	51·9	1·05	100	100	100
1920–1	100·0	1·26	160	188	85
1925–6	116·0	1·40	167	171	98

gains in *per capita* production have coincided with an increased volume of immigration. Moreover, the new increments to the population come mainly from the excess of births over deaths. The guess may be hazarded that New Zealand has not yet gained an "optimum" population, and that increases in numbers still normally cause a gain in productivity, other things being equal.(24)

The check to productivity disclosed after 1910 is to be explained by other reasons than an increasing population. It was, moreover, in the quantity, not the value, of production per head. As long as prices continued to rise it was a matter mainly of academic interest; but with a falling trend of prices it becomes a matter of real and very practical concern. Such an untoward trend of prices lays bare the fact that the productive organisation of the Dominion had slackened considerably in the days of easy prosperity. The causes of that slackening are to be found mainly in the speculative trafficking in land values, and in the public borrowing for development purposes upon which it was based. Subsidiary causes may possibly be found in the extension of State enterprise, the elaboration of welfare legislation, and the tendency to over-elaborate regulation of wages and industrial life generally. It is at any rate clear that after a remarkable spurt in production, New Zealand drifted, after 1910, into a somewhat precarious reliance upon rising prices rather than more effective organisation. In this most recent period there has also been a decided check in the rate at which New Zealand's population has increased. Both the sister Dominions, Australia and Canada, increased at a perceptibly faster rate in the decade 1910 to 1920.(25)

CHAPTER VIII

THE TRIUMPH OF THE FREEHOLD

Reversal of the Leasehold Policy

There seems for some time to have been a good deal of misconception prevalent concerning the extent and importance of the leasehold system of land tenure in New Zealand. It has been argued in earlier chapters that the dominant form of land tenure has always been freehold, and that rural organisation has from the time of earliest settlement proceeded mainly on that basis. Before the tenurial controversy became the outstanding political issue of the nineties, the great bulk of the best land of New Zealand had passed into private ownership. Moreover, the leasehold system introduced by Rolleston in 1882 and extended by the Liberal-Labour legislation of the next decade was very half-hearted. The conservation of the public lands was always regarded as secondary to the encouragement of closer settlement. It was for this reason that Rolleston was forced to insert a purchasing clause in his 1882 measure providing for perpetual leases, and McKenzie ten years later agreed to the compromise tenure known as the lease-in-perpetuity.

Perhaps because these forms of leasehold tenure, and the renewable leases to be described below, were mainly used in settling small farmers on better-class land, the tenurial controversy has centred round them. They were alternative forms of tenure to freehold in those lands which were most in demand for closer settlement. Yet a close examination of the statistics will disclose the fact that they have never been really important as compared with the freehold areas. Five million acres is probably the maximum amount that has ever been held by small farmers on these tenures. It is difficult, indeed, to resist the conclusion that the magnification of their importance has been due to the superficial habit of most investigators in lumping together all forms of leasehold held from the Crown. The mere statement that at March 31, 1927, there were 37,055 Crown tenants holding 20,153,026 acres conveys quite a false impression, unless it is pointed out that of this total 9,619,931 acres of very poor land was held on pastoral lease by 643 tenants and 2,715,241 of rather better pastoral country was held in 853 "small grazing-runs". If to these figures are added the holdings o deferred payment which are being made freehold, the much larger area held on the tenure known as "occupation with right of purchase", and the large but poor "educational endowments", the total land held in relatively small areas upon the tenures which have been the subject of heated controversy approximates to the five million acres mentioned above. This is perhaps a fourth of the area of freehold land.(1)

For some obscure reason the pastoral leases escaped controversy until within very recent years. They also seem to have escaped the notice of most investigators. Yet it is upon the lands held by this tenure that the evils of the leasehold system have been greatest. This point needs a good deal of emphasis, since it has been the cause of much confusion in the whole tenurial controversy. It will therefore be raised again later in this section.

It has been argued in Chapter VI that the vigorous measures of closer settlement initiated by John McKenzie as Minister for Lands in the Liberal-Labour Ministry were the chief means of breaking through the economic deadlock created by the land monopoly which existed prior to 1890. It was further argued in Chapter VII that more favourable economic circumstances after 1895 caused a great increase in productivity and that this increased production was supplemented by a rising price-level. The prosperity which ensued was general and was shared by the small farmers, who had been put on the land by McKenzie's leasehold policies. Hardly a decade had passed, therefore, before the Crown tenants began to feel in a position to demand the freehold of their farms. Many arguments were advanced for the change. A competent observer has summarised the chief reasons urged in favour of the freehold as:

(1) That it would pay the colony to sell the freehold and expend the money received in purchasing large estates for subdivision and closer settlement, instead of borrowing millions from abroad for this purpose and remitting the greater part of the rents to the foreign money-lender by way of interest.

(2) That the restrictions as to cropping, personal residence on the

property, and other covenants in their leases were vexatious, and by purchasing the freehold they could farm their lands as they wished.

(3) That the labour unions and single-tax advocates were agitating for reappraisement of the rents of the lands leased for 999 years.(2)

These are, however, merely rationalisations of what must now be regarded as the real reason for the freehold agitation, viz. the desire to be free from Governmental restrictions in order to participate in the speculative land-selling that began at this time to dominate farming in New Zealand. As the sequel will show, there have been solid advantages in the leasehold system, particularly the freeing of the tenant's capital and the escape from taxation; but against these must be set the lure of rising values. It is true that the leaseholders could realise on the goodwill of their leases; but they were hedged about with restrictions of area, occupation and improvement conditions, Governmental oversight, and difficulties in the valuation of improvements. Speculation is far easier with freehold land in a time of rising prices, especially when sale and transfer is made easy and cheap as it is by the Torrens system of land transfer. It is not surprising, therefore, to find that an agitation for the freehold grew up among the Crown tenants and was strongly supported by the much more numerous class of freeholders.

By 1905 even Seddon could no longer resist the pressure. A departmental committee had considered the land laws in 1904, but a Royal Commission was appointed also in the following year.(3) Its members proved to be equally divided on the freehold and leasehold issue. The question was temporarily shelved; but Seddon's successor had to face it in 1907. The legislation of that year, followed as it was by amendments of the arbitration system in the year following, represents the first important break in the Liberal-Labour policies of State Socialism. Both were obviously due to the growing political power of the small dairy-farmers in the north island.

The revision of land legislation at this time is contained in three Acts, all passed in 1907. The Land and Income Tax Assessment Act is more conveniently discussed in the next section. It was intended to compensate for the virtual administrative abandonment of the policy of repurchase and subdivision which had become too costly a means of inducing the closer settlement of great estates, and was in any case less urgently needed than it had been when it was first introduced in 1894.(4)

By this time, also, the lease-in-perpetuity which McKenzie created in 1892 had few defenders. It had all the demerits of a compromise and was popular neither with freeholders nor with leaseholders. By the Land Laws Amendment Act of 1907 this peculiar system was abolished and tenants were given the right of freehold purchase.(5) This concession to freehold sentiment was more gesture than reality, since doubt immediately rose as to the meaning of the rather vague "price equal to the capital value of the said land at the time of purchase thereof".(6) Since many existing holders had bought the goodwill of the leases from previous tenants they naturally objected to paying for the land over again. Future settlement of Crown lands was to be under "renewable leases" for 33 or 66 years, with perpetual right of renewal upon revaluation. This tenure has proved to be attractive and successful. Up to March 31, 1927, it has been taken up by 7,971 holders of 2,151,465 acres, and of this total only 237 holders of 40,397 acres have availed themselves of the right to acquire the freehold provided by subsequent legislation.(7) It is too soon yet to anticipate what may happen as the period of revaluation approaches.

The third part of Sir Joseph Ward's revision of the Liberal land legislation has been the least successful. By the National Endowment Act, 1907, an area of 7,000,000, to be later raised to 9,000,000, acres of land, was proclaimed as an endowment in perpetuity, to be disposed of only on leasehold tenures.(8) The revenue from this endowment, after defraying costs of administration and certain local body subsidies, was to be applied to the costs of education (70 per cent.) and old-age pensions (30 per cent.). The endowment has, however, proved to be more visionary than real. For the financial year 1926–7 the gross rental received was £138,040, while the expenditure on education was £3,910,241 and on old-age pensions £982,356. The 9,000,000 acres was reached in 1920; but subsequent legislation has reduced this area to 6,750,000, mainly by proclaiming 1,690,300 acres to be forest reserve.(9) The lands are of poor quality, and in accordance with the freehold policy of the Reform Government, lessees have recently been granted a somewhat restricted right of purchasing the freehold. The author of the endowment rather pathetically protested that its potential value "a thousand years hence" should be considered, but such long views have little appeal in New Zealand.

Various education reserves, which had been set aside by different provinces from 1862 onwards and had come under the control of the Central Government in 1877, after the abolition of the provincial system, were administered, until 1908, by school commissioners in each district concerned. The Education Reserves Act of 1908 consolidated this legislation, and an amending Act two years later abolished the commissioners and vested the lands in the ordinary land boards.(10) The lands concerned vary in quality, but large areas are poor. At March 31, 1927, there were 819,732 acres held by 4,035 tenants and returning an annual rental of £127,130.(11)

The only other Act of any importance passed at this time was the Land Settlement Finance Act, 1909, intended to facilitate the purchase of land by co-operative credit guaranteed by the Government after due investigation of the transaction proposed. The measure was intended to encourage closer settlement and has been moderately successful, 46 associations being in existence at March 31, 1927, involving 303 holders of 42,511 acres. No transactions have been made, however, since 1917.(12) The conditions with which such schemes are necessarily hedged about are very cumbrous, restrict the transference of land in many ways, and are generally unattractive in a time of rising prices and easy credit, though such conditions have ensured the success of the schemes started.

The legislation described above has proved to be the last dying effort of the Liberal-Labour defenders of the leasehold system. In the election of 1912 the economic development of the north island, which had created a numerous and successful class of small freehold farmers, confident in their prosperity and intolerant of anything resembling State Socialism or land nationalisation, brought about a change of Government. The new Premier, Mr. Massey, who was to hold office thenceforward till his death in 1925, came into power pledged to grant the freehold to Crown tenants. He himself took the portfolio of lands, and in his first session of office introduced and carried the Land Laws Amendment Act, 1912, by which lands held upon the lease-in-perpetuity were made purchasable upon terms that were very favourable to the tenants.(13)

Hardly a year has passed since without an amending land Act, and throughout this mass of legislation the principle of the freehold has been steadily extended.(14) Even the sacrosanct national endowment lands have (with some restriction) been thrown open to purchase by the tenants. At the same time there has been a consistent effort to liberalise the conditions of the pastoral leaseholds.(15) A great deal of the severest criticism of the leasehold system has in recent years been directed against the predatory farming encouraged by the short leaseholds without adequate compensation for improvements which have been the rule on most of the pastoral land held from the Crown. The strongest critics frankly admit that their strictures do not apply to the "renewable leases" of 1907, which are in fact classed as a "good tenure".(16)

In the case of the pastoral leaseholds, however, there are good grounds for criticism. When almost ten million acres of land return a rent averaging 2·32 pence per acre, something is seriously wrong. Moreover, as a competent critic has pointed out, "while all the lands with freehold rights have steadily improved in productive capacity and in monetary value since the country was first occupied, the pastoral runs have steadily deteriorated in production and value".(17) This deterioration has largely been due to the fact that the leases have been too short and have not protected the lessees' improvements. Predatory farming and overstocking have resulted, lessees have not cared to wage the necessary relentless war upon the rabbits, the pastures have in consequence deteriorated, and in many cases erosion and denudation have thereby been facilitated. The greatest damage of all has been done by unskilled or careless tenants burning off the tussock at the wrong period of the year. Burning is necessary to prevent the country from becoming rough; but if done carelessly it destroys the pasture. The Province of Otago, which has the greatest area of these pastoral leaseholds, has been the worst sufferer. There is no room for doubt that this has been the main cause for the relatively slower increase in the population of this province.

While there is substantial basis for these criticisms of the pastoral leaseholds, responsible officials of the Lands Department point out in reply that the spread of rabbits and over-

LAND TENURE IN NEW ZEALAND

burning were at least as important as insecurity of tenure in causing deterioration of the pastures. The recent improvement is due, in their opinion, as much to suppression of the rabbits, more careful burning, and attempts at regrassing as to improved tenure. Moreover, they suggest that many concessions made to the leaseholders in the form of lower rentals and better terms of lease have been as much due to organised agitation as to genuine grievances. It is probable, however, that a large part of the more efficient farming of the last few years has been due to more liberal conditions attracting experienced farmers.

LAND TENURES HELD FROM CROWN, 1913–27

Tenure.	1913.		1927.		Converted to Freehold.	
	No.	Acreage.	No.	Acreage.	No.	Acreage.
Deferred payment	24	2,668	2,773	336,361	10,660	1,253,494
Perpetual lease ..	739	72,225	174	8,902	3,101	862,785
Occupation with right of purchase	5,791	1,829,536	3,994	1,198,214	4,791	1,237,640
Lease-in-perpetuity	10,990	2,296,730	7,649	1,651,065	3,115	525,533
Renewable leases..	3,513	967,235	7,734	2,111,068	237	40,397
Agricultural leases	17	550	9	282	1,408	140,896
Miners' district leases	651	23,749	709	19,190	126	4,069
Homestead ..	—	—	—	—	61	80,453
Pastoral licences (mining) ..	702	153,113	699	155,989	76	16,409
Small grazing-runs	914	2,425,227	853	2,715,241	49	59,631
Pastoral runs ..	645	10,808,013	643	9,619,931	4	6,155
Miscellaneous ..	5,215	961,290	6,704	1,158,844	115	11,611
Rotorua leases ..	331	4,05	316	2,038	15	162
Education endowments	382	772,353	4,035	819,732	4	81
Other endowments	898	403,310	763	356,169	4	5,019
Total	33,812	20,720,056	37,055	20,153,026	23,766	4,244,335

In order to investigate this whole problem of deterioration a Royal Commission was set up in 1920, and upon its report legislation was introduced in 1921 and 1922, by which the right of freehold purchase was extended to pastoral tenants.(18) Little advantage has been taken of this legislation, however, and in fact the whole effect of the freehold legislation of recent years has been surprisingly small. This is well indicated by the table above, showing the situation of the various tenures upon which Crown lands were held at March 31, 1913, and 1927.(19) In reading this table it is to be remembered that 1,028,023 acres had been purchased under the deferred-payment system which was abolished in 1892, leaving only 225,471 acres which have been converted into freehold since the reintroduction of the system in 1912.(20) The conversion of perpetual leases into freehold also occurred almost wholly before 1912, and the same statement is true of the agricultural leases and the homestead tenures. The "occupation with right of purchase" tenure was never a leasehold system. With these tenures deducted it will be seen that the granting of the freehold since 1912 has mainly resulted in offering a specially favourable bargain to the tenants upon lease-in-perpetuity. It is to be remembered, however, that there is still time for a good deal of conversion to take place.

The reasons for the comparatively small results of this reversal of policy are not far to seek. First it may be re-emphasised that the leasehold versus freehold controversy has been waged over the remains rather than the body of the land system of New Zealand, which always has been and is mainly a freehold system. Then it is clear that, except in the specially bad case of the pastoral runs, there are few criticisms of leasehold farming which might not be equally urged against the freehold when conducted under speculative conditions as it is in New Zealand. It is significant that in the heavy depression of the last three years, 1924–6, freehold land amounting to 193,785 acres, and private leasehold land amounting to 181,502 acres, has gone out of cultivation, while the area of Crown leasehold has slightly increased.(21)

Finally it must be stated that the incidence of taxation described in a later section gives very real advantages to Crown tenants, many of whom until recently escaped both the land and the income taxation which presses hardly upon other classes in the community.

The Progress of Closer Settlement

The statistics of landholding in New Zealand in the last thirty years show a consistent tendency to subdivision of holdings; but this tendency is difficult to measure accurately, because of the variety of uses to which the land may be put. The table below, which ignores holdings of less than ten acres and shows the different subdivisions with cumulative percentages both of the total number of holdings and of the total area held, gives as fair a picture of the trend as may be gained in any way short of a series of Lorenz curves.

STATISTICS OF LAND OCCUPATION IN NEW ZEALAND, 1895 AND 1926 (22)

(*Percentages*)

Area of Holdings. Acres.	1896.		1911.		1926.	
	Holders.	Acreage.	Holders.	Acreage.	Holders.	Acreage.
Over 50,000 ..	0·27	30·5	0·16	20·2	0·06	11·0
20,000–50,000 ..	4·0	45·5	0·4	30·6	0·3	22·9
10,000–20,000 ..	9·0	56·3	0·9	39·9	0·7	31·6
5,000–10,000 ..	1·8	62·6	1·8	48·5	1·5	41·6
1,000–5,000 ..	8·0	77·4	10·0	72·1	10·0	68·2
640–1,000	12·0	81·8	17·0	79·4	16·0	66·2
320–640	24·0	89·2	32·0	89·1	31·0	87·0
200–320	37·0	93·3	45·0	93·6	42·0	92·2
100–200	58·0	97·4	64·0	97·6	64·0	97·0
50–100	74·0	99·0	78·0	99·2	80·0	99·1

In interpreting this table a good deal of caution is necessary. The trend towards closer settlement is definite and clear. It may be illustrated by quoting the smaller number of large holders, the decrease in the average size of their holdings, the increased percentage of landholders in the lower medium range, and the greater increase in the areas held by them. It must be remembered, however, that there are two principal types of farming in New Zealand, and that the area of a small sheep-farm is considerably greater than that of a dairy-farm. Within these main types there is, of course, a wide variation of size according to the quality of the land.

The development of the dairy industry in this period would have caused a great deal of subdivision if no other factors had been operating. The table above shows that the tendency towards subdivision on this account was stronger in the latter half of the period than in the earlier years. In 1926 there was a substantially larger proportion of farmers holding from 11 to 320 acres. The decline in the number of landholders having between 11 and 50 acres occurred in the first period and is due mainly to increased prosperity giving small owners an opportunity to expand, at the same time doing away with the necessity for village homesteads intended to relieve unemployment. If the table is summarised the drift becomes clearer.

Percentages

Acres.	1896.		1911.		1926.	
	Holders.	Acreage.	Holders.	Acreage.	Holders.	Acreage.
Above 5,000 ..	1·8	62·6	1·8	48·5	1·5	41·6
1,000–5,000 ..	6·2	14·8	8·2	23·6	8·5	26·6
320–1,000	16·0	11·8	22·0	17·0	21·0	18·8
1–320	76·0	10·8	68·0	10·9	69·0	13·0

There is nothing in this table to lend support to the idea that land aggregation has been occurring in New Zealand since the reversion to the freehold system in 1912. On the contrary there seems clear evidence that the tendency towards smaller holdings has been definitely accelerated. The statistics lend strong support, therefore, to the contention repeatedly expressed in these pages that economic rather than political forces are mainly responsible for shaping the development of the Dominion. Land is now held in smaller areas primarily because dairy production pays better than sheep-farming on much of the land. Large holdings persist in other areas because the most profitable use of the land is found in sheep-raising by intensive methods.

A review of the recent land legislation emphasises this conclusion. Attention has already been drawn to the virtual abandonment of the leasehold system after 1912, and to the increasing expense which compelled a slowing up of the Liberal-Labour repurchase policy at an even earlier date. Of the total area (1,997,870 acres) purchased and subdivided under this policy up to March 31, 1927, two-thirds was purchased before 1913. The remainder has consisted of smaller properties than those acquired in the earlier period, the average size and price being 1,119 acres at £10 8s. per acre, as compared with 5,598 acres at £4 15s. per acre prior to 1913.(23)

An interesting and important development of the repurchase policy was the settlement of discharged soldiers upon land purchased under the Discharged Soldier Settlement Act, 1915, and its amendments. The financial aspects of this development have been less satisfactory than in the case of the older policy. Altogether 1,427,490 acres were purchased. Of the total amount (£8,973,995) advanced by the Government to returned soldiers towards the purchase of farms, market-gardens and orchards, and discharge of mortgages, £2,584,296 has been written off capital and mortgage values by the Revaluation Board set up in 1923.(24) These figures indicate clearly that the repatriation policy, while very costly owing to the purchase of land by voluntary negotiation at the very peak of land values in the post-war boom, was more important as an agency of closer settlement in the post-war period than was the older purchase policy under the Lands for Settlements Act. In the absence of definite statistical evidence concerning the extent of subdivision it is impossible to measure the degree to which either contributed to closer settlement. There is no reason, however, to believe that they were more than contributing factors to the powerful tendency to subdivision engendered by the post-war boom, particularly in dairying lands.

The Efficacy of Taxation

Sir Joseph Ward, in advocating his legislation of 1907–8, laid great stress upon the efficacy of the land taxation, which he stiffened considerably by the Land and Income Tax Assessment Act, 1907. The earlier working of the graduated tax on the unimproved value of land was described in Chapter VI. There is a good deal of evidence that "before the year 1907 the scale of taxation in force had no very marked effect in breaking up the big estates".(25) It is of considerable interest, therefore, to analyse the effect of the stiffer graduation and checks to evasion introduced in 1907. Such analysis, however, is complicated not only by the complexity of the land-tax schedules, which have changed a good deal in the last twenty years, but also by the interaction of these schedules with the income-tax system.

The land-tax system of New Zealand from 1907 to 1917 consisted of an ordinary non-graduated tax of a penny in the pound of unimproved value and an additional graduated tax.(26) In 1917 both rates were combined in a single progressive tax rising from one penny to sevenpence in the pound, plus a super-tax of 50 per cent., and a further 50 per cent. on the total amount in the case of absentees. The years from 1915 to 1923 represented the peak of land taxation, since in those years rates were highest, and in addition farmers paid income-tax on the income derived from land. In the financial year 1921–2 the maximum was raised to $7\frac{17}{20}$ pence in the pound (27); but the super-tax was lowered from 50 per cent. to $33\frac{1}{3}$ per cent., and a rebate of 10 per cent. of the whole tax was allowed for prompt payments. In the following year the super-tax was reduced to 10 per cent., and it was removed entirely the year afterwards, while farmers were again exempted from income-tax. A further reduction of 5 per cent. was made in the year 1924–5.

This bare outline of the major changes made, necessarily omits all details of graduation and exemptions. Even then it is clear that the system is an intricate one, difficult to estimate in its incidence and effects. Certain outstanding facts may, however, be noticed briefly.

In the first place Crown land is exempt from taxation and, since their scale of operation is relatively small, the lessees of most Crown land escape income-tax also.

When the legislation making farmers subject to income-tax was repealed in 1923, the pastoral lessees were freed also, but in the following year income-tax was reimposed on the Crown lessees of small grazing-runs and pastoral runs. There is little doubt that the favoured position of the smaller leaseholders in regard to taxation was one of the main reasons for the small extent to which they took advantage of the right to convert their leases to freehold after it was given to them in 1912.

It is difficult to estimate the relative incidence of land and income taxation. Cases may be constructed such as the following, which was argued to the writer by an expert in rural finance in defence of the recommendation made by the Royal Commission of 1922 urging the abandonment of the land-tax and the substitution therefor of income-tax:

For example, take a man owning £150,000 worth of land and stock, and having in addition an income of £5,000 a year drawn from other sources. Assume for argument's sake that he is making, say, $7\frac{1}{2}$ per cent. on his landowning venture before taxes are deducted. This means that he has a total income from his land of £11,250 a year. He only pays Land Tax on the unimproved value of his land. His stock, plant, and improvements would probably account for £60,000 of the £150,000, leaving him £90,000 on which he has to pay Graduated Land Tax. His tax on this comes to £2,043 15s. Then he will have to pay Income Tax on his remaining £5,000. His Life Insurance and other exemptions will probably come to, say, £400, and his taxable income is £4,600, on which the rate is 3s. 7⅕d., and the tax £1,035. His total tax, therefore, is £3,078 15s. Under the proposals of the Commission he would pay no Land Tax, but he would pay Income Tax on £16,250. This would have to be paid at the maximum rate of 5s. 10⅖d. in the £, which is £4,766 13s. 4d.

This shows that he is now getting off with £1,687 18s. 4d. less tax than he would have to pay if he were paying Income Tax only.

Few people realise the great change that was made in the system of taxation when the Graduated Income Tax was introduced during the war. Prior to that we had what was practically a flat rate, with reduced rates on the very small incomes. Where there is a flat rate it does not matter into how many portions an income is broken up, but with the graduated system the rate is fixed in proportion to the size of the income. It is therefore necessary to ascertain what the income is, and bring the whole income together in one amount.

The figures quoted in this supposititious case check consistently with the average proportions and relations of valuation and income, and there is no reason to assume that the argument is fictitiously strengthened by selection of the figures used. Moreover, in a time of rising prices and probably at any time in a developing country, valuations tend to lag behind the market value of land. Estimates have placed this lag as high as 23 per cent. in a comparatively stable period, and it must have been much greater in the post-war boom.(28)

Various authorities have remarked upon the efficiency of the New Zealand valuation system; but closer examination of their data reveals the fact that, being separated from the facts by long distances, they have almost always relied upon official statements and reports. Naturally the Government valuers claim accuracy, but there has been no independent scientific check upon their claims, and it is common knowledge in New Zealand that there is a wide disparity between Government valuations and selling prices. It is true that the Government valuation has some influence in determining mortgage capacity; but the possibility of repurchase as a check to correct valuation has been for many years almost non-existent. Here, as elsewhere, a sympathetic administration has not pushed a drastic law to its logical extreme.

It will have been noticed that the argument in the case cited is twofold. A comparison of the rates of taxation will show that income taxation is relatively heavier, except possibly in the highest ranges of unimproved land taxation (£100,000 and upwards). It seems clear, therefore, that the burden of taxation in the medium range of incomes, say from £500 to £5,000, has been relatively heavier upon business and professional classes than upon farmers. This probability is greatly increased by the fact that under the New Zealand system of income-tax, joint-stock companies are taxed as if they were individuals, so that shareholders in such companies must pay at maximum rates even though their incomes be relatively small.(29) The only mitigation of this inequity lies in the fact that since certain businesses are necessarily carried on in large-scale units which are all taxed at maximum rates there is a clear tendency for income-tax under these circumstances to be shifted to consumers and producers. Such shifting is difficult, if not impossible, to estimate. Even admitting this tendency, the incidence of company taxation decidedly strengthens the argument that moderate investments in land (as well as in private businesses) are more lightly taxed than similar investments in joint-stock companies.

In addition to this disparity of tax rates there is the argument, which is well illustrated in the case cited, that wealthy individuals can minimise the effect of progressive taxation by dispersing their investments. In New Zealand a wealthy man, by investing in several small businesses paying less than the maximum rate of income taxation, as well as in tax-exempt Government bonds, in debentures subject to lower tax rates, and in land, may very greatly reduce his total burden of taxation without any semblance of evasion whatever.

It is difficult, therefore, to see how the progressive land taxation, heavy as it apparently is, can be regarded as penal, except possibly in the very highest ranges of valuation. Direct taxation, especially of income, is high, and progression is steep. On the other hand, land valuations lag behind the market, while income returns show actual income received.

There are, however, two outstanding exceptions to this general argument that the progressive tax on land has not been nearly as burdensome as it appears to be and therefore has played a much less important part in breaking up landholdings than might reasonably have been expected. The first exception is obviously to be found in the period from 1915 to 1923, when farmers paid both land and income taxation. In these years the land-tax was penal in its incidence; but as events turned out, this penal effect was masked by an extraordinary rise in land values which greatly accentuated the normal lag of official valuations behind market prices. The chief effect of the land taxation at this time was therefore to intercept for the State some share of the rising land values caused by the currency depreciation of the war period and accentuated by the land boom after the war.

When the crisis of 1920–1 put a sudden end to this inflation of land values the farming community quickly complained of the injustice and inequity of the taxation to which they were subjected. A Taxation Committee was appointed in 1922 and was succeeded by a Royal Commission in 1924. The Committee, representative chiefly of farmers and business men, reported that "it had become unprofitable to hold land in large areas". This rather naïve finding was put forward in more guarded language by the Royal Commission in its conclusion that "the graduated land-tax was originally designed to break up large estates. There is no evidence to show that it is required any longer for this purpose, and there was much evidence showing that it is now preventing the development of large areas of land requiring a considerable amount of capital expenditure to break in".(30) Before the Commission's report, the farming community had been relieved of income-tax in 1923, and this relief brought to an end the only period when the pressure of the land-tax upon any but the largest holdings was visibly drastic. It may reasonably be concluded that except for this brief period between the fall of prices in 1920–21 and the remission of income-tax in 1923, the only disadvantage the landowners suffered from the progressive land-tax was the rather problematical effect it had on the largest estates. Over the great bulk of rural landholding, its incidence was relatively lighter than income taxation would have been.(31)

On city properties there is, of course, a different story to tell. The statistics of landholding calculated from the tax returns show the following division between rural and urban lands.

LAND TAX RETURNS, 1926–7 (32)

Occupation of Taxpayer.	Number of Taxpayers.	Total Unimproved Value.	Taxable Balance.	Total Amount.	Tax Assessed per £100 of Unimproved Value.
		£	£	£	s. d.
Farming and allied pursuits	25,470	142·4	8·25	603,205	8·6
Professional	2,886	8·0	4·0	26,119	6·7
Manufacturing and industrial	2,549	8·9	5·9	46,428	10·5
Commerce and trade ..	3,831	20·1	14·4	145,937	14·6
Banking	41	2·5	2·5	66,568	52·5
Transportation	430	1·0	0·6	4,138	8·3
Miscellaneous and unspecified	16,299	50·9	36·2	245,864	9·8

This table reveals the extent to which the burden of the land-tax, especially in the upper ranges, falls upon urban rather than rural property. More detailed returns show that practically all the land owned by banking firms fell into the class with an unimproved value of £10,000 or more; rather more than half the land used in commerce, 40 per cent. of the manufacturing land, and rather less than 37 per cent. of farming land was in this class. Of the 38,540 farming returns, no less than 10,871 fall into the class where tax is paid upon an unimproved value between £1,000 and £2,000. There is another modal point at £10,000–£15,000. It is unfortunately not possible to make a complete tabulation of the extent to which the farming community escapes or pays land taxation, because of the large "miscellaneous" group of taxpayers, many of whom are farmers.

As far as the city returns are concerned it is obvious that the progressive taxation of unimproved values is a true penal tax, since it is additional to income-tax paid also at progressive rates. Moreover, a far larger proportion of city lands pays at the higher scale than in the case of farming land. Since the unimproved value of land in boroughs has increased by more than 50 per cent. in ten years, it cannot be argued that such heavy taxation has unduly depressed values. It has, in fact, intercepted for the State some portion of the unearned increment, and as an instrument for so doing it is sound public finance. The only possibility of any part of this taxation being shifted would seem to arise when the business using the land is enabled by a monopoly position to pass on taxation to its customers. The only important case in which this is likely is presented by the close association of the six banks operating in New Zealand. In the case of competitive businesses the land-tax takes for public purposes part of the increasing land values which have been created by urban concentration and rising prices. This appears to be a true example of the appropriation of an "economic surplus" without disturbing the equilibria worked out by competitive forces.

It is to be remembered also that since the Rating on Unimproved Value Act was passed in 1896, local bodies may adopt this principle in local taxation if it has been affirmed by a referendum of ratepayers. (33)

In 1926, 74 boroughs out of 119, representing more than two-thirds of the borough population, had adopted the system.

In summing up the results of land taxation, therefore, a great many conflicting and interacting factors must be taken into account. The incidence of the system is clear in the important case of city lands under both local and national taxation. Any tendency towards undue concentration and overbuilding is easily checked in New Zealand by elaborate and capably administered building regulations and factory inspection.

The efficacy of the tax in bursting up great holdings of rural land must be regarded as unproven, in view of the complex interaction with the system of income taxation, the lag of valuations in a time of rising prices, and the probability of amortisation.

There was a good deal of subdivision reported just prior to 1907 in anticipation of the new tax rates, but this has not been continued. Any effect the increased tax had was largely discounted at an early stage. It is true that the Commissioner of Taxes gave evidence before the Royal Commission in 1924 indicating that subdivision was being induced by taxation. This evidence was given in another connection and was not supported by specific statistics. As argued above, the tax was obviously penal after the slump of prices in 1920–1, and in addition was blamed for the other effects of the slump. Its efficacy, doubtless, was greatest at that time; but over the period 1907–26 as a whole no definite evidence of its achieving its primary object is discoverable. No statistical proof can be attempted. It is easily possible to show that the number of large holdings is being somewhat reduced(34); but many factors are at work, and the effect of land taxation cannot be isolated even in theory.

The progressive intent of the tax is again complicated by the possibility of escape provided by the income-tax system. It was argued in an earlier chapter that the chief effect of the land-tax immediately after its inception in 1891 was to give a relative advantage to those farming industries, particularly dairying, in which costs arising from the land were smaller than in the more extensive pastoral farming. Before the war income taxation was low and the scale of graduation was fairly flat. After 1915 the rates and the scale of progression were drastically raised. This has largely neutralised the effect of the steep rise in land-tax rates and progression after 1907. Between urban and rural incomes, therefore, it is even truer of the later than of the earlier period that the weight of direct taxation is on the towns. Against this may be set the fact that some considerable part of the income taxation on large companies is shifted back to the farmers in increased charges. More important still is the generally recognised truth that urban industries and services catering for a local market, as in New Zealand, can pass on increased costs, such as arise from a rising cost of living, to the rural producers.(35) There can be little doubt that the prosperity of the twenty-five years 1895–1921 enabled this shifting of costs to be met by the farmers with equanimity. It is equally clear that the check to prosperity since 1921 has made the burden of taxation more obvious and distressing; but it is the burden of taxation as a whole, and not the land-tax in particular, which is the trouble. The average farmer is not grievously injured by land taxation.

Whether the smaller farmers gain the same relative advantage from a progressive rate of land taxation as formerly is doubtful. The large landowner cannot escape progression by subdividing his land and retaining the ownership of it. But he can and does spread his capital over urban as well as rural investment, thereby minimising his taxation. In this he would appear to have a relative advantage over the small farmer, whose necessarily limited investments are almost wholly in freezing companies and quasi-co-operative trading concerns.

All of these are necessarily large-scale enterprises which pay income-tax at maximum rates, and must either pass on this burden in greater charges to their owner-consumers or fight a losing battle against the competition of specialised trading firms subject to lower taxation. On the other hand, the wealthy landowner can spread his investments among debentures, tax-free Government bonds, and smaller trading concerns. It may well be concluded, therefore, that the subdivision of large holdings has resulted more in diverting rural capital into these smaller trading concerns and gilt-edged securities than into the closer settlement types of farming.

The whole subject is so complex and so little capable of precise measurement that conclusions must be very tentative and guarded. This in itself indicates that the achievement of social aims, such as closer settlement and equalisation of wealth, is difficult even in such a comparatively simple economic organisation as that of New Zealand. Economic change is too rapid and the ingenuity of profit-seekers too great for crude legislative panaceas to be very effective. It is probable that land taxation has settled into a permanent element of the New Zealand tax system; but it is difficult to discover, except in the case of city lands, any very clear evidence of its superiority over other forms of direct taxation. More recent New Zealand experience amply confirms the sane judgment expressed by Scheftel in 1916: "Not as a panacea, then, for all social evils and economic maladjustment, although its influence may be beneficial with regard to these, but as a tax, must the expediency of the tax on land value be determined." (36)

Farming for the Property Market

It has been argued that the dominant form of landholding in New Zealand is freehold, and that under this tenure there has in recent years been a strong tendency to subdivision and closer settlement. Reasons have been offered for believing that neither land legislation nor the pressure of taxation upon the unimproved value was as influential in promoting settlement in the twentieth century as in the last decade of the nineteenth. Despite the lessening of these pressures, closer settlement proceeded faster in the later than in the earlier period. The obvious explanation is that other forces of an economic character were more potent. The chief of these has already been stressed in the emphasis laid upon the advance in dairying production. The great strides made by this new industry, quickened as they were after 1900, were in themselves sufficient to account for the great bulk of the subdivision that went on.

Attention must now be drawn to other factors mainly connected with the financing of rural enterprises. Before doing so it is necessary to make clear the importance of the very simple system of land registration and transfer which New Zealand shares with the Australian States. The Torrens system of land registration received its name from the Collector of Customs, who devised it in South Australia and succeeded in having it passed into law there as early as 1858. Two years later a Land Transfer Act was passed in New Zealand, but it was not until 1870 that the system became really effective. Successive amendments have been made in the law, culminating in the Land Transfer Act, 1924, designed to bring all the land of New Zealand within the scope of the registration system within a limited period.(37)

The essence of the Torrens system is that the registration, after due enquiry concerning the title to a piece of land, affords a complete assurance of validity. The title so secured is backed by a State guarantee and by what amounts to a State system of insurance of titles. At any time the ownership of the land may be ascertained beyond all doubt by inspection of the entry in the register of the Land Transfer Office. This obviously means a very great ease and certainty of transference, together with a great reduction of conveyancing costs.

Not all the land of New Zealand is registered in this way. Before the Torrens system was made effective a great deal of land was alienated under the property law of the colony. From 1841 onwards, provision was made for the registration of deeds and similar instruments secured on land. Such registration is not essential to the validity of the instruments, but is important in securing priority of security. In 1924, 18·6 per cent. of the land was dealt with and titles secured under this earlier system of registering deeds rather than titles. A marked tendency had appeared for the proportion of land so dealt with to increase; but the Land Transfer (Compulsory Registration of Titles) Act, 1924, has been operative in checking this tendency. Land registrars have been directed to investigate all land titles not already registered and issue certificates of title either limited or unconditional. It is therefore only a matter of time before the whole of the land will be registered and will be almost as readily saleable as any other form of property.

In a time of steadily rising prices the temptation to speculation offered by a freehold system based upon such simple and transferable titles becomes almost irresistible. There is a strong tendency in any case to follow the will-o'-the-wisp of price changes as between the various farm products. This is very clearly illustrated in the wheat-growing activities of the Canterbury farmers. Crops grown to take advantage of expected high prices have generally defeated their object. There is a clear and rather pathetic correlation between high prices and large production in the following season.(38) Farmers forget that price movements go faster than the processes of nature, and they are only too often chasing prices—a season behind. The tendency is clearest in the wheat industry, but is well marked, if not so measurable, in other forms of farming. Under the speculative farming practised in New Zealand it takes much self-control to abide by the ups and downs of the market and organise production upon the lines best suited to the capacity of the land. Yet in farming, more than in any other industry, the dictum of Henry Ford is irrefutably true in the long run.

> In the end speculation will kill any manufacturer. Give him a couple of good purchases on which he makes money, and before long he will be thinking more about making money out of buying and selling than out of his legitimate business, and he will smash.(39)

Few farmers, however, can resist the lure of prices. Each man backs his judgment in estimating relative prices, and most of them necessarily lose on balance, if only because their land is not worked to the fullest capacity.

The interference with normal organisation of production caused in this fashion is connected with and largely due to the far more important tendency to speculation in the ownership of the land itself. Discussions of land speculation in other countries tend to be concerned mainly with the holding of urban or suburban property in order to gain profit from subdivision.(40) This form of speculation exists in New Zealand, but is checked by the taxation of unimproved value and still further by the additional taxation specially devised to force land of this kind into use.(41) In the Dominion it is the trafficking in rural land actually under cultivation which is the more important, and which is in fact the outstanding characteristic of rural organisation on the freehold tenure.

There is an extraordinary turnover of landholding in New Zealand. A careful estimate by an economist who has specialised upon this problem places the proportion of land that changed hands in the ten years 1915–24 as rather less than half the occupied area, even allowing for retransfers.(42) When allowance is made also for the large area held in great holdings upon pastoral lease the extent of turnover in the small-holdings is obviously considerable. It is true that land speculation was especially feverish during a great deal of this period, but even in normal times there is a very great turnover. In the period of rising prices before, during, and immediately after the war this speculative element was naturally more marked than it has been in the years since 1921, when land values have tended rather to fall than to rise.(43)

The speculative trafficking in land values was most obvious and most harmful in the smaller holdings. It was directly encouraged by the comparatively light taxation and generous exemption of mortgages in the lower ranges of the land-tax system.(44) The lavish borrowing of overseas capital for the construction of public works also encouraged speculation by adding fortuitously to the already marked effect upon land values of a rising level of prices. The money borrowed for the repurchase and subdivision of land has had the same result far more directly. The most conspicuous example of this form of Government encouragement to speculation in recent years has been the repurchase by voluntary negotiation of large areas for the settlement of returned soldiers upon the land. In effect the Government turned loose in the real estate market 22,585 new purchasers armed with £22,627,864 of borrowed money.(45) Little provision was made to control the advance in land values resulting from this increased demand. Both town and country lands were affected and on both there have been losses not yet finally determined. Up to the end of the financial year 1926–7, reductions in capital and mortgage value had totalled £2,584,296. In addition the Government had negotiated reductions in private mortgages, and was still engaged in investigating the more difficult problem of advances upon current account.

Besides these losses to the Government there were the losses of the soldier settlers themselves and in some degree of their private creditors. It is impossible to estimate with any accuracy the total loss involved in the abandonment of holdings and also in the reduction of equities. Amortisation proceeds rapidly and secures the Government advances in greater degree as the years go by. Up to March 31, 1927, £5,764,770 had already been paid off the principal. But this repayment, while safeguarding the Government against further loss, is quite consistent with a fall in land values, reducing the settlers' equities. In specially bad cases this reduction in equity may even include part of the money already paid off the Government and other loans.

This somewhat extreme case of Government lending has been cited first, as the clearest example of the encouragement to land speculation resulting from freehold (and certain kinds of leasehold) farming with easy credit. It has been urged at various times that the whole system of State advances inaugurated in 1894 and steadily extended since has had the same effect. Discussion of State advances is deferred till the following section on the organisation of rural credit; but it is relevant here to point out the comparative ease with which Government loans of this kind are transferred when the land is sold. They offer cheap credit upon good securities and have certainly not operated to restrict land speculation.

This is not due to any inherent quality of the Government loans, and can hardly be regarded as a valid criticism of the system. The private mortgages and advances of various types have been far more potent in promoting speculative activity. The fact is that land speculation in New Zealand is firmly rooted in the desires of the farmers themselves. Certain elements of the taxation and financial systems of New Zealand encourage those desires, and it is possible to conceive ways in which such encouragement might be lessened; but so long as the progress of settlement and a rising level of general prices tempts the farmers to regard the appreciation of land values, rather than improvements in production, as the goal of their endeavours, so long will land speculation remain the outstanding characteristic of New Zealand farming.

Such speculation is always one-sided. There are no "bears" on the real estate market. It is always a rise in values that is sought. This fact in itself is sufficient to explain why the organisation of rural credit is devised in such a way as to tempt farmers in times of rising prices to take up obligations which are often beyond the productive capacity of their land at current prices. The inevitable result is that in a time of violent speculation, such as that which followed the war, there is a clear tendency for the creditor class to take an increasing share of the returns from farming. The freeholder, under such circumstances, exchanges the landlord for the mortgagee. He works hard for smaller remuneration upon his capital and for his (and his family's) labour than his fellow-worker in the town. If, after a period of years, a rising price-level enables him to capitalise the "unearned increment" of his land, he retires well content. If, however, prices should trend downward his position is thereby the worse. There are thousands of farmers and ex-farmers in New Zealand at the present time who plume themselves upon their farming and financial ability when in reality they have gained fortuitously from speculation in land values upon a rising market. There are, unfortunately, thousands of others who have already lost heavily, and thousands more whose chances of selling at appreciated values have receded far from their hopes of a few years ago. Only those who view farming as a permanent productive business and the rise and fall of land values as windfall gains and losses are on a thoroughly sound economic basis.

It is, unfortunately, not possible to measure with any exactitude the burden of indebtedness carried by the rural producers of New Zealand. What statistics exist relate only to the more measurable mortgages upon fixed security, and it is difficult to estimate the degree to which changes in the amounts of such mortgages are paralleled by changes in the more elusive forms of credit advances. Moreover, the mortgage statistics must be used with caution, since many mortgages, and the discharges of many more, are not registered, while some are registered for indeterminate amounts and others are registered many times in different land districts. Of the total mortgages outstanding in 1923–4 (£258,000,000) an expert estimate of the "live" mortgages upon rural lands was £136,000,000. The validity of this figure is supported by an independent estimate of £140,000,000, supplied from official sources and based upon mortgage figures in the land-tax returns. At the height of the land boom in 1920 the rural mortgages registered were three times the value of those on urban lands; but the proportion is now approximately equal, indicating that available mortgage money has in recent years flowed into city rather than country securities. There has at the same time been a marked tendency towards higher rates of interest. It is only too obvious that rural finance has become more difficult since 1921.(46)

The farmers, having pitted their judgment of speculative values against that of the financial experts, have in recent years been forced to realise that they have lost in the gamble. A rising level of world-prices, resulting ultimately in higher land values, is no longer present to produce the illusion that their financial judgment is at least on a par with that of merchants and bankers. Faced by this situation they display a very natural tendency to blame the Government, the banks, the merchants, the Arbitration Court, the trade unions, or any one else but themselves for the financial straits into which their own speculative activities have brought them. This is a large part of the real background of the agitation for improved rural credit, co-operative marketing, and the amendment of the arbitration system. It must be said, however, that the great increase in primary production in the last few years, without any increase in the farming population, is proof that the actual working farmers are facing the situation resolutely and successfully.

The Organisation of Rural Credit

No system of comparatively small-scale freehold farming could exist without an elaborate system of rural credit. In New Zealand, despite the great extension of Government advances in recent years, the bulk of the credit supplied to farmers is provided by non-Governmental agencies. The expert estimate noted in the preceding section placed the "live" rural mortgages in 1924 as £136,000,000. In that year the total amount of the loans made by the Advances to Settlers Department was £25,481,065, of which £14,329,018 had been repaid. Since that time there has been a considerable expansion of the Department, the corresponding figures in 1927 being £36,500,000 and £17,200,000.(47) These loans are made mainly on rural land; but they are available also for purchase of homes in the cities, and some part of the total is made up of advances upon the security of stock and farm implements. When these facts are taken into consideration it will be seen that Governmental loans account for perhaps 10 per cent. of the rural mortgages. The small average of the loans granted in earlier years has been appreciably raised by the liberalising of the system in the last three or four years, and is now beginning to approximate to the average value of mortgages registered on rural lands. It must be remembered, however, that the State advances are made as first mortgages upon ample margins of security, whereas the registered mortgages include many smaller amounts of second, third, and later mortgages upon indifferent security.

Viewed as a business enterprise the system of State advances is well established and soundly administered. It pays income-tax upon its profits, but enjoys a differential advantage over private lenders in escaping any taxation upon debenture issues such as would be necessary to provide capital in a private concern.(48) It was established originally by borrowing overseas so that the gross public debt included, on March 31, 1927, an amount of £19,342,780 on account of advances to settlers alone. Considerable additions are made to this sum yearly and there is constant pressure to enlarge borrowing for this purpose. From a narrow financial point of view it is obviously good business to borrow cheaply upon State credit in overseas markets and lend within the Dominion at rates sufficient to leave a small margin on the transaction. Whether the indirect economic effects, particularly in the inflation of land values, would justify a sudden large extension of borrowing is another matter.

In addition to the new funds made available by borrowing,

the Department now has at its disposal the repayments made upon previous loans. The system has become a revolving and increasing fund. Moreover, in recent years the Department has been given the use of other public moneys, such as the Public Debt Sinking Funds, and has reinvested its own sinking fund. In using these funds it is of course merely diverting investment into rural channels and not adding to the investment funds available in the Dominion.

The security of the loans is sound by reason of the wide margin of valuation insisted upon. This margin is steadily increased as repayments are made at regular half-yearly intervals. The Department has in consequence avoided losses and, on the other hand, has built up reserves and sinking funds, paid income-tax, and shown a slight profit. Within the limits of its operation it must be regarded as sound public finance, and it is obviously capable of expansion as time passes. Proposals for sudden expansion by large borrowings, however, involve economic problems, especially in regard to land speculation, which require very careful consideration. These are discussed in connection with public finance in a later chapter.

It has already been argued that the Government loans have, by adding to the credit resources of the Dominion, tended to encourage speculation in land values, but that in this respect they are at least no worse than the private credit agencies. The outstanding merit of the system is its insistence upon a predetermined scale of regular repayment of principal. By this insistence it regularises and in the end considerably cheapens the use of credit for productive purposes.

When all this is said, the fact remains that the great bulk of the rural credit needed in New Zealand is supplied by private agencies. This is true of the long-term credit necessary for the purchase of land, and even truer for the shorter term and floating credits used in purchasing implements and stock and for current expenditure.(49) The average farmer in New Zealand works upon overdraft, generally with the commercial organisation which handles his produce and supplies his material. Any wealth he has is for the most part represented by his equity in the land he farms. If he is a substantial financier of conservative leanings, he will use any extra returns in good times first to reduce his overdraft and then to readjust his mortgages. He will be greatly tempted, however, to extend his landholding rather than do this. The freehold farmer whose land is unencumbered by mortgages and who works upon a credit balance, while not absolutely unknown in the Dominion, is a rare bird.

Any mortgages beyond those of the State Advances Department must be sought in a market which is curiously unorganised. Investment companies, trust funds, solicitors, private individuals, some Government departments such as the Public Trust Office, insurance companies—all have mortgage money in varying amounts and on varying terms. The rate of interest is fairly well based upon bank rates; but the margin of security varies with individual judgment. The term of rural loans is usually short—from three to five years—and the expenses of renewing the loans are heavy. There is therefore solid ground for the efforts made in recent years to provide some more effective organisation of rural credit.

An agitation arose among the farming community immediately after the drastic fall in export prices of the season 1920–1. The demand was for more credit. The credit stringency in the slump period was very real, and the demand that the Government should provide some way of relief was very human. The fact remains, however, that the main cause of the farmers' troubles was too much rather than too little credit, and while a further extension of loans would undoubtedly have relieved a difficult situation, it would have been at the cost of greater difficulties later on.

The first result of the agitation was the passing of the Rural Credit Associations Act, 1922, a measure which did little to satisfy the farming community.

Under it, any association of not less than ten persons may be formed, and then proceed to work between the banks and the farmers, in the manner of a loan and finance company. Provision is made for deposits being taken from members at rates of interest to be fixed, and the association may borrow additional money, to be loaned out again for most of the purposes for which capital is required on farms. Members of the association are to be jointly and severally liable for the whole of the liabilities of the association. Within its limits the Act might possibly have proved a useful addition to the credit machinery of the country, but the maximum loan any member may obtain is £500, and this in itself indicates how little likely the Act was to help the particular trouble in which farmers found themselves during the slump. Actually it has been a dead-letter. The principle of joint and several security in itself is a drastic limitation upon the extension of credit by means of the new associations.(50)

The agitation continued, and in 1924 a political crisis was shelved only by the appointment of a Royal Commission to investigate the problem. The commissioners included the chief protagonist of the agitation, a prominent banker, and the retiring head of the Treasury. After a world-tour a voluminous report was produced(51); but in the meantime prices had improved and the opinions of the commissioners were somewhat chastened also by a realisation of the fact that nowhere in their travels had they found rural credit as cheap or as abundant as in New Zealand. The net result of their recommendations was the Rural Advances Act, 1926, constituting a new branch of the State Advances Department, with power to raise funds by the issue of bonds, stock, or other securities, and to apply the proceeds to rural loans on first mortgage.(52) The limits within which loans may be granted are somewhat more liberal, but in all essential respects the Act is merely an extension of the State advances system.

In the following year the Rural Intermediate Credit Act, 1927, was passed, creating a Dominion board of seven members, including the Public Trustee. This board also has power to issue debentures and may utilise grants from the Consolidated Fund. It works through district boards in advancing, to co-operative credit associations of not less than twenty members, limited short-term loans upon approved security, such as live stock or farm produce.

In addition, the Bank of New Zealand was empowered by legislation in 1926 to create, by the issue of debentures, a Long Term Mortgage Fund, to be utilised solely for the purpose of making advances on first mortgage of freehold or leasehold lands.(53) In this way a credit foncier department is created separate from but under the same management as the deposit business of the Bank.

It is obviously too soon to test the efficacy of any or all of these expedients. They have been evolved as a result of a particular credit situation and are essentially conservative. From them may well come some improvement in the long-term organisation of rural credit, but they will do little or nothing to relieve the immediate stringency. Schemes for co-operative credit, including the rural intermediate credit associations provided for in the Act of 1927, assume a degree of permanence in farming and landholding which has not hitherto been exhibited in New Zealand.

Of these various measures only the intermediate credit associations even approach the most awkward and extensive part of the problem—namely, the situation created by the excessive loans of commercial institutions in the boom period. The most usual, almost the inevitable, method by which a New Zealand farmer purchases stock and operates his holding is by negotiation through one of the various agency companies. These are in some cases quasi-co-operative concerns, in others private proprietary companies. Their business is a combination of merchandising and banking. They buy materials for their clients, and in the case of the quasi-co-operatives, conduct extensive retail selling to the general public also. On the other hand, they handle their clients' produce on commission. Inevitably competition forces them into financing prospective purchasers. Every such concern has a real estate department, and in addition the number of specialised land agents in a boom period is legion. After the war, and in every similar boom period, farms were bought on a minimum equity, so that not only the bulk of the purchase-money for the land but the credit required for stock, implements, current expenses, even household expenses, was necessarily made available by the agency firms. For every subsequent purchase made, the farmer draws a cheque on his overdraft. The extension of credit caused in this way during the boom has been a principal cause of the economic difficulties of the Dominion in the years since 1920.

In normal times it is possible that this system is as workable as any that can be devised for providing independent freehold farmers with short-term credit. It has many advantages of flexibility and of practical judgment by expert farm financiers, and it has certainly provided an abundant volume of comparatively cheap credit with a minimum of restrictions. Any more restricted system would involve a degree of financial discipline which the average New Zealand farmer would quickly resent. When all is said and done, the chief reason for the excessive issues of credit in boom periods is to be found in the demands of the farmers themselves. It is true that competition is keen between land agents and agency companies. It is equally true that the public interest demands earlier restrictions of credit issues by the joint-stock banks and perhaps more effective public control by some such means as a heavy licence fee upon the operation of land agents. Banking legislation might also be devised to limit the powers of the agency companies to act as deposit bankers without assuming any of the ordinary responsibilities of bankers in regard to reserves and liquid assets. But even if all these precautions were taken, they would probably avail little to prevent the small farmers from becoming the victims of their own cupidity in a time of rapidly rising prices and land values.

Adventures in Agrarian Socialism

The various post-war extensions of Governmental activities into the field of export marketing form the most characteristic recent expression of the opportunist use of the powers of the State in New Zealand, and of the readiness with which those powers are invoked in support of sectional interests. There had been few significant extensions of State enterprise in the industrial and financial fields during the preceding twenty years.(54) Any tendency towards State Socialism as a general policy had long since disappeared and the labour influence, which was largely responsible for the earlier experiments, had been in active opposition to the Government of the day, at least since 1906. The recent control and marketing experiments, as well as the credit legislation outlined in the preceding section, reflect the political power of the small farmer. They offer the clearest possible illustration of legislation in the supposed interest of an economic group. While the Labour Party supported them on general principles the initiative came directly from farmers who were faced with a temporary economic situation of great difficulty, and therefore brought pressure to bear upon the Government to find a way out.

The background both of the economic difficulty and of the

idea of State intervention is to be found in the war commandeer of primary products. For five export seasons, beginning with 1915–16, the chief products of New Zealand were bought by the Imperial Government Supplies Department. (55) This voluntary commandeer included in its scope wool, frozen meat, cheese, sheep-skins, butter, scheelite, glaxo (a dried-milk preparation), condensed milk, rabbits, hides, and calf-skins. It involved regulation not only of exports, but of supplies to the local market. In the case of butter it led to an "equalisation fund", by which the proceeds of an export-tax were used to keep down the price of butter in New Zealand. (56) The organisation of the commandeer was effective largely because of the patriotic spirit with which the merchants as well as the growers co-operated in its administration. Such co-operation rested also upon the fact that everyone concerned was getting larger rewards from the constantly advancing prices which accompanied war inflation of the currency. There is little exaggeration in the statement made at the time that the operations of this Department saved New Zealand from the risk of bankruptcy early in the war.

The various commandeers, with the exception of butter, ended prior to the season 1920–1. This first year of uncontrolled marketing saw a disastrous fall of prices, and the farmers not unnaturally associated boom conditions with control and depression with the speculative operations of free marketing. The slump was primarily due to the general contraction of credit in every country following the crisis in Japan in 1919, and the action of the Federal Reserve Board in the United States in 1920. It is difficult to imagine how it could have been wholly avoided. The dairy industry, partly owing to the continuance of the commandeer, did not slump till the season 1921–2, but when it, too, faced a drastic fall in prices the farmers were convinced of the necessity for concerted action to stave off the worst effects of the crisis.

The need for some measures of temporary control was obvious enough, if only because of the accumulation of stocks which still remained in the hands of the Department of Imperial Government Supplies. A quantity of wool considerably greater than a season's clip had been bought but not used. The prospective liberation of these stocks, together with the necessity of disposing of a considerable unsold portion of the 1920–1 wool-clip, hung over the market, and there were the most gloomy predictions of depression extending for years ahead. Nearly all of these predictions failed to take into account the rapid recovery of manufacturing demand in Europe, by which the length of the depression was fortunately reduced. The formation, in January 1921, of the British Australian Wool Realisation Association (Bawra) Ltd. was primarily an Australian matter, but the new organisation took over 772,943 bales of New Zealand wool.(57) It was faced, in the season 1921–2, with New Zealand stocks still on hand amounting to 720,000 bales. These were augmented by a further 200,000 bales unsold from the previous season and the wool-clip of the year, estimated at 550,000 bales. The successful marketing of these accumulations was a great achievement, even aided as it was by a remarkable recovery of the market. Further depressions in prices in the years 1925 and 1926 hindered the complete realisation of the stocks until the season 1927–8.

As the main activities of Bawra drew to a close its controller, Sir John Higgins, laid a scheme for permanent organisation before a large and fully representative meeting of wool-growers and merchants at Melbourne in December 1922. Despite his presentation of prospective advantages and economies in marketing practice, the meeting without discussion summarily rejected the whole project. The wool industry, therefore, has reverted completely to its highly individualistic and competitive organisation.

The New Zealand farmers, however, particularly the smaller dairy-farmers, persisted with the notion of reorganising their marketing arrangements. In the session of 1921–2 a Meat Export Control Act was passed, setting up a board, to be elected by the meat exporters, and giving that board the widest powers of control over the whole export trade.(58) After the creation of the board, export was allowed only upon licence; the board was given power to negotiate rates of freight, insurance, and similar charges, to regulate marks, packages, shipment, and, if necessary, sales upon the London market. This constitutes a remarkable delegation of power, and the organisation it creates is an experiment of considerable interest, in so far as it incorporates within the State machinery organised bodies of economic producers. It is too soon yet to estimate the full importance of this step towards functional devolution. At least one early incident indicated the far-reaching possibilities of the change. The meat-freezing industry was very much overcapitalised during the war and post-war boom, and a good deal of readjustment has been necessary after the slump. The Meat Board refused an export licence and thereby stopped the sale of a freezing-works to a company which it deemed to be a subsidiary of the American meat trust. A former refusal of the Government to grant an export licence became an international incident, in that Washington addressed enquiries to London upon the subject, and, while of comparatively minor importance, it is sufficient to indicate the wide extent and potential importance of the administrative powers conferred upon this sectional body. (59)

The political import of this development has not attracted as much attention and criticism as the possibility of far-reaching economic innovations in marketing. The political aspect of the experiment, however, may well appear the more important to future students of the subject. This probability is rendered greater by the fact that in practice the Meat Board has avoided the dangerous experiment of "absolute control". From the first it has been influenced by the large sheep-owners and the other large-scale interests involved. It has therefore eschewed any attempt to devise a wholly new system of marketing, but has preferred to negotiate with and work through existing mercantile agencies. A large part of its work has consisted in removing competitive anomalies such as the multiplicity of trade-marks and brands, the elimination of small lots, the improvement of grading, loading and discharging cargoes. In all these respects it can act more directly and with more initiative than the Department of Agriculture. The question of overlapping is bound to arise in the future, and it may well be that this new organisation, which is so much more directly responsible to the farmers, may take over many of the functions now discharged by the Department. The way seems clear for this development along guild rather than State Socialist lines.

The greatest claims made so far by the Board are that it has succeeded in regulating shipments over the year, so as to avoid glutting the London market. Thereby it claims to have reduced the range of speculation. It has also negotiated general rates of freight, insurance, railway charges, unlading and storage charges in London, and freezing charges. The claim is made that these reductions are equivalent to 5s. 5d. on every sheep, 3s. 11d. on every lamb, 60s. 7d. on a bullock, and 9s. 6d. on every pig exported.(60) Granting the possibility of some exaggeration in these estimates, and the fact that reductions would probably have come in any case with falling prices, it is probable that the Board has rendered service at this point. Its potentialities in promoting greater production, higher quality, and better organisation of the industry within New Zealand are as yet undeveloped; but they are much greater than the gains possible from reducing intermediate costs of this nature.

The history of the Dairy Produce Export Control Board has been far more chequered. The Board was brought into existence by a poll of the producers under an enabling Act passed in 1923. Many of its first members, including the chairman, had committed themselves to a policy of absolute control and had talked very freely, both about the "iniquitous" speculation of the London traders and about their intention to "cut the middlemen out" by a system of regulated sales in London. The Board, as a whole, reflected the lack of business experience general among its constituency. The whole theory of its operations sprang from the delusion that the troubles of the dairy-farmers were not due to their own rash land speculations, but to a bad marketing system. The established success of the co-operative method in butter and cheese production gave support to the theory of co-operative marketing. Many grotesque calculations were current of the extent to which speculators on the London market were robbing the New Zealand producers.

The policy of absolute control became effective during the export season 1926–7. Unfortunately it met a bad market owing to economic conditions in Britain, and it was faced also with the undisguised hostility, amounting to a boycott, of the London traders. In the meantime opposition among the dairy-farmers themselves, many of whom had always been fearful of absolute control, developed to such a degree that an amending Act changed the basis of representation in 1926 from the number of suppliers to the number of tons produced in a factory. Under the new regulations elections changed the composition of the Board, and in face of the hostility of the merchants both in London and in New Zealand the Board abandoned its heroic policy and reverted to the same routine functions as those developed by the Meat Board. The most awkward legacy of its experiment is the loss of good will on the part of the traders and to some extent of the consumers in Great Britain. There are some indications that this has taken a permanent form by the diversion of capital into the promotion of alternative sources of supply such as Canada.

The remaining experiments in marketing set up under the Fruit Control Act, 1924, the Honey Export Control Act of the same year, and the Kauri Gum Control Act, 1925, are of minor importance.(61) Wheat-growing, now almost wholly a domestic industry, was placed under Governmental control and guarantee in the post-war period, and in 1927 extracted from the Government increased protective duties on a sliding scale.(62) The dubious economics of this particular form of Governmental interference cannot be expected to stabilise an already disturbed industry.

At the present time, therefore, it seems very clear that freehold farming in New Zealand has resulted in economic problems of considerable magnitude. Land monopoly is no longer a main cause of difficulty, though one still hears the old slogans re-echoed. The real problems of readjustment in this period of falling prices are those which have been created by the over-optimism of the small farmers in their speculative land transactions. It is true that the fictitious increase in prosperity based on boom prices was reflected in extravagance and laxity in many other directions, particularly in increased taxation and other overhead costs, and that there is a great deal of readjustment necessary in many departments of economic life. It is evident also that the farmers have turned desperately to agitations for rural credit and improved marketing largely in the quest for relief from their own involved finance. It will be seen in a later chapter, also, that much of their agitation against the

Arbitration Court is driven by this same desire to find an external cause for their misfortune. One is tempted to quote the realist, Cassius, who pointed out to Brutus the fallacy of blaming the stars when the cause of his misfortunes lay nearer home.

CHAPTER IX

BORROWING FOR DEVELOPMENT

Opening Up the Country

The construction of roads, railways, bridges, and other means of communication is one of the major tasks confronting the pioneers of settlement in every new country. In New Zealand this task was undertaken almost of necessity by the State. It is conceivable that private enterprise might have been induced to undertake certain portions of it, such as the construction of railways in suitable localities. There can be no doubt, however, that development would have been greatly delayed, and would have taken a different course, if transport and communication had awaited the initiative of private capital. There are good grounds also for believing that in the long run private enterprise would have been more costly to the community as a whole. New Zealand is a very difficult engineering country. It has few stretches of open plain. Most of the land is broken by rough mountain ranges, nearly all of it was heavily forested; over large sections of the country, also, there are peculiar engineering problems, such as those of the soft "papa" country of the north island, where road metal is lacking and railway construction is subject to constant danger from slips.

These peculiarities have resulted in the railway system, and to a less extent the roading, of the Dominion involving a series of remarkable engineering feats.(1) New Zealand has the longest railway tunnel in the British Empire, as well as a double spiral and a gradient so steep that it requires specially constructed locomotives using a centre rack rail. The great bulk of the system, in the north island particularly, is built up of curves, gradients, and tunnels in disconcerting succession. The cost has in consequence been heavy, both because of the difficulties themselves and because they have involved a high standard of heavy construction. It is very improbable that private enterprise would have persisted, as State enterprise has done, in opening up the country in accordance with a simple and unified scheme built round the trunk lines which run north to south in both islands.

This continuity and unified planning of construction is a

definite advantage resulting from Governmental construction, not only of railways, but of other public works also. It is easy to point out aberrations from the general scheme; but it is broadly true to say that the Government engineers have planned simple effective national systems of surveys, telegraphs, telephones, and hydro-electric works, and are now devising an effective system of main highways. The hydro-electric construction of recent years illustrates this advantage very well. Where private enterprise would have pursued the line of immediate profit, the public service has planned an integrated system whereby the various undertakings are co-ordinated into what will eventually be linked up into a connected chain of power units in each island. (2) There are few persons in New Zealand who remain unconvinced of the wisdom of public control and planning of such important social monopolies.

Moreover, public enterprise, in following this general planning rather than the lure of immediate profit, has contributed greatly to the opening up of the country. In doing so it has sometimes been more costly than a more narrowly conceived policy might have been; but in the long run it has resulted in great gains to the community as a whole. On the other hand, it has saved the Dominion from domination by great vested interests in control of essential services. Not only construction policies, but freight and passenger rates, and indeed all management decisions, have been made primarily on grounds of public rather than sectional interest. There has been political log-rolling, but there are no railway companies to dominate politics. Mistakes have been made in plenty, rates have been fixed for political reasons; but there is no problem of rebates or concessions to interlocking economic interests.

Reasons such as these make the possibility of private ownership of public utilities seem remote, almost fantastic. But it must be admitted that they are largely afterthoughts. The primary reason why public opinion forced the State into such economic activities was the lack of any practical alternative. The settlers were not content to wait until sufficient private capital should have accumulated within New Zealand itself. Nor were they willing to yield the control of their economic destinies to outside capitalists by granting large areas of land, as was done in the United States and Canada. The two experiments in this direction were not reassuring. In the case of the Midland Railway Company the Government had eventually to take over the contract and with it the land grant.(3) The Wellington-Manawatu Company was more successful. Its line was completed, and its land was sold profitably; but until its purchase in 1908 it remained an obvious complication in the trunk line system of the north island.(4) These two experiments have reinforced the conclusions which the settlers drew from the experiences of Great Britain and the United States in private construction of railroads.

To recount the salient features of road, railway, telegraphic and public works construction would be to sketch the economic history of New Zealand from the angle of transport facilities. The aspect of that construction which concerns us here is its connection with the public finance of the Dominion. It must suffice, therefore, to point out that until the inauguration of Vogel's national policy of public works and immigration the opening up of the country was largely the concern of the provincial assemblies and local bodies. The initiation of Vogel's policy quickly raised the issue of local or national control, an issue which within six years caused the complete destruction of the provincial system. Local bodies retained much of the responsibility for roads, and in later years have greatly extended the construction of such public works as harbours, tramways, gasworks, and electric-lighting systems, which are primarily matters of local concern.(5) The great national services, however—railways, telegraphs, telephones, education, electric-power stations, and in more recent years highways for motor transport—have become a function of the Central Government. The Department of Public Works is therefore of first-rate importance, and its activities have always occupied much of the attention of Parliament. The "roads and bridges" member is, in fact, the principal type of Parliamentarian, and acts as advocate-in-chief for the needs of his district. It is an accepted practice that the responsible Ministers of the Crown always notify the members concerned of any local requests, deputations, or grants.

Since public works were so largely provincial concerns before 1870 it is natural to find that the richer south island provinces got a long start in the construction of roads and public buildings.

The problems of road construction were simpler in the open plains of Canterbury and the downs of Otago. The preponderance of population in these provinces, when the Vogel scheme of developing public works and immigration was put forward, enabled them to get the lion's share also of the borrowed money. By 1890, therefore, they were comparatively well provided with roads and railways. Much of the construction of public works in this period was based on over-optimistic expectations of rapid economic progress. Many of the branch lines which connect up with the main trunk line between Christchurch and Dunedin have never paid interest on their construction costs. They provide the best illustration in New Zealand of the fact that premature opening up of the country by public works may retard its progress for a long period.

The economic burden caused by this premature development might have been considerably greater if the onset of depression in 1879 had not caused more sober reconsideration of schemes already authorised. The outstanding example of this was the authorisation of the central line which was to connect up the back-country of Canterbury from Oxford to Temuka. Altogether there remain 162 miles of line in Canterbury and Otago authorised in 1879 for which no money has ever been voted.(6) This was the remnant of the boom proposals in regard to which better judgment prevailed when the slump began. It would have saved the railway system a considerable burden of unprofitable construction if other proposals had similarly lapsed.

During the depression of the eighties, and indeed throughout the whole period of railway development, there have been heavy losses also from the system of piecemeal construction. Large amounts of capital have been locked up in uncompleted works, while parochial rivalries have constantly prevented any effort to concentrate upon particular lines so as to get them into profitable usage at an early date. The outstanding example is again to be found in the south island, but it is merely an extreme case illustrating the general rule. The Midland line from Christchurch through the Southern Alps to Greymouth was begun in 1886 and not completed till 1924. The construction involved building a five-mile tunnel, besides difficult viaducts and similar works; but even allowing for this and for the fact that private contractors held up progress till 1895, the length of time taken was hopelessly uneconomical.(7)

By the year 1908, when the north island main trunk line was completed, the main railway system was practically laid down. Since the financial year 1908–9 only 490 miles have been added to the 2,674 then in existence. Naturally enough the greater part of this recent construction has been in the north island, where economic development was proceeding so much more rapidly. It is obvious that the expenditure of public money has in turn accelerated that development, as it did in the south island in earlier periods. Provincial jealousies have always been a source of trouble to Government officials and Ministers; but a detached analysis of the situation will show that public expenditure depends upon the electorate, and that population shifts in accordance with economic opportunity, so that it is broadly true that public works are usually being pushed ahead most rapidly in the areas where they are most needed. Revenue returns show convincingly the financial importance of north island development in recent years. This is as true, though not as easily demonstrable, of other public works as it is of railways.

A glance at any public works statement as it is presented to Parliament every year will show the very unusual variety of expenditure controlled by the Public Works Department. Approximately half the expenditure from the general funds of the Department has been made upon railway construction, while 16 per cent. has gone to the building of roads. The remainder is spread over such purposes as public buildings, telegraphs, land purchases, departmental working expenses, loan charges, and a wide variety of subsidiary charges.(8) In addition to the £101 millions spent from this fund in the years 1870–1927, there must be reckoned the considerable amounts expended by local bodies and the expenditure of the Central Government upon hydro-electric undertakings. Of the moneys expended from the General Purposes Account, 85 per cent. was borrowed, and only 15 per cent. was raised by taxation. The great bulk of public works construction has depended, therefore, upon public borrowing.

This is even truer of the Governmental expenditure intended to encourage closer settlement, practically all of which has been provided from borrowed money. At March 31, 1927,

£25·5 millions of the public debt was due to expenditure on land settlement and forests, in addition to £19·3 millions on account of advances to settlers. (9) If these amounts are added to the money spent by the Public Works Department and the assets of the local bodies, as well as expenditure on hydro-electric undertakings, the construction of public works and advances of a developmental nature will be seen to have cost New Zealand at least £208 millions since 1870. (10) Of this total, approximately £195 millions were borrowed. The financial result of this public works policy is therefore a matter of considerable importance.

The Growth of Indebtedness

Together with the public assets of the provinces, the Central Government in 1876 assumed their liabilities, including the provincial debts, which were very unevenly distributed and remain to this day a subject of grievance in certain provincial districts. Before 1870 the public debt, swollen by the substantial sum of £2,357,000 incurred on account of the Maori wars, amounted to £4,543,316. In addition, the provincial councils owed £3,298,575. (11) Besides the sums spent from loan money upon public works there was a substantial amount not easily ascertainable which had been derived from revenue, especially from land sales. The receipts from the sale of the national estate were mostly reinvested in roads and similar public works.

The main outlines of the Vogel period have already been sketched, and need not be recapitulated here. By 1880 the gross public debt had grown to almost £24 millions. The expenditure upon public works continued to be heavy throughout the eighties, so that by 1891, when the Liberal-Labour Government took office, the total had reached £38·8 millions. (12) The position of the public debt at this time may be seen in the following table (p. 276).

Ballance took office in 1891 pledged to a non-borrowing policy. It was not likely that this policy would be adhered to for long, but in the ten years following, less than ten million pounds were added to the net public debt. Thereafter there was some tendency towards expansion of borrowing, which was warranted by the increased prosperity which had come with rising prices. There was, however, no marked extension of borrowing for developmental purposes until Sir Joseph Ward took office as Premier after Seddon's death in 1906. The political situation at that time was uncertain, and the increased expenditure of borrowed money was probably inevitable. It is, however, worth noticing that the check to productivity mentioned in a previous chapter should have set in soon after the resumption of freer borrowing policies.(13) The advent of the European War necessitated much heavier borrowing still, and this was continued into the post-war boom. The table opposite, therefore, shows the position of the public debt at these crucial dates.

EXPENDITURE OF THE PUBLIC LOANS BEFORE 1891

	Millions.	Millions.	Per Cent.
Directly Reproductive—	£	£	
Railways	14·6	—	—
Telegraphs and telephones	0·8	—	—
Lighthouses and harbours	0·5	15·8	41
Investments—			
Purchase of Native lands	1·5	—	—
Loans to local bodies	0·3	1·9	5
Indirectly Productive—			
Roads, bridges, etc.	5·1	—	—
Immigration	2·5	—	—
Development of gold- and coal-mines	0·6	8·1	21
Unproductive—			
Public buildings	1·8	—	—
Maori war	2·4	—	—
Defence	1·6	—	—
Deficiencies in revenue, loan expenses, etc.	7·2	13·0	33
Total	—	38·8	100

The outstanding fact revealed in these statistics is the great growth of the unproductive debt because of the borrowing for war purposes between 1914 and 1918. Apart from this obvious fact there are several features of the table which deserve notice. The first is the very great increase of expenditure in the post-war period on public works of various kinds. Some part of this increase was due to the slowing up of public works

ALLOCATION OF THE PUBLIC DEBT OF NEW ZEALAND, 1891–1927 (14)
(*In millions*)

Class of Expenditure.	1891.	1906.	1914.	1919.	1927.
Productive Works—	£	£	£	£	£
Railways	14·6	20·4	28·4	32·0	50·3
Telegraphs, etc.	0·8	1·1	2·2	3·3	7·8
Hydro-electric power ..	—	—	0·2	0·5	6·0
Lighthouses and harbours ..	0·5	0·5	0·6	0·7	1·1
Miscellaneous	—	0·2	0·5	0·5	2·4
Total	15·8	22·2	31·9	37·0	67·6
Per cent.	41	36	34	21	28
Land Settlements and Forests—					
Land for settlement ..	—	5·0	7·2	8·3	8·6
Discharged soldier settlement	—	—	—	0·9	9·7
Native land settlement ..	—	—	0·9	2·1	3·9
Purchase of Native lands ..	1·5	2·2	2·7	2·7	1·9
Miscellaneous	—	—	0·4	0·6	1·4
Total	1·5	7·2	11·2	14·6	25·5
Per cent.	4	12	12	8	10
Investments—					
Advances to settlers ..	—	3·4	8·7	9·3	19·3
Advances to workers ..	—	—	2·5	2·4	8·1
Loans and advances to local bodies	0·3	2·5	6·1	6·3	6·3
Miscellaneous	—	1·0	1·8	2·4	2·3
Total	0·3	6·9	19·1	20·4	36·0
Per cent.	1	11	20	12	15
Indirectly Productive—					
Roads and bridges	5·1	6·1	8·1	9·5	16·0
Immigration	2·5	2·5	2·5	2·5	2·8
Irrigation, etc.	—	—	—	—	1·5
Miscellaneous	0·6	0·8	0·9	1·0	1·7
Total	8·2	9·4	11·5	13·0	22·0
Per cent.	21	15	12	7	9
Unproductive—					
War and defence	4·0	4·3	6·4	74·6	79·7
Public buildings	1·8	4·6	6·1	7·7	11·9
Revenue deficiencies ..	7·2*	7·6*	8·5*	8·7*	3·0
Total	13·0	16·5	21·0	91·0	94·6
Per cent.	33	26	22	52	38
Grand totals	38·8	62·2	94·8†	176·1	245·9

* Includes loan expenses distributed in latest returns to the various accounts.

† Excluding £4,976,000 raised in 1913–14 for redemption of loans falling due early in 1914–15.

construction during the war, but a great deal of it reflects the boom conditions of the post-war period. Every item in the first category of expenditure—that on productive works—is greatly swollen. The totals were enlarged by the fact that this was a period of very high prices, one of the most costly periods during which public works could have been undertaken.

The only significant increase in the next category is the comparatively large sum devoted to settling returned soldiers on the land. If this item is taken logically with the expenditure on advances to settlers and advances to workers, it will be seen that the public debt increased on these accounts from £12·6 millions to £37·1 millions in the seven years 1919–26. Here is the most important cause of the post-war land boom. If to the borrowings for advances are added the large sums derived from the accumulated surpluses of war taxation which were used for the same purposes, it is evident that very large sums of credit were diverted by Government policy to rural investment immediately after the war. The large borrowings and expenditure from revenue for public works construction also pushed the level of costs higher than it might have been, and contributed indirectly to the further enhancement of land values. The post-war period was a time of expanding currency and inflated credit in almost every country. The credit boom in Great Britain caused very high prices in New Zealand's chief export market. The only way in which the extra gains of such prices could be transferred to New Zealand was by an expansion of credit within the Dominion.(15) In any case, therefore, the years following 1918 would have seen rising prices, wages, and land values in New Zealand. Into this situation, however, the Government injected the most vigorous borrowing policy since the days of Vogel. Between 1919 and 1927 the public debt increased by almost £70 millions. In addition a large surplus of revenue accumulated in the war and post-war years, amounting approximately to £25 millions up to the last year of large surpluses (1920–1), was expended mainly in advances to returned soldiers. This extra Governmental expenditure came on top of an ordinary budget approximately double pre-war figures. Even when full allowance is made for the needs of an increasing population, for the arrears of repairs and new construction to be made up after the war, and for higher levels of prices, it is clear that there was a very considerable expansion of Governmental expenditure. The slump of 1920–1 brought a check, and after the reconstruction of the Government in 1925 a firmer Treasury control was evident; but commitments had been accepted which made it difficult to reduce expenditure and borrowing. Such reduction and control as there was caused political difficulty, and contributed to the unpopularity of the Government evidenced in the elections of 1928. It is significant that the Liberal Party was galvanised into new life and gained increased popular support on what was essentially a borrowing policy. This circumstance reinforces the abundant evidence that borrowing, like all other policies tending to the enhancement of land values, is firmly rooted in popular support.

Before one can appreciate the full extent of Governmental expenditure in this post-war period the local body statistics must be added to the national figures of increased debt, accumulated surplus, and expenditure from taxation. There was a notable increase, also, both in local body borrowings and in rates. The following table gives a graphic summary of the great extent to which the public-purse strings were unloosed in the post-war boom.

PUBLIC EXPENDITURE IN THE POST-WAR BOOM(16)

(*In millions*)

Year ending March 31st.	Increase in Net Public Debt.	Total of Accumulated Surplus.	Total Expenditure from Consolidated Fund.	Expenditure from Public Works Fund.	Increase in Local Body Debt.	Local Body Expenditures.
	£	£	£	£	£	£
1914	4·2	0·4	11·8	2·8	1·4	6·8
1919	24·3	15·2	18·7	1·4	0·4	7·3
1920	23·8	17·5	23·8	2·2	2·0	10·9
1921	3·6	8·6	28·1	3·7	1·6	12·8
1922	10·7	7·5	28·5	6·9	4·1	15·1
1923	1·2*	5·6	26·3	4·7	5·8	15·7
1924	1·6	5·0	26·1	4·7	3·0	16·5
1925	5·7	4·2	27·4	5·5	6·6	19·4
1926	22·3†	4·4	23·6	5·9	6·0	20·9
1927	6·8	3·7	24·4	5·5	4·6	21·7

* Decrease.

† Caused by transfer of accrued sinking funds to Public Debt Redemption Fund.

It is not possible to add the amounts of this table either horizontally or vertically, but the individual items are in themselves sufficient to show the remarkable increases in public expenditure after the war. Since the relations between the various accounts which involve overlapping and double-counting remained much the same throughout the period, it is legitimate to calculate that public expenditure increased between 1914 and 1920 roughly in the proportion of 27·0 to 75·0. There was some readjustment of the national accounts in the year 1926–7 which had the effect of slightly swelling the totals of the Consolidated Fund; but the figure corresponding to those quoted above is 64, and is not greatly overestimated. Increase of population and higher levels of prices need to be taken into account, but if corrections are made for them the figures show an increase in the volume of public expenditure amounting to 58 per cent. between 1914 and 1920, and reduced to 27 per cent. by 1927.(17) It may reasonably be argued, therefore, that beyond increases to meet the needs of a greater population and higher prices, Governmental expenditure in 1920 was half as much again, and in 1927 still remained 25 per cent. greater than in the pre-war period.

This consists only in part of expenditure from borrowings, and a good deal of the borrowing was from local as distinct from overseas sources. In 1913–14 the proportion of the public debt held overseas was 83 per cent.; by 1918–19 the flotation of local war loans had reduced this proportion to 56 per cent., at which figure it has since remained. This means that at March 31, 1927, £109·3 millions of the public debt was held in New Zealand.(18)

It is comparatively easy, therefore, to demonstrate that the increase of public expenditure in New Zealand is primarily a matter of local consideration. Much of it has come from heavier taxation, another large part from increased local borrowing, and the remainder from overseas loans. There is no evidence of anxiety on the part of overseas investors concerning the security of their loans. New Zealand financiers have been careful to meet the requirements of the London Money Market in regard to information in their loan prospectuses. Resort is had to overseas borrowing in comparatively moderate degree, and consequently the credit of the Dominion stands enviably high. Loans are easily floated at favourable prices, and this fact in itself is sufficient to negative the idea that the financial authorities in London have any qualms about lending to the Dominion.

This is true, even though provisions for repaying the public loans are always being tinkered with. In 1879–80 the sinking funds had accrued to £1,805,231, which was 7½ per cent. of the total debt. In that year, however, they were reduced, and after slow growth they were again raided from time to time until they reached their lowest point, £751,932, less than 2 per cent. of the total debt, in 1894–5. Thereafter they increased slowly until 1910, when they were £1,503,225, which was almost exactly 2 per cent. of the outstanding debt. In that year Sir Joseph Ward introduced his Public Debt Extinction Act, by which a payment was made each year of "an amount equal to the sum which, if invested at compound interest at 4 per cent. per annum for seventy-five years, would repay the whole of the public debt as at the preceding March 31st".(19) As a result of this Act the sinking funds grew by 1925 to £13,462,839, or almost 6 per cent. of the outstanding debt. The Repayment of the Public Debt Act, 1925, substituted a method of purchasing securities at advantageous periods.(20) Under this Act the greater part of the existing sinking funds were transferred to a capital fund to be held intact, but not increased. The interest on this fund, which amounted on March 31, 1927, to £24·7 millions, is used to provide part of the moneys required each year for debt redemption. These are "equal to ½ per cent. of the debt affected as at March 31st, plus ½ per cent. of the total amount previously repaid or redeemed under the provisions of the Act. To this is added a sum equal to interest at 3½ per cent. per annum on the debt paid off under the scheme." By this means the total debt affected (£174 millions in 1927) will, if the scheme is adhered to, be repaid in sixty years. The catch in the scheme lies obviously in the gradually increasing amounts which must be provided as the debt is paid off. The theory is that the interest saved will be devoted to further repayment, but future Finance Ministers will be tempted to use the savings in other ways and find ingenious alternative schemes of repayment in a still more distant future.

The remaining portions of the debt are provided for in other ways. The large advances accounts have their own internal reserves, the hydro-electric undertakings have been financed on a repayment basis, and the war debt owing to the British Government was funded on an annuity basis which will extinguish the liability by 1959. Nominally, therefore, there are repayment provisions for the whole debt. If they are not interfered with, the existing debt will be extinguished in due course, but past experience does not make one optimistic of repayment keeping pace with new borrowings. The virtues of compound interest upon which sinking funds are based are mainly prospective. The particular method of repayment matters little, providing the community is willing to live within its income.

The local bodies are by statute required to maintain adequate sinking funds, usually on a thirty-year basis. This means that each generation pays for its own expenditures, and the local governing authorities, unlike the Central Parliament, cannot seek relief by postponements. As sinking fund payments accumulate, the rates must be adequate to meet them. Such an expansion of local services as that which has been proceeding since the war brings, therefore, an early and cumulative increase in local taxation. (21)

The "Stimulus" of Borrowing

While it is clear that the overseas investor in New Zealand loans has little reason to fear for the security of his investment, this fact does not in itself justify a heavy borrowing policy. Overseas investors in London are encouraged by the provision of the Colonial Stock Act, 1900, to subscribe to Dominion issues. This Act does not give any guarantee, or even stamp the approval of the British Government upon such loans, but it does place them among the securities available for trustee investment, and in so doing it opens a great fund of credit to the Dominion Governments. The relatively lower rate of interest at which such loans are floated is a most substantial form of imperial preference, far and away more valuable than tariff alteration could be. There may be grounds for arguing that the policy needs reconsideration from the point of view of British industries, but there is no reason to assume that the investor has any fear, or need have any, for the safety of his investment. Calculations of public assets or private wealth to ascertain their adequacy as security for overseas loans are hardly worth making.(22) There is no question as to the solvency of New Zealand public credit.

The more debatable aspects of Dominion borrowing concern its relation to domestic development, to the distribution of wealth within New Zealand, and to the interference with economic equilibrium which results from State advances and activities disturbing the flow of capital into the usual competitive channels. These are very real issues of domestic importance. They are demonstrated most clearly by the rapid increase in the burden of taxation. This increase is greatly swollen by the larger loans of recent years, and also by the fact that renewals of loans falling due have had to be made at higher rates of interest. The heavier departmental expenditure is also due largely to the expansion of State activities, which is mainly based on borrowed money. The tendency for taxation to increase faster than productive capacity is clearly shown in the following comparison:

INDICES OF PRODUCTION AND TAXATION, 1900–26 (23)

1913 Base = 100

	1900.	1913.	1920.	1926.
Production	55	100	173	201
State taxes	51	100	290	303
Local body taxes	40	100	175	280
Total taxation	49	100	261	297
Taxes as a percentage of production	11	13	19	19

It is usual for apologists of public borrowing to contend that, since the proportion of local loans has so largely increased in recent years, the burden of debt is much exaggerated; that interest is merely transferred within New Zealand from one individual to another. This argument has some force in respect of the burden of overseas payments and the balance of trade; but this is not a problem of real concern. It has no relevance to the real problems of borrowing which arise from the disturbances of economic equilibrium within the Dominion.

Before any attempt is made to estimate the domestic effects of the borrowing policy it is necessary to review the different categories of expenditure for which the debt has been incurred. A large portion, totalling £40 millions at March 31, 1927, is classed as Investments, mainly in the form of advances to settlers, workers, and returned soldiers. With the possible exception that further losses may be disclosed on the advances to returned soldiers, this debt is amply secured, is returning a full rate of interest, and is amply provided with reserves which are at the present time being reinvested. From the narrow financial point of view, therefore, this debt is soundly situated. It involves no net burden on the taxpayer.

On the other hand, it must be recognised that these advances have had some effect in diverting resources to rural industry. This is clearly the position in so far as sinking funds and taxation surpluses have been used. The diversion has been of relatively slight importance compared with the total of rural credit available to the farmers, but it is a definite example of administrative policy forwarding the interests of a dominant electoral group.

A good deal of the expenditure has come from overseas loans floated at comparatively low rates of interest. The use of the credit of the whole community to provide cheaper capital for small working farmers is defensible as sound economic strategy. It has brought into the Dominion a good deal of capital badly needed for development. It must be borne in mind, however, that this has contributed incidentally to the promotion of speculation in land values. The effects of borrowing for this purpose depend clearly upon the degree to which it is undertaken. In amounts that can be readily absorbed there is little doubt that the State advances policy contributes to closer settlement and greater productivity; but undue expansion of loans, as in the post-war period, accelerates the tendency to speculation and decreases productivity.

Another large section of the public debt is that incurred for the construction of public works which are expected to be directly reproductive. Railways, telegraphs, telephones, hydro-electric stations, harbours, State coal-mines, tourist resorts, come in this category. The theory is that commercial prices are charged for the services rendered, so that the loan interest is not really a net charge upon the taxpayers. Any survey of the various services undertaken by the State in New Zealand will disclose great variations in the translation of this theory into practice. It is next to impossible to sum the net cost which has fallen upon the taxpayer by reason of the failure of State enterprises to be operated on a strictly commercial basis. The nature of the public accounts made it difficult, if not impossible, until the year 1925–6 to estimate the extent to which each public service was meeting, or failing to meet, the full interest, depreciation, and repayment charges upon its capital expenditure. There is room for legitimate difference of opinion as to whether rates should be fixed on a commercial basis, or whether such services as the railways should be operated to achieve social values even at the cost of some financial loss. There is little room for difference of opinion as to the desirability of frank statement of any losses incurred in this way.

The railways offer a typical and important case of failure to achieve full commercial rates. The problem of railway rates is always a difficult one, but the peculiarities of New Zealand history and the pull of various political interests have resulted in some curious anomalies, such as the carriage of many farmers' requisites at low rates, or even free. A striking case in point is the favourable treatment accorded to dairy produce when the industry was struggling in the nineties. These low rates were carried on long after the industry had grown to be the most important in the Dominion.(24) Proposals to increase the rates would be regarded at any moment as an injustice and an economic infliction upon the dairy-farmers, who are always struggling; but the ultimate effect of low rates has obviously been to increase the value of dairy lands. Adjustments would quickly be amortised in a further fall of land values in dairying districts.

Because of such anomalies, and still more because of the provision of services for which there is insufficient commercial demand, but mainly because the railway system is saddled with heavy capital liabilities dating from the boom period of the seventies, the revenue has never really been adequate to meet all the costs of the service. For many years the aim was to return a nominal rate of 3 per cent. on the capital cost. This objective was raised to 3¾ per cent. in 1909–10; but even this higher rate was insufficient to meet the real capital charges. Though the rate of interest actually earned averaged £3 16s. 6d. in the twenty years 1908–27, the railways remained a net burden on the taxpayer, if only because quite inadequate allowances were made for depreciation, renewals, and repairs. In accordance with the recommendations of the Royal Commission of 1924 a new system of accounts was inaugurated on April 1, 1925. Under this system a Working Railways Account was established, into which all earnings are now paid and from which all payments are made, including working expenses, superannuation subsidies, and interest on capital. Interest is charged according to the actual rates payable on the various loans. In order to give the railway system a fair start it was, however, agreed that the losses on certain lines constructed in the boom of the seventies should be met by subsidies from the Consolidated Fund.(25) This heavy recurring burden on the taxpayers indicates one of the clearest possible examples of the way in which premature and misdirected expenditure from borrowed money may become a hindrance instead of a help to productivity.

Within the last three or four years there has been a definite and sustained attempt to extend this principle of commercial operation to all the public services. The Post and Telegraph Department has normally returned profits more than sufficient to pay interest on its capital, while the State Fire and Government Life and Accident Insurance Departments began operations without capital upon a Government guarantee. Another great commercial department whose activities are growing rapidly by accretion, the Public Trust Office, is similarly placed. All of these departments are disturbing factors for good or ill in the economic life of New Zealand, but they do not contribute directly to the increasing burden of taxation.

The expenditure of hydro-electric undertakings is an interesting case of State enterprise.(26) The great generating stations built and operated by the Public Works Department are soundly financed. The initial stages of these enterprises are always the most difficult. Few other industries are so clearly subject to the law of increasing returns. As demand increases and diversifies, the heavy overhead expenses are spread over a wider revenue. In New Zealand the system has been well planned so that each large station has been strategically placed to supply current for the steady and diversified demands of a large city. It is satisfactory, therefore, to find that the revenue and expenditure of the Government enterprises, allowing for full capital charges and sinking funds, were almost balanced in 1926–7. This is sound finance at such an early stage of operation.

The generation of current is, however, not the whole story. Transmission, especially in the scattered country districts, is a more costly process. Immediately after the war there was somewhat extravagant optimism concerning the possibility of supplying cheap electric energy to farmers as well as to city people. Electric power boards were set up in 1918 which now make electric supply available to 64 per cent. of the total population. These local bodies have constructed works from loan moneys after polls of the ratepayers, which in every case were carried by substantial majorities. Capital outlay is already approaching the total of £10 millions.

In the first optimistic period many schemes were advocated, and some were constructed, without due appreciation of the heavy overhead cost of reticulating country areas where the consumers are scattered and where demand is concentrated in peak loads at the milking hours of the day. It is difficult to estimate the financial results of the system of power distribution as a whole. The official statistics show at March 31, 1927, nineteen boards returning a net profit and fourteen showing losses. The total profits of £93,639 are built up very largely by the profit of £62,639 returned by the Auckland Board, which handles the city demand of Auckland. It is not possible from the table to judge the adequacy of the amounts set aside for capital charges. The total amount shown is £673,163, which is 7·15 per cent. of the capital cost. The total revenue received from the sale of electricity gives a return of 13·2 per cent. on the capital outlay, which seems hardly adequate to provide for maintenance and depreciation charges as well as interest and sinking funds. Experience shows also that maintenance increases with extension to less profitable areas and with the age of the plant. There is some ground for believing, therefore, that a number of the power boards will have difficulty in conducting their finances without recourse to subsidies from taxation.

There are individual cases in which such recourse has already been necessary. The outstanding case is that of the Southland Power Board, which began supplying current in 1925 with a capital cost of £1,558,087. The area supplied is mainly a dairying district, and the distances to be covered are long. The expenditure in 1926–7 amounted to 13·3 per cent. of the capital cost, including 7·4 per cent. capital charges. Revenue, however, fell far short, so that the Board showed a loss on the year's working of £70,287, of which £67,451 was recouped by a general rate of seven-eighths of a penny in the pound on the unimproved value of the land in the district. This is a heavy imposition, and must result in a tendency for land values to fall in the area affected.

Moreover, the power boards have had to revise their ideas of supplying cheap power. As the costs of transmission were revealed to be greater than was generally anticipated, the rates charged for current were adjusted to the commercial necessities of the enterprise. While exact estimation is difficult, the balance of evidence is that precipitate construction in a period of high costs immediately following the war may result for a time in some net loss to the community as a whole. There can be no reasonable doubt that the development of New Zealand's resources of hydro-electric energy is a justifiable economic proceeding, and that it is good business to proceed with that development by raising loans abroad. But it is equally clear that such a policy needs to be handled with caution, and that there is a very real possibility that premature development may result in impeding productivity. The facts quoted above show that this has undoubtedly occurred in certain districts where the local boards embarked on ambitious schemes which were out of relation to the real needs of their constituency. If the officers of the Public Works Department had capitulated to all the impressively staged local agitations there might have been many more such clear cases of economic loss through premature construction. As it is, there is some doubt as to the net result of the development of water-power viewed in its entirety.

Quite clearly the initiative and responsibility in this matter rests with the electorate. Where the engineers of the Department were most firmly in control, in the provision of central generating stations, the financial results are satisfactory. The losses are to be expected in the local units of administration, though it will be surprising if such losses do not cause a demand that the generating stations lower the prices at which they sell current in bulk to the power boards, thus throwing some of the financial burden on to the State.

This rapid summary of some of the main reproductive enterprises is sufficient to show that apart from indirect effects upon economic development there has been in times past a considerable net burden left upon the taxpayer in consequence of the failure of the State activities to be fully remunerative. Obviously this burden is still clearer in the expenditure upon works which are classed as indirectly productive. Roads, bridges, immigration assistance, irrigation, mining development have added £22 millions to the public debt, and in addition large sums have been expended by local bodies. None of this expenditure returns any direct revenue to the Government. The theory is that by opening up the land it increases general productivity, and so indirectly increases the revenue raised by taxation.

The last category into which the public debt is divided is the unproductive expenditure upon war and defence, revenue deficiencies, and public buildings. Here, again, both local and national expenditure are involved. However justifiable such expenditure may be on general grounds, it is clear that it results in a heavy deadweight burden upon the taxpayer.

It should be clear from this summary of the various categories of expenditure that the taxpayer carries a considerable net burden in the interest arising from unproductive and indirectly productive expenditure, and from the difference between the actual revenue and the real capital charges of reproductive services. It remains, therefore, to examine the evidence available as to the effect of this financial situation upon the productivity of the Dominion.

The table on the following page puts together the principal statistics of productivity as estimated by the Government Statistician.(27)

This official estimate of changes in productivity needs cautious interpretation. In the first place, the statistical information on which it is built must necessarily be imperfect. For this reason the total value of production is omitted in the table given below, since it is the comparability rather than the absolute amounts of production that are to be relied on. In comparing the figures from year to year it must be noted that the base year, 1910–11, was a year of normal effort following recovery from the crisis which demoralised New Zealand industry and trade in 1908–9. It is possible that the peak of productivity shown in that year is somewhat exaggerated.

NEW ZEALAND PRODUCTIVITY, 1900–26
BASE 1910–11 = 100

Year.	Production per Head.	Index of Value, 1910–11.	Wholesale Prices, 1910–11.	Index of Productive Activity, 1910–11.
	£			
1900–1	39·45	80	93	85
1905–6	42·73	86	102	85
1910–11	49·54	100	100	100
1915–16	64·45	130	136	96
1918–19	75·08	152	165	92
1919–20	81·85	165	179	92
1920–1	79·35	160	188	85
1921–2	69·58	141	174	81
1922–3	75·24	152	163	93
1923–4	79·33	160	168	95
1924–5	84·96	171	174	99
1925–6	82·85	167	171	98

There seems little reason, however, to doubt that productivity increased markedly in the years prior to 1910, that some slackening was in evidence in the years immediately before the war, and that the decline in productivity became marked in the boom period immediately following the war. There is support for these deductions in the railway statistics, which reflect general trading conditions. The tonnage of goods and live stock carried on the railways shows a larger increase between 1901 and 1911 than the Government Statistician's figures of productivity, and a still greater increase in the decade 1891 to 1901. It is noticeable that all of this increase dates from the financial year 1895–6, when prosperity and progress were assured by the favourable turn of the price-level. From that year to the year of the greatest productivity per head fifteen years later, the *per capita* tonnage of goods carried on the railways almost doubled.(28)

After 1910 there is obvious check to this increase, and it is clear that a period of productive stagnation was then masked by a rising price-level. This is even clearer when the indices of productivity begin definitely to fall in the war period. The fall was continued into the post-war boom years, and the subsequent recovery had by 1925–6 failed to bring productive efficiency per head of population back to the figures of 1910–11.

This serious decline is only revealed when the statistics are corrected to allow for the influence of rising prices and increasing population. It is significant that the trend of real wages should have suffered a check at this time, and it is very evident that the continually rising monetary values of the war and post-war period have carried New Zealand along on a wave of fictitious prosperity. With lower levels of value since 1920–1 the decline in productivity has stood revealed as the chief problem confronting the Dominion.

It is not possible to estimate to what extent this decline is traceable to inflation of values due to excessive borrowing. So many factors are at work in the economic structure of the Dominion that the mere coincidence of heavier borrowing and falling productivity is not necessarily proof that the one causes the other. Both may be due, or partly due, to a common cause, such as the rising price-level reaching a point about 1910 where speculation was encouraged to an unprofitable point. The fact that a similar check to productivity appears to have taken place in Australia under somewhat different conditions should call for caution in attributing the New Zealand phenomenon to purely local causes.

The whole problem affords an interesting example of what Stamp has called "economic stimulus". The fact that productivity declined heavily in the only similar period of heavy borrowing and active speculation in New Zealand's history, the period of the Vogel boom from 1879 to 1880, leads one to suspect that there is a point beyond which an undue amount of stimulant decreases instead of increasing productivity. Economists in Australia and New Zealand have developed the theory of an "absorption point" beyond which immigration causes a disturbance of economic equilibrium. It is fairly obvious that there is a similar absorption point at which the importation of borrowed capital sets in motion forces of speculation and unsettlement which more than counteract the extra productivity to be expected from improved equipment. New Zealand has ignored that absorption point with unfortunate results in her two periods of boom, the years following 1870 and the years following 1910.

The circumstances of these periods are different, and in neither is it possible to separate the effects of excessive borrowing from the speculation induced by variations in the price-level. This is especially true of the later period during which New Zealand gained a continuous advantage from the drift of prices in favour of her producers. It is mainly for this reason that her economic position at the present time is so much sounder than it was in 1879, when a severe crisis brought a disastrous termination to a borrowing policy which had persisted through at least five years of falling prices. The similar crisis in 1920–1 followed a period in which prices had been rising, and it is only in respect of the continued borrowing after that time that the two periods are strictly comparable.

Economic interactions are so complex that it is impossible to argue with any exactness concerning the causes of the most recent decline in productivity. The farmer will point to physical causes, such as the diminishing fertility of land. Other causes may be found in labour policies, in shifting levels of commodity prices, in the extension of Governmental activity, in heavy taxation, in the growth of protected industry, and the sheltering of economic groups within the community. Every aspect of economic life and of related social policies, such as education, contributes some influence. But it seems clear that in both Australia and New Zealand there has been a marked check, and even decline, in productivity since 1910–11, both absolutely and relatively to the statistical measurements made in other countries.

It is a reasonable deduction from the economic history of New Zealand that the chief cause of this decline was land speculation induced by rising prices. There were many subsidiary causes—such as a great expansion of overhead costs, a tendency towards the development of urban industry, and a protected standard of living—and a marked increase in national and local Governmental activities. How far the increased borrowing after 1910 was cause, and how far it merely reflected the speculative temper induced by rising prices, no one can determine.

Whatever the combination of causes, it is at least clear that the combined stimuli of rising prices and cheap overseas capital caused a steady and cumulative increase in productivity between 1895 and 1910, so that the "economic stimulus" in this period fell into the class A 1, distinguished by Stamp as returning increasing or cumulative permanent gains to each dose of stimulant.(29) After 1910 the returns to larger doses fell into class B, in which increased productivity is followed by reaction. The war supervened, and the even greater doses of stimuli in the post-war period caused the returns to drop into class C 2, which shows permanent partial loss.

One further comment is necessary. Apart from the diversion of resources into other competitive channels and the loss consequent on premature and misdirected development, there arise the more subtle costs of uncertainty and variability resulting from development by spasms of boom and depression. These costs bear particularly harshly upon the classes least able to bear them. In the slump following the break of prices in 1920–1 there has been unemployment and social distress worse than any experienced for forty years. This situation is more conveniently discussed with the problems arising out of State regulation of wages by the machinery of the Arbitration Court.

It is difficult to measure the extent to which the distribution of incomes between individuals has been changed in the period of speculation. Statistics of income exist in the returns of income-tax, but their value is impaired by the fact that exemptions are numerous, and include the important farming class, except in the period 1915–23. The New Zealand system of taxing companies as if they were individuals also complicates the problem. Lorenz curves showing the degree of inequality of income among the individual taxpayers indicate clearly that there was greater inequality at the end of the post-war boom than there was before the war.(30) The heavy taxation on joint-stock companies naturally had the reverse effect, but since much of the taxation on these companies was really borne by the shareholders with moderate incomes, this proves rather than disproves the thesis. There is ample statistical evidence, therefore, to support the conclusion mentioned in another connection that there has been a tendency in recent years for a transference of wealth to the creditor classes in the community. This tendency involves a worsening of income distribution.

In view of all these facts the cautious estimate of an Australian writer may well be applied to New Zealand. After arguing that Australia was able to sustain its burden of debt with comparative ease, he concluded with the observation that

> it is, however, quite another question to suppose that it was beneficial to have incurred it or that it would be wise to increase it. The figures of national income per head for over the past sixteen years, when reduced to pre-war values, are not so encouraging as to make it certain that the large expenditure of loan moneys on development has produced corresponding benefits in production.(31)

Mr. Reeves, who combines the prestige of a bank chairman with that of a close student of New Zealand conditions, puts forward a very similar estimate of the position. In closing his review of the economic and financial condition of New Zealand in 1928 he concludes:

> It cannot be said that New Zealand as a whole is suffering from low prices, dear money, and high costs of production. So far as she is suffering at all it is from the results of dear land, heavy taxes and rates, too much public borrowing persisted in for many years, and, still more, from too much private debt.(32)

CHAPTER X

THE ECONOMIC FUNCTIONS OF GOVERNMENT

The Extent of Public Enterprise

The number of public servants in New Zealand is estimated by the Government Statistician as "the huge total of nearly 82,000".(1) This is approximately 10 per cent. of the employed population of the Dominion. Upon examination, however, the figures appear to need considerable modification and interpretation. The somewhat unfortunate epithet "huge" is apt to carry with it the implication that State activities in New Zealand are extraordinarily numerous, and perhaps undesirably so. This implication is strengthened by the attention given to State Socialist experiments by writers who have described the Liberal-Labour regime in the nineties.

Despite the confident expectations of certain visitors of Socialist leanings, New Zealand never went far in the conduct of State enterprises. There has from the foundation of the colony been a steady policy of public operation of utility services, such as railways, telegraphs, and, in more recent years, hydro-electric power. The fact that practically all the best land has passed, in three-quarters of a century, from public to private ownership has carried with it heavy obligations which have required, and still require, large numbers of public servants. In the same way the public works required for opening up a new and difficult engineering country have been extensive. New Zealand has preferred to see those works undertaken by Government engineers rather than by private contractors. In all these respects, and also in the provision of education and similar social services, democratic Governments in young countries necessarily build up large corps of public servants.

The fact has often been stressed that practically all of these functions of Government, which still account for the great majority of the public employees, were in active operation before 1890. In addition, the colony's isolation and lack of financial organisation prompted more novel extensions of State enterprise at a very early stage. There was a State bank with a monopoly of all banking functions from 1850 to 1856. This was urged upon the colonial Government by responsible officials at home, but was abandoned as soon as there was a reasonable prospect of private enterprise meeting the colony's financial needs. In 1869 the Government Life Insurance Department was authorised to begin operations in the following year. Three years later the Public Trust Office was established. For both, the precedent was cited of the Post Office Savings Bank established in England by Gladstone in 1861 and copied in New Zealand four years later. The House was unanimous in the insurance venture, and there was virtual unanimity in setting up the office of Public Trustee. The obvious necessities of the colony justified these departures, even at a time when *laissez-faire* theories were accepted as beyond criticism.

In the same way the Land Transfer Office, which does most of the conveyancing in New Zealand, was established in 1860 and greatly strengthened by the legislation of 1870. It works in with, and supports, the various departments of the Government dealing with land questions. This group of departments has always been, and still is, important in New Zealand economic life.

The construction of public works and railways on a national scale also dates from 1870, when Vogel's policy of borrowing for immigration and public works was initiated. In the same way the Education Act of 1877 took over from the province the responsibility of elementary education, and after 1885 the State provision for hospitals, mental asylums, and charitable aid was systematised and greatly extended.

The summary table opposite of the public departments and their employees clearly shows that the Governmental activities mentioned above, all of which were established early in New Zealand history for practical rather than theoretical reasons, still remain the most important functions of the State.

The so-called State Socialism of the nineties involved practically no new departure as far as State enterprise is concerned. In particular, the trading ventures in economic fields already taken up by capitalist organisation, which are generally suggested by the phrase "State Socialism", are conspicuous by their absence. Fire and accident insurance activities were added in 1901 and 1903, and a State Coal Mines Department was established in 1901. Later sections of this chapter will indicate the very restricted scope of these enterprises, which, except for minor and incidental undertakings, such as the development of tourist resorts, conclude the story of New Zealand experiments in this field. It is to certain Australian States rather than to New Zealand that one must look for experiments in State shipping services, brickworks, butchers' shops, bakeries, fisheries, etc.

PUBLIC SERVANTS IN NEW ZEALAND, 1915 AND 1925 (2)

	1915.	1925.
Railways	14,614*	17,246
Posts and telegraphs	5,958	10,384
Education	5,627*	9,845
Administrative departments ..	7,519	8,647
Public works	6,108	6,583
Defence and police	941†	2,243
Other departments	450‡	930‡
Local body employees	16,502	25,969
Total	60,000 (approx.)	81,847

* Plus an indeterminate number of temporary employees.
† Police only; numbers of military employees not given in war period.
‡ Not subject to Public Service Commissioner.

The same story can be told of New Zealand municipal activities. The provision of public utilities, such as waterworks, tramways, gasworks, electric lighting and power works, is generally regarded as a proper municipal function; but any experiments in municipal trading are jealously watched. In this respect at least New Zealand has yielded what leadership it ever had in State Socialism to Australia.

The fact is that the New Zealand colonists were forced to a reorientation of their notions of the functions of government. Empirically and entirely without conscious theory they departed from the *laissez-faire*, or "policemen", theory of the State. In their distinction between the "agenda" and "non-agenda" of economic activities suitable for State activity they were guided by political opportunism. (3) Generally speaking, they have not allowed the State to encroach upon the field of private enterprise, except in the case of public utilities, which are regarded as natural monopolies. In this case they anticipated and took a direct path to the socialisation of public utilities that is proceeding by various methods in almost every country.

The list of State departments is at first reading rather impressive; but in reality these departments encroach very little upon the important spheres of capitalist organisation. "Socialisation of the means of production, distribution, and exchange" is a conception very remote from practical politics in New Zealand. Where, as in banking, the Government has been fortuitously placed in possession of unexpected opportunities for socialisation, public opinion has approved the support and regulation of private enterprise rather than State administration.

On the other hand, successive Governments have embarked freely upon regulative policies. The elaborate labour code, State regulation of wages, a free use of the taxing system, to say nothing of legislation and regulations intended to control monopolies and other business practices which were deemed anti-social—in fact, the whole trend of New Zealand legislation is aimed at the regulation rather than the supplanting of capitalist enterprise.

In addition, New Zealand has deliberately embarked upon extensive and expensive social welfare activities. Education, hospital and charitable aid systems, pensions, child welfare activities, demand an increasing number of public employees.

In a period of increased prosperity, such as followed the favourable turn of prices in 1895, it is natural also to find some tendency towards the increase of Govermental services, and some slackness in their performance. This is especially true of the local governing bodies. The people of New Zealand have come to expect better roads, drainage, sidewalks, tramways, street lighting, postal deliveries, and similar conveniences, all of which have required an increasing number of public employees. A wealthy community can demand and pay for such luxuries. It is the multiplication of such services as these, rather than any very novel experiments in State Socialism, that has accounted for the relative increase in the number shown by recent census returns as occupied in Governmental and professional callings.

The Conduct of Public Utilities

Any detailed description or criticism of the various State enterprises would extend far beyond the limits of this chapter. Each great undertaking, such as the railway system, the co-operative contracting system of public works construction, the hydro-electric undertakings, the multifarious services of the Post and Telegraph Department, which include banking, remittance, radio, cables, telephones, and in the country districts almost all minor Governmental jobs—each great public service should be viewed as a business with its own peculiar problems. It is, however, beyond the limits of this chapter to discuss the technical problems of organisation involved in each of these enterprises.

There are certain general problems arising from Governmental operation of industries which are common to most of the State ventures. The financial aspects of State enterprise have received some attention in the previous chapter. It has there been argued that as a whole the extension of State enterprise has resulted in a net cost to the taxpayers, and that this cost has been so heavy in recent years as to cause, or at least be connected with, a relative decline in the productivity of the Dominion. In addition to this virtual subsidising of the State services from the proceeds of taxation there are financial advantages accruing from the use of State credit, and in certain instances from freedom from taxation. Some of the State trading departments, notably the insurance offices and the Public Trust Office, have built up large businesses without the necessity of providing capital. Backed by the credit of the State, which would have had to make good any losses that might have occurred, they have built up reserves and carried large risks. This does not appear to be a valid argument against State enterprise, however irritating it may be to competing private agencies. The use of State credit in this way is a genuine economy providing, other things being equal, cheaper and more efficient service in important public utilities.

The advantages of some departments in freedom from taxation, particularly from the heavy income-tax as levied upon companies, is rather more debatable. It is arguable whether public undertakings should be charged with taxation as if they were private enterprises. Any such charge is purely a matter of book-keeping. It is essential to remember, however, that the financial aspect of such enterprises as the railway system would be very different if income-tax were calculated, and calculated as in the case of private companies, upon gross rather than net profits.

The various construction departments are also heavy importers of materials upon which Customs duties are not levied. Even in those departments, such as the State Advances Department, which pay income-tax, it is admitted that less is paid than would be paid by private concerns of like magnitude. The profits of such State enterprises, whether actual net profits or social benefits conferred upon the community, need to be discounted by the amount of the taxation which would have been received if these utilities had been allowed to develop in private ownership. This is one of the arguments always used in New Zealand in favour of the present position of the Bank of New Zealand, in which the Government is a large shareholder and has a controlling share in the management, but which is conducted and taxed as a private company.

Even more debatable is the privileged position of certain departments in regard to the legal requirements exacted from competing private concerns. The most outstanding examples of such privilege are the exceptions to trustee law made in favour of the Public Trustee. It may be true that "this trustee never dies or runs away, never mistakes the trust funds for his own, never speculates or endangers the property of his wards, never becomes disqualified or involved in private quarrels, and never makes any but the most moderate charges—barely enough to cover the actual cost of the service".(4) It is also true that many of the functions thrust upon him are such as private trustees would not be likely to welcome. He cares for great numbers of small estates, and acts for the State in such matters as the administration of the affairs of patients in mental hospitals. In order to give him freedom to handle his multifarious and ever-growing tasks, the Public Trustee has sought and obtained from acquiescent Parliaments considerable amendments of the trust law enabling him to do what in private practice would be breaches of trust.

Most of the criticism of the Office in recent years has gathered round this exceptional legal position of the Public Trustee and around the practice of throwing the proceeds of most estates into a Common Fund which virtually averages the return from his investments.(5) Instead of administering each estate as a unit, the usual practice, unless specific directions to the contrary are made in the will, is to realise the estate and place the proceeds in the Common Fund, from which loans are then made in suitable amounts. Various public moneys, such as sinking funds, have also been included in this Fund at times. Loans from the Fund are made at the ordinary commercial rates upon first-class security, so that the Public Trust Office has grown to be one of the important lending departments of the Government. The practice has been followed of declaring an arbitrary rate of dividend on this Common Fund which is allocated *pro rata* to the various estates and moneys represented. This rate of dividend has consistently been much lower than the average rate of return received from investments.

In this way the Public Trustee has been enabled to show a profit and carry out large building programmes despite a rapid growth of staff and probably of overhead costs. There is no way of estimating the relative efficiency of his staff. Some services are performed free, or at low cost, for private individuals, such, for example, as the making of wills; but only when the Public Trustee is named as executor. Charges for administering estates are on a commercial basis. Other services, such as the care of estates for patients in mental hospitals, are carried out by the Public Trustee for the State. The present system of making all such net costs virtually a charge upon estates in the Common Fund, as well as the averaging of return upon all the estates in that Fund, is open to debate. Attacks upon it come almost wholly from the legal profession, and are apt to be discounted as mere expressions of animosity from disgruntled competitors. As in so many other State activities, there is little popular knowledge or criticism, and the Public Trust Office is usually accepted as a clear example of successful State enterprise. It is obvious, however, that by manipulating the rate of interest declared upon the Common Fund, the Public Trustee can always make a good financial showing. This does not detract from the value of his services to the community. It does make it impossible to discover the efficiency of those services in relation to their cost.

The growing power and importance of the Public Trustee is an excellent example of the tendency in New Zealand towards a marked expansion of bureaucratic influence. There are, on the other hand, obvious cases, particularly in the construction of railways and public works, where political interference markedly diminishes the responsibilities and efficiency of the expert departmental officers. The local agitations for uneconomical extensions of hydro-electric undertakings are a clear case of such political interference. Most of the unprofitable railway lines of the Dominion owe their inception to similar political agitations, pursued either with the ostensible object of relieving economic distress and unemployment, or frankly in local interests at the expense of the general community. This is a well-marked weakness of State enterprise under the ordinary forms of Parliamentary control.

Generally speaking, however, the tendency in recent years has clearly been towards an increasing measure of bureaucratic influence. In certain departments, such as those dealing with education and hospitals, this influence is open to strong criticism. Under a system of non-expert recruitment and promotion by seniority these important departments have largely passed under clerical, routine domination, the natural and inevitable result of which has been stagnation. The case of the great engineering departments has, however, been different. The colonising genius appreciates the material results of expert engineering practice, and values the trained engineer much more readily than the more elusive and less measurable social values of the educator, the research scientist, or the physician.

The planning of the important public services, such as surveys, railway development, hydro-electric supply, has been remarkably well done. New Zealand has profited from the labours of a succession of conscientious, able, and public-spirited explorers, geologists, surveyors, and engineers. Some of the most eminent scientific names in New Zealand history have been those of public servants. Not only in the natural sciences, such as geology and biology, but even more in the recording of Maori lore and the elucidation of ethnological problems, officers of the Government have made remarkable contributions. There has been an extraordinarily high level of attainment among the men who have planned the groundwork of New Zealand development. This tradition is continued by the New Zealand born and trained engineers and administrators who are now coming into control of the great constructive departments.

While the general planning and administration of the public services is efficient, there are many executive details in which the State enterprises are open to criticism. They share with all large-scale business enterprises the ever-present danger of slackness and unprogressive policies. For example, almost every commission or committee of enquiry that has investigated the railway service has stressed the inadequate and out-of-date equipment of the railway shops. In part, such a defect is due to the inadequate co-ordination of responsibilities between a Minister subject to Parliamentary criticism and the permanent head of the department. Largely, however, it comes, as does the common failure to adapt to local situations, from the general tendency to centralisation. The Public Works Department, necessarily treating each construction task as a problem in itself, has generally escaped both of these pitfalls. Since the appointment of a General Manager of the Railway Department, and the vigorous decentralisation and businesslike policies initiated after the report of the Railway Commission in 1924, there has been considerable improvement on the railways also. The challenge of the motor competition has not altogether been met, but it has at least stimulated a much greater degree of efficiency, and the recent changes have incidentally produced an *esprit de corps* which is new and quite remarkable.

The chief problems of the State enterprises, however, arise from the methods of recruitment and staffing. There has, in the period of prosperity, been some tendency to overstaffing. Departments grow by accretion, if only because every increase aggrandises the senior official. This is a minor problem, however, in comparison with the wider questions of efficiency, and one that can easily be handled over a series of years. There is considerable evidence that in the financial stringency since 1921 there has been a general tightening up of staff conditions.

Since 1886, Civil Service appointments in New Zealand have been made upon the basis of competitive examination. The junior officers entering the various departments have therefore been of a calibre rather better than the average ability. In many cases, indeed, the Civil Service, with its comparatively easy conditions, but lack of large prizes, has proved a convenient stepping-stone for ambitious youths. It is a remarkable fact, on the other hand, that until very recently practically no provision was made for training of officers after appointment. The Public Trust Office and the Railway Department provide specialised courses of training for their juniors, and the Telegraph Department necessarily trains its operators; but in the administrative departments as a whole the officers are allowed to grow up in the routine practice and traditions handed down by their seniors without any systematic formal teaching.

Since control of the public service was vested in commissioners in 1912, encouragement in the form of extra salary increments has been given for passing certain university and other examinations. There has been little co-ordination between the departments and the university, and it is probable that the chief effect of such encouragements has been to assist ambitious junior officers to qualify for the professions outside of the Service. More important still, the commissioner system of control under the statutory limitations within which it works in New Zealand has fastened on the services the tendency, always marked in Government departments, for promotion to depend largely upon seniority. The quite inadequate provision made for expert divisions in certain departments has not combated this tendency effectively. Recruitment and promotion are therefore almost wholly from below. In most departments the possibility of introducing highly trained and well-paid experts in the higher ranges of the Service is very limited. There is no system comparable with the divisions by which the British Civil Service admits young men of exceptional ability and prolonged training into the higher executive offices of Government with large responsibilities at an early age. The New Zealand system, under which every officer is entitled to promotion to a vacancy immediately above him unless he can be shown incapable of discharging its duties, or in default to a position of equal remuneration, tends to promote departmental inbreeding and to place a premium on routine unadventurous mediocrity. It says a great deal for the calibre of the public servants of New Zealand and for the general standard of education that, under such conditions, the level of efficiency should be so high. Corruption and "graft" are all but unknown, and are always met with condign punishment. High standards of courtesy and conscientious administration are maintained, and it is only in regard to initiative and resourcefulness that criticism is heard.

The lack of training facilities is largely due to the failure of the university to model its methods upon the necessities of colonial rather than British conditions, and to its lack of prestige in the general community.(6) There is a larger proportion of university graduates in the Government services than in private business, but except in the strictly professional degrees, such as medicine and law, graduation has in many cases meant rather the passing of examinations than training for any particular or general sphere of usefulness.

There was at one time, during the later years of Seddon's regime, considerable, if vague, criticism of the "Civil Service vote" and its manipulation in the Government interest. There has never been anything approaching the "spoils" system which is so common in America. Civil Service appointments are permanent during good behaviour. But there was a good deal of innuendo concerning appointments of Government supporters, and much talk of disclosures concerning "Seddonism", when the Opposition got "access to the pigeon-holes". No such disclosures were ever made, and it is unlikely that there were any serious lapses to be disclosed. Any such possibilities were removed once for all by the appointment of Public Service Commissioners in 1912.(7)

It is difficult to estimate the degree in which the Civil Service vote has influenced the course of politics; but, except in the case of the organised trade unions, such as the railway and postal unions, which have developed affiliations with the political Labour Party, it is probable that the Civil Service vote has been divided and has exerted little direct political influence. The Civil Service organisations have carefully abstained from the appearance of political affiliation or support. The railway unions and postal workers, however, have had direct contact both with the trade union movement and with the political wing of the labour movement, though the latter has been less obvious than the former. An awkward situation is created when, as in 1919 and again in 1924, a great body of public servants goes on strike with the support of the trade union movement and the vocal sympathy of the official Labour opposition in the House. Inevitably the strike takes on a political rather than an economic complexion. It says a great deal for the restraint of both sides and for the non-revolutionary character of the trade union movement that such a difficult situation should have terminated amicably and resulted in bringing the railway servants within the scope of the compulsory arbitration system.

Experiments in State Trading

It should be clear from the preceding sections of this chapter that the chief extensions which New Zealand has made in the sphere of public enterprise have been in the control and conduct of public utilities, in the provision of social welfare services, such as education, hospitals, health regulation, and in the administration of departments intended to regulate private enterprise. New Zealand opinion includes not only the railway and postal services, but also the various lands departments, the Public Works Department, and the Public Trust Office, as public utilities properly provided by the State. In the same way local bodies undertake gasworks, tramways, electrical supply, and waterworks, as coming within the same category of services suitable for public operation as drainage and road construction.

The lending departments of the Government which provide advances to settlers and to workers are justified partly as public utility services, partly as social welfare activities, and partly because they are regarded as a form of State competition checking the development of monopoly. Of these justifications the second probably looms largest. It is the wisdom, from a social point of view, of placing small farmers on the land and assisting workers to buy their own homes which is the real basis of the lending departments' support in public opinion. At the same time it was easy to argue that in providing financial assistance for small farmers and workers the Government was merely extending the public utility principle which it had already followed in creating State insurance, public trust facilities, and a Government savings bank. In essentials this principle is the same as that which justifies the State in building railways and other public works on the ground that private enterprise is inadequate to provide these needed public services.

The fear of monopoly control of industry, and especially of financial monopoly, has also been a definite factor in New Zealand public opinion. There is no doubt that it entered into the support given to the creation of lending departments. The provision of cheap credit on easy terms of repayment through the Advances to Settlers and Advances to Workers Departments would not have been necessary if the existing financial institutions had been deemed capable of meeting the demands. Since 1895 the principal financial institution of the Dominion, the Bank of New Zealand, has been under Governmental control, but the fear of financial monopoly has not been altogether removed.

The only State trading departments established in New Zealand have owed their origin to this belief in the use of State enterprise to check monopoly. Both in the insurance ventures and in the establishment of the State coal-mines, other factors entered in, but in both cases the desire to establish competitive standards was dominant.(8) There have been a few other minor examples, such as the State butchers' shops run for a year in Auckland City in 1917, but the range of State trading has been remarkably limited in New Zealand.

The Government Life Insurance Department began operations in 1870 without capital but under a State guarantee.(9) It entered a very profitable field, since New Zealand death-rates are the lowest in the world, and the volume of insurance carried is extraordinarily great. For many years it had little competition from private concerns, but on the contrary had great advantages in being linked up with schemes of Civil Service retirement annuities. Its tables, calculated upon the low rate of interest prevailing in Britain, left substantial margins of profit when the proceeds were invested at the higher rates of interest ruling within New Zealand. These fortuitous advantages led to a rapid increase of business in the early years of the Department's history, but they proved to be merely temporary, and subsequent developments have greatly qualified the hasty conclusion of early observers that the Department's success had proved beyond question the efficiency of State operation of insurance.

There is a clear tendency in recent years for the Department to lose ground as compared with private firms. This is mainly because experience has confirmed the belief of the larger clients that bonus dividends in certain companies compare more than favourably with those of the Government office, and that this difference more than compensates for the State guarantee and for the somewhat lower premiums. The comparative failure of the Department to secure a proportional share of new business, despite its use of all the ordinary commercial methods, was noted by Le Rossignol and Stewart as early as 1908. Subsequent experience has proved the validity of their conclusions. In 1925 the Government Life Insurance Department obtained approximately 20 per cent. of the new business, mainly in smaller policies. The Australian Mutual Provident Company alone, with slightly fewer new policies, obtained new premiums more than 50 per cent. greater than the Department secured in the year 1925.

LIFE INSURANCE BUSINESS IN NEW ZEALAND

	1907.		1917.		1925.	
	Policies Out-standing.	Amount Assured.	Policies Out-standing.	Amount Assured.	Policies Out-standing.	Amount Assured.
	No.	£ (millions).	No.	£ (millions).	No.	£ (millions).
Government Life Insurance Dept. ..	46,945	10·9	53,058	12·9	63,775	18·0
Percentage	38	36	32	30	28	25
Private companies ..	75,989	19·3	111,085	30·0	159,283	54·4
Total ..	122,924	30·2	164,143	42·9	223,058	72·4

The State Fire Insurance Department was established in 1903 only after bitter and prolonged controversy.(10) The chief argument urged in its favour was the existing high and uniform rate of premiums, which was regarded as proof of the existence of an "insurance ring". At this time the Government's experiment in life insurance was commonly regarded as having proven the success of State enterprise at least in the insurance field. Enthusiasts of the period—mainly Radical visitors—had prematurely concluded that the State "had beaten private companies in fair competition".

At the beginning of the century the fire risks in New Zealand were greater even than they are now. In the days before ferro-concrete, not only dwelling-houses, but offices, factories, and shops were built mainly of wood. The large building in which the Governmental offices at Wellington were, and for the most part still are, housed was often referred to with pride as the largest wooden building in the world. The insurance companies therefore felt that New Zealand risks were more speculative than usual in a field of insurance which in any country is much less certain and calculable than life insurance. They pleaded that there was no real analogy between fire and life insurance, and that their rates were not unreasonably high in view of their risks. Popular support was, however, behind the Government's determination to enter the field. The first Bill drafted went so far as to make fire insurance compulsory on all buildings and optional for stock and effects. The Act establishing the Department in 1903 did not go as far as this; but the mere establishment of a competitive State office aroused strong and even bitter opposition. The Department did not begin operations till 1905, when it was immediately met by a boycott from the private companies, which refused to share risks in which the State office held a part, or to accept reinsurance. Mr. Seddon met the boycott by sending an officer to London to arrange for reinsurance with Lloyd's. The boycott gave way in New Zealand shortly afterwards, and gradually the State office has taken its place as one among the competing fire insurance agencies of New Zealand. It is now criticised more for identifying itself so completely with the methods and policies of the private concerns than for its rashness in undercutting them or departing from established practice.

The very hostility with which it was first met has provided the chief argument urged in its favour. It proposed immediately to cut the premium rate by 10 per cent., to which the companies retorted by reducing trade risks in the same proportion, and cutting the rates on dwelling-houses, furniture, and similar risks by 33⅓ per cent. These further reductions were accepted by the Department, so that the immediate effect of its entry was a substantial reduction of premiums. In the succeeding few years there was much criticism of these lower rates, and the Department suffered some substantial losses. The rates of premium at this time were admitted in official reports and Parliamentary debates to be too low for safety. No increase of rates took place, however, and the financial position both of the companies and of the State office was steadily improved by the increasing use of insurance spreading risks over a greater volume of business and, until the year 1921, by a marked diminution in the incidence of fire risks. So great was the improvement that by 1923 the State office was in a position to make rebates of from 10 to 15 per cent., which have since been continued. The private companies immediately fell into line; but they have also made very substantial profits, which are the object of much criticism, particularly by the Labour Party.(11) The challenging statement is made that "the statistics reveal that a large proportion of the benefits of modern fire-fighting appliances and adequate water-supply is being diverted to the shareholders in private companies by way of abnormal dividends on an insignificant capital outlay".

Examination of the financial situation of the fire insurance companies yields convincing evidence that for several years past they have been among the most profitable forms of investment within New Zealand. High dividend rates plus large transfers to various reserve accounts have been supplemented by generous bonus share distributions. It is at least obvious that the State Department, which in 1925 obtained only 13 per cent. of the premiums paid, has not operated in such a way as to be ruinous to private business. It is equally clear that it has failed to obtain for the insuring public such minimum premium rates as would have brought the companies' profits down to a parity with commercial institutions in general. Investors in New Zealand have known that insurance and banking offer sound, non-speculative securities yielding more than average returns over a period of years. Yet these are the financial spheres in which the Government has competitive power. The situation is complicated by the fact that the private companies accept risks and make investments outside New Zealand; but their New Zealand business has not been jeopardised by State competition.

The only other important experiment in State Socialism has been the State coal-mining venture on which Mr. Seddon embarked in 1901.(12) Fear of monopoly was again a considerable factor in the Government's decision to promote this enterprise. The responsibility for providing the railways with adequate coal-supplies was another important factor. The effort to reduce the cost of living by opening State coal depots in the various towns indicates the force of the humanitarian trend of Mr. Seddon's later years. Candour compels one to point out also that the chief coal area of New Zealand lies in what was Mr. Seddon's own beloved province, Westland. He never forgot completely the rôle of miners' advocate in which he first entered the House. Under his vigorous administration the State reserved some of the best coal areas, and opened up two collieries in addition to several retail depots. The railways and other Government services have always been the chief users of the coal produced, which reached its maximum quantity (249,442 tons, or 13 per cent. of the total production) in 1909. In the last year for which statistics are available (1926) the production was 174,754 tons, or rather less than 8 per cent. of the total number of tons raised in the Dominion.(13)

This decline of importance is due to a combination of factors, chief among which is the administrative attitude of more recent Governments. The financial results of the experiment cannot be clearly ascertained, owing to the fact that it has been so tied up with the freight rates charged by the railways and the prices charged for coal supplied to the railways and other Government departments. There seems no reasonable doubt that there has been some net loss transferred to the taxpayer. It is probable, however, that the militant activities of the coal-miners' trade union, which often affected the State mine after 1906, were the chief cause of the lukewarm attitude of succeeding Governments towards the experiment. Certain seams worked out earlier than had been expected, and the Reform Government which came into power in 1912 was not sufficiently imbued with State Socialist ideas to seek ways and means of reinvigorating the enterprise.

The administrative apathy, if not hostility, which after 1912 took away the last possibility of making these trading ventures into really effective experiments in State Socialism is a true reflection of majority opinion in New Zealand. The fact that Cabinet Ministers, contrary to British practice, retain their directorates without offending public opinion is proof enough that this opinion is not hostile to private capitalist enterprise. In recent Governments, Ministers have continued to act as directors of coal-mining, insurance, and frozen-meat companies, while the Cabinet of which they were members has had to supervise State coal and insurance departments and the meat export control boards.

The fact is that New Zealand abandoned at a very early stage the attempt to monopolise, or even to compete effectively, in fields already organised by private enterprise. Certain public utilities remain in the hands of the State, and the trading departments have not been altogether abandoned, though their scope and initiative have been greatly restricted. The public opinion of the country, never Socialistic, has at times supported Governmental ventures intended to break through monopoly situations; but generally speaking it supports the regulation rather than the suppression of private enterprise.

The Regulation of Private Enterprise

The interference of modern Governments with economic life necessarily increases. In new countries, where institutions and policies are in the making, and where few traditions and vested interests exist to confine Governmental activities within narrow bounds, Governmental contact with economic life is maximised. In New Zealand, at least, this fact does not demonstrate any Radical theory so much as immaturity of economic development and empirical opportunism in politics. The only theoretical basis of Governmental policy is a vague humanitarian belief in the priority of personal over commercial considerations.

There is also to be reckoned with the very well developed Parliamentary tradition of competence to deal with any and every subject that may come before the House. The miscellaneous collections of lawyers, journalists, farmers, and professional politicians who make up the Lower House seldom seems to feel any doubts of its ability to deal with any matter requiring decision. It will cheerfully legislate for the university or the learned professions, face measures dealing with contagious diseases or borderland cases of insanity, or set up any other form of political or economic machinery. It accurately reflects the New Zealand democracy in paying little attention to experts, and is therefore almost wholly at the mercy of the bureaucrats who control the Government departments. Fortunately for New Zealand the departmental heads maintain a high average level of ability; but from the very nature of their work they cannot be specialists. These facts, very seldom stated, but obvious to every critical observer, do not deter the legislators from a free exercise of their constitutional powers. As long as economic prosperity continues, little harm is done, but there is always the possibility of temporary depression leading to a ready acceptance of quack remedies, the fallacies of which are obvious to expert eyes, but which catch the attention of legislators as likely to appeal to public opinion. The New Zealand statute-book records many such nostrums, most of which were fortunately allowed to drop quietly into disuse after their immediate causes passed away. There is, as in most democracies, a general feeling of apathy concerning political questions, broken only when some proposed legislation touches a sectional interest.

Much of the routine of legislation necessarily affects the economic life of the country. The various forms of taxation, for example, especially those which call for returns of income or property, involve interference with economic organisation. When, as in the New Zealand graduated taxation of land and income, the taxes are used for social as well as fiscal purposes, such interference may become marked. It is an easy step from taxation of this sort to various licence fees and stamp taxes, the payment of which is accompanied by Governmental inspection and regulation of industry. There has been a marked tendency in New Zealand to assert the principle that all economic activities are social and must submit themselves to public investigation and control. There are few countries where the old catch-cry that a business man has a right to organise his own business in his own way has as little weight as it has in New Zealand.

There is also a very minute code of factory legislation backed up by detailed and efficient Governmental inspection to ensure the maintenance of minimum standards. Shops and offices and various special occupations are subject to equally rigid scrutiny. The Labour Department carries out a long and detailed list of inspectorial duties, involving hours of labour, apprenticeship conditions, and trade union preference, as well as working conditions. In the same way the Health Department controls the registration of medical practitioners, nurses, midwives and maternity nurses, masseurs and plumbers, supervises the sale of food and drugs, and protects the public from quackery and fraud.(14) The Agricultural Department has inspectors to check the spread of noxious weeds and diseases, and pests such as rabbits. It has wide power, which it exercises to prevent the spread of disease, as, for instance, by ordering the destruction of animals affected with tuberculosis, bees with foul brood. It also inspects all meat and dairy produce. The Marine Department is responsible for inspection of machinery and of ships to ensure safety of life at sea, and the Mines Department has similar important duties in its industry. New Zealand development has tended to throw upon the State departments the onus of protecting the public interest. The risk of petty officialdom and regimentation involved in such a policy has been fairly well safeguarded by the good sense of the administrators and the co-operative attitude of the people generally; but there is naturally some grumbling among business men concerning the interference with normal routine and the cost of preparing numerous returns for different departments.(15) There are few, however, who would countenance the possibility of returning to a system of unregulated industrial competition.

The Government departments have been most successful where they have been able to enter into co-operative relations with those engaged in industry. A particularly fruitful relationship has been built up between the farmers and the Department of Agriculture. Constructive measures of immediate assistance have led naturally to practical regulative measures such as the inspection and grading of export produce, being securely based upon understanding and group assent. The farmer willingly submits to restrictions when he understands that their loyal observance by the whole farming community will add to his wealth. The Departments of Industry and Commerce and of Forestry, as well as the various export control boards, are following the same line of development. The Labour Department, except in its provision of unemployment bureaux, has a much more difficult task, since it must work between two well-organised and suspicious groups, the trade unions and the employers' associations.

Regulation of private enterprise in the public interest leads logically to the outlawry of commercial practices which are deemed to be anti-social. In New Zealand the responsibility for such action is generally thrown upon the State. Many responsibilities, which in such a country as Great Britain or the United States would be undertaken—if undertaken at all—by individual businesses or trade associations, are in New Zealand made the subject of legislation or administrative action. There are clear cases, such as the elimination of much quackery and fraud in the medical sphere, and the virtual suppression of subcontracting and homework, where Governmental action is very effective and wholesome. There are other respects in which its efficacy is debatable. Of these the chief example is probably to be found in the efforts made to control or prevent monopoly organisation of important economic functions.

Two New Zealand expedients for combating monopoly have already been discussed—the assumption by the State of public utilities, and spasmodic efforts made at State competition. Less successful than either has been the effort to control monopolies by legislation.

The first Act for this purpose was the Monopoly Prevention Act, 1908, which was quickly followed by the Commercial Trusts Act of 1910.(16) These Acts go into considerable detail in the definition of monopoly practices, such as secret rebates, commissions for exclusive purchases, and boycotts. The Act of 1910 defines a "commercial trust" in very wide terms as any association having as its object that of controlling, determining, or influencing the supply or demand or price of any goods in New Zealand, or creating within New Zealand a monopoly, whether complete or partial, in the supply or demand of any goods. Under the terms used in this Act a determined Government might have put an end to almost all local as well as overseas associations of suppliers or consumers. The theory upon which the Act was drawn was the most completely logical application of *laissez-faire* individualist competition.

In actual practice the Act has been a dead-letter. Specific cases were adduced before the Royal Commission on the Cost of Living in 1912 of boycotts, rebates, and similar practices associated with monopoly(17); but no effective action was ever taken, although evidence given before the Commission definitely invoked the provisions of the 1910 Act. This is a very clear case in which legislation appears much more important than subsequent administration has allowed it to be.

In 1915 what appeared to be an even more important measure was passed. The Cost of Living Act of that year created a Board of Trade, which was given control of price-fixing and was entrusted with the administration of the Commercial Trusts Act, 1910.(18) In the war years the Board of Trade functioned with some vigour, fixing maximum prices, controlling the prices of important monopoly products like sugar, importing wheat, and launching systematic investigations of important industries. In the general extension of State activity during the war period these functions were accepted without much question, and on the whole safeguarded the public interest at a difficult time. There is ample evidence to show that during the war years prices rose less in New Zealand than in most countries, and this was largely due to the control of important prices by the Department of Imperial Government Supplies on the one hand and the Board of Trade on the other.(19) The effective steps taken by the Board to control sugar prices were made easier by the fact that it was negotiating with a monopoly organisation, but in the light of after-events it is clear that wartime regulation must be judged as a problem *sui generis* with little relation to normal industrial organisation. It was not long after the war before the Colonial Sugar Company felt itself powerful enough to bring effective pressure on the Government to secure an increased amount of tariff protection and practical freedom of operation.(20)

The Board of Trade Act, 1919, passed in the first session after the war, consolidated and extended the powers of the Board. Like so many New Zealand Acts, it was drawn in the widest possible terms, giving the Board power to do almost anything in the way of investigating, and, if necessary, controlling, the economic life of the Dominion. The regulation of profiteering was added to its functions, and price tribunals were set up which had as little real importance as the tribunals in England, on which they were modelled. The first case of any importance challenged the principle of selling goods at prices fixed by the manufacturers, but after elaborate argument concerning replacement values and profits based upon them the cases were dismissed without conviction.(21) After one or two minor cases, in one of which an unfortunate chemist was convicted for charging a rate of profit which did not seem to be excessive when allowance was made for his skilled labour and the slow rate of turnover in his business, the profiteering tribunals lapsed into a forgotten episode.

The rejuvenated Board of Trade in its first year or two of independent life showed admirable energy in the investigation of important industrial situations. It appeared likely that its main function would turn out to be that of a business audit. There were many advantages to be expected from such a development, and the first published report on the coal industry, in which the Board had the collaboration of an eminent economist, was a fine practical piece of work. Other investigations were undertaken, but their publication was interdicted when the slump of 1920–1 overtook the Dominion. In the campaign for public economy after the slump the Board of Trade suffered heavily. Its members were allowed to resign, until the Board of Trade Amendment Act, 1923, abolished the Board and vested its power in the Minister of Industries and Commerce, while its functions, greatly shrunken in practice, were taken over by his department. The Act, however, in all its potentialities remains on the statute-books as a trap for future historians, and possibly for future politicians.(22)

It may be said, therefore, that New Zealand, after half-hearted administration of apparently important and almost revolutionary legislation, very quickly abandoned any attempt to fix prices or control business organisation. The legislation remains on the statute-books, and occasionally some surviving administrative regulation becomes a source of irritation to the commercial community; but the "economic judiciary" which was to parallel and supplement in the field of prices the State regulation of wages by the Arbitration Court remains only a dream in the minds of a few ardent Socialists. Meantime businesses operate in New Zealand which come obviously within the wide definition of monopoly incorporated in existing legislation. The Merchants' Association still uses its monopoly of certain proprietary lines of merchandise and its agreement with the Colonial Sugar Company as the corner-stone of its distribution system.(23) The American system of the manufacturers fixing resale prices (both wholesale and retail) operates unchecked, and in many other respects it is evident that the legislation of 1908–10 has done nothing to regulate such practices. It is abundantly clear also that public opinion at the present time has lost any effective expression of whatever resentment it had against monopoly in these forms.

New Zealanders, however, are conscious that their isolation and their extreme dependence upon overseas trade leaves them peculiarly open to monopoly depredations. Import monopolies of consumers' goods, export monopolies of the great staple products of the country, or a straddling of communications by a great shipping combine—any or all of these prospects will arouse alarm even among Conservative politicians. It is significant that it was largely fear of the great American combinations for the manufacture of farm machinery, the oil combine, and above all the Meat Trust, which prompted the legislation sketched above. There does not seem to be any very lively fear of a shipping combination, although it is generally known that there are agreements, and even some measure of interlocking ownership, between the local companies and great shipping organisations overseas, and that coal and other interests are drawn in. Even during the shipping shortage of the late war period the New Zealand Government refused to embark upon a State shipping service as Australia did.

The co-operative system of manufacture in the main primary products is probably the best guarantee against overseas monopolies controlling the export trade. The local freezing companies are largely owned by the farmers, and the great majority of butter- and cheese-factories are true co-operatives. The farmers need only be loyal to their own organisations to prevent overseas traders from getting a foothold. Nevertheless it is obvious that somewhat exaggerated fears of monopoly have entered largely into the agitation which has since the war created control boards in the main export industries with the exception of wool. The control boards bargain with shipping and insurance companies for lower standardised rates. The whole procedure is based upon the belief that the farmers are dealing with associations of firms in which there exist understandings and gentlemen's agreements, if not definite monopolistic control of rates and division of markets. The farmers support the boards largely in the belief that they enable them to present a united front in such negotiations.

A further step has been taken in fear of the dreaded Meat Trust. The export licence system, which originated under the war commandeer by the Department of Imperial Government Supplies, has been taken over by the semi-official export control boards. Reference has already been made to the early refusal of an export licence to a firm which was deemed to be a subsidiary of the Meat Trust and to the enquiries made in the matter by the State Department. The subsequent refusal of the Meat Export Control Board to sanction the sale of a freezing-works which was in financial difficulties to a firm which was thought to be a subsidiary of the Trust, raised the policy once more into clear relief.(24) There were serious questionings as to the effect which such a refusal might have upon the market value of shares, not only of the particular company concerned, but of meat companies in general. These questionings were the greater because of the over-expansion of freezing-works in the post-war boom, which has left many of them, particularly the farmers' co-operative concerns, in financial difficulties. The Government and the Board, however, stood firm in refusing to grant the licence.

The Government and the Bank of New Zealand

It is a curious fact that the relations between the Government and the Bank of New Zealand have not been adequately treated by writers on the State Socialism of the Dominion. The episode of 1894–5, by which the Government obtained a share in the ownership and management of the Bank, is well known. It has been fully described by Drummond, and with rather different emphasis by Lloyd,(25) but the subsequent development of the relationship thus begun has largely escaped attention. In many ways, however, it furnishes a touchstone by which to test the nature of Governmental policy. Here is a Government, avowedly pledged to a policy of State Socialism, placed suddenly and by accident in the position of controlling the largest financial institution in the Dominion, supplying fresh capital, guaranteeing new issues, passing legislation to facilitate the transfer of frozen assets to a separate institution, and in return accepting preferred shares and a majority on the directorate. Obviously such a situation might have led a determined administration a long way towards nationalisation of credit, or at least to the control of this dominant institution in such a way as to secure the maximum advantages to the banking public of competitive credit agencies.

The actual course of development is illuminating. In retrospect it is perfectly clear that the Seddon Government in 1894–5 was taken completely by surprise, that it had no previous intention of coming to the rescue of the Bank, but was forced to do so by the disclosure that some immediate and drastic action was necessary if the Bank was to be saved from closing its doors and the colony from a terrible financial crisis. There is no doubt that the steps taken were courageous and wise, and that the Government's action averted much suffering and loss. But there was no plan or theory beyond the immediate crisis, and no consistent policy was developed as the Bank gradually regained its financial stability. At the earliest possible moment the shareholders made efforts to be released from Government participation, and did succeed in reducing the Government's rights to share in the growth of what was becoming a most profitable enterprise. As prosperity increased, however, the Government slipped into the rôle of a complacent sleeping-partner with a junior interest. It shared in the dividends and distribution of bonus shares, for which legislation was passed from time to time, and in every respect identified itself completely with the shareholders' interests. It continued, and still continues, to appoint four of the six directors, including the chairman, as well as the auditors; but there has never been any attempt to use this power to direct banking policy in the interests of the banking public or the public finances. Throughout the whole period the Bank has followed "sound conservative banking policy" on strictly orthodox lines. It has, moreover, participated fully, and even taken a leading part, in the close and systematic arrangements worked out by the associated banks for uniformity of exchange rates, rates of interest, discount and overdraft, and of banking policy generally. So far from being a State bank, or even a strongly competitive institution, it must be regarded as the leading member of a close monopoly organised on conservative capitalistic lines.

The details of the crisis of 1894–5 have been so fully described by Drummond and Lloyd that only the barest summary is necessary here. The Bank of New Zealand was founded in 1861 after the abandonment of the previous State bank of issue.(26) At its foundation it was the second bank operating in the colony, and the only locally owned institution. It therefore received the custody of the Government balances, and from that time to this it has acted as the Government's agent. The profits of the gold-rush period and the handling of large sums of Government money in the Vogel boom placed the Bank in an enviable position, but as the land speculation of the seventies got out of control it was drawn into unsound banking policies. The financing of developmental schemes upon the security of non-liquid assets, such as land values, was strongly criticised by financial authorities in London; but it was a policy in which all the Australasian banks shared, and was vigorously defended as perfectly sound and safe in a new country. The banks of issue were, moreover, in competition with the stock and station agencies, and more dangerously still, were forced to act as the ultimate reservoir of credit upon which those companies drew to make good their unsound advances at the height of the speculative boom.

It is probable that, despite its great advantages as the Government bank, the Bank of New Zealand was rather less wisely administered in this period than the older Australian banks, which were its competitors, and which had their investments and liabilities spread over a wider range of business in Australia as well as New Zealand. All, however, were caught badly by the depression of values which followed the falling price-level after 1874. The Australian banks paid the price of their mistakes in the bad crisis of 1893.(27)

Even before this date the Bank of New Zealand was struggling in serious difficulties. Its affairs were involved with a mass of sheep stations which had recoiled on its hands as mortgagee, and with a developmental company floated as a subsidiary enterprise. The existence of this company and of an Estates Company floated to administer the Bank's propertied holdings enabled a good face to be put upon the affairs of the Bank itself. Shares in the subsidiary companies were shown at values sufficient to maintain an appearance of solvency in the main enterprise which justified the payment of dividends throughout the worst period of the crisis. In 1888–9, however, at the depth of the depression the directors were forced to take some steps towards meeting their real position. A committee of shareholders was set up, and on their recommendation the whole of the reserve fund (£625,000) was written off, as well as £300,000 of the paid-up capital. In addition, £500,000 of new capital was raised; but these measures were quite inadequate, and in 1890 a further £300,000 of capital was written off. All this time, and indeed up till the Government intervention in 1894, the Bank continued to present balance-sheets showing profits and to pay dividends.(28)

Prices continued to fall, and business conditions got steadily worse. In 1893 the Bank's reserve of coin fell below the legal amount, but though attention was called to this fact by the Government, no pressure was brought to bear on the Bank. Early in the following year, however, an experienced banking officer was sent out from London, whither the head office of the Bank had been removed in 1890, and on June 25th this officer disclosed to the Government the fact that the Bank would close its doors almost immediately if the Government did not come to its rescue. The disclosure was practically an ultimatum.(29) The Bank's representative asked for legislation, and added, "If the Government finally determines to go on with the measure it should be put through to-day". He intimated on the Friday of the week in which his disclosures were first made that the Bank could not reopen on the following Monday if it were not helped in the meantime.

The Liberal-Labour Government had no particular reason to befriend the Bank, which was not popular among the workers and small farmers, and with which many of the opponents of the Government Party had in past years been associated.(30) It was no time, however, to dally with a situation which might have involved the worst financial crisis of the colony's history.

A Banking Bill was prepared, after consultation with representative leaders of the House, including the leader of the Opposition and Sir Robert Stout. The Bill was put through all its stages in both Houses at a single sitting, and signed by the Governor the same night. When the Bank opened on the Saturday morning it had been reconstituted with a Government guarantee.

A new issue of share capital, with preference over all ordinary shares, amounting to £2,000,000 was guaranteed by the State, and the Bank, in addition to arrangements safeguarding the Government against any loss from its guarantee, agreed that without Government consent no dividend should be paid on ordinary shares as long as these preferred "A" shares had currency. Of the new money thus made available, half was to be used in the Bank's ordinary business and half retained for investment approved by the Government. In addition, the Bank was instructed to call up half its reserve capital, amounting to £500,000, within twelve months.

These measures were sufficient to allay any possibility of a panic run on the Bank; but its troubles were only half-disclosed, and the State, having come to its rescue, was forced to further large commitments after more thorough investigation. The details of the rearrangement of the involved finances of the Bank, the Estates Company, and the Auckland Agricultural Company were further complicated by the amalgamation of the Colonial Bank with the Bank of New Zealand, and the Colonial Bank in turn was intimately connected with subsidiary companies, some of which were financially involved. During 1894 and 1895 a joint committee of both Houses of Parliament investigated the whole situation.(31) Feeling ran very high, and there were not wanting charges of improper action on the part of the Government, and particularly of Sir Joseph Ward, the Colonial Treasurer, some of whose private affairs were closely connected with the Colonial Bank. It would serve no useful purpose at this distance from the events to revive the acrimony of this controversy. Sir Joseph Ward resigned his ministerial post, but was triumphantly re-elected, and has subsequently served with distinction as a prominent member of the Seddon Ministry, as Prime Minister from 1906–12, as Minister of Finance in the National War Cabinet from 1915–19, and again as Prime Minister in 1928. It is clear that public opinion in New Zealand has never taken seriously the charges made against him in the heat of the banking crisis, even though such charges were made the subject of judicial comment.

The actual details of the rearrangements of the Bank's finances defy any short summary. In broad outline it may be said that legislation was passed by which the landed properties which were encumbering the legitimate banking business were taken over by an Assets Realisation Board, for which the Government also supplied extra capital. This Board gradually realised the estates, and its operations were wound up in 1906, the Bank contributing regularly out of its profits to the writing-off of losses made in the realisation.(32)

Freed from this incubus, tided over the panic period by the Government guarantee, and provided with new capital, the Bank had no difficulty in developing along profitable lines. The whole of its capital had been written off, together with a further call on the reserve liability of its shareholders. Except for the liability to contribute towards writing off the losses of the Assets Realisation Board and similar past commitments, the Bank had a fresh start. Its officials repeatedly acknowledged the fact that this would never have been possible but for the prompt and effective action of the Seddon Government and the financial skill of Sir Joseph Ward.(33)

When rising prices and general prosperity had floated New Zealand, and with it the Bank, into calmer and easier circumstances, the bargain between the Government and the shareholders was reconsidered. The arrangements, almost amounting to receivership, necessary in the crisis were revised in 1898 and the present system was inaugurated, by which the State appoints four out of six directors, including the chairman. In 1902 a dividend of 5 per cent. was paid again, and in the following year legislation was introduced by which the Government-guaranteed stock was redeemed, and also the Government's preference shares, the Government receiving in their place new preferred shares to the nominal value of £500,000. These shares were to rank with the ordinary shares up to 5 per cent., and in profits over this rate the shareholders and the Government share in the proportion of two-thirds and one-third.

The subsequent history of the Bank has been one of uninterrupted prosperity. In 1913 the ordinary capital of the Bank was increased to £3,000,000. The shareholders conducted a powerful agitation for the termination of the Government's share in the management and its right to participate in the profitable issues of new capital. The agitation was unsuccessful in its main object, but the Government's participation in new issues was reduced from one-half to one-third. By 1920 the Bank's business had again increased to the point at which a further call upon the shareholders for new capital was made. At the same time the £10 shares were replaced by £1 shares, and £1,125,000 was transferred from reserve as a bonus distribution to shareholders. In 1923 the ordinary share capital was increased by a further £750,000, each shareholder being entitled to one share at par for every three shares held. In 1926 the Bank secured further legislation, enabling it to create a department for long-term advances on rural securities, and to issue shares and debentures for that purpose, the Crown having a right of participation.(34)

The present position, therefore, is that the Government owns £1,875,000 of the Bank's subscribed capital of just over £6,000,000.(35) On £500,000 of this the Government receives a maximum of 10 per cent., and a slightly higher rate for the remainder. Its interference in the affairs of the Bank thirty years ago has therefore returned a good profit, and no losses have resulted therefrom.

This, however, is a long way from State Socialism, and is indeed its antithesis, viz. the support and buttressing of capitalist enterprise by the use of the powers of the State in an emergency. The Government has been far from making a hard bargain, and equally far from introducing any revolutionary changes in management. The extremity of the Bank was such in 1894–5 that it must have acceded to any terms demanded of it. Every new issue of shares and change in management has necessitated legislation, giving Parliament the power to review the whole arrangement. A policy which over thirty years has accepted for the Government the position of shareholder and justified the changes made as "good bargains", has no revolutionary portent. Its passive acceptance by the electorate must be regarded as public approval.

There is no evidence whatever that the Government has used its power of nominating the chairman and a majority of his board of directors as a means of influencing banking policy. There have been, and still are, substantial criticisms of a responsible character concerning important aspects of policy. It is to be remembered that banking is a closed field in New Zealand. No bank can start operations except with a Royal Charter, or an Act of the New Zealand Parliament.(36) The six banks operating work openly in the closest association, with regular and frequent meetings to lay down policies and decide on rates. There is no country in the world where credit is so easily and satisfactorily regulated as in New Zealand, which works under a "credit-exchange" standard of currency that places decision entirely in the hands of the banks.(37) It is true that their decisions must come within the limits of broad economic movements, but it is the bankers who interpret those movements.

To many readers (and apparently to the majority of people in New Zealand) this system, by which currency and credit movements are regulated in accordance with economic necessity by skilled bankers, will appear more sensible than any proposals for political control or semi-political control through a State bank. It is at any rate perfectly clear that successive New Zealand Governments for more than thirty years have been, and still are, in a position to dictate the policy of the largest bank in the country, but have not taken any steps to do so. The public finances might have been relieved, the Bank might have been given a monopoly of credit and note issues, the margin between borrowing and lending rates of interest might have been reduced, the lending rate itself might have been manipulated for political purposes, the margin between buying and selling rates of exchange might have been narrowed, and those rates might have been manipulated also. If the Bank of New Zealand had taken action along any or all of these lines the competing banks must have followed suit or lost business.

In practice the Government nominees on the board of directors have acted with fullest freedom along lines that are ultra-orthodox and conservative. Banking in New Zealand, therefore, has been as unfettered as if the Government had not owned an important interest in the largest bank. It is in fact less fettered than in most countries. The various Acts and charters carefully limit the right of note-issue in accordance with the tradition of the mid-nineteenth century, when the unregulated issue of bank-notes was the chief cause of banking failures. There is no statutory recognition of the enormous change that has taken place in the development of credit issues and the relatively minor importance of bank-notes in a modern credit system. In the issuance of credit the bankers of New Zealand are regulated only by their own good sense and banking traditions.

The price which New Zealand pays for this banking freedom is a natural tendency so to regulate charges that profits may be maximised. A chart of share prices, in which allowance is made for redistribution of capital, will show that the financial shares, of banks and insurance companies particularly, have in the last thirty years climbed away from the general movement of securities. Investors know that their capital returns better interest over a long period when invested in such financial securities as bank shares. This obviously means that the disclosed bank profits, to say nothing of the reserves tucked away in buildings and properties written down to almost nominal values, are great enough to allow of reduction of profit margins in exchange and interest rates without impairing the financial stability of the enterprise. Such reductions have not taken place to any important extent, and certainly not to the extent of affecting the bank's financial position.

Unfortunately most of the criticism of the banks on this point is ill-informed. Farmers often clamour for a lower interest rate, or calculate what an adverse exchange means on every bale of wool. These rates, however, must be regulated with the supply and demand of the market. It is in the margins between buying and selling, and their discrimination between securities, that the bankers, fortified by a position of semi-monopoly, make their profits. Pressure at these points could easily result in benefiting the customers of the banks at the expense of the shareholders. The lack of pressure has enabled the shareholders to profit in much greater degree than they would under competitive conditions, or than is usual in other countries. (38)

CHAPTER XI

STATE REGULATION OF WAGES

An Established Institution

The system of compulsory arbitration in labour disputes, introduced by the Industrial Conciliation and Arbitration Act, 1894, is probably the most important, and certainly the best known, of the legislative experiments that have been made in New Zealand.(1) Unlike other experiments, it has had a vigorous tendency to expand rather than diminish in scope and importance. Thirty-five years after its inception it appears to be more firmly established than ever. Its functions have altered considerably, its friends and enemies have changed sides more than once, criticism of its operations has never been wanting; but the very fact that it has for more than thirty years been an important factor in the economic life of the Dominion makes the possibility of its abolition almost unthinkable to the generation which has grown up in its shadow.

Apart, therefore, from its intrinsic economic interest, its development as a function of government is extremely significant. The Arbitration Court, which is the heart of the system, very quickly developed a life and characteristics of its own, quite different in many respects from those designed for it by its author. No student of social development can fail to be interested by the way in which it has made adjustments to its environment. By limiting its functions in some directions and expanding them in others, it has adapted itself to the practical demands and possibilities of its constituency. In this way it has developed a somewhat unexpected resiliency and power of survival.

This fact is more apparent when it is remembered that in its thirty-five years of existence the Court has encountered very considerable changes in economic and political conditions. As a result of these changes there have been considerable shifts in criticism from various quarters. The trade unionists, who in 1900 regarded the Act of 1894 as "part of their religion", were craft unionists.(2) Four years later Siegfried noted with interest and surprise the complete absence of revolutionary unionism or class warfare in New Zealand,(3) but within a very short time after his visit class warfare of the most definite variety was preached and practised by a large section of the labour movement.(4) When this new factor in the situation appeared, the majority of the employers, who had in any case been convinced by this time that the Court was not an instrument of social revolution, rallied to its support. From 1908 to 1913 the greatest criticism of the Court was from the labour side. A lingering trace of this situation remained after the war, when in 1921 the secretary of the Alliance of Labour made public his opinion that "the whole caboose should be knocked on the head".(5) The same vigorous controversialist took sharp issue with the statement that in the difficulties caused by falling prices, clear-sighted labour leaders were again turning to the support of the Court. Less than five years later, however, he was the accepted spokesman of the labour delegation to the National Industrial Conference of 1928, and as such, eloquently pleaded the cause of the Court and described as "disastrous" any proposal to take away its compulsory powers.(6)

On the other side, a perusal of the 1928 conference proceedings will show that a large number, though not all, of the employers' representatives were anxious to restrict or even abolish the compulsory powers of the Court. These powers of compulsion were rightly regarded by Mr. Reeves, the author of the Act of 1894, as the very marrow and essence of the whole system. The employers were hostile to compulsion in 1894. They were constantly appealing to the compulsory powers of the Court while there was a strong revolutionary labour movement from 1908 to 1913. Some of them have now reverted to their earlier position.

Moreover, the chief demands for abolition of the whole system at the 1928 conference were voiced by representatives of the organised farmers. Complaints were made during the conference proceedings that the delegate of the dairy-farmers had previously written condemnations of the labour movement that made co-operation difficult, if not impossible, on the part of the trade union leaders. The farmers' advocates also put forward very strong anti-protectionist views. The original Arbitration Act was passed by a Government which depended for its support upon an alliance between the trade unionists and small farmers, and tariff protection ranked with labour and land legislation as the important items in this Government's programme. It is obvious, therefore, that the former allies have now become political enemies.

One further illustration may be cited of the unexpected twists which the arbitration system has taken because of changed economic and political conditions. No principle laid down by the Court called forth more bitter comment and hostility from the employers than the "preference to unionists" clause embodied in the first award. The clause was made the subject of action before the Supreme Court and the Court of Appeal, and the employers were only restrained from taking their appeal to the Privy Council by the fear that the Government of the day would pass special legislation if necessary to enforce the principle. (7) Such legislation was actually embodied in the Amending Act of 1900, though individual unions like the seamen's had to struggle for the privilege for some years afterwards. (8) It is therefore of considerable significance now to find strong critics of the Court and the trade unions openly defending preference to unionists as "a most useful implement of discipline over recalcitrant unions" and "a suitable reward to any union which loyally discharges its responsibilities". (9)

Such reversals of opinion indicate the necessity of studying the arbitration system against the local economic and political background. No other New Zealand experiment has been the subject of so much library "research"; but in none is the human element so important and so subtle in its influence on actual administration. It is, however, very clear that, through all the shifts of personal and group opinion and all the changes in economic circumstances, the Arbitration Court has developed a quite unexpected power of adaptation. As early as 1901 an acute critic prefaced his review of the system by the apt quotation from Machiavelli: "Let no man who begins an innovation in a State expect that he shall stop it at his pleasure or control it according to his discretion." (10) He had in mind particularly the rather unforeseen development of the Court into a tribunal for the judicial fixation of wages and labour conditions. The quotation may just as aptly refer to the Court's powers of survival and adaptation. The whole organisation of large sections of New Zealand industry has in the last thirty-five years accommodated itself to the arbitration system. The ramifications of that system extend into minute details of industrial life, and upon its working both employers and trade unionists have built their organisation. The Court has also taken over special functions, such as the administration of the Workers' Compensation Act. Theorists may dissect the illogicalities and weaknesses of the system, and interested third parties may protest against their involvement in it, but those most directly interested find themselves dependent almost parasitically upon it and fear to face any considerable change. The trade union leaders "are afraid to take any risk of a drastic change", and even those employers who are convinced of the necessity for drastic changes—and not all employers are so convinced—recognize that "the industries—the patients—have been under the influence of a drug for thirty-five years, and you cannot suddenly take away that drug entirely from industry".(11)

The New Zealand system of compulsory arbitration must therefore be regarded as having proven itself to the extent that it has become engrafted into the Governmental system of the country. Its general acceptance at the present time is partly due to the practical way in which its administrators have fitted its working to the economic and political limitations of the country. They have not extended its operations to the basic primary industries, nor have they allowed it to become an instrument for regulating or sharing out profits. Its scope has been fairly strictly confined to the minute regulation of wages and labour conditions mainly in the secondary urban industries. In some degree also, it is accepted as an established institution, because in the course of thirty-five years other institutions, such as trade unionism, have adapted themselves to it. As long as no violent fluctuations disturbed New Zealand's economic life, there was little effective opposition, and even in the violent post-war fluctuations of prices and industry the Arbitration Court has gained rather than lost prestige. Indeed, as later sections of this chapter will show, the wholesome stabilising influence of the Court in a time of violent price fluctuations has constituted one of its greatest services to New Zealand.

The Establishment of Compulsory Arbitration

The circumstances under which the Arbitration Act of 1894 was passed, and its operation before the revolutionary trade union movement appeared in New Zealand, have been described so often and in such excellent detail that only the barest summary is necessary here.(12) Scholefield, writing in 1909, and Le Rossignol and Stewart two years later, describe the first phases of the labour revolt from the Court; but both of these statements were written before the challenge was definitely thrown down in the bitter Waihi Strike (1912) and Waterside Workers' Strike (1913).(13) A later section of this chapter is therefore devoted to a description of the period of labour discontent. The story is then brought up to date by an analysis of the wage-regulating functions of the Court in the war and post-war years.

The New Zealand Act of 1894 created the first and for some years the only system of compulsory arbitration of labour disputes by a State tribunal. The Act was modelled largely upon a Bill which had been introduced earlier into the South Australian Parliament by Mr. C. C. Kingston; but Mr. W. P. Reeves, who sponsored the New Zealand measure, must be given the credit for initiating the experiment and insisting upon its most vital feature—compulsion to enforce the Court's awards. His Bill was rejected many times because of its compulsory clauses, but these he considered vital to its success and insisted upon retaining.

It is perfectly clear, and Mr. Reeves has frankly admitted the fact, that the measure was intended to throw the burden of industrial disputes upon the conciliation boards and to keep the Arbitration Court as an ultimate tribunal for the settlement of intractable disputes. The comparative lack of opposition to the passing of the Act, and the contemptuous sneers of practical men at what they deemed the ill-considered work of a theorist, indicate that the Court was not expected to take on such practical importance as it actually did. It was at first expected that a Judge of the Supreme Court would be called upon occasionally to act as president of the Arbitration Court; but it was not expected that his whole time would be taken up and that the Court would quickly develop into a tribunal in continuous session, regulating the minutest details of industrial life.

The opposition of the employers, who in many cases refused to appoint representatives to the conciliation boards, was the chief cause of this development. It was natural also, after the trade unionists had drawn first blood by securing a substantial success in the first case brought before the Court, that there should be a tendency to promote disputes and to press them past the conciliation stage.(14) The energetic secretary of the Labour Department, Mr. Edward Tregear, and a succession of sympathetic Ministers, watched over the development of the Court, and brought in amending legislation where necessary.(15)

The amending and consolidating Act of 1905 closed the first period of experimentation with the machinery of the Court. During that period were decided most of the important questions of administrative principle which the Court has since followed. In almost every case the decisions came out of rulings of the Court on practical issues raised in specific cases. On important points where the law appeared to be ambiguous or ineffective it was amended either to support the Court's decisions or to overrule them. In this way definitions were arrived at and procedures determined.

The most important developments in the law were in the definitions of industry, worker, employer, and industrial dispute. In every case those decisions resulted from attempts by the employers to limit the scope of the Court's jurisdiction. After the first few disputes in 1896 and 1897 one question after another was raised. The inclusion in the first award of a clause granting "preference to unionists" was used as a basis for challenging the Court's authority, which was, however, upheld on appeal and put beyond all question by an amending Act in 1900. It was at this stage that a series of decisions by the Court virtually limited its jurisdiction to the manufacturing industries and declared in succession that "wharf labourers, tramway men, grocers' assistants, and livery stablemen" were not engaged in undertakings "of an industrial character".(16) The amending Act of 1901, therefore, drew definitions of employer, industry, worker, etc., in the widest terms.

The next important challenge to the Court came in the attempt to limit the term "dispute" to acute industrial situations involving the risk of a strike instead of allowing any difference of opinion between workers and employers on minor matters to be regarded as a dispute capable of being brought before the Court. This point, which was finally settled against the employers by a decision of Judge Cooper in 1906, indicates the trend of the Court's development.(17) By 1905, when the legislation was compiled into one Act, the Court had evolved into a tribunal sitting continuously to legislate upon the minute details of wages, labour conditions, holidays, apprenticeship, and all other labour questions. In 1900 its powers had been increased by the amendment that all awards were to remain in force until fresh awards were made. In the same year an extra Judge of the Supreme Court was appointed, with the understanding that he would give his full time to arbitration work. In 1901 a further very important step was taken in allowing disputes to be taken direct to the Court instead of their having first to be considered by the conciliation boards, with which there was at this time much dissatisfaction.

It will be apparent from the foregoing brief summary that the Arbitration Court had by 1905 developed ample machinery for the continuous regulation of labour conditions in the industries for which awards had been made. It is equally clear that its grip over those industries was tightening. The factory inspectors of the Labour Department acted as Inspectors of Awards, and the Secretary of the Department made no secret of his sympathy with the trade union movement and its aspirations.

In two important respects, however, the Court shrank from the logical development of its purposes. The illogical opportunism of New Zealand politics is nowhere better illustrated than in these reservations. To the great disappointment of Mr. Tregear and the disgust of many trade unionists, the judges of the Court steadfastly refused to allow its awards to take on a profit-sharing character. While they were prepared to take into account the general prosperity of the industry in deciding what was a fair wage, they made it clear that they had no intention of attempting to control the rate of profit or to fix wages in such a way as to enable the workers to share in the larger profits of prosperous years. Mr. Tregear saw clearly enough that this decision would reduce the Court to an instrument for interpreting and standardising wage rates in terms of the cost of living. Successive judges were equally clear on the point, and one of them later stated the position very emphatically in conversation with a visiting American economist.

> The judge said [writes Professor Hammond] that he did not see how the Conciliation and Arbitration Act could be made an effective instrument for bringing about a better distribution of wealth. The Act assumed the continuance of the wage system. The Court, he thought, could not do more than establish a minimum wage, and he believed it was the intention of Parliament to establish by means of this minimum wage a level below which the competition of employers was not to be allowed to reduce wages. Any attempt to bring about a better distribution of wealth must be made outside the sphere of the Court, and by such means as profit-sharing, co-operative production, and Socialism. (18)

Here was a drastic limitation of the Court's power arising from the familiar legal processes limiting and narrowing the scope of legislation which departs far from established usage. But unlike the series of decisions quoted above, which narrowed the definition of industry, this limitation was allowed to stand. No amending legislation has ever been passed which might extend the functions of the Court into the sphere of profits and management. New Zealand public opinion stopped short of this development in the direction of State Socialism.

The second drastic limitation of the Court's functions did not become explicit until 1908, when the Court refused to grant an award on the application of the Christchurch Agricultural and Pastoral Labourers' Union. (19) This refusal, which has since been supported by other similar rulings, made perfectly definite the implicit assumption upon which the Court had worked prior to 1908, that its operations were confined to the organised and unionised secondary urban industries. In New Zealand this meant that the great staple industries of the country were exempt from the direct operation of the Court's awards. In recent years breaches have been made in this principle by the granting of awards to unions of shearers, drovers, threshing-mill hands, musterers, and packers. In addition, the farmers have a vital interest in the secondary manufacturing processes of meat and dairy production, which are regulated by the Court in respect of their labour conditions. It is still true, however, that the farm-labourers in general and the small working farmers who are by all odds the most important groups of producers in the Dominion are exempt from the Court's awards.

In this limitation, again, public opinion, as represented by Parliament, supported the Court's decision. An amending Act in 1908 specifically recognised the right of the Court to refuse an award, even though all technical conditions had been complied with, "if it considers that for any reason an award ought not to be made in the matter of that dispute".

By 1906 the net effect of the administrative decisions summarised above was clear. The Court (for the conciliation machinery had been virtually abandoned) had become an instrument for standardising in minute detail the wages and labour conditions of the secondary industries of the Dominion. Its operations were not confined to those industries which enjoyed tariff protection; but such industries provided an important part of its work, while, on the other hand, the great primary industries were affected only indirectly by the awards of the Court.

Bearing these facts in mind, and remembering also that the Court began its work at the lowest depth of a prolonged industrial depression and continued into a period of steady prosperity based securely on rising prices and increasing production, it can readily be understood that its awards were very welcome to trade unionists in the early years of its operation. Until its procedure became standardised and the pace of economic progress began to slacken about 1906, the Court was able to grant successive wage increases and improvements in hours, holidays, and working conditions. It is doubtful whether, after the first year or two, the wage increases much more than kept pace with a steadily rising cost of living (20); but it may reasonably be argued that the rewards of labour taken as a whole improved considerably up till 1906.

These gains, moreover, were achieved without the necessity of striking for better conditions. The fact that from 1894 to 1906 New Zealand was completely free from industrial conflicts was an enormous gain. During this critical period of economic development the Dominion was able to take advantage of its opportunities without domestic strife complicating its problems. The worker gained by regularity of employment, by the standardising of wages as between industries and among employers in each industry, by the stamping out of sweating and subcontracting, and by sharing in the general prosperity of the country, which made the normal rates of wages substantially higher than the minimum award rates in a great majority of cases. These were substantial gains, and the trade union leaders rightly attributed them to the beneficent influence of the Court.

The employers, on the other hand, gradually withdrew from their position of hostility to the Court. They became convinced that it was not an instrument of socialisation, that its awards were reasonable and not destructive of industrial enterprise, and that they gained substantially from the industrial peace which it ensured. There still remained the complaint that the minuteness of its regulations harassed and hampered the employer in the management of his business; but a large part of this complaint was academic, and in very few cases was it possible at this stage to quote definite examples of the harm done to industrial organisation. The benefits of the system clearly outweighed its defects, and by 1906 even the employers were becoming convinced of its usefulness.

There was no doubt of its popularity in the country generally. It was associated in the popular mind with prosperity, it had brought industrial peace for twelve years, and there was no evidence of any harmful effects arising from the Court's awards. The primary industries were prosperous and the town industries prospered with them. Moreover, there was apparently a complete absence of class warfare. The lion had lain down with the lamb. Unionism was accepted, the membership of the unions, helped by the preference clauses in most awards, steadily increased, the secretaries worked with and through the Court and maintained cordial relations with the employers. To many observers, especially to visitors, the labour situation in New Zealand immediately after 1900 seemed almost like an industrial millennium.(21) It was unfortunate, therefore, that the advent of revolutionary, class-conscious, industrial unionism in 1908 should have coincided with the achievement by the Court of a *status quo* which seemed to the workers to present an effective barrier to any further improvement of their economic standards. The next period in the Court's history, the years from 1906 to 1913, saw a determined challenge to the Court's authority from the industrial wing of the trade union movement, a challenge which culminated in the bitter and costly "general strike" of 1913.

The Revolt of the Militant Unions, 1906–13

Labour dissatisfaction with the Court's awards became acute in 1906. There had, however, been much grumbling before this date, and Broadhead records expressions of disapproval as early as 1901.(22) Dissatisfaction was based primarily on the fact that the Court was increasingly taking up the attitude that no further advances of wages were possible and refusing to grant new awards. It was clear that the first immediate gains from levelling up and standardising wages had been reaped, and that the Court had no intention of embarking upon any steps which would advance the standard of living of the workers. The consistent refusal of the Court to consider anything resembling compulsory profit-sharing meant in effect that the workers were bound by the arbitration legislation to accept nominal wage rates based upon the standard of living of 1900. The Court would not consider means to improve that standard, and the workers were bound not to use the direct methods of collective bargaining and the strike. Sir Robert Stout had prophesied that the arbitration system would mean a reversion from contract to status, and when the trade unions began to realise what this meant in a time of general prosperity, rising prices, and rising costs of living, they became very restive. The substantial benefits which they secured from industrial peace, continuity of employment, the tendency for wages to advance beyond the minimum wage rates, improvements in holidays, hours, and labour conditions, did little to counteract the psychological effect of their feeling that they were tied to inadequate standards of living as expressed in wages.

Naturally enough the dissatisfaction was often given a personal turn by attacks upon the distinguished judges who acted as presidents of the Court. The growing tendency to legalism, inevitable in a tribunal which had accumulated precedents and rules of procedure, was a source of constant irritation. The fact that the virtual abandonment of the conciliation machinery had since 1901 thrown upon the Court a much greater volume of work and responsibility accentuated this situation.

From time to time strong attacks were made upon the judges and also upon the Government for appointing them. About this time, also, the old alliance between the small farmers and the trade unionists was obviously breaking down. A Political Labour League was formed in 1904, following a resolution of the trades and labour councils in 1902, and only Seddon's personal prestige prevented an open rupture. After his death in 1906 the organisation of a separate Parliamentary Labour Party was assured. One candidate was elected in 1908. The Political Labour League went out of existence after the election, but the New Zealand Labour Party was formed in 1910 at a meeting of the trades and labour councils. Four candidates were elected in 1911, and in 1912 the United Labour Party was formed and conducted a vigorous political propaganda.

Apart from these general expressions of dissatisfaction, however, there was a very definite and specific cause of labour discontent in the rising cost of living, which began to appear as a new phenomenon to be reckoned with in all labour negotiations. In 1904 Mr. Tregear, as Secretary of Labour, sent the Prime Minister a remarkable memorandum, in which he drew attention to this fact, and went on to state in the most vigorous terms that:

> There is a third hand in the game besides the employer and the employee, and it is this third man—the non-producing ground landlord of the city and suburban property—who alone will rise a winner in the end. The chief devourer of the wages of the worker and of the profits of the employer is excessive rent. That an equitable payment for the use of land and dwellings should be made to their owners is, under the present constitution of society, proper and desirable, but a greedy, rack-renting system which transfers gradually almost the whole of the earnings of the industrial and commercial classes into the pockets of the non-producer is indefensible. (23)

It is difficult to discover what purpose these strong words were intended to serve. It is obvious that by far the larger part of the gains from rising prices have gone into increasing land values in New Zealand. It is also clear that the workers were involved in a losing effort to keep their wages commensurate with the increasing costs of living. So far from wage rates keeping the standards of 1900, they tended to lose ground. The only result of Mr. Tregear's memorandum, however, was a half-hearted housing scheme. As far as the Arbitration Court was concerned there was no possibility of any steps being taken to do more than register past increases in the cost of living wage awards. As far as the award wage rates were concerned, the workers appeared to be losing ground.

Actually they were sharing substantially in the general prosperity which always accompanies rising prices in New Zealand. A later judge of the Court has argued this point very clearly:

> Admitting that the award rates did not in every case keep pace with the rising cost of living, there were many factors beneficially affecting the real earnings of the workers. Employment was plentiful, and there was a great diminution of casualness of employment. The award rates were true minima, and very many workers received substantially higher wages. Overtime was regularly worked, and was paid for at higher relative rates than in pre-war times. In many occupations young lads became self-supporting almost as soon as they left school, and so relieved their parents of the burden of their maintenance. Hours of work were shortened, and conditions of employment were improved. Unskilled and semi-skilled workers were often able to command skilled workers' rates of pay. All these factors must be considered before we can affirm that wages did not, during the period of rising prices, keep pace with the increasing cost of living. When we make proper allowance for these matters we cannot say that the real earnings of the average worker did not keep pace fairly well with the increased cost of living during the period of rising prices except, possibly, for a few months at the peak of prices. The volume of retail trade, the increased attendances at entertainments and race meetings, and the general appearance of prosperity, all indicated that purchasing power was not diminished, but rather enhanced.(24)

In view of these facts it is not surprising to find upon close examination that the discontent with the Court between 1906 and 1913 was very largely the result of the importation of doctrinaire revolutionary theories into the labour movement. The apparent stagnation of wage awards provided material for the propaganda of direct actionists, whose attack was not so much upon the Arbitration Court as upon the capitalist system. Despite a measure of disappointment that the Court had not fulfilled all the idealistic hopes they had placed upon it, the great majority of the craft unionists represented in the trades and labour councils remained free from the doctrines of class warfare and loyal to the principles, if not always to the practice, of the arbitration system.(25) The revolt was confined to such strongly organised and militant unions as the miners, waterside workers, seamen, and slaughtermen. Among such workers theories of direct action always have a stronger appeal than among the more conservative and weaker unions formed primarily to defend the privileges of skilled craft workers.

The origin and point of entry of the revolutionary doctrines is quite clear. Its centre and rallying-point throughout the whole period was the mining industry. Discontent among the miners had been vocal at least as early as 1901–2, when prolonged agitation to shorten working hours and virtually increase wages by the inclusion of a "bank-to-bank" clause, calculating working hours from the time of entering the mine instead of the time of arrival at the working face, had been unsuccessful before the Court, but successful in Parliament, which passed a statute granting the demand. The miners, therefore, had proof of their ability to secure concessions which had been refused by the Court.

The first strikes for twelve years had occurred in 1906 and 1907, in defiance of the Court's awards and compulsory powers of enforcement. There was a general feeling that the Arbitration Act was on its trial and needed amendment. In the session of 1908, therefore, an important amending Act made two major changes. An effort was made to revive again the conciliation procedure which had failed, but this time Conciliation Commissioners were appointed—civil servants who quickly developed both skill and ability to gain the public confidence. They have acted as chairmen of conciliation councils convened *ad hoc* for the particular disputes needing investigation. While this procedure has not altogether fulfilled the hopes of those who looked for a reversion to the original plans of Mr. Reeves for a system under which conciliation should settle the majority of disputes and the Arbitration Court become merely an ultimate tribunal of appeal, it has gone a long way in that direction. There is little doubt that this wise step taken in 1908 has been the salvation of the arbitration system. It is reported that in recent years the conciliation councils have settled more than ninety per cent. of the disputes, while the Court has fixed minimum rates and laid down general policies.(26) It can therefore be said that after 1908 the system became what it was originally intended to be, a system of voluntary conciliation supplemented by judicial fixation of wages.

The second major change introduced in 1908 was the imposition of more effective penalties for strikes and lockouts, designed to prevent such outbreaks as had occurred in the two previous years. The penalties have not achieved their object, even though after 1912 an unsympathetic Government made strong efforts to enforce them. Such sanctions are of little avail in practice, since the working of conciliation and arbitration depends ultimately upon good will and not upon force.

Beyond these the legislation of 1908 made no really effective changes in the law. A distinguished member of the Ministry made public suggestions for the greater use of piece-wages or "exertion wages", but the suggestion fell on deaf ears.(27) By this time the die was cast as far as the miners were concerned. The theories of industrial, syndicalist unionism propagated among them were based largely upon the American movement known as the Industrial Workers of the World.(28) A strike at Blackball in 1908 had already revealed a new temper in the labour movement. The striking union was fined by the Court and efforts were made to recover the sum by distraint upon the personal possessions of individual miners. The official auction sale of the goods distrained gave the miners an excellent opportunity of ridiculing the Court and the Government. The auction was made a joke, and the total proceeds were 12s. 6d. The Government then had to attach the workers' wages in order to collect the fines, which it did eventually. Though the men had to accept defeat and return to work, the purpose of the revolutionary leaders in challenging the Court had been achieved, and the organisation of the new industrial movement spread rapidly. Registration of the unions under the Arbitration Act of 1894 had always been voluntary, and many of the stronger unions now proceeded either to cancel their registration or to allow it to lapse by failing to send in the required returns. As the same time, they organised a Miners' Federation of Labour following the Blackball Strike in 1908 and expanded this into the New Zealand Federation of Labour in 1909. This Federation specifically adopted the theory of the class war as expounded in the Communist Manifesto of 1848. When it adopted a revised constitution in 1912 it used the preamble of the Industrial Workers of the World, which in turn repeated the phrases and ideas of Marx and Engels.

The working class and the employing class have nothing in common. There can be no peace so long as hunger and want are found among millions of working people and the few, who make up the employing class, have all the good things of life.

Between these two classes a struggle must go on until the workers of the world organise as a class, take possession of the earth and the machinery of production, and abolish the wage system. . . .

Instead of the conservative motto: "A fair day's wages for a fair day's work", our watchword is, "Abolition of the wage system".

It is the historic mission of the working class to do away with capitalism. The army of production must be organised, not only for the everyday struggle with capitalists, but also to carry on production when capitalism has been overthrown. By organising industrially we are forming the structure of the new society within the shell of the old.(29)

In thus attributing the introduction of the new class-conscious note in industrial affairs to the revolutionary activities of a comparatively few labour leaders, the economic historian needs neither to pass judgment upon their actions nor to state anything beyond what is printed in their own official record of the period. This record, printed and widely distributed under the title *The Tragic Story of the Waihi Strike*, contains many bitter references to the arbitration system, and ends with such statements as: "Until the toilers of New Zealand absolutely smash the Arbitration Act the thing will be for ever in the way, tripping them up and betraying them."(30) It should be stated that these words were writen in the heat of a bitter struggle and after a new and hostile Government had developed the tactic of using the arbitration machinery to discipline recalcitrant unions. But there is ample evidence that the industrial unionists claimed for themselves, and gloried in, the distinction of having broken through the period of industrial peace. Whether or not they were justified is a matter of opinion; the initiative was undoubtedly theirs.

Between 1908 and 1912 the Federation of Labour grew rapidly. The miners' unions provided a fighting nucleus, and they were joined by many of the industrial as distinct from the craft unions.

The West Coast Labourers had been the first to come in. The Auckland General Labourers followed. Then came the Auckland Tramwaymen, for whom the Federation won such substantial increases. The Waterside Workers of Westport next added their membership to the strength of the Federation, and soon after the Shearers and nearly the whole of the

Waterside Workers of New Zealand came in. Then came the Westport Labourers, the Flaxmillers, and other organisations.

At the last Conference (May 1912) the membership stood at 15,000!

The officers of the Federation and the Organiser (R. Semple) went everywhere, hunting every Labour heresy, nailing every Labour lie; its speakers spoke in nearly every town, faced every Capitalistic opponent; on every field improved conditions of labour were won—shorter hours here, higher wages there. The efforts of these officials have been herculean; their activities prodigious.

Never before in the history of the Southern World was the rise of an organisation so rapid and so firm.(31)

It was inevitable that so powerful an organisation should seek and find an arena of conflict worthy of its powers. On the other side were employers' associations who readily accepted the challenge, having come quickly to the conclusion that the "Red Federation" was a menace, to be strangled in its cradle.

The number of industrial disturbances that occurred between 1906 and 1913 is much exaggerated by the system of recording the official statistics by districts. The slaughtermen employed in the freezing-works struck twice, in 1906–7 and in 1912–13; but the statistics record twelve strikes on the former occasion and nineteen on the latter.(32) The number of actual conflicts was very few; most of the industries continued under the arbitration system without recourse to strikes even in this period of discontent. There were occasions, indeed, when the warfare between the industrial and craft unionists was pursued with more rancour than the class warfare between the unions and the employers. The fighting policy of the Federation, however, enjoined upon it the necessity of coming to the support of all strikes, whether of "arbitration" or of industrial unions. Its prestige was greatly enhanced by this fact and by its successes in winning conditions which in many cases had been denied by the Court. One fact was demonstrated beyond all doubt in this period, that the strongly organised unions, given conditions of general prosperity and a fair degree of solidarity in their own ranks, were able to obtain better terms by collective bargaining than could be obtained under the arbitration system. The weaker craft unions, on the other hand, even at this time, remained steadfastly of the opinion that the Court was their shield and defence.

The series of strikes in which the Federation of Labour took part was not very large; but its culmination in the Waihi Strike of 1912 and the Waterside Workers' Strike of the following year indicated the seriousness of the industrial situation thereby created. The Waihi Miners' Union had affiliated to the Federation in 1909 and cancelled its registration under the Arbitration Act in 1911. Almost immediately the Federation officials obtained for them substantially improved wages and conditions. In the following year a new situation arose when a section of the engine-drivers formed a union which applied for registration under the Court. The Miners' Union took this up immediately as a challenge, declared the union "scab" and a mere device of the employers. A strike was called in protest, demanding the disbandment of the new union and the recognition of the miners' organisation as the only union with which the employers should deal and to which all the mine-workers should belong.

The strike began on May 13, 1912, and was continued, with the support of contributions from other unions in Australia and New Zealand, until the formation of a "loyal" union enabled the mines to be reopened on October 2nd. The strikers were beaten and capitulated at the end of November.(33) In the course of the strike there had been the ugliest clashes between strikers and police, leading on one occasion to the death of a striker. Many other strikers, including all the prominent officials of the Union, had been imprisoned. There was no doubt left of the hostility of the new farmers' Government to the industrial labour movement, and feeling ran very high.

After Waihi there was a brief period during which overtures were made to compose the differences separating the two wings of the trade union movement. The Federation of Labour had, up till this time, maintained an uncompromising attitude, refusing to modify its preamble or abate its class-warfare doctrines. The older craft union organisation retained control of the various trades and labour councils. Throughout the Waihi Strike these councils had refused to countenance the Federation's tactics and had even warned the Australian unions—fruitlessly as it turned out—against supporting the strikers.(34) The bitterest recriminations ensued, and were not lessened by the fact that the United Labour Party, formed by the trades and labour councils and the Political Labour Party at a so-called Unity Conference in Easter week, 1912, had placed in the field a powerful rival organisation. The United Labour Party was distinctly right-wing, and commanded the support of many bourgeois Radicals. Its programme was essentially Parliamentary, and its organiser, a voluble and ubiquitous American "Professor", W. T. Mills from Milwaukee, was no believer in the class war. (35)

After Waihi, however, the Federation of Labour sought alliance with its rival. A preliminary conference was held in January 1913, and the real Unity Congress, convened in the following July, worked out a basis of agreement. Two organisations were agreed upon: a Social Democratic Party to represent the political wing of the movement, and the United Federation of Labour to work in the industrial field. After a long fight the preamble proclaiming class warfare was dropped, but the honours of reorganisation lay with the militants. (36) The strike policy adopted was too obviously revolutionary to command the real support of the craft unionists, and the life of the Federation was not very long. The Social Democratic Party also dwindled quickly into a mere local unit which was later absorbed by the Parliamentary Labour Party. The Waterside Workers' Strike, which began at Wellington on October 20th, resulted in a decisive defeat for the Federation of Labour and its principles of industrial direct action. The wave of patriotic enthusiasm which swept New Zealand at the outbreak of war completed its destruction. The United Federation nominally survived until it was replaced by the Alliance of Labour in 1920. The miners in the meantime decided that their interests would best be served by alliance with the Australian miners rather than with the New Zealand craft unionists. The United Federation of Labour was never a fighting organisation, therefore, after the Waterside Workers' Strike. The Alliance of Labour by which it was replaced after the war retains some of the industrial philosophy of the Federation. It will affiliate only nationally organised unions which will agree to its theory of an industrial Parliament, but in practice it has co-operated with the craft unions and accepted the arbitration system, albeit rather ungraciously at times. The real end of the revolutionary challenge to the Arbitration

Court is to be found, therefore, in the defeat of the Federation of Labour at the time of the Waterside Workers' Strike in 1913.

This finale of the revolutionary movement was quite dramatic. The dispute of the Wellington shipwrights, out of which it grew, was trivial enough, but the contest soon developed into a death-struggle between the Federation of Labour and the Employers' Federation.(37) On this occasion, though many of the craft unionists were at least lukewarm, there was nominal solidarity in the trade union movement. Levies were paid and the strategy first of the isolated, then of a sympathetic, and finally of an attempted general strike, was faithfully followed under the direction of the Federation officials. The result was a complete defeat, in which the most important factors were the response of the farming community to the call for free labourers, and the uncompromising attitude of the Government in enrolling special constables for their defence.

Besides breaking up the Federation of Labour, this strike had very important results in tightening up the administration of the Arbitration Act against the trade unions. A Labour Disputes Investigation Act on the Canadian model was passed in 1913 and was made more stringent in its operation by successive measures of war legislation in succeeding years.(38) Under its operation, strikes were practically outlawed as an instrument of industrial policy. Even more important, however, was the development of the tactic, first used at Waihi and a little later at a local waterside strike in Timaru, of enrolling free labourers in unions which were perfectly eligible to apply for registration under the Arbitration Act and to seek from it an award which thereupon became legally binding upon the whole industry for a term of three years.

Backed by a Government which was hostile to the class-warfare theories and practices of the militant unions, this tactic became a powerful instrument for bringing the unions once again under the Court's discipline. The circle had been completed. Those unions which, confident in their own bargaining powers, and disgusted at the stabilisation of the standard of living, had cancelled their registration, were driven back within the competence of the Court. Even the miners have since found themselves subject to this pressure. At the outbreak of war in July 1914 it may therefore be claimed that the arbitration system had successfully withstood a prolonged and well-planned challenge from the side of militant labour, and had emerged from this trial more firmly rooted in popular support and with its machinery not only tested but strengthened. War conditions were to test that machinery from another angle altogether.

A Legal Minimum Wage

During the war period New Zealand was exceptionally prosperous and, despite a war effort that was creditable in proportion to the size of the population, wage-earners generally were in a fairly favourable position. The level of real wages measured in food, as far as the awards of the Court are concerned, fell throughout this period, but the shortage of many types of skilled and unskilled workers led commonly to earnings above the award rates laid down by the Court. It is difficult to measure the extent to which these minimum award rates become the maximum, but in normal times, especially for certain classes of unskilled workers such as building tradesmen, employers are generally prepared to pay something above the award rate. In times of prosperity and labour shortage this tendency is naturally more pronounced.

Moreover, unemployment, which is normally of small volume in the Dominion, was almost completely absent during the war and the post-war boom, while opportunities for overtime were plentiful.

Hence it was not unnatural to find that, despite wage increases that always registered something short of the increase in the cost of living, labour was on the whole contented and quiescent until the credit inflation (towards the end of the war and immediately afterwards) caused a steep rise in the price-level, so that the cost-of-living problem became acute and the Arbitration Court was forced to take more account of it.

The War Legislation and Statute Law Amendment Act (1918) gave power (Section 18) to the Court to take increases in the cost of living into account during the currency of awards. Acting upon this power the Court took a step that was the logical development of its evolution from a mere tribunal to settle occasional disputes into the economic arbiter of a large part of the industrial life of the community. It instituted for all industries a legal minimum or basic wage.

Awards of the Court generally have a currency of three years, and the workers, in a time of rising prices, had to suffer the increase in the cost of living over that period. This was naturally a source of friction when the rise in the cost of living steepened, and advantage was quickly taken of the powers conferred on the Court, under the 1918 Act, to review awards during their currency. Applications poured into the Court, which was almost inevitably forced to take them *en bloc* and devise some scheme for a standard minimum wage which might serve for all industries as a basis upon which future increases might be calculated as cost-of-living bonuses. The Court made its first general pronouncement under the new Act on April 19, 1919. After explaining that it would fix minimum rates and then announce periodic bonuses or reductions in bonuses as the cost of living changed, it fixed the basic rates as(39):

Skilled workers	1s. 7½d. per hour
Semi-skilled workers	1s. 4½d. to 1s. 6d. per hour
Unskilled workers	1s. 3½d. per hour

In the words of the Court, "these wages are substantial increases, for the different classes of workers, upon the wages prevailing immediately prior to the war, and to some extent, although not wholly, compensate the workers for the increases in the cost of living up to the time of the passing of the recent Act".

A year later, on April 27, 1920, when announcing the third bonus, the Court reviewed the basic rates in what has come to be known as the Gisborne Pronouncement.(40) The readjusted rates were then:

Skilled workers	2s. per hour
Semi-skilled workers	1s. 8d. to 1s. 10d. per hour
Unskilled workers	1s. 7d. per hour

Until 1923 the Court held to these basic rates for all industries and the battles fought before it were, therefore, of two main kinds. First, there was the bonus itself. Secondly, in any particular industrial award there was a good deal of skirmishing concerning the classification of workers in the industry concerned into the three grades recognised by the Court. This classification was obviously the main source of disagreement, since the basic rates were fixed for all industries.

The procedure adopted by the Court, once the basic rates had been decided upon, was to make a half-yearly pronouncement (usually in May and November) of the movement in the cost of living during the preceding six months (October to March and April to September). Upon that basis was calculated the bonus to be paid for the ensuing six months.

When the movement in the cost of living had been ascertained, the bonus due was calculated as a number of pence per hour upon the basis of the wages of a semi-skilled worker for a 48-hour week. The bonus thus arrived at was given as a flat rate to all three groups—skilled, semi-skilled, and unskilled.

The first bonus of 2½d. per hour was granted in April 1919, at the time of the first pronouncement concerning basic rates of wages, and was intended to compensate for the rise in the cost of living between the passing of the 1918 Act and the first pronouncement. In January 1920 a further 1d. per hour was granted, and in May 1920 a further 1½d. At this stage, however, the Court was convinced that its basic rates were too low, and therefore incorporated part of the bonuses in a new scale of basic rates (given above under the Gisborne Pronouncement), at the same time adding a further bonus of 3d. per hour.

The history of the subsequent bonuses illustrates clearly the difficulties besetting any system for the judicial fixation of wages at a time when violent fluctuations of economic conditions are likely to occur. When the next bonus fell due (November 1920) it was calculated as 1¾d. per hour; but it was disclosed that in the calculation of the bonus granted in January 1920 an error of calculation had resulted in 1d. per hour being paid in excess. The resultant over-payment was rectified and the total bonus payable corrected by reducing the new bonus granted to ¾d. per hour.(41) Following the usual custom the Court announced the bonus due and then heard the case argued before making a general order putting the new rates into force. Already there were indications that the post-war boom was drawing to a close, although the cost of living continued to increase rapidly. The workers' advocates stood firm for a further rise in wages, based on the increased cost of living; the employers called evidence, including that of the

Chairman of the Bank of New Zealand, to show that a crisis was near at hand and would render the industrial position precarious.

Before the Court made its next pronouncement the crisis was well developed. Upon the basis of the cost-of-living figures it appeared that a further 1¼d. per hour or 5s. per week should be added to the bonus. But in the meantime the war and post-war prosperity had given way to the anxiety of a severe crisis. Inflation and land speculation had gone to great lengths between 1918 and 1920, and the first fall in the price of export products was bound to prick the bubble of artificial prosperity. New Zealand is in fact peculiarly dependent upon the prices of her exports in the markets of the world. Over 90 per cent. of these exports are derived from the pastoral industry, or, in other words, from the sheep and the cow. Wool, butter, cheese, frozen meat, hides, skins, tallow, and many other allied commodities and by-products, are sold as raw materials or foodstuffs and provide the purchasing power with which the people of the Dominion may command the manufactures and exotic goods they need. As the prices of these export goods rose rapidly immediately after the war, large credits were heaped up in London, which were used partly to finance heavily increased imports, partly to loosen credit advances in New Zealand. A policy of borrowing on the part of the Government assisted the inflationary process, and heavy commitments were entered on every hand. The repatriation scheme for returned soldiers launched thousands of new buyers with Government credit to draw upon into a land and housing market already excited and buoyant. As a natural result, both urban and rural land values increased rapidly. In the same way, new enterprises sprang up all over the Dominion, and existing enterprises were greatly extended. There were, for example, many new freezing-works built, numbers of which were soon in difficulties.(42) The Government also embarked upon extensive public works that had been delayed by the war, especially upon hydro-electric development. The local secondary manufactures were unwontedly prosperous, and at the same time the importing merchants enlarged their orders to meet the apparently insatiable demands of consumers.

But with the fall in the price of wool the merchants found

themselves with heavy stocks bought at high prices, while the purchasing power of the most important section of the community, the farmers, was crippled. The continued high price of butter and the guaranteed price of wheat alone saved the farming community from serious disaster. In these circumstances the employers once again strenuously opposed the granting of any further increases in wages. The labour delegates, on the other hand, claimed that the workers were justly entitled to the extra 1¼d. per hour, since they had suffered the increased cost of living during the preceding six months. Ultimately the Court decided to embark upon a scheme of stabilisation, to withhold the bonus due, but to offset it against the reduction that might be expected to follow in the next six-monthly period.(43) By this scheme wages were kept stable from November 1920 to May 1922, over the worst period of the credit stringency and economic depression. This stabilisation certainly mitigated the severity of the crisis in no small degree. The labour costs of production were stable and calculable for months ahead in a most trying time, and the purchasing power of the labouring section of the community was unimpaired. A drastic reduction of wages, such as would probably have followed unrestricted competition, would inevitably have produced reactions in the shape of unemployment, lowered purchasing power, and a vicious circle of pessimism.

The subsequent history of the cost-of-living bonuses was comparatively uneventful. Wages were stabilised at the same figure from November 1920 to May 1922. At the latter date, when the worst period of the crisis was over, the Court issued its preliminary announcement that the fall in the cost of living justified a reduction of 1¼d. per hour or 5s. per week. The labour delegates before the Court naturally argued against any reduction and based their argument on two main reasons—the necessity of maintaining the standard of living and the fact that under rising prices wages had not kept pace with the cost of living. Mr. Justice Frazer's reply to the second argument has already been quoted; the first he discussed with some elaboration, although his main line of defence was that since the proposed reduction was in strict accord with the lower cost of living, the standard was not affected.(44)

The employers urged the necessity of much greater reductions totalling 13s. per week, made up of the 5s. proposed by the Court, an extra 2s. which was really included under a misapprehension, and a further 6s. which it was urged should be taken off the basic wage. In support of these reductions strong evidence was put forward concerning the serious economic position of many industries, and also concerning the increase of labour costs through slackness in the workshop.

The Court, however, rejected both sets of arguments, and, the employers' assessor dissenting, adhered to its decision to reduce the bonus by 1¼d. per hour or 5s. per week.

In the following pronouncement (November 1922) the cost of living had again fallen, and without much argument the Court authorised a further reduction of bonus amounting to ¾d. per hour or 3s. per week. By this time conditions were very much more stable, and neither side made a great fight. It so happened that in the two following pronouncements the movement in the cost of living was so slight as to justify the Court in keeping wages stationary.

The net result was, therefore, that during the whole period of post-war adjustment and depression following the boom, over a period of three years, from May 1921 to May 1924, the general level of wages in the Dominion had but two changes, amounting together to a reduction of 2d. per hour on all wages, whether skilled or unskilled. There can be but few countries in the world where labour came through the depression so lightly. There was a certain amount of unemployment, but its volume was surprisingly small. Not only was there stability of the general level of minimum wages, but the normal relationship between wages in the different industries was, by the provision of a legal minimum wage, fairly well sustained. There was no such upturning of the industrial system as that which in Great Britain, for example, destroyed the normal relationship between the wages of organised skilled labour and those of the relatively less organised and less skilled labour which in the past had had to be protected by the trade boards. A certain amount of readjustment in accordance with the variant conditions of different industries necessarily took place. For example, the engineering industry became stagnant and therefore the minimum award rates of the Court tended to become the maximum, while there was a good deal of unemployment. The building trades, on the other hand, were prosperous even after the slump, and wages were much higher than the award rates. Such readjustments as these, however, compare very favourably with the wholesale wage reductions and widespread unemployment of other countries, and not less with their piecemeal and fortuitous character, which so often resulted in the most extraordinary reversals of position between different trades.

The Strain of Falling Prices

Having successfully established itself as an integral and important part of the Governmental and economic machinery of New Zealand the Arbitration Court had before 1914 staved off challenges first from employers and then from revolutionary labour organisations. In the war and post-war period it had come with considerable credit through a trying succession of price disturbances. In order to minimise the effects of these price movements the Court adopted a bold and well-considered basic or minimum wage-scale applicable to all industries, and reviewed this scale at frequent intervals. It is difficult to find valid objections to the claim that by this action, and especially by the effective stabilisation of wages during the violent price fluctuations of the crisis period 1920–4, the Court saved New Zealand a great deal of industrial conflict and prevented a great deal of hardship to the less powerfully organised workers. As an emergency measure the stabilisation scheme was wisely conceived, thoroughly planned, and carefully executed.

At the expiration of the last basic wage award in May 1924 the Court reverted to the practice of making individual awards for each trade. It was clear that the worst immediate effects of the fall in prices were past. Prices of the main exports were higher once more, and there was a general expectation that "the corner had been turned". Little beyond the general theoretical criticism to which the Court has always been subject was to be heard, though there were indications that the farming community, never very enthusiastic about what they consider the pampered lot of the town worker, were ready to blame the Court for their financial troubles.

The dilemma in which the Court was placed by falling prices

had already been illustrated very clearly by the only breach made in the stabilisation scheme.

In order to effect the stabilisation of wages during the depression, it had been necessary for the Court to withhold in May 1921 a bonus that was due according to the increase in the cost of living during the preceding six months. Naturally the trade unions had not accepted the scheme with any great cordiality, and a strong appeal was made to the Court to reconsider its pronouncement. This the Court refused to do, and in its decision the workers' assessor supported his colleagues. Some doubt, however, existed concerning the Court's power under the law to fix wages for such a long period ahead, and therefore a proviso had been added to the pronouncement, carefully worded as follows:

> It is not intended to take away the right of either party to an award or industrial agreement to make application to the Court under the existing legislation; but the Court will require proof of extraordinary circumstances before departing from the principles herein laid down, unless the parties agree to a modification.(45)

It was not long before this formula proved a source of serious difficulty. The excitement concerning the stabilisation scheme had barely passed from the public mind when the invocation of the proviso in the case of a dispute between shearers and sheep-owners reopened the whole question and did more to shake the established position of the Court than any other dispute during the last twenty years.

It should be remembered that the great bulk of the trades that lie within the Court's jurisdiction are those town industries that in New Zealand are commonly and significantly called "secondary industries". The higher standards of wages and working conditions and the protection of workers by labour laws are widely, if somewhat incorrectly, regarded as part of an industrial scheme of which tariff protection to the industries concerned is the external complement. The industries and occupations affected by the Court's decisions find a domestic market; even the nascent manufactures have little or no export trade. The result is that changes in wage rates are easily adjusted and diffused over the economic organisation of the Dominion.

But the rural industries are in a very different position. The bulk of their produce is for competitive world markets, so that they cannot pass on wage rates that have become disproportionate to their receipts. The Arbitration Court and all the other measures of State Socialism adopted in New Zealand during the last thirty years have undoubtedly resulted in some net cost to the community, and that cost has for the most part been passed back on to the shoulders of the farming community. While the level of prices continued to rise and prosperity was abundant the burden was easily carried, but as soon as a sharp fall in prices plunged the primary producers into difficulties the cost of the experiment was bound to be revealed.

The fixing of prices by the Arbitration Court is equivalent to pegging down part of the economic machine, and any sudden movement of the rest of the mechanism causes strain. So when the price of wool fell drastically in the season 1920–1, the sheep-owners came to the Court to protest that the wages of shearers must be reduced, since they could not possibly pay them when their wool-clips were unsaleable. The shearers, on the other hand, asked for an increased piece rate; but the President of the Court and the employers' assessor were convinced that "extraordinary circumstances" in terms of the Court's proviso had been proved and therefore departed from the stabilisation scheme by ordering a reduction of approximately 20 per cent. in the wages of shearers.(46) The workers' assessor, who had held his position since 1908, resigned in protest against what he considered to be a breach of agreement, a view of the case to which the other two members took strong exception. The trade unions insisted upon re-electing him despite his reluctance to stand, and he finally consented to hold the fort until a successor was appointed. He adhered, however, to his refusal to take permanent office again, and after a few months his successor took his place and the controversy gradually died down. It had, however, shaken the confidence not only of many trade unionists, but also of many other people to whom the very fact of controversy brought the Court from its assured position as part of the Governmental machinery of the country once again into the category of debatable policy. The shearers attempted a strike; but there is always a fluctuating reserve of labour in the ranks of the small farmers, and the

Maori shearers were not disposed to stand by the union, so that the strike was little more than a demonstration.

When prices fell again in 1925–6 all economic problems were greatly accentuated. The Dominion was suffering from the after-effects of a prolonged period of speculative activity based upon the expectation of a continuously rising price-level. The ultimate repository of over-valuation is the land, and lower price-levels which promised to be permanent had disclosed a serious economic position on the part of great numbers of farmers. The first sharp effects of the 1920–1 crisis—bankruptcies, compromise of mortgages, abandonment of farms to the mortgagees—had not been adequate to right the situation, and the recovery of prices in 1923–4 had tempted many people to believe that the setback was only temporary. The further severe fall in prices, with the prospect that, despite recoveries, it might be the precursor of lower if not falling prices for a long period, made it impossible any longer to blink the hard economic fact that rural lands and all their superstructure were not worth the valuations that had been placed upon them.

It is only too easy in such a situation to focus attention upon one particularly obvious weakness in a complicated organisation. The financial and economic strain through which New Zealand has been passing is less than that which most countries went through in the crisis of 1920–1. The stabilisation scheme of the Arbitration Court and similar measures postponed a good deal of the reconstruction which in other countries was brought about by the harsh operation of bankruptcy and wage reduction. The result is that the financial strain which remains in New Zealand is not a question merely of inflated land values, of rural credit, arbitration wages, excessive taxation, over-borrowing, or inflated overhead costs, but a combination of all these and other related factors. There is no really effective short cut to a solution of problems as complicated as this. To focus interest on one aspect of the problem and neglect others is not very helpful.

Despite a considerable element of truth in their reasoning, therefore, the recent attack by the farmers upon the Arbitration Court as an agency which interferes with the natural adjustments of prices and wages is not a very convincing explanation of the economic difficulties of the farming community. Statistical measurement of such an involved problem is all but impossible. It may be shown that the cost of labour employed on farms is very small and in any case is mostly outside the Court's jurisdiction. It may further be shown that the prices of farm materials have moved in a manner relatively favourable to the farming community in recent years.(47) This does not, however, dispose of the fact that the level of wages as fixed by the Arbitration Court remains substantially above the level of export prices when both are compared with pre-war standards.(48) The exact extent to which the maintenance of these higher wage-levels is responsible for high farming costs is impossible to estimate and still more impossible to measure.

There can be no reasonable doubt that the Court, by setting wage standards, affects the costs of urban distributing and manufacturing businesses and also of Governmental services. The farmers are not likely to be argued, by index-numbers, out of the belief that if the wages of County Council and other employees were lower, their taxation would be less. The connection is so obvious indeed, and so liable to be exaggerated, that it becomes easy to forget such other factors in the situation as the expanded margins of profits, the slackness in efficient organisation, capital expansion for purposes not really necessary and now rendered definitely uneconomical by falling prices and higher interest rates. In fact one may turn the argument completely round in defence of the Court by pointing out that wages offer such an easy target for attack that as early as the crisis of 1920–1 there would in all probability have been a "raid on wages" if the stabilisation scheme of the Court had not prevented that unjust and uneconomical method of obtaining relief from a difficult economic situation.

There is no denying the seriousness of the situation created by the disparity between farm costs and prices (including interest and taxes and rates). Farms have been abandoned, the use of fertilisers has been reduced, the deterioration of land in certain north island areas was so obvious that a Governmental commission was set up to investigate the problem. Moreover, the restricted financial resources of the farmers, coupled with the high wage rates ruling, made it impossible for them to absorb surplus labour in improving their lands. There has in fact been the unfortunate contrary situation of farm employment being drastically reduced. Even when economic conditions have forced greater efforts at rural production, the high wage rates have encouraged the improvement of farming technique and a greater use of machinery rather than greater employment of labour. This is the main, though not the only, cause of the bad spell of urban unemployment since 1925. The Arbitration Court chose to maintain high wage rates, and in default of other price adjustments, the natural result has been to throw a substantial margin of workers out of employment. Such a result is not inevitable, but it is very general because of the greater resistance to change shown by other economic factors, such as the rate of interest and land values.

While it is arguable in theory that lower wages would place the farmers in a somewhat better position to absorb more labour, the practical result is very doubtful. The farmers' inability to provide employment is due only very slightly to the rate of wages. Many farmers are tied up with mortgages, and all find that such heavier costs as taxation combine with the lower levels of prices to reduce their range of expenditure very greatly. It is probable that the extra employment given would not compensate for the wages lost by the whole body of workers. The latter, at any rate, are convinced that this would be the case. The unemployment problem is undoubtedly accentuated greatly, if not mainly caused, by the curtailment of rural employment, but in this curtailment arbitration wages figure as a minor factor.

The conclusion seems warranted therefore that, while the arbitration rates of wages are a contributory factor in the farming depression which is the root of New Zealand's difficulties, an attack upon those wages or upon the Court would not be a hopeful way out of the trouble. It would relieve the farming community very slightly, and this relief might well be absorbed in such ways as increasing land values. Reductions of wages also involve such probabilities of industrial disturbance, especially if made outside the Court's jurisdiction, that the problematical gain would be more than lost in the interruptions to production, all of which would recoil largely upon the farmers' pockets if not heads. To the economist it appears as if the farming community has pursued will-o'-the-wisps in its efforts to control the supposed gains of the speculator in marketing, in the agitation for rural credit facilities, and in the attack on the Arbitration Court. In all of these post-war movements there has been an element of reality and some positive contructive reform to be made—but none of them was capable of yielding as much economic relief as the same amount of thought and energy might have achieved if it had been directed to the improvements of the productive processes of farming. The individual farmer works hard and works at a high level of efficiency, but there are still great ranges of organisation related particularly to the utilisation of applied science, where co-operative effort is needed. The farmer, as well as the worker, tends to spend time trying to improve his share of the national income which would be more profitably spent in trying to increase its sum total.

Apart from the criticism of the Court which arises out of its comparative rigidity in fixing wage rates when other prices are fluctuating, the case against its work depends almost wholly upon the personal political theories of its critics. (49) The recent National Industrial Conference (1928) disclosed the fact that the representatives of the trade unions, including the secretary of the Alliance of Labour, who indeed acted as spokesman for the labour side, were (at least in public) unanimous in their support of the Court. It is an open secret that many leaders of the stronger unions were not as enthusiastic for the Court as their public statements would lead one to believe. Their closing speeches clearly revealed the fact that their stanch opposition to the employers' proposal that the compulsory powers of the Court should be reduced was based on the fear that the inevitable result would be reductions of wages. In 1920–1 it required a little more imagination than some labour leaders possessed to foresee the fact that in a time of falling prices the Court's awards would necessarily be as conservative in reductions as they had been in wage increases when prices were rising. Sufficient time has since elapsed to demonstrate even to the labour critics of the Court that in a time of falling prices the worker gains by having his wages fixed for three years at a time.

The basis of the employers' proposals was the criticism which has consistently been made against the Court since its inception, that the minuteness of its awards has a hampering influence in industrial organisation. Professor Murphy referred, in passing, to the waste of time and irritation caused when the Court had to decide whether the spreading of jam on sponge-cakes was or was not skilled work. This reference was rather irritably discussed as if it were a piece of misplaced humour on the Professor's part, but he was able to produce the exact reference where the learned judge decided that the work was unskilled. (50) A Chamber of Commerce questionnaire revealed the fact that 77 per cent. of the replies received from employers considered the minuteness of the Court's regulative powers a hindrance. It may well be queried, however, whether the Court is any more detailed in its regulation than collective bargaining would be and is when conducted by powerful trade unions. The freedom of the American employer sometimes leads to paternalism, but it often leads to labour conditions which have little appeal to Australian, New Zealand, or British observers who are used to strong trade union action, buttressed in the case of the two Dominions by the judicial authority of the Arbitration Courts. (51) It has been argued that this tendency to minute regulation is one of the factors responsible for the check to productivity which has been noticeable in New Zealand. It is probably a contributory factor, but since so large a part of the Dominion's production is outside the competence of the Court and can therefore be affected only indirectly, it is reasonable to assume that its influence in this respect is very small. New Zealand opinion generally assumes that the abolition of the Court or the weakening of its powers of compulsion would result in efforts to reduce wages and consequently in industrial conflict. The risk of lowered productivity from this cause is deemed greater than the present burden of over-regulation.

It is perfectly conceivable that many of the valuable functions now performed by the Court could be taken over by other bodies. The Supreme Court could administer many functions, including the important duties arising from the Workers' Compensation Act; the Labour Department might administer the conciliation machinery; a revived Board of Trade might fix a basic minimum wage without applying it in detail to individual industries. These steps have been advocated with the logical corollary that collective bargaining should be resorted to for the determination of detailed wage rates and labour conditions. (52)

Labour opposition to any such steps arises from a knowledge that the numerical strength of the trade union movement conceals a weakness of organisation and an almost total absence of fighting spirit. The strongest trade unions would have little difficulty in adjusting themselves to such a change. In favourable times these unions might even hope to gain a good deal by collective bargaining, but in a time of falling prices and economic stringency they are more likely to be forced into accepting lower wages after industrial conflict. The weaker trade unions organised on a craft basis, which after all comprise the majority of trade unionists in New Zealand, are even more keenly aware of their dependence upon the Court.

The conclusive argument in common judgment lies outside the realm of economic measurement and is in fact the humanitarian plea that the Court safeguards the living conditions of workers with little power to protect themselves. It has been argued throughout this volume that empirical opportunism rather than doctrinaire theory is responsible for the various New Zealand legislative experiments. This is particularly true of the arbitration system. It was introduced when the public memory of sweated labour conditions was very recent and very clear. In the thirty-five years of its operation such conditions have disappeared. General economic prosperity may have been more responsible for this fact than any work done by the Court, but the Court's operations supplementing an elaborate labour code admittedly make any repetition of sweated conditions impossible. Against this personal, humanitarian consideration, buttressed in detail by the widely known weakness of the smaller unions, the argument that the Court may have some problematical and immeasurable influence in slowing up production carries very little weight. It is not proven that it does slow up production as much as industrial conflict might do, and even if this were proven, New Zealand majority opinion would regard the cost as well repaid by the safeguarding of the standards of living of the economically weak. It may be admitted that the small working farmer has a case for the defence of his standards also, but it is difficult to see how the substitution of collective bargaining for arbitration awards would greatly help him.

This is not to argue that compulsory arbitration is proven a panacea by New Zealand experience. It should be apparent that the New Zealand system has fitted itself by adaptation into a particular environment, that its operations are restricted to a definite group, mainly of urban workers, and that it has been administered with remarkable ability and tact. British traditions of judicial impartiality have been well sustained, and in addition many judges, among whom the president of the Court at the present time, Mr. Justice Frazer, is conspicuous, have shown remarkable economic insight and imagination.

Wise administration of this order is matched in New Zealand by a readiness to accept the law which is not always found in labour organisations. The almost complete absence from the proceedings of the National Industrial Conference, 1928, of any hint of class warfare may not indicate that no warfare exists or even that no belief in it exists. It does indicate a readiness to accept facts as they are and to work for what is possible with the machinery that exists. Trade unionists in New Zealand realise that their position in a country whose interests are dominantly rural is economically weak. They are glad to have a powerful ally in such an established organ of government as the Arbitration Court and its subsidiary machinery.

CHAPTER XII

MATERNAL LEGISLATION

The Background of Law

If New Zealanders can be stated to have any social or economic theories, pride of place must undoubtedly be given to the general theory that human considerations should take precedence of economic progress, or perhaps that true economic progress can in the long run be based only upon human welfare. The origin of this humanitarian trend of thought is probably to be found in the character of the men and women who first settled the colony. Included among their number were many men of fine scholastic and cultural attainments, in whose standards of value wealth did not rank very high. Communities whose leadership was in the hands of men like Bishop Selwyn, Sir William Martin, Sir George Grey, William Swainson, John Robert Godley, Dr. Featherston, Captain Cargill, and many others of like ability and ideals, were bound to carry differences of opinion to great lengths and to commit great mistakes, but little likely to subordinate social welfare to economic gain. The very choosing of illustrative names is invidious. Among the first settlers were many cadets of landed families, and there were also many trade unionists and chartists at a time when those movements were sacrificial and idealist. There was, moreover, a notable spirit of piety, explicit as in the Church organisation of Canterbury and the Free Kirk contribution to Otago, or less definitely organised as in many individual leaders and groups in every settlement. The natural consequence was that from the very beginning of colonisation the demands of education, and social services generally, received much consideration.(1) In the spirit of the time education was conceived by the early colonists as closely allied with religion, and works of humanity as a natural consequence with both. In the pressure of material activities such aspirations were often enough relegated to the background, and it was not long before the necessities of early colonial life devolved both education and humanitarian works upon the State in default of any other community organisation adequate to undertake them. It is true that in many districts gallant efforts were made to support hospitals by private charity as in England and that church schools pioneered the way for a State system. Neither form of voluntary effort was satisfactory, and the nationalisation of these important social services became inevitable at an early date.

The simple and direct spirit of the pioneers, rising above forms and vested interests, is nowhere more clearly reflected than in the legal provisions drawn up for the governance of the colony at its very inception. It would be out of place in an economic treatise to enter at any length into the legal history of the Dominion; but some general and simple facts need to be stated as a background for the consideration of the social legislation which is so marked a feature of New Zealand economic life. The first Attorney-General, Swainson, and the first Chief Justice, Sir William Martin, set a fine example in simplicity of procedure and language. Swainson's drafting of the essential ordinances dealing with legal procedure, marriage, conveyancing, and similar fundamental subjects provided the basis upon which subsequent legislators and draftsmen have built the simple but effective New Zealand system of law. The economic importance of such work is so fundamental that it tends to be taken for granted and forgotten.

New Zealand is fortunate in the possession of a legal and judicial system of almost unquestioned integrity and inexpensive simplicity.(2) The greatest care has been taken from the beginning of the colony to provide for the inviolable independence and permanent status of the Judges, with the result that the integrity of the Bench is taken for granted. In the same way there has, since the abolition of the provincial system, been a permanent police force under centralised control.(3) While individual deficiencies of ability and sometimes of character are bound to occur there is no suspicion of anything approaching corruption. In the earlier heated controversies arising from the anti-liquor agitation there were charges of police connivance with breaches of the law, but the very nature of the charges brought before the Royal Commission of 1909 is eloquent of the high standard New Zealand expects of its police.(4)

New Zealand is, therefore, a well-governed and law-abiding community. Swainson's simple procedure was further simplified by the Supreme Court Act of 1882. Recourse to justice is easy and not expensive. The natural result is some tendency for the courts to be used for minor offences and for the collection of small debts. This tendency, supplementing the marked elaboration of social legislation, tends to swell the number of cases and convictions. When the statistics of "crime" are analysed, it is very clear that many New Zealand offences would not come before courts in other countries.

At the same time there has been a cautious but definite liberalising of the law in regard to juvenile offences in which magistrates sit privately and have considerable latitude, in the probationary system which has existed since 1886 and was considerably extended in 1920, in the classification of prisoners, open-air forestry camps for minor offenders, the provision of indeterminate sentences for habitual criminals, and the work of the Prisons Board, which has power to remit reformatory sentences. (5)

Prison reformers, especially those who stress the importance of psychological factors in criminality, would not, however, admit that New Zealand has gone far in the scientific treatment of crime. It is to be remembered that the humanitarianism of the Dominion is of a conservative rather than a radical nature, based upon experience rather than scientific theory.

The Feminine Influence

It is noteworthy that the first point at which New Zealand social legislation definitely began to diverge from English models was in the Divorce Act of 1898, which went some distance in giving women equality of divorce rights. This Act, affecting the most fundamental of human relationships, came within five years of the granting of woman suffrage. In the same year the Old Age Pensions Act was passed, which inaugurated the long series of welfare experiments. With these results so quickly evident, it is difficult to explain why so many critical observers should have considered the effects of the women's vote to have been so slight. On the contrary there appear to have been very definite and important consequences of the activity of women in political affairs. The extent of these consequences has possibly been masked by the fact that feminine pressure upon Parliament has taken its own characteristic form and has worked with and through sympathetic male legislators. It is true that no woman has ever sat in the New Zealand Parliament, though women have had votes since 1893. It is, however, impossible to imagine that Parliamentary candidates since that date have not been greatly influenced by the knowledge that one-half of their prospective constituencies have consisted of women. The increasing attention given in the last generation to education and its allied services, involving steadily increasing education votes, is largely traceable to feminine influence. As early as 1877 women began to sit upon school committees and their natural interest, particularly in primary education, had marked results after 1893. In the same way the steady liberalising of the hospital and charitable aid system of the Dominion, together with all the allied pension, provident fund, family allowance, and similar experiments is directly traceable to the woman's vote. Women take an increasing share in the local administration of hospitals and charitable aid boards.

More characteristic still, the influence of organised women's bodies, centring in the Dominion organisation of the National Council of Women, has kept steady watch and incessant and ultimately irresistible pressure upon details of legislation and administration which tend to work social injustice, particularly to women and children. The President of this Council placed before the first Pan-Pacific Women's Conference in 1928 a list of forty-four Acts in which the organised effort of women voters had had an effective influence. Included in this list were Acts of general humanitarian application, such as the measures providing for old-age pensions, the licensing Acts, the establishment of technical schools, the National Provident Fund, as well as the Factories and Shop Assistants and Workers' Compensation Acts. While the origin of some of these measures precedes woman suffrage and all of them are in general conformity with the humanitarian trend of New Zealand thought, women have supported and extended their application and in some cases have gained specific amendments of importance to women and children.

This is even clearer in the majority of the other measures cited, a summary list of which is worth quoting. The influence of women was claimed in measures relating to:

Infant life protection.
The adoption of children.
Industrial schools.
Illegitimacy.
Legitimation.
Widows' pensions.
Divorce and matrimonial causes.
Summary legal separation.
Slander of women.
Testators' family maintenance.
Destitute persons.
Married women's property.
State maternity hospitals.
Aged and infirm persons' protection.
Crimes amendment.
Extension of the probation system.
Establishment of Juvenile Courts.
Juvenile smoking.
Raising of the age of consent.
Repeal of the Contagious Diseases Act, which placed responsibility upon women for the spread of disease.
Temperance instruction in schools.
Education amendment.
Female law practitioners.
Women medical inspectors of schools.
Establishment of dental clinics for schools.
State Infant Welfare Department.
Women assistant hospital inspectors.
Payment of prisoners who have dependents.
Women appointees on the Board of Health, and on the picture censorship appeal Board.
Pensions for the destitute blind.
The Child Welfare Act.
Children's courts with women associate magistrates.
Appointment of women Justices of the Peace.
The equal right of women to guardianship of infants.(6)

The mere recital of these achievements is sufficient to prove that the doctrinaire, radical, and uncompromising attitude described by Siegfried in his account of an early meeting of the National Council of Women has not been characteristic of later developments.(7) On the contrary the women have added to the opportunism which is characteristic of New Zealand a feminine preoccupation with practical details of immediate importance in home and family life. It is precisely because they have concentrated upon legislative and administrative amendments in detail, rather than sweeping theoretical programmes of legislative reform, that they have acquired the wholesome respect of the average politician, leading to the substantial successes indicated.

The fact that women form half the electorate has had considerable influence also in extending and elaborating the various measures which form the New Zealand code of labour legislation. The more recent codifications of these measures in 1901 and 1908 have shown a marked tendency to extension of scope and functions; but here again New Zealand's primacy is a matter of history rather than present achievement. Social workers know that "New Zealand is not in the forefront of legislation in the matter of industrial hygiene".(8) This is particularly true in regard to the lack of compulsory health examinations, the absence of sickness and unemployment insurance schemes, the inadequate provision of women factory inspectors and their lack of any specialised training. These are aspects of industrial regulation in which New Zealand has been left behind. The general average of labour conditions is remarkably good; but it is a general average which will not compare with the best results achieved in some other countries.

It is in the field of infant welfare, however, that the efforts of New Zealand women have been concentrated, and in this field they have achieved remarkable results. The work of the Royal New Zealand Society for the Health of Women and Children goes back to 1907, when Dr. (now Sir Truby) and Mrs. King began education work in infant welfare with the aid of a small but influential committee of women in Dunedin. After years of strenuous effort the work of this Society (popularly known as the Plunket Society, after the Governor's wife who first gave it social prestige) has convincingly demonstrated the ability of New Zealand women to plan sustained and constructive co-operative organisation. The Society now has sixty-six branches throughout New Zealand, as well as many smaller centres visited from the main branches. In 1927–8 it operated 6 hospitals for sick babies, employed 115 trained baby-nurses whose advice was available both for expectant mothers and for nursing mothers, and carried out a thorough educational campaign reaching into every corner of the

Dominion. The aim of the Society is "to inculcate a lofty view of the responsibilities of maternity and the duty of every mother to fit herself for the perfect fulfilment of the natural calls of motherhood, both before and after child-birth, and especially to advocate and promote the breast-feeding of infants".(9)

For the achievement of this aim the Society has worked out characteristic methods of organisation and education almost entirely by the voluntary services of women. The effect of the campaign so intensively carried on is not precisely separable from the consequences of improved general prosperity and better education; but there can be no reasonable doubt that the credit for New Zealand's extraordinarily low rate of infantile mortality must go in large measure to this voluntary women's movement. Certain of the common infant diseases which are directly traceable to malnutrition or improper feeding have been reduced to the point of elimination. The effect of such improvements is naturally reflected in the rate of infant mortality for the whole Dominion, which in the nineteen years 1908 to 1927 has fallen from 67·89 to 38·74 per thousand.(10) This exceptionally low rate is much lower than the Australian rate, which comes closest to it, and is still falling steadily. It is obvious that much needless loss of infant life has been averted. Moreover, since the incidence of children's diseases bears little if any relation to vitality, it is not possible to argue that the Society's work keeps weaklings alive. Rather it has the contrary effect not only in saving life, but in avoiding the general weakening of stamina caused by disease and malnutrition. Its positive contribution to the economic welfare of New Zealand has been immense. Selected population is the Dominion's greatest need, and the safeguarding of infant life is the best of all ways of increasing the population. The fact that a baby born in New Zealand has on the average more chances of living than a baby born anywhere else in the world is a significant economic fact, of far more importance ultimately than any other single fact recorded in any economic survey of the Dominion's resources. After exhaustive investigation the special investigator of the United States Children's Bureau gave his considered opinion that "the most important influence in the reduction of the infant mortality rate is undoubtedly the work of the Royal New Zealand Society for the Health of Women and Children". The credit for this achievement must therefore go to the women of New Zealand. It is eloquent of their practical and essentially conservative outlook that their main effort has gone into education for motherhood, even though their country was the first to open political activity to women.

The infant welfare work of the Dominion remains, and is likely to remain, largely in the hands of the Royal New Zealand Society for the Health of Women and Children. The funds of the Society are now subsidised by the Government, and the Departments of Health and Education, the various hospital boards, and the medical profession are cordial in their support of the movement.(11) The Society has lived down some very natural suspicion on the part of the medical profession, and this in itself is indicative of its practical character. Its activities comprise the education of secondary school-girls in baby nursing, the training of baby-nurses, ante-natal clinics, hospitals for sick babies, a complete system of visitation of mothers after child-birth, and a continuous propaganda for natural feeding and hygienic clothing. These activities are so thoroughly organised that the Society is able to extend its co-operation to the campaign being developed against the high rate of maternal mortality.

In 1925 the Child Welfare Act was passed, constituting a Child Welfare Branch of the Education Department, which had already gone a considerable distance in making provision for physical welfare. In 1912 a school medical service was initiated which in 1920 was given legislative authority for compulsory medical examination of school-children. This was supplemented in 1921 by the School Dental Service.(12) The establishment of a Child Welfare Branch, under Sir Truby King, is an effort to complete the organisation. The 1925 Act brings under the control of this department all the Dominion's destitute, neglected, and delinquent children, as well as orphans and afflicted children. It establishes the principle of dealing with juvenile offenders in privacy and on remedial instead of penal lines. Child welfare officers also investigate all cases of illegitimacy and either place the child in a foster-home or advise the mother concerning affiliation proceedings or concerning employment. In all, 5,592 children were under the department's care in 1926.(13)

This very summary outline must serve to indicate the completeness with which, under constant pressure from the women of the country, provision has been made for the physical welfare of the children of New Zealand. This result is in itself a striking vindication of the political sagacity of the women. New Zealand, under their guidance, has achieved the desirable economic position of a population increasing as rapidly as the country demands (more rapidly than any other country), with a low birth-rate and a relatively high age at marriage, but the lowest death-rate in the world. The economic gain from this situation is considerable, since the human capital of any country is its most important asset. The improved status of womanhood and the minimising of the suffering and cost involved in producing an increased population as a result of high birth and death rates, add to the gain. It must be added also, that in New Zealand home duties occupy the largest proportion of her women. This material fact must be borne in mind when the national income is compared with that of other countries, such as the United States, where a larger proportion of women, both married and unmarried, earn cash incomes which swell the statistical calculations, but do not necessarily connote a larger measure of social welfare. Under these circumstances New Zealand's *per capita* cash income, which is one of the highest in the world, is a remarkable indication of prosperity and social welfare.

The Prevention of Poverty

One of the chief impressions which observant visitors carry from New Zealand is that of physical health, happiness, and absence of poverty. It is easily possible to exaggerate this impression, and local social workers are keenly conscious of the existence of substantial problems of overcrowding in certain cities, social delinquency, unemployment, and similar causes of distress. Yet the bad spots in the towns are small and not typical, conditions of life are freer and substantially better than in most countries, and extreme poverty is fortunately at a minimum. Even if they may be accused of missing some of the darker spots, the visitors are not far wrong in their impressions, which correspond well with Montague's description of the Dominion troops in France as "startlingly taller, stronger, handsomer, firmer in nerve, better schooled, more boldly interested in life, quicker to take means to an end and to parry and counter any new blow of circumstance".(14)

There seem to be three main reasons for this happy state of affairs. Two of these should already be obvious from the preceding chapters of this volume. New Zealand's social health depends primarily upon the quality of the stock from which the present generation has been recruited. Physically, mentally, and morally, the original stock was rigidly selected. To find any parallel to the chosen bands of emigrants who laid the foundations of New Zealand it is necessary to go back to the Puritan fathers of the New England colonies. Britain sent of her best to the new land. Moreover, with rare exceptions, subsequent immigration has maintained a high level of quality. Standards were rather let down for a short time at the height of the boom in the seventies when assisted immigration was pushed to great lengths; but normally the flow of new immigrants has been steady, and drastic tests have accompanied any Governmental assistance. The overwhelming bulk of the immigrants have come from Britain and it takes imagination, nerve, health, and some resources to venture half-way round the world. There has therefore been no rush of unselected labouring immigrants to cause a lowering of economic, social, or political standards.

With strictly controlled immigration of this character and a steady cumulative increase in the native-born population, the physical quality of the people is naturally high. This in itself is a guarantee of economic progress and welfare. When such a people is placed in a new and rich land, with natural advantages in the industries which demand outdoor rural activity, it would be extraordinary to find any great amount of poverty. The two chief causes of New Zealand's physical and social health are to be found, therefore, in the highly selected quality of its people and the natural wealth of the country. For neither of these causes is any special credit due to the present generation.

There is, however, a third element, part cause and part effect of the absence of poverty and social distress. The Governmental machinery for the prevention and relief of poverty is a factor of some importance. In older lands it presents a burdensome and often baffling problem. It is partly New Zealand's good fortune, but partly also her sound policy, that reduces poor relief to minor proportions. The chief measures of her social policy are outlined below. It is interesting, but perhaps futile, to speculate to what extent they would survive harsher economic conditions. It is probable that the compromise of principles embodied in the hospital system would be severely tested. The loose and unorganised forms of outdoor charitable relief have already been strained by the recent distress consequent upon unemployment. They could hardly survive in a country where such distress was chronic. The liberality of the various pensions schemes might not be possible in a poorer country, and this is equally true of the boarding-out of orphan children and similar costly but effective social expedients. Such speculations, however, do not invalidate the conclusion that, New Zealand being as prosperous as she is, her liberal policies of "preventive social medicine" are thoroughly sound economically. The amount spent by all the charitable aid boards in both indoor and outdoor relief was in 1925–6 approximately £250,000.(15) While this is by no means the total cost of relieving poverty, it is indicative of the fact that New Zealand effort and money go into prevention rather than relief.

The causes of chronic poverty as distinct from the occasional distress due to individual misfortune or economic calamity in most countries are fairly well recognised though inadequately met. It is clear that sickness, old age, dependency in early childhood, and social delinquency such as drunkenness and wife desertion, add to the poverty and distress which in every land is due to individual weakness, inefficiency, disease, and criminality. It is probable that in New Zealand these factors are reduced to proportions lower than in most countries. It is also true that the best of all remedies is a comfortable standard of living such as New Zealand workers enjoy. But there remain substantial problems to be dealt with either by preventive or by remedial measures, or by a combination of both.

Before dealing with the particular policies adopted it should be pointed out again that the elaborate and effectively administered code of social legislation greatly diminishes many of these causes of poverty. Sickness is reduced by the factory code and by stringent measures of "preventive medicine", as well as by the constructive work in the fields of infant welfare and education, including school medical and dental treatment. Social delinquency is checked very considerably by the changes inserted in the criminal code and the legislation affecting women and children and family relationships, upon which women's organisations have concentrated their political activity. Constructively also, the activities now gathered together in the Child Welfare Department salve much of the damage that might otherwise result from broken homes. All of these measures find remarkably unanimous support in public opinion.

There is one outstanding cause of poverty, however—the social delinquency resulting from drunkenness—which has given rise to controversy and in which progress towards an accepted solution has been slower. While the extent of drunkenness in New Zealand is as small as one would expect from such a community, social workers are practically unanimous in their view that it remains the outstanding uncontrolled cause of such poverty as still exists.(16)

In the last generation substantial progress has been made towards eliminating the most obvious abuses of the liquor traffic. The closing hours of hotel bars have been placed earlier until six o'clock closing is now the law, the employment of barmaids is eliminated save for a few remaining on the register, the issue of new licences for the sale of liquor is strictly controlled and the tendency is towards reduction of licences, police inspection is strict and generally effective. Upon the administrative side, therefore, there has been steady progress towards the elimination of gross abuses.(17)

The great effort of the social reformers has, however, gone into the "no-licence" or "prohibition" movement, and this movement, especially since the war, has met with little success. In the early nineties it had all the fervour and proportions of a crusade. Its initial successes in winning the legislation providing for local and ultimately national referenda on the subject, and in securing both reductions and certain local extinctions of licences, were due largely to the first enthusiasm of a new crusade. The evangelical Protestant churches, the Radicals, and the newly enfranchised women, gave it uncompromising support. The spirit of the times, which had a rather naïve belief in the power of legislation to promote social welfare, was in harmony with the proposal to abolish the liquor traffic.(18)

The beginnings of legislation date back to 1881, when the administration of the licensing law was transferred from nominated boards to committees elected by ratepayers, and these committees were given power to veto new licences and refuse renewals on the ground that they were not required. The real beginning of the prohibition movement, however, was in 1893, when popular referenda placed the power of local option in the hands of the electorate. The first election saw the closing of seventy licensed houses and complete "no-licence" in one electorate. The reduction of licences went steadily on till in 1918 this issue was eliminated from the ballot-paper. In all, thirteen districts have at various times voted for no-licence, of which only two have reverted (in 1925 and 1928) to restoration of licences.

The concentration of the movement into a regular political campaign for national prohibition at every triennial election has resulted in a distinct setback. The causes of this setback are to be found partly in the increasingly effective solidarity of the vested liquor interests, but mainly in public revulsion from the political manœuvring and bargaining which became manifest. The virtual abandonment of local campaigns in favour of the national struggle placed a premium upon the organisation of advertising, and similar methods of mass-appeal for which the vested interests had more money and obvious advantages of motive and cohesion. It removed the question also into the realm of abstract moral principles rather than local individual experience and feeling. In both respects, and also in the wider educational aspects of the movement, it was a major mistake in strategy.

As interest centred in the national polls, the concentration upon political manœuvres rather than popular education was intensified. The movement lost its crusading qualities and became involved in lobbying and political manipulation. Routine educational activities were pushed to one side in the campaigns for the popular vote. Leadership passed into the hands of men with less fervour and more belief in organisation. The collection of funds, promotion of legislation involving bargaining and compromise, and whirlwind electoral campaigns, brought existing resources to a peak immediately after the war, when a majority within New Zealand favourable to prohibition was overturned only by a decisively unfavourable vote from the soldiers overseas.

Since that near approach to success by the heroic, frontal method of attack, the prohibitionists have steadily lost ground. At each triennial election from 1919 onwards the majority against prohibition has increased. In the 1918 referendum they were within 10,000 votes of success; ten years later they lost by more than 140,000 votes in a poll of 734,231. The reasons for this setback are complicated. Distrust and dislike of the American methods, or even the appearance of following America's example, enter into the situation. More directly, the average man resents the political activity and bargaining methods of the new phase of the movement. Over and above the minor factors, however, it is clear that the prohibitionists are paying the price of their attempted short-cut to success. Their preoccupation with politics and neglect of education has cost them the support of the younger generation of voters. It will take at least a generation of routine educative work to regain the lost ground. An institutionalised movement with a professional bureaucracy finds it difficult to face the facts and turn from the excitements of political intrigues. Meantime other issues have arisen and the fight is no longer clear cut between crusading reformers and defenders of a vested interest. New Zealand has definitely turned from the simple solution of the liquor problem by the enactment of prohibition. The issue can hardly now be regarded as one of "social morality" and in the meantime other methods must be sought to deal with the poverty which is a by-product of alcoholism.

The Care of the Sick and Indigent

The association of hospitals with charitable aid arises from the obvious connection of sickness with poverty, and is reinforced by the modern conception of both as due largely to social ill-health. The administration of these related services in New Zealand has a long history of compromise between the tradition of individualism supplemented by charity which the colonists brought with them from Britain, and the trend towards nationalisation which arose in New Zealand earlier than in most countries because of the lack of private organisation in a new community.

To trace the detailed development of the hospital system from the various local origins is unnecessary. Certain broad tendencies are very clear. In the early days of the provinces local hospitals were organised. In the latest of the settlements, indeed, such hospitals formed part of the plan of colonisation along with schools and churches. There was at the time considerable feeling that hospitals were best controlled by voluntary boards on the model of the great English charitable hospitals. The necessities of the new land, however, drove every community steadily to a recognition of the necessity for public effort, so that even before the passing of the Hospitals and Charitable Institutions Act of 1885 the provinces had virtually shouldered the burden of caring for the sick.(19)

The Act of 1885 was part of the reorganisation of local government rendered necessary by the abolition of the provincial system. It was a sound piece of legislation, one of many which New Zealand owes to the fine legal and administrative sense of Sir Robert Stout. It provided for the systematic organisation of hospital boards with control also over charitable aid. The combination of hospitals with charitable aid was achieved by instituting three different types of board. The Act did, however, consolidate a great deal of voluntary charitable effort under a single, popularly elected board in each district. In the same way, although it compromised between the principles of local and central finance, and between nationalisation and commercial operation, yet it made as great advances as were possible at the time. The financial arrangements of the boards were definitely fixed and a long step was taken towards the public provision of hospital and medical service as a right of citizenship.

There has been little advance upon the principles of 1885, except in detailed amendment embodying the fruits of experience as the system has worked out. The activities of the hospital boards have steadily widened. A hospital board now has power to establish, control, and manage any of the following institutions: Hospitals, charitable institutions, maternity homes, convalescent homes, sanatoria, habitual inebriates homes, reformatory institutions for the reception of women and girls, and any other institutions for any purpose which the Governor-General, by Order-in-Council, may declare to be a public charitable purpose. It may grant charitable aid to indigent, sick, or infirm persons; may provide medical, surgical, and nursing attention for persons not inmates of an institution; and may grant financial assistance to medical and nursing associations and private philanthropic institutions approved by the Minister. (20)

By means of this organisation New Zealand has a fairly complete system of hospitals and allied institutions. Private hospitals are also strictly regulated under licence from the Health Department, and the same Department operates seven maternity hospitals in different towns.

The hospital boards operate many benevolent institutions, including old people's homes, maternity and refuge homes for women and girls, orphanages, homes for the infirm or afflicted, "prison gate" homes, and an institute for the blind. This official work is supplemented by that of religious bodies and other benevolent associations depending upon private support. It is intimately connected also with the activities of the Child Welfare Branch of the Education Department.

One other complete system of hospital care is controlled by the Department of Mental Hospitals, which operates seven institutions caring for over five thousand patients. There is only one small private mental hospital in the Dominion, so that mental diseases are cared for almost exclusively by the State. This has the great advantage of simplifying the legal arrangements for committal, providing for adequate inspection and control of abuses, and making the care of patients' estates obligatory on the Public Trustee. (21)

This bare description of the network of institutions for the care of the sick will indicate that New Zealand is well provided with machinery for this purpose. The cost both to the State and to local bodies has been growing rapidly in recent years as the institutions have embarked upon expensive modern equipment such as radium and X-ray plants. The financing of the hospital system has not progressed beyond the double compromise of local and central taxes, and free public service and commercial fees. The result is a peculiar system of control in which representatives of ratepayers, especially from country districts, exercise a majority influence. Efforts are made to keep down expenditure and to collect fees from patients. At the same time most hospitals have borrowed from the English hospitals the system of honorary surgeons and medical officers for specialist work.

Compromise systems of this type are never wholly satisfactory. The routine treatment in New Zealand hospitals keeps a good average standard; but there are obvious weaknesses of operation, particularly on the scientific side. None of the public hospitals is able to maintain adequate staff or equipment for routine laboratory tests, to say nothing of research, while the appointment of paid specialists such as dietitians, radium and X-ray experts is recent and has not gone very far. Another weak spot is the small degree to which the hospitals are linked with the university medical school at Dunedin, which turns out excellent technical medical practitioners, but sponsors almost no scientific research.

There must inevitably be pressure to bring modern scientific methods of diagnosis and treatment within the reach of all classes of people. This involves concentration of expert workers and expensive technical equipment in institutions. American hospitals have gone far to solve the problem by enlisting the professional spirit of medical men in co-operative "community hospitals" run frankly on commercial lines, so that the best modern treatment is available and poorer classes of patients have differential treatment, subsidised in part from the receipt of fees from wealthier patients. Such a system runs counter to New Zealand tradition; but both the medical profession and hospital administrators seem to balk at the prospect of nationalising the hospital service by providing free treatment at the cost of taxation in the same way as free education is provided for the whole community. Caught in this dilemma of policy, New Zealand can hardly expect to keep pace with the best modern practice.

It must be frankly admitted, moreover, that New Zealand pays the penalty of isolation, and to some extent of prosperity, in a decided intellectual lag. It will be argued in a later chapter that the theory of New Zealand leadership in constructive social thought has little foundation; but that on the contrary the Dominion is decidedly an intellectual backwater, particularly in education and scientific thought. The hospital situation illustrates this fact, and the position of the mental hospitals adds point to the illustration. The institutional management of the hospitals is excellent. There are few abuses, and on the contrary a high level of efficiency and consideration is steadily maintained. But, on the other hand, there is no special training beyond that of experience; modern psychological and psychiatric practice is only just beginning to penetrate to the Dominion, and as a natural consequence remedial treatment lags behind the best practice of other lands. This situation is paralleled in the prisons and in the educational system.

It is equally clear in the provision of charitable aid. There is generous provision of outdoor relief, often in the form of cash subsidies or in orders for provisions. Indoor relief is given in old people's homes and orphanages. New Zealand's wealth and the comparative absence of poverty make possible a generous provision of relief without inquisitorial enquiry or any very skilled or specialised administration. The problem is not large enough to call for the scientific organisation and skilled technique demanded in other lands. Whenever, as in the early nineties or in the recent strain of post-war unemployment, the demands for charitable aid are greatly swollen beyond the average, the inadequacies and weaknesses of the system become manifest.(22)

Pensions and Family Allowances

The various pension and superannuation schemes now in force in New Zealand have a clear connection with the charitable aid system of the Dominion.(23) They are essentially measures of preventive legislation aimed directly at eliminating the poverty caused by old age, widowhood, and unduly large families. Like many other experimental measures they have a long history before their enactment into law. It was sixteen years from Sir Harry Atkinson's first pension proposals in 1882 before the Old Age Pensions Act was passed in 1898. It is very significant, therefore, that legislation awaited the advent of woman suffrage. Both the initial enactment and the subsequent liberalising and extension of the pensions system may be directly traced to the interest of women voters in these matters.

The point of origin of New Zealand interest in old-age pensions is fortunately clear. In 1879 the Rev. Canon Blackley, of Winchester, contributed an article to the *Nineteenth Century* on "The Prevention of Poverty". In this article he advocated a universal compulsory scheme of contributory payments into a fund which would provide both sick benefits and provision against old age. The social welfare policies of Bismarck had directed attention to the practicability of such schemes. The first German State Insurance Law was passed in 1881, and successive extensions of the Law came quickly in the years following.(24) It seems to have been Canon Blackley's article, however, which was most widely discussed in New Zealand and which provided the basis of Sir Harry Atkinson's contributory pension scheme in 1882.(25)

It was a time of depression in New Zealand and there was a good deal of poverty and unemployment. In moving his motion before the House in July 1882 the Premier earnestly advocated a contributory scheme of regular payments to be made in early life to provide a fund from which both sickness and old-age pensions should be drawn. The Liberal Opposition attacked the proposal on various grounds, including many of those afterwards used by their opponents against Seddon's scheme in 1898. In the following year, 1883, Atkinson stumped the whole country advocating his scheme, but found little popular support.(26) In the Financial Statement of 1883 the scheme was mentioned again, but met with the derisive laughter of the House. In the following year Atkinson went out of office, and with him went any possibility of a contributory pension scheme.

It is indicative of the close connection between the whole question of pensions and charitable aid that the Stout-Vogel Ministry's reconstruction in 1885 of the hospital and charitable aid system should have been regarded as an effective alternative proposal. The next development came from the severe criticisms levelled by Dr. McGregor, in his capacity as permanent head of the Health Department, against the evils of indiscriminate outdoor relief. So great was the depression of the early nineties that the provision of relief was altogether inadequate. Particularly in his report for 1892, Dr. McGregor urged that some substitute should be found for the system of outdoor relief.(27)

The Danish law of 1891, providing for universal old-age pensions payable out of general taxation, attracted much attention also, so that the question was a live one at the 1893 election, which gave the Liberal-Labour Party a sweeping majority. By this time the various progressive Liberal associations, trades and labour councils, and similar bodies were very active. Lectures and pamphlets on old-age pension schemes began to multiply and popular interest was effectively roused in the subject.(28)

The Liberal-Labour Government was very cautious. The Financial Statement for 1894 included the following passage:

> The question of Old Age Pensions still remained unsolved. The grant of a State pension to all arrived at a certain age would not only necessitate a greatly increased taxation, but would also add to the burden of those least able to bear such increase. If the pensions were to be granted to those only who could prove need, it would be difficult to separate the recipients from the non-recipients without injustice, and without discouragement of thrift. Nevertheless the aims of the friends of the scheme are so high and noble that they must have the warmest sympathy of all humane minds. A Select Committee is now sitting to consider the subject, and it is hoped they will be able to make some practical suggestions.

The Parliamentary committee referred to, after sitting for many weeks, merely recommended the appointment of a Royal Commission. This time-honoured procedure of escape from a difficult situation aroused the Liberal organisations to effective action. The Liberal movement of the time was strongest in Canterbury, and a scheme basing pensions upon increased death duties was drawn up and widely circulated by the Canterbury Progressive Liberal Association early in 1895.(29)

There seems little doubt that Reeves's statement that "the Government, boldly moving in advance of public opinion, suddenly brought down a Bill containing a pensions scheme" does something less than justice to the persistent agitation which had created a strong public opinion on the subject.(30) The measure brought down in the session of 1896 was in reality a kite to test the strength of opinion on this subject. Seddon had previously conferred with representatives of the friendly societies, hoping to find some way of administering a pension scheme with their help; but the conference was fruitless. The Bill of 1896 therefore provided for pensions as of right, payable through a State department to all persons over the age of 65 whose income was less than £52 yearly and who fulfilled certain qualifications. A hostile amendment making the pensions universal caused the Bill to be dropped, and Seddon immediately had an Act passed providing machinery to ascertain the cost of a pensions scheme.(31)

Old Age Pensions provided an excellent rallying-cry for the progressive forces in the 1896 election, and their victory made the passing of some measure certain before the next election. The Legislative Council, however, killed the Bill which passed the Lower House in 1897, and it was not until the session of 1898, and after new appointments had been made to the Legislative Council, that the Act was finally passed.

The stormy passage of the Bill through the Lower House culminated in the famous committee sitting of ninety hours, during the whole of which, from the Wednesday to the Saturday night, with only brief respite at the meal hours, Mr. Seddon sat at the chairman's table, snatching what sleep he could, as the stonewall dragged on. It was the last dying effort of the old Conservative Party, and Seddon himself always referred to the passage of the Act as his crowning achievement. Nor was he slow to put the law into actual operation. By March 1899 the first pensions were being paid out.(32) Naturally enough, the Government secured an overwhelming majority at the ensuing election.

The subsequent history of the old-age pension law is one of extension and liberalising. The sums paid in charitable aid have not decreased, but the apparent increase is due to a combination of causes, among which the most important are the rising level of prices, a more effective and extensive organisation of charitable aid, and a more normal age-grouping of the population with larger proportions of aged people and very young children.(33) Allowing for these factors it may reasonably be argued that the cost of old-age pensions is well repaid by reason of the minimising of the demoralising forms of charitable aid.

There is now no opposition of any consequence to the pension system. The politicians who in the nineties voted against the scheme found it increasingly difficult in later years to explain away their votes or to defend their arguments. New Zealanders are convinced that old-age pensions do not appreciably discourage thrift, diminish filial piety, or cause an undue strain on the Exchequer. The numerous amendments liberalising the old-age pension administration afford sufficient proof of popular support for the principles embodied in the system. The original Act provided for a maximum pension of £18 yearly when the applicant had fulfilled stringent conditions, including public examination to prove that he was not in receipt of an income greater than £34 per year. The present rate of maximum pension under the Pensions Amendment Act, 1925, is £45 10s. yearly, reducible by £1 for every complete £1 of income over £52, and £1 for every complete £10 of net capital value of accumulated property.(34) The law has become more complex as it has been necessary to meet special cases, and the general tendency has been to make the pension right easier and the claims less public. The broad principle now is that a married couple's income shall not exceed £143 and an individual's income £97 10s. annually, including pension. The definition of income, however, does not include many important receipts, and net accumulated property is defined with equal liberality to exclude a property on which a pensioner resides, life insurance policies or annuities, or other life interests in the capital sum of which the applicant has no interest beyond the income derived therefrom. The number of recipients and the cost of the pension scheme have steadily grown, until in the financial year ending March 31, 1928, 24,875 pensioners drew an average of £40 12s. 6d., amounting to £1,010,575. This sum is approximately eight times the original annual cost, the average payment to each pensioner having been approximately trebled and the conditions greatly liberalised.

In 1911 a considerable extension of the pension system was made by the passing of the Widows' Pensions Act, which also has been steadily liberalised by subsequent amendments. The maximum pension now payable for a widow with six or more children under the age of fifteen is £208 per year. The cost of widows' pensions in the year 1927–8 was £304,066, paid to 4,098 recipients with 8,933 children.

In 1912 a Military Pensions Act made provision for Maori war veterans, and in 1915 a Miners' Phthisis Act provided similarly for victims of miners' phthisis contracted in New Zealand. The Act provides also for the widows of men dying from this complaint.

The War Pensions Act, 1915, was the next large instalment of the system, providing liberally for disabled members of the New Zealand forces and for the dependents of disabled, deceased, or missing members of those forces. Payments on account of war pensions reached a peak of £1,886,952 in 1920–1, but have since diminished rapidly to £1,151,797 in 1927–8.

Other pension schemes exist for South African War veterans, members of the Defence Forces, victims of the influenza epidemic of 1918, persons afflicted with blindness, and miscellaneous Civil Service pensioners.

Payments under all these schemes are now made in accordance with the consolidated Pensions Act, 1926. They are made as of right to applicants who can prove their eligibility. There is no stigma of charity and still less of pauperism attached to them, and all are on a non-contributory basis, funds being provided from general taxation. The modest cost of the first full year of old-age pensions was £157,342; for the last financial year on record (1927–8) the total cost of the various pension schemes was £2,613,770, and no expenditure from the public funds meets with less criticism.

Various contributory pension and superannuation schemes add to the State's financial burden. Superannuation schemes were provided for the police force (1899), railway servants (1902), teachers (1905), and the public service (1908). The Public Service Superannuation Act, 1927, consolidates the legislation other than that relating to the railway scheme and to local authority schemes established under the Local Authorities Superannuation Act, 1908. In all of these funds, and also in the National Provident Fund established in 1910, the Government has paid subsidies and must in some cases pay further subsidies to make the funds actuarially sound. All of the funds are clearly and adequately described in successive issues of the official year-book.

The latest extension of the pension system was contained in

the Family Allowances Act, 1926.(35) In this case the legislation was passed almost without public recognition and certainly without adequate public discussion. Unlike the Old Age Pensions Act, there was no widespread public demand for such a measure. The women's organisations, it is true, had for some years discussed in vague terms the endowment of motherhood and other proposals looking toward a greater degree of economic independence for women. The actual origin of the 1926 Act is to be found, however, in an electioneering tactic just prior to the election of 1925. The propaganda conducted in Australia by Mr. A. B. Piddington, K.C., aroused virtually no interest in New Zealand; the various schemes of family wages introduced in continental Europe mainly by employers' associations are of quite different character from the New Zealand measure. In the same way it is difficult to see how the New Zealand Act can be regarded as providing in any adequate way the increased measure of feminine independence which is the basis of all schemes for the endowment of motherhood. It merely provides an allowance of 2s. per week for each child in excess of two wherever the total family income does not exceed £4 weekly plus 2s. for each child in excess of two.

The conclusion is obvious, that the Family Allowances Act of 1926 is nothing more than an extension into a specific field of the pensions legislation already so far developed in New Zealand. It might even be regarded as an extension of the charitable aid system, or, more correctly, as another form of preventive pension designed to relieve the charitable aid payments and to obviate their demoralising effects.

With these drastic limitations the scheme can hardly be regarded as having any revolutionary significance. It was designed to relieve distress arising from a particular cause, the burden of dependent children upon families receiving very small incomes. The Arbitration Court professes to fix its basic rates of wages upon the "statistical family" of a man, wife, and two children. The family allowances are designed to afford extra relief to families where the number of children is in excess of two. In the first year of operation the number of family recipients has been 3,000.

The total sum paid was £37,652. In view of these facts there seems a good deal of hyperbole in the epithets used to describe such a modest measure, which hardly suffices "to restore the Dominion's title to the rank of pioneer in social and economic experimentation". A title resting on such a basis would be empty of any great significance. Neither does there seem to be any justification for the opprobrious epithets, of which "dole" seems to have been the most popular.

The scheme is a soundly conceived measure of minor importance for the relief of a particular form of poverty. Its effect upon the general level of wages is negligible, except in the possible contingency of the allowances influencing the Arbitration Court in its determination of a standard wage. Since the allowances are avowedly in supplement of the basic wage, and the latter by tacit tradition is mainly determined by the cost of living, such a contingency would seem to require a degree of perverseness not hitherto disclosed by the Judges who have presided over the Court. Nor is it likely that the extra two shillings a week will have much effect upon the birth-rate. To suppose that it might, involves the belief that economic motives are much more powerful in such matters than any modern economist, since the "economic man" went out of fashion, will admit.

It is obviously true that a future Government with socialistic or feministic principles might extend the operations of this Act until it really became a revolutionary measure. Such a Government might also use existing legislation to make the Bank of New Zealand an instrument of financial revolution, the Board of Trade an economic judiciary for all industrial activities, and the export control boards soviets for the nationalisation of the primary industries. These things have not happened in New Zealand and are not likely to happen. The conservative temper of the people is such that experimental legislation is never allowed to reach its logical revolutionary conclusion. The Family Allowances Act may be liberalised as the other elements of the pension system have been, the allowances may be increased—in a time of depression the cost of the scheme may go up; but it is difficult to see what revolutionary principle is involved in the measure as it now exists.

Housing and the Standard of Living

The standard of living of a whole community is too vague a conception to be capable of accurate measurement.(36) Comparisons of wages either with other countries or within the same country at different times are obviously inadequate. Variations in the size and make-up of the family, the extent of supplementary earnings, and similar factors make comparisons almost meaningless and are extremely hard to take account of except in the broadest and most unreal form of types or averages. In the same way differences of price-levels are not easy to adjust in any very satisfactory way.

Even if, as has sometimes been done, more or less typical groups of workers are compared by estimating the standard wages and the prices of selected articles of consumption such as the main food-stuffs, there still remain immeasurable factors.(37) One of these, at least, is important in New Zealand. In any comparisons with a nominally high standard country such as the United States, or a lower standard country such as Britain, the smaller extent to which New Zealand women act as wage-earners and their greater degree of freedom to discharge their home duties must be taken into account. On the contrary any historical comparisons within New Zealand itself must reckon with the greater opportunities in recent years for women to enter a wider variety of wage-earning occupations.

While the effort to make any precise test of the real standard of living in the Dominion is hardly worth making in the present state of economic and statistical information, there is some evidence that the standard is comparatively high. One of the best tests is that of physical health and especially of infant mortality, to which some attention has already been paid.(38) There is ample evidence that in the first necessity of existence—food—there is little lack either in quantity, quality, or variety. The same may be said of clothing.

Definite statistics exist in regard to the third necessity of economic life—shelter—and these give colour to the idea that there can be few countries in the world where a relatively high national income is so evenly distributed among the whole population. The latest figures available at the time of writing are those of the 1921 census, which show that the total number of married, widowed, and divorced males was at that time approximately 260,000, almost exactly equal to the number of females in similar conjugal classes. The total number of private dwellings and tenements (260,229) coincides remarkably with this figure, which may be taken as approximately the number of families in the Dominion. This is sufficient to make clear the first general conclusion. There may be instances in the towns of more than one family occupying a dwelling, but the general rule in New Zealand is that each family occupies its own home.(39)

Of this total number, 250,254 were private dwellings and 9,975 were tenements or flats. Despite the tendency in recent years for flats to appear in the cities, especially in Auckland and Wellington, the great majority of New Zealand families live in detached wooden houses. Almost two-thirds of these houses consist of five rooms or more. Sixty per cent. are owned or partly owned by their occupants, more than 20 per cent. are owned outright, the remainder being in course of purchase or encumbered by mortgages.

These bare statistics indicate an unusually high standard of housing for the general population. From this high standard, however, there has apparently been a distinct tendency to decline in the most recent years, a tendency which the 1926 census returns may reasonably be expected to disclose as having been considerably aggravated by the economic difficulties since 1921. The New Zealand definition of overcrowding has been set higher than in most countries at one and a half persons per room. Judged by this standard the city tenements and flats using more expensive sites tend to show a fair amount of overcrowding; but it is significant that the percentage of the population affected by overcrowding is much higher in the country districts than in the towns. This coincides with the fact that the amenities of country houses are on the average less than those of similar dwellings in the city.

The economic stress of the post-war period is indicated also by the fact that the 1921 census was the first since 1886 to show an increase in the number of persons per inhabited dwelling. It may safely be assumed that the 1926 census will show a further increase, just as the similar figure increased steadily in the previous period of falling prices and economic stringency from 1871 to 1886.

Something should be said in conclusion of Governmental efforts to maintain a high standard of housing welfare in the Dominion. Those efforts fall into two distinct classes: the encouragement to ownership given by the State advances schemes, and the efforts made from time to time to carry out more or less ambitious schemes of State construction.

The latter and less important line of State activity may be taken first. The Workers' Dwelling Act of 1905 was partly the result of the memorandum by the secretary of the Labour Department drawing attention to the important Arbitration Court decision which effectually standardised wages in terms of the cost of living. Mr. Tregear, as has already been noted in another connection,(40) drew the Government's attention to the fact that this meant that the workers could not improve their standards, and went on to speak of the ground landlord abstracting a larger and larger proportion of the weekly wage. The Act of 1905, however, under which the Government would build houses of a standardised type for workers whose wages were not more than £175 per year, was not of great importance. Even as amended in 1910 and in 1914 it had little appeal. Workers who were in a position to face regular payments for the purchase of a house preferred the greater freedom of choice given them by other avenues of purchase. Between 1905 and 1919 only 657 houses were built under these Acts.(41)

In the post-war year 1919 a more ambitious scheme was put forward by the Housing Act of that year. The Housing Board, created under this measure, showed signs for a short time of expanding into a substantial construction department. The Government took power to borrow large sums, the limits of wage-earning capacity and of the value of the houses to be constructed were raised, provision was made for loans to local bodies. Four hundred and twenty houses were built under this Act before the depression of 1921 overtook the Government and caused a retrenchment campaign, one of the results of which was the curtailment of the housing scheme, which was absorbed in the Advances to Workers Department by the Advances Act of 1922.(42)

The lending activities of the Government since the passing

of the Advances to Settlers Act in 1894 and the Advances to Workers Act in 1906 have been much more influential in promoting the marked tendency for workers (and all other classes) to own their own homes. Since it is possible to take advantage of the Advances to Settlers Act to raise a first-mortgage on a dwelling-house, it is impossible to state with precision the full extent to which Government loans have encouraged ownership. The Advances to Workers Department alone, from its inception in 1906 to March 31, 1928, had granted 30,724 loans totalling £14,870,000, of which amount almost 29 per cent. had been repaid.(43) These figures indicate that loans have been extended to a substantial proportion of the total number of dwellings in New Zealand and a still higher proportion of those dwellings in course of purchase.

Under the Act as it now stands, loans may be granted up to £1,250, which must not be more than 95 per cent. of the total value of the security. Worker is defined as a person who is not in receipt of more than £300 per year plus £25 for each of his children. The scope of the Act is therefore wide, and applications under it are normally in excess of the money available. The Department has been cautious in valuations and in actually granting the loans. There has been no net loss to the State. Amortisation payments quickly increase the margin of security in the property, and as far as the financial aspects of the scheme are concerned there seems little ground for criticism. The Government borrows in the cheapest market abroad and relends on good security at a rate sufficient to cover the loans and working expenses of the Department. The financial position is even stronger since in recent years the repayments and internal reserves of the Department have become available in increasing amounts as a revolving fund for fresh loans, naturally at higher rates of interest than those carried by the original loans.

The social advantages of stability and thrift induced by the possession of property, and the necessity for regular payments of interest and reductions of capital, are also to be reckoned on the credit side. But various indirect consequences are not so clearly favourable to the scheme.

In the first place the Government Statistician's comment on the 1921 census figures of householding as showing a trend away from rental to purchasing ownership suggests doubts as to the free choice of many workers.(44) One of the penalties of the Act's success has been to decrease very greatly the number of houses built for rental. Speculative builders exist, it is true, but they sell instead of letting their houses. This means that a worker who wants a home must buy, sometimes on terms that he really cannot afford. The easy transferability of the Government loans also facilitates speculation in urban as well as rural property. The Government valuations are such that in many cases a purchaser has to find an extra mortgage for the last difficult portion of the price he is forced to pay.

On balance it seems true to say that the social advantages of the scheme are great, but that they would be difficult to obtain in a country where the standard of income was lower than in New Zealand. Where a worker has a margin above bare necessities such that he can buy a section of land, the liberal Government loans are of great assistance in enabling him to purchase a home. His income enables him to meet the strain of interest and capital repayments, and his equity in the property steadily grows.

The dangers of the system are worst in a time of rapidly rising prices and land speculation. The shortage of houses, combined with over-adequate lending facilities in the post-war period, caused excessive prices to be paid. It needs only a small marginal surplus or shortage of houses to cause great variations in price. Even a brief period of boom, therefore, results in overborrowing, and the subsequent fall of prices transfers a large part of the community's wealth to the creditor classes.

Other aspects of the housing situation have never been adequately investigated. It is possible that the costs of construction are made higher by the piecemeal construction and inefficient methods of small cottage contractors working for private owners. Such methods play into the hands of combinations of merchants controlling essential supplies like timber and cement.

In essentials, therefore, the system of freehold ownership of houses has much the same virtues and defects as those connected with the freehold ownership of farms. There are social advantages of ownership, but disadvantages of finance and speculation.

CHAPTER XIII

IMPERIALISM AND FOREIGN AFFAIRS

The Imperial Sentiment

There are many reasons why a survey of New Zealand's economic and social development would not be complete without some reference to the leading features and events of her imperial and foreign policy. The economic implications of her geographical position are such that overseas trade is her very life. Her remote isolation makes possible also a far greater degree of control over immigration than is usual. The character of her population, the most important factor in economic production, has therefore been largely determined by Governmental policy. In the same way, shipping and tariff policies, taxation, the trading facilities given to nationals of countries outside the British Commonwealth, have all been affected by the imperial sentiment which has dominated the Dominion throughout its history. One of the most important illustrations of this fact is to be found in the conscious direction of both public and private borrowing for developmental purposes.

New Zealand, more definitely than any other part of the British Empire, has striven to think and legislate imperially. She has had a long succession of leaders to whom citizenship in the British Empire has been of more vital importance than local considerations. This was natural enough at the very beginning of the colony's history, but the succession is too marked to be regarded as merely an accident. Vogel, Seddon, Ward, and Massey took the same essential attitude as Wakefield, Selwyn, and Grey, and for the same basic reasons. There have been times, it is true, when the attitude of New Zealand statesmen has been in conflict with the strongly expressed policies of the Colonial Office. During the whole Wakefield period there was conflict. In the period of the Maori wars also, relations were strained for a time until Weld carried through his "self-reliant policy" in 1863. Again in the early seventies, when the several colonies of Australia and New Zealand were struggling for freedom to make reciprocal tariff treaties with each other, Vogel boldly, and to the dismay of the Colonial Office, carried the doctrine of fiscal autonomy to its logical conclusion.(1) The same bold political thinker pressed hard for more forceful British policies of annexation in the South Pacific a decade later, and alarmed the Colonial Office by declaring New Zealand's readiness to act in Samoa and Tonga at any moment.(2)

In all these cases, however, the action of the New Zealand leaders foreshadowed the later development of imperial policy to which the Colonial Office in time had to conform. Indeed, it may fairly be claimed that in this first period of what has been called the Second British Empire, New Zealand often played an effective leading rôle in the development of imperial relations. That leadership seemed to pass when the economic development of the larger Dominions made it increasingly difficult to conceive imperial policy in federative terms. With the advent of colonial nationalism, first in Canada and later in Australia and South Africa, New Zealand's position has tended to become that of a conservative defender of the existing order rather than that of a leader towards a new conception of imperialism.(3) What has recently passed for initiative in imperial affairs, as far as New Zealand is concerned, has been a succession of acts, such as Seddon's offer of troops in Samoa in 1899 and next year in the Boer War, and Ward's offer in 1907 of a battle-cruiser for the British fleet—acts intended to demonstrate New Zealand's unity of policy and sympathy with the Motherland.

Through both these periods, however—the period of initiative looking towards imperial federation, and the more recent period of identification with the policies of the Motherland—there runs the same essential theory. This theory of the necessity for imperial solidarity has always been powerful in New Zealand. In part it is a legacy from the political ideas of the first colonists. In larger part it is an essential corollary of the economic position in which New Zealand is placed by her remoteness from the chief market for her produce. Both origins need to be taken into account.

On the political side it is necessary to recall the fact that the Wakefield settlers came to New Zealand urged by a sense of privilege and mission. Voluntarily and deliberately they had left the Motherland to plant a new Britain overseas. Their numbers included many idealists who sought freer opportunities in a new land—some among them were younger sons of noble families; others were trade unionists and chartists, or members of the infant Free Kirk of Scotland, but none was driven from the land he loved by persecution or misgovernment. In consequence they were loth to regard themselves as exiles. They were still British, and in their new far-away home their only fear was lest they should lose touch, and perhaps be forgotten, in the politics of Britain. No one can read their letters, their first poems, their public speeches, without realising how large a place their continued British citizenship claimed in their thoughts.(4) One must remember, too, that they were politically minded above the average. The first Parliaments, both Provincial and National, disclosed a quite unusually high level of political thinking and forensic skill. It is hardly to be wondered at, therefore, that the first public reference to the possibility and desirability of imperial federation which the historian of the British Commonwealth was able to find was in John Robert Godley's farewell address to the settlers of Canterbury in 1852.(5) It was essential in Godley's thinking that some means should be found by which active citizenship might be exercised under the British constitution even in far-away New Zealand. In an age which had not been disillusioned of Parliamentary democracy it was natural that federation and Parliamentary representation should have appeared to his mind as the ideal of his desires. Indeed, it is not long since this ideal, impractical as most people now recognise it to be, was still agitated in responsible quarters in New Zealand. Political imagination in the Dominion has not always remained at Godley's high level, nor kept pace with the times.

Despite great economic and political changes, this passionate loyalty to the British Crown and to common citizenship in the British Empire (the term "Commonwealth" is not very often used in New Zealand) remains the basis of the Dominion's imperial and foreign policies. The exclusiveness of the original Wakefield settlements was broken down by the gold-rushes of the sixties and the assisted immigration of the following decade, which brought in a flood of new settlers who had scant sympathy with the somewhat aristocratic ideal that lay behind Wakefield's theories. As the government of the colony passed into the hands of the new-comers the social and political ascendancy of the original settlers was destroyed; but their imperial ideals and aspirations have persisted. In more recent years it has become evident that the population of New Zealand has begun to develop characteristic qualities reflecting its origin and environment. Three-fourths of the people are native born, and in recent generations the legend of high endeavour and noble aspirations so characteristic of the first Wakefield settlers has become a powerful formative agent in the teaching of citizenship in the schools.

It is to be remembered also that New Zealand, in proportion to its size, has a comparatively heavy volume of immigration, and this immigration is almost wholly from Great Britain, so that nearly 99 per cent. of the population is British. The total population is now approximately 1,500,000, and new settlers from Great Britain average more than 10,000 annually in normal years, so that the connection with the Motherland is kept fresh by constant new contacts.

The close connection of the Motherland and her farthest Dominion has other varied aspects. The newspapers have direct cable services and print surprisingly large quantities of British news; British journals (and few others) circulate among a people which reads more on the average than most communities; the university colleges and many other educational institutions are largely staffed from British universities; literature, music, and art, even politics, are apt to be influenced very directly by judgments and happenings in the Motherland. To some among the younger generation the closeness of these ties savours of intellectual tutelage.(6) It is probable that the development of a distinctive New Zealand literature and art has been delayed by the acceptance of British forms and standards. But with most people, and until recently, such a thought has hardly risen into consciousness.

The closeness of these spiritual ties is reinforced in a very practical way by economic interest. The very smallness and remoteness of the Dominion are important both economically and politically. New Zealand politicians are apt to be very proud of the fact that they can boast the highest value of international trade per head of any country in the world. For the year 1927 the exports amounted to approximately £33 9s. per head, and the imports to £30 18s. The very size of these figures, however, indicates that the small New Zealand community is dependent to an uncommon degree for the necessities of its life upon overseas trade.

Moreover, this trade is necessarily all sea-borne, and the greater part of it must go half-way round the world to its chief market, which is, of course, Great Britain. Seventy-six per cent. of the total exports of New Zealand produce in 1927 went directly to Great Britain, either for consumption or for re-export, and from Britain was derived 48 per cent. of the total imports. In certain important exports the proportion taken by Great Britain is considerably higher, and this is particularly true of the great bulk cargoes—wool, meat, butter, and cheese. These facts go far to explain the insistence of New Zealand's political leaders upon policies calculated to strengthen the British Navy.

It must be added that British shipping shares with local companies a virtual monopoly of overseas trade; British financial institutions supply the circulating capital which shifts this trade half-way round the world, and the commercial transactions arising out of the trade centre in London. It is not too much to say in addition that the overwhelming bulk of the overseas capital invested in the Dominion is British. It would hardly be politically possible for a New Zealand Government to follow the example of certain Australian States and borrow upon the New York market. On the contrary both the national Government and local bodies are supported by public opinion in deliberately accepting British tenders which are, within a reasonable margin, higher than competing tenders from foreign countries. This sentimental preference is in addition to the tariff discriminations under the policy of imperial preference. In the same way, though not to the same extent, there is a predominance of British interests in the overseas capital which is invested in industrial and commercial enterprises. There is a widespread, if not well-founded, distrust of foreign investment, and it is not many years since the United States Government felt bound to enquire about the discrimination which certain anti-trust legislation was alleged to have effected against an American firm.

Such facts as these, vital as they are in the sentiment and economic interest of the Dominion, are quite adequate to account for the characteristic attitude which responsible New

Zealand statesmen have consistently taken on imperial questions. This attitude may be summed up briefly as a fervent loyalty to the British Crown, distrust of constitutional changes within the Empire, lukewarmness towards the League of Nations, and readiness to co-operate in imperial, and especially in naval, defence. There can be no reasonable doubt that on all of these points public opinion has generally supported Governmental policy. It is significant that there is little effort in the educational system to awaken a local patriotism. New Zealand history has only recently come to occupy even a slight place in the educational curricula. The loyalty which is taught in New Zealand is to the Crown as the symbol of imperial unity. The patriotic orator never dreams of appealing to such a catch-cry as Australia for the Australians, White Australia, or Canadian Nationalism. His appeal is not even to the British Commonwealth!

Occasionally, indeed, amusing problems of terminology arise, as when an association of firms engaged in trading with Great Britain, anxious to capitalise New Zealand's imperial sentiment and yet afraid of Canadian and Australian competition, had to abandon the word British and invent the slogan "Be English, Buy English", which immediately gave offence to many patriotic Scots in the Dominion. This, however, is a commercial perversion of New Zealand's real sentiment. The New Zealand catchwords are concerned with the Empire and the Navy. Imperialism, which in other lands is more often than not a term of reproach, is never anything but a proud title of distinction in New Zealand's public life. (7)

New Zealand's Island Empire

The interest of successive generations of New Zealand statesmen in the outlying Polynesian and even Melanesian islands, together with a steadily deepening feeling of separatism from Australia and dislike of any policy, such as federation, which appeared likely to merge New Zealand's identity with that of her larger neighbour, have reinforced the strong feeling of dependence upon the Motherland and have contributed materially to the formation of the characteristic New Zealand attitude upon imperial and foreign policy. The people of New Zealand regard themselves as the custodians of the British imperial tradition in the south seas, but, unlike their Australian neighbours, they have not yet converted this tradition into any very real feeling of nationalism. On the contrary the increased responsibilities of their island empire, which, as an American geographer has recently pointed out,(8) stretches from the Equator to the Pole, add to the dependence upon the power and diplomacy of the British Empire which New Zealanders feel so strongly as a consequence of their isolation and remoteness.

The tradition of New Zealand's responsibility for the scattered Pacific islands traces back in clear succession to the utterances of Bishop Selwyn and Sir George Grey. The letters patent appointing Selwyn to the missionary bishopric of New Zealand in 1841 contained a curious error illustrating the vague geography in vogue in Government circles at that time. His diocese was defined as extending to 34 degrees north instead of 34 degrees south latitude. While he drew his mandate for missionary activities in the Polynesian and Melanesian islands rather from his archbishop's farewell letter of instructions, the letters patent enabled him to keep within the legal limitations of his office.(9) As soon as his work in New Zealand was fairly started he began a series of missionary voyages to the various islands, primarily with the object of gathering students for St. John's College at Auckland. He saw this college as the centre of missionary training for the whole South Pacific, and much of his thought and planning went into its early work.

On the political side Grey dreamed the same dream. The bishop and the Governor were on terms of intimacy, and one of their many common interests was the noble vision of a federation of the Pacific islands under New Zealand leadership as an integral part of the British Empire. Grey vehemently protested against the passivity of the British Government in face of French activity in the Pacific, especially in regard to the occupation of New Caledonia in 1853.(10) The Colonial Office, however, has never at any time given real support to the view so strenuously advocated by Selwyn, Grey, Stout, Vogel, Seddon, and later leaders, that the South Pacific, and even the North Pacific, islands were a rightful preserve of the British Empire, in which any activity by other Powers should be regarded as intrusive, if not hostile.

The history of the Pacific islands and of British diplomacy in connection therewith has been written in careful detail by a New Zealand historian, and there is no need here to go over the same ground.(11) In brief it may be said that both New Zealand and Australia viewed with alarm and protested to the Colonial Office in no uncertain terms against every step taken by foreign Powers towards annexation of any of the islands. First France, and later Germany, became the object of their fears and suspicions. As Siegfried rightly pointed out, the presence of the French in New Caledonia has never seemed quite natural or right. The condominium which Britain and France exercise over the New Hebrides is, and always has been, a subject of much criticism and heart-burning in both Australia and New Zealand.(12) Since the European War the former German possessions in New Guinea and Samoa have fallen to the administration of the Dominions as mandatories of the League of Nations; but satisfaction with this result is somewhat marred by uneasiness concerning the similar Japanese mandate for the islands farther north. New Zealand and Australia, in fact, have dreamed of a Monroe Doctrine in the Pacific. Siegfried put this very clearly when he wrote(13):

> According as the policy of colonial expansion developed among the Powers, they realised, as a sure instinct had from the very first warned them, that it was necessary for them to remain, as far as possible, alone and without troublesome neighbours in the South Pacific. In this way the programme "Australasia for the Australasians" developed into "Oceania for the Anglo-Saxons".

The most vehement protests from New Zealand were called forth by German colonising activity, especially in Samoa. Vogel had taken upon himself the mantle of Grey, and at intervals throughout the sixties and seventies he put forward proposals for a federation which should bring all the southern islands, including Fiji, Tonga, and Samoa, under British rule, with New Zealand as the leading member of the federation. In a memorandum dated April 5, 1876, Vogel stressed the danger of allowing any foreign Power to occupy Samoa; but his representations had little or no effect, and German traders became active there soon afterwards.(14)

In 1883 a powerful Samoan chief, Malietoa, in difficulties owing to German support of his chief rival, entered into correspondence with Sir George Grey. Grey, at that time a private

Member of Parliament, introduced and carried a Bill to enable New Zealand to accept the federation of any of the island races of the Pacific which should ask for such union. This Bill was clearly beyond the powers of the New Zealand Parliament at that time, and never received the Royal assent. It provided the occasion, however, for much agitation. Individual members of the Lower House, apparently Aucklanders moved by the prospects of trade with the islands, took active steps to prepare the ground for annexation in Samoa itself, to the annoyance of Bismarck and the great embarrassment of the British official representatives in the islands.(15)

In the following year, 1884, Vogel participated on behalf of New Zealand in an inter-colonial conference prompted mainly by alarm in Australia over the German annexations in New Guinea. The Stout-Vogel Ministry was in power, and to the consternation of the Colonial Office declared itself ready to assume the cost of annexing both Tonga and Samoa, and of combining both with Fiji in an island federation. It was even proposed that the Government steamer, with Vogel himself aboard, should visit Samoa "to accurately ascertain Samoan feeling pending a reply from the Colonial Office".(16) There was no result from this rather outspoken declaration of New Zealand policy, and the British Government proceeded to negotiate the Samoan Convention of 1884–5.

This Convention, however, extinguished other German claims in the South Pacific, and New Zealand demanded permission to take in hand the administration of the remaining islands, which had been left to British influence. The chief group concerned was the Cook Islands, which as early as 1864 had petitioned for annexation. It was not until after the second Colonial Conference of 1897 that their request was granted. An order-in-council of May 1901, proclaimed under the authority of the Colonial Boundaries Act of 1895, included the Cook and other islands within New Zealand's jurisdiction.(17)

This tardy concession to New Zealand's imperialist claims in the south seas did not come until after Great Britain had acquiesced in the annexation of part of Samoa by Germany in 1899. Samoa forthwith became, in the minds of many local politicians, a New Zealand irredenta. British acquiescence was doubtless part of the diplomatic game being played in this troubled period just before the Boer War; but it was a sore blow to New Zealand dreams, and Seddon spoke in no uncertain terms of his disappointment.(18) The record of British diplomacy in the islands of the Pacific is, in fact, singularly unenterprising for a supposed imperialist power. Seddon in his characteristic way had called upon President McKinley and his Secretary of State, as he went to the Colonial Conference of 1897, and had bluntly informed them of New Zealand's interests in Hawaii. His subsequent representations on this subject in London were of no avail, and Hawaii was annexed by the United States in 1899.(19) The New Zealand imperialists contemplated with some feeling the remnant of islands which fell to their share in 1901, and thought regretfully and resentfully of Downing Street's unwillingness to forestall French, German, and American expansion in the Pacific.

The subsequent administration of the Cook and other islands seems to have been reasonably successful.(20) There has been no marked economic development, such as the Americans have forced in Hawaii; but the interests of the native race have been conserved, the population is increasing, and there have been no serious difficulties of administration. Government is carried on by island councils, which include native chiefs. The fruit and copra export is mainly directed to New Zealand, which also controls the bulk of the import trade. It is not long since the New Zealand House of Representatives listened with evident appreciation to the Minister for External Affairs, himself a Maori, reading a list of names of local fruit-growers, many of them obviously foreign in origin, and denouncing their petition that tomatoes from the Cook Islands should be made subject to import duty.

As far as these islands are concerned it may fairly be claimed that successive New Zealand Governments anticipated the principles of the mandate system, and cared for the welfare of their native peoples as "a sacred trust of civilisation". Whether the Dominion's administration record could have been as well sustained if her responsibilities had been larger may well be doubted in view of her recent experience with the mandated territory of Western Samoa. Her dream of a Monroe Doctrine for the South Pacific came to naught against the failure of the imperial authorities to give it serious consideration when larger issues were at stake. Most of the southern islands now acknowledge her jurisdiction; but Tonga is merely a British protectorate, Fiji remains a Crown colony; the Tahiti group is under French rule, and the United States has only in 1929 completed its annexation of that part of Samoa which contains the fine harbour of Pago-Pago. New Zealand's island possessions are therefore much less than she desired; but the more limited responsibilities attaching to them have been faithfully discharged.

The Mandate for Western Samoa(21)

Passing reference has already been made to New Zealand's interest in Samoa and the disappointment felt in the Dominion over Great Britain's failure to forestall foreign competition for the control of the islands. The group is small in area, resources, and population; but it has more than once figured as the centre of international rivalries and friction. The almost continuous native feuds lend themselves admirably to this situation, and, as Robert Louis Stevenson long ago remarked, offer excellent opportunities for discontented white people to stir up trouble. It was through the intervention of three great Powers in a tribal feud that Samoa first became a subject of diplomacy.

British missionaries had settled in Samoa in 1830, and eight years later a commercial treaty was signed with Britain, followed by a similar treaty with the United States the next year.(22) In 1847 Britain appointed a consular agent; the United States followed suit in 1853, and Germany in 1861. As in New Zealand, tribal and personal feuds were intensified by the disturbing influences introduced by the white traders. A particularly prolonged feud began in 1869, and, partly as a result, petitions for annexation were sent to Britain in 1877 and the United States in 1878, but both were declined. The United States did, however, take steps in that year to secure a naval and coaling station at Pago-Pago, the best harbour of the whole group. The two other interested Powers followed suit in 1879.

Thenceforward the history of Tutuila, the island on which the American naval station is situated, was comparatively simple. Though the Samoans still retain their unity of language, customs, and nationality, Tutuila has remained in effective American occupation, which in 1928–9 was finally turned into definite annexation, transferring the island from naval to civil Government.

Despite protests from New Zealand, the British Government adhered to the Samoan Convention of 1884–5. Following this a tripartite neutrality agreement was signed at Berlin in 1889, and yet both Britain and the United States concurred in the definite annexation by Germany of Western Samoa in 1899. New Zealand opinion was distinctly hostile to this agreement and it became customary thenceforward to refer to German Samoa as New Zealand's irredenta.

The opportunity which the Dominion had long awaited came with the outbreak of the European War. On August 29, 1914, a New Zealand Expeditionary Force landed at Apia, and the former German territory remained under its military administration until the League of Nations gave New Zealand a mandate for the territory.

In setting forth New Zealand's claim to the mandate much credit was claimed for the colony's government of the Maori race and of the Cook Islands people, both of whom are close kin to the Samoans.

During the debate in the New Zealand House on the acceptance of the Samoan mandate Sir Apirana Ngata, the acknowledged leader of the Young Maori Party and the orator of the House, paid an impressive tribute to the justice and the generosity with which the Maoris have been treated.

> The Samoans [he said] may be congratulated that they have come under the wing of the Anglo-Saxon race, and they are extremely fortunate in that they have come under the direction of the Government of New Zealand, because there is no better representative of the British conscience of administration in a just way of the native races than the Government of this country. I can speak with experience, sometimes with a little bitterness, as to the treatment some of the Maoris have received in New Zealand at the hands even of our own Pakeha people. But the Maoris have a saying "that is between you and me", and take it by and large, take it over the century, no native race has been so fortunate as the Maoris of New Zealand.

With such experience as this at its disposal, the apparent failure of the New Zealand Government to make a success of its trust in Samoa needs explanation. After less than ten years of civil administration it was found necessary to deport three of the leading European residents, one of them a member of the Legislative Council. The Administrator also found it necessary to deprive Samoan chiefs of their hereditary titles and banish quite a large number from their own homes to other parts of the island. Later, cruisers were despatched from New Zealand in order that sailors might be landed to effect the arrest of several hundred members of the Samoan organisation known as the Mau, which had been formed to offer passive resistance to the administration.

The Mau leaders were duly arrested, but were shortly afterwards released as an act of executive clemency. Passive resistance continued even with the advent of a new Administrator, there was a widespread refusal to pay taxes, and economic production seriously declined. In the meantime a change of Government aroused fresh hopes among the Samoan malcontents; but a firm statement by the new Premier was quickly followed by the arrest of the prominent chief who was leader of the Mau, and by his incarceration in a New Zealand gaol. Such events as these warrant a careful examination of the grievances expressed by the discontented Samoans and their allies among the white traders.

The mandate for the former German colony of Western Samoa was issued by the League of Nations to "His Britannic Majesty for and on behalf of the Government of New Zealand" on December 17, 1920. It contains the usual provisions stressing the material and moral welfare of the native inhabitants; prohibiting slave-trading, traffic in arms, military training, fortification, and the sale of alcoholic liquor; and stipulating freedom of religious teaching.(23)

The Government of New Zealand, consistently with its characteristic attitude in imperial affairs, pursued a strictly constitutional course in accepting this mandate under the authority of an Act of the British Parliament, the Foreign Jurisdiction Act, 1890.(24) The procedure, however, was more legalistic than vital. The acceptance of the mandate is essentially a contract between the League and New Zealand, which is one of its Member States.

The legal basis of the government of Samoa under the mandate is the Samoa Act, passed by the New Zealand Parliament in 1921, and subsequently amended in 1923 and 1927.(25) Section 45 of the main Act delegates power to the Governor-General (of New Zealand) to make regulations by Order-in-Council for the peace, order, and good government of Samoa. The following section grants power to the "Administrator acting with the advice and consent of the Legislative Council of Western Samoa" to make ordinances, provided they are not repugnant to the regulations mentioned above, or to any Acts either of the New Zealand Parliament or the British Parliament which are in force in the territory.

The Administrator has the advice and assistance of a legislative council, which may consist of not less than four and not more than six official members appointed by the Governor-General, and three unofficial members elected by the European residents. In addition there is a Fono of Faipules, or native parliament, consisting of leading chiefs from every district, which meets twice yearly and has the power of submitting recommendations to the Administrator. These Faipules are appointed by the Administrator.

The government of the territory, therefore, is vested very largely in the person of the Administrator, since neither the Legislative Council nor the Fono has executive authority, and both are very largely bodies of his creation.

In New Zealand itself a special Department of External Affairs was created, and the Administrator is directly responsible to the Minister in charge of that Department. New Zealand also has a Department of Native Affairs, which is concerned with Maori matters. There is, in addition, a Cook Islands Department, created to administer the Cook and other islands which were annexed in 1901. These three Departments are presided over by three different Ministers and have no direct connection one with the other, although the natives both of Samoa and of the Cook Islands are of the same blood as the Maoris. The administration of the Cook Islands has been conducted without apparent friction by means of local administrators and councils very much of the same type as those which were created for Samoa. For many years the responsible Minister in charge was a Maori member of the Cabinet, Sir Maui Pomare.

One of the most surprising features of the recent difficulties which New Zealand has experienced in Samoa is the apparent lack of co-ordination between the departments which are responsible for the government of the three sections of the Polynesian race. This was dramatically illustrated when Sir Maui Pomare, speaking as a Maori, although he was Minister-in-Charge of the Cook Islands, strongly, and to the evident chagrin of his colleagues, opposed the actions of his own Government in Samoa.

Active opposition in Samoa to New Zealand's administration can be dated definitely from a public meeting held in Apia on October 15, 1926.(26) This meeting, convened by the three non-official members of the Legislative Council on the eve of the triennial election, was attended not only by the European voters, but also by natives. From it sprang not only the so-called Citizens' Committee, but also the native organisation known as the Mau, or League, which has acted in liaison with the Citizens' Committee.

After some delay, on account of which he has been charged with bad faith and broken promises, the responsible Minister of External Affairs arrived from New Zealand on June 3, 1927, to investigate complaints which had finally been gathered together in a petition to the New Zealand Parliament of May 5, 1927.(27) Throughout his visit he took a position of uncompromising opposition to the demands of the petitioners, and indicated quite definitely and unequivocally the "strong" policy which the Government of New Zealand intended to pursue if the agitation continued. The Administrator whose actions were under criticism, reinforced by the Minister's stand and empowered by an Order-in-Council to do so, immediately threatened the leader of the agitation with deportation.(28)

In the following month there was a prolonged debate in the New Zealand House of Representatives on the Samoa Amendment Bill, which was introduced on July 23, 1927, and which gave extended power to the Administrator to deport European residents to the islands and banish Samoans to areas within the islands. The Labour Opposition fought persistently, but the Government majority, reinforced by the Liberals (who took the attitude of throwing responsibility on to the Government in the matter), ensured the passage of the Bill.(29)

At the Administrator's request, however, a Royal Commission was appointed on September 5th, and after taking voluminous evidence in Samoa, reported to the Governor-General on November 29th. The Commission's report is, on the whole, an emphatic endorsement of the legality of the Administrator's actions, and has been claimed by the Government as a complete vindication of its policy. It did not, however, settle the agitation by any means. The Mau movement, indeed, grew into thoroughly organised passive resistance to the administration, which was perhaps best described in the words used by the Prime Minister in justifying the subsequent orders.

> In Samoa to-day the native people are seriously disunited; a large section of them are in a state of passive resistance to constituted authority; so far as they are concerned the King's writ is not running; they are refusing to obey orders and summonses of the Court, even though serious indictable and criminal offences are involved; they are refusing to pay their taxes; they are failing to search for beetles or to account for those collected; they are neglecting their plantations; they are keeping their children from the Government schools, and, perhaps the most serious of all, they are rejecting medical help and neglecting similar precautions. It is impossible to ignore the serious position that exists to-day, and has existed for some months past, and it is not too much to say that sufficient mischief has already been done to prejudice the prosperity of Samoa and the Samoans for many years to come.(30)

The decision of the Government in face of these facts was to strike at the root of the agitation and deport the European leaders of the Citizens' Committee. The three men deported included the wealthiest trader on the island, a Swedish-Samoan half-caste, the Hon. O. F. Nelson, member of the Legislative Council. The order was issued on December 22nd, and Mr. Nelson was duly deported in January, being given a most impressive farewell by his native supporters.

The native situation by this time had become so much worse that cruisers were sent from New Zealand on February 18th, landing sailors and arresting four hundred leading members of the Mau organisation. By this time the agitation had centred round the personality of the Administrator, Sir George Richardson, and the chief Samoan demand was for his removal. His resignation was announced in March, and shortly afterwards he left the islands for New Zealand, whence he proceeded to Geneva to give a statement regarding his administration before the Permanent Mandates Commission. His place was filled by the appointment on March 22nd of Colonel S. S. Allen, whose military title was gained as a member of the New Zealand Expeditionary Force during the Great War, but who is not a professional soldier. It is too soon to determine whether the change of administration has had the effect of quieting down the natives. As a measure of clemency the four hundred Mau prisoners were released on March 9th prior to the departure of Sir George Richardson, but the exiled trader, Mr. Nelson, is a person of considerable wealth and influence, and his native blood gives him a commanding position with the Samoans, so that the agitation for the transference of the mandate from New Zealand to Great Britain continues, and seems likely to continue.(31)

The Permanent Mandates Commission of the League of Nations naturally took special interest in the report of the New Zealand Government upon these events. Both Mr. Nelson and the Administrator were present in Geneva, but the Commission refused to allow the former to appear personally before it. The result of the cross-examination of the officials representing New Zealand was an emphatic endorsement of their policy. The commissioners put their conclusions into clear and unmistakable language(32):

> It is the considered opinion of the Commission that none of the charges of any importance against the Administration which have been made in the various petitions has been substantiated, and that none contains any evidence of policy or action contrary to the mandate.
>
> On the contrary, the local Administration seems to have made every effort to improve the conditions of life of the native population, notably in regard to public health and education, as well as in regard to agricultural production and commerce.
>
> The Commission cannot too strongly condemn the action of Mr. Nelson and those associated with him, who seem to have been inspired less by a desire for the public welfare than by personal ambition and interests. By unworthy means they have worked upon the minds of an impressionable people, who prior to their propaganda showed no disquieting signs of discontent. The Commission is satisfied that the Administrator acted with great patience—if not perhaps always with sufficient psychological insight—and showed a forbearance and confidence in the people which may have been misunderstood, and so to some extent may have undermined his authority. The lamentable absence of sufficient means to enforce the law which it was his duty to uphold placed him in an extremely difficult

situation. This situation was made all the more delicate by the uncertain attitude of the Government.

The Commission has noted with satisfaction the action taken by the mandatory Power in setting up an impartial commission of enquiry and in communicating to the League its very full report. This report, with the evidence on which its conclusions are based, were of great assistance to the Permanent Mandates Commission in forming its own judgment. The presence before it of General Richardson, the responsible Administrator from 1923 to 1928, and the frankness of his statements were also very useful.

In view of the statement that the unrest in Samoa will probably continue until the League of Nations comes to a decision, the Permanent Mandates Commission considers it of the greatest importance that it should be clearly understood that the mandatory Power alone is responsible for maintaining law and order in accordance with the mandate.

The Commission is assured that adequate means for that essential purpose are now at the disposal of General Richardson's successor, and it trusts that the Samoans, when they realise that they have been misled, will resume their former attitude of confidence in the Administration, and that the mandatory Power will soon be able to re-establish peace and prosperity in Western Samoa by a policy both firm and liberal.

In the meantime Mr. Nelson had carried his case to the highest legal authority in the British Empire; but the Privy Council dismissed his appeal against the legality of his deportation. The policy of New Zealand appeared to be vindicated; but Samoan discontent remained. A new Government in New Zealand itself showed no signs of reversing the established policy; but instead authorised the arrest and imprisonment within New Zealand of the high chief Tamasese, leader of the Mau. An action for his release on a writ of *Habeas Corpus* was denied by the Supreme Court, so that once again the legality of New Zealand's action was affirmed.

The report of a Civil Service Commission concerning the efficiency of administration in Samoa was released to the Press on February 21, 1929. The commissioners, taking an extremely narrow view of the situation, commented in strong terms upon many weaknesses which they had unearthed. Their report presents a superficial case to the Government's critics, but cannot be held either to substantiate the charges of financial imposition on the Samoan people, or to prove more than specific cases of inefficiency. The whole tenor of their report is that New Zealand has embarked upon costly experiments in native welfare, which have burdened the New Zealand taxpayer. Publication of the report merely complicated and embittered a situation which had already become too much involved in factious party political strife. Its leading recommendation, that the Samoan Civil Service should be regarded as essentially part of the public service of the Dominion, is distinctly retrograde in character. The largest single cause of the Samoan troubles has been the lack of officials with specialised training to fit them for the difficult tasks of native administration. The average New Zealand civil servant, admirable as he may be at home, has neither the training nor the temperament for such tasks, involving as they do much subtlety of understanding, and at the same time a dignified, impressive presence.

The troubles in Samoa, therefore, are far from solved still. They may well be considered first as those arising from the discontents of the white traders, and secondly, and more important, as those which arise from native grievances.

Discontent with New Zealand's administration of the mandate is of long standing on the part of the European residents and half-castes.(33) In considering the grievances of the traders and their friends in Samoa it should be noted that the course of events following the acceptance of the mandate by the New Zealand Government not only keenly disappointed the hopes of residents, who looked for a programme of commercial exploitation and development after the war, but actually committed Samoa to commercial decline, and the traders, in some cases, to poverty. Imported labour was reduced to the minimum, the enemy population largely repatriated, and their estates, representing 90 per cent. of the plantation and a substantial portion of the mercantile interest, were taken over, in some cases abandoned, and in nearly all cases absorbed with indifferent success, in the organisation known as the Reparation Estates. The effect of these policies upon a small community can well be imagined, especially when the Reparation Estates bought and sold outside of Samoa, replacing the numerous business contacts with local interests that existed before. The policy of the Government was similar; enterprises were taken over and run under State ownership, while a purchasing department practically eliminated the local merchants from participation in the enlarged activities of the Government.

Again, it is a truism that a successful commercial policy and a sympathetic native policy do not make good bedfellows. The local white inhabitants felt that the Government was over-indulgent to the natives, and neglectful of the interests of those others who had made the islands their home. The result has been that at no time since the establishment of civil government has there been much real sympathy or collaboration between the Government and the non-Samoan population. The latter were often bound by ties of blood or friendship to the Samoans, and their quarrel with the Government contained endless possibilities of trouble.

The grievances may be placed in three categories. The first of these is the total prohibition of the sale of alcoholic liquor to Europeans and natives alike. New Zealand has taken this provision of the mandate seriously, and has incorporated total prohibition into the Act under which Samoa is governed. The responsibility therefore lies with the New Zealand Parliament. The verdict of the Royal Commission, presided over by the Chief Justice of New Zealand, himself a sturdy opponent of the prohibition movement in New Zealand before his elevation to the Bench, is that the prohibition has been reasonably effective. There are 446 persons of pure European blood and 1,916 persons of mixed blood in the islands, according to the census of 1926. It would be difficult to enforce prohibition on the natives alone.(34)

A more substantial grievance has been the interference of the administration in the economic life of Samoa. In the years since the mandate was accepted this question has presented very different aspects. Upon the verdict of an impartial authority, writing in 1922, the civil Government was considerably harsher to the former German traders than the military administration had been.(35) The large German estates on which copra was produced by plantation methods were taken over by the administration as a State enterprise. There is therefore a considerable quantity of copra, the property of these Crown estates, which must be disposed of by the administration.

In the year 1920 violent controversies arose in New Zealand itself over the decision to import indentured Chinese labourers to work on the Crown estates in order to keep down the ravages of the rhinoceros beetle.(36) This decision was strongly criticised by the Labour Party as a breach of the provision in the mandate prohibiting the slave traffic. Attention was also drawn to the moral abuses of the indentured labour system in past times. The protest, however, was unavailing, except, perhaps, in causing greater care both in the provisions of the contract under which the Chinese labourers were introduced, and in the rigid insistence upon strict control and ultimate repatriation of these labourers.

The decision of the Administrator in February 1926 to assist the natives to market their copra through the agency of the New Zealand Reparation Estates caused a storm of protest from the private traders of the islands. These traders, including their chief spokesman, the Hon. O. F. Nelson, a Swedish Samoan, had for a time during the war and before civil government was introduced been greatly enriched by the elimination of the Germans. They had developed a system of virtual monopoly in the buying of copra, under which there was not only no competition in the price, but no grading of the product. It is clear that the Administrator had ample legal power to take the steps which he did. Whether it was wise on his part to incur the hostility of such powerful local personalities is another matter.

It is only just to state that Mr. Nelson and his fellow-critics have repeatedly disclaimed any grievance over prohibition, or over the Government's trading activities. Their recently published statements rest their case wholly upon alleged native grievances which they are anxious to see put right purely on unselfish grounds. In view of the Royal Commission's judgments, and still more in the light of earlier statements, it is difficult to accept such an attitude at its face value.(37)

The third grievance of the European community is also one of long standing. It is the increased cost of government which has followed the efforts of the New Zealand administration to improve the health, education, and economic status of the natives. The evidence offered on this point by European traders before the Royal Commission was unfortunate in its preparation. The Commission reported the grossest errors betraying what at best was inexcusable carelessness. "So gross were their mistakes, and so numerous, that it is difficult to understand how they came to be made. The report and its conclusions were rendered perfectly useless as supporting the conclusions of its authors on the grounds adopted by them."(38)

The castigations of this evidence by the Royal Commission were apparently well deserved. There is, moreover, no evidence of dishonesty or inefficiency on the part of the administration, but this is not the real point.(39) Indeed, the grievance may be said to rest rather upon the undue efficiency than inefficiency of the Civil Service. It is urged that neither the Samoans nor the European traders wished for the expensive methods of modern efficient government, that improvement has gone too fast and too far.(40) This statement appears valid, even in face of the report of the three prominent officials sent from New Zealand to investigate the Civil Service arrangements of Samoa. They disclosed weaknesses in accounting, and some evidence of slack finance; but it is essential to remember that any wastage was of New Zealand, not Samoan, money.

The annual subsidy paid over by the New Zealand Government to the Government of Western Samoa was definitely given for extension of the educational, health, and wireless services in Samoa. This was done at the representation of the Government of Western Samoa that its revenue was unable to take care of any more than what had been the normal expenditure for these services. Similarly, a gift of a capital sum by the New Zealand Government was principally for capital expenditure on hospitals.

Moreover, the point of view of the commissioners and all their recommendations were avowedly those of strict accountants with little or no regard for the difficulties of tropical administration. They condemn the administration because at New Zealand's expense it has embarked upon unprofitable educational and health work. Their report is likely to furnish ammunition for the Government's critics, but can hardly commend itself to those who are anxious to improve the welfare of the natives.

Against such criticism must be set the verdict of Dr. S. M. Lambert, of the International Health Board of the Rockefeller Foundation, as stated in such passages as the following:

> The vital question as to whether the decline of native Pacific races can be checked and their numbers brought back has been answered brilliantly by the New Zealanders in Samoa, by intensive efforts against hookworm

disease and yaws, especially with good hospitalisation and establishment of confidence in their Government in the Samoan mind. In a period of less than three years a birth and death rate practically equal has been changed to a birth-rate of fifty-five and a death-rate of twenty-two, with an infant mortality rate that many civilised countries might envy.(41)

To sum up this aspect of the Samoan situation it may be said that apart from the question of prohibition, which is outside the control of the Administrator, the other grievances resolve themselves down to the fact that during the last two years of his term Sir George Richardson was not able to carry with him the confidence and support of the leaders of the local trading community. He acted strictly within his legal powers. There is no charge of personal inefficiency or dishonesty, and even his opponents have not questioned his desire to improve the conditions of the native race.

These facts, however, are quite compatible with the alienation of the sympathy of the traders. A small community living under tropical conditions is peculiarly liable to such personal strains and disagreements. There was a battle for supremacy between the Administrator and Mr. Nelson. Backed ultimately by the armed forces of New Zealand, the Administrator won his victory and Mr. Nelson was deported. In the struggle, however, a large section of the native race, always prone to intrigue, has sided rather with the merchant benefactor of their own blood than with the official. Mr. Nelson in exile may well prove a romantic figure parallel in the Samoan mind with the former champion for whom their ancestors built the Road of the Loving Heart.

The Samoan natives have repeatedly been referred to as "the aristocracy of the Pacific". They are a branch of the Polynesian race which is scattered all over the southern and eastern Pacific islands. The reputation which they have for aristocracy does not seem to rest upon any very definite achievement or anthropological evidence, and their record of adjustment to the demands of European civilisation will not compare with that of the Maoris. They have, rather, been content to carry into the twentieth century the habits and organisation of the pre-European period. They have a well-deserved reputation for gossiping intrigue, continuing the traditional village fighting which was their chief occupation in former days. The former

German administration was continually faced with this tendency, and American Samoa has not been free from it.

The New Zealand administration of Western Samoa has not been popular with sections of the natives ever since the military occupation and subsequent trading depression.(42) The unfortunate incident by which the influenza epidemic entered the mandated territory, with disastrous results, has left on the native mind an impression that is not readily wiped out. It is true that subsequent health measures have been far-reaching and effective, so that by the census of 1926 the population had almost caught up the losses then sustained, but such developments have not served to wipe out the memory of the scourge of 1918.(43)

The first object of the Mau, therefore, is avowedly to rescue Samoa from the rule of New Zealand. The Mau leaders talk bravely of self-government, at other times they indicate a preference for the rule of Britain; but they are quite clear that they would prefer any rule to that of New Zealand.(44)

The second object of this native organisation has been to bring the present administration into discredit by a systematic policy of passive resistance. The effectiveness of this policy may be judged by the serious tone of the Prime Minister's statement quoted above. It is probable that the first enthusiasm of the Mau members may die down, but much damage, as the Prime Minister pointed out, has been done already.

The specific grievances of the natives are difficult to get at. The Royal Commission, with its businesslike methods and legality, claimed to have given every opportunity for the natives to express their grievances; but it is at least doubtful whether the Commission was in a mood to enter into the rather childish and half-formed discontents of a primitive but vain people. The Prime Minister of New Zealand subsequently justified the severity of deportation by throwing all the blame for the native discontent on to the malicious propaganda of a few European traders, whose interests were prejudiced by the policies of the administration. There is much evidence in the Royal Commission's report to support such a view, and it may be taken as a fact that the Citizens' Committee was unscrupulous in stirring up rebellious attitudes among the Samoans as a tactic in its quarrel with the Administrator.

The fact remains, however, that discontent exists on such a scale as to jeopardise the good government of the territory and the welfare of the native peoples. In the battle of wits between the administration and the self-constituted Citzens' Committee, the latter so far won, if the welfare of the natives is taken as the test of good government provided in the mandate. The theory behind the deportations is that with the source of trouble removed, discontent will die down; but such a theory appears on the surface to be a little too simple.

There is no reason to detail the involved points of discussion concerning the appointment of Faipules to the Fono, the right of the Samoans to representation on the Legislative Council, the banishment of disaffected chiefs, and the deprivation of titles.(45) On all these points and the vague charges of interfering with native customs there always has been and always will be scope for agitation and discontent.

The Fono, representative of every important district in the territory, has been emphatic not only in defence of the Administrator, but in categorical condemnation of those who are stirring up trouble.(46) The leaders of the Mau retort that the Faipules are creatures of the administration and in no way representative of the people. It is impossible, now, to determine whether their appointments were made with the real good will, or merely with the formal assent, of the villages, or whether they have subsequently lost the good will they once had. It is difficult, also, to measure the real strength behind the party of rebellion as compared with the supporters of the administration.

In the same way, it is perfectly true that the power of banishment—a severe punishment in a communal society—is a Samoan custom which has been vested in the European Government ever since the islands came under German rule. The recent amending Act of the New Zealand Parliament even safeguards the position of the prospective banishee more than before.(47) But as the Royal Commissioners hint, the whole issue lies in the justice and tact with which the power has been used and the ability of the Administrator, in whom it is vested, to retain the confidence and respect of the natives.

The claim of the Samoans for complete self-government may be dismissed as extravagance. Their whole history shows their incapacity for such organisation as will preserve their race under modern conditions. Unlike the Maoris, they have produced no outstanding leaders in European culture, medicine, and government. They are a child race needing tutelage.

The astonishing feature of the whole situation is the way in which New Zealand has neglected its own traditional experience with native races. As the experience of the Cook Islands shows, New Zealand has men at its command wise in the ways of the Polynesians and apt for their rule. Many of these men are themselves Maoris, blood-cousins of the Samoans. Others are descended from the early missionary and governing families having long experience and sympathy with the Maoris. A little imagination on the part of the New Zealand Government in the appointment of Samoa's rulers might have made the territory an object-lesson to the world instead of an object of anxiety.

This is not quite as true of the minor appointments as of the major. The truth is that present-day New Zealand (adequately represented by its Government) is almost blind to its historical tradition. The Maori race has reached the point where it can fight its own material battles; but there is an almost complete neglect of its possibilities. A few Maori scholars have at last managed to get the Maori language and literature recognised as a subject of university teaching; but there is no chair of Anthropology in the university, and the only systematic studies of native life are carried out under the auspices of the Maoris themselves. The result is that there is almost no body of young New Zealanders with the insight into native psychology demanded by such a situation as exists in Samoa. The departments of the Samoan Civil Service, including the schools, are staffed by men drawn without any particular qualifications from the New Zealand Civil Service.

It is evident that the congratulations offered by Sir Apirana Ngata to the Samoan race when they came under the control of the New Zealand Government were at least premature, if only because the Government, when dealing with the Samoans, forgot that it had available a rich store of experience with the Maoris and the Cook Islanders. It is a sad commentary upon Sir Apirana's message to find fourteen years later another Maori, Sir Maui Pomare, Minister for the Cook Islands, rising in his seat in the House, to the unconcealed chagrin of his

Cabinet colleagues, in order to defend and plead for the Samoans.(48) Warning the House of the troubles that followed the unjust banishment of the man who afterwards became the cruel and fanatical rebel leader Te Kooti, Sir Maui ended an eloquent speech with the appeal of Portia, "The quality of mercy is not strained".

His appeal for understanding and patience on behalf of a child race is convincing and likely to meet response; but it remains to be seen whether the Government's action in deporting the powerful Swedish-Samoan trader, Nelson, has removed the irritant or merely left a festering sore of discontent.

One other aspect of the Samoan situation demands attention. In New Zealand, as in most other mandatory Powers, public opinion tends to regard possession of the mandate as virtually equivalent to annexation, or at least to permanent control, subject only to the scrutiny of the League. There is even some tendency to resent too minute scrutiny on the part of the League's Permanent Mandates Commission. In 1925 the Australian and New Zealand representatives at Geneva successfully resisted the proposed extension of the Commission's powers. During the course of the recent agitation also, the Administrator of the mandated territory permitted the circulation of a catechism for use in the native schools. The catechism attempted to state the powers of the Government in simple terms that the natives could understand; but the phrasing was unfortunately open to the criticism that it minimised the position of the League of Nations almost to the point of ridicule.(49) While explanations of this misconception are possible, it remains true that there is a widespread feeling in important circles in New Zealand that little difference exists between a mandate and an actual possession. A leading Government organ stated quite bluntly in its editorial columns that "New Zealand's administration of Western Samoa derives from the Allied and Associated Powers, not from the League of Nations. The fact that a mandatory has to make an annual report to the League does not affect the position."(50) Whatever the origin of the mandate, however, it would seem that any attempt to minimise the ultimate authority of the League of Nations strikes at the heart of the mandatory system. It is not likely that the League will go beyond investigation and public criticism; but a perfectly clear distinction must be drawn between the unrestricted authority exercised in a possession and the stewardship which is required in a mandated territory.

The Samoan troubles have been detailed at some length because they are of international importance greater than their somewhat trivial origins. They have been reported and commented on in newspapers all over the world. New Zealand will be known and judged by her success or failure in Samoa more than by almost anything else.

Moreover, the attitude of New Zealand in these difficulties reveals important characteristics which deserve notice. There is a general feeling of puzzlement, almost of dismay, mixed with some chagrin, that such untoward difficulties should have occurred in spite of vague good intentions towards Samoa. Public opinion in the Dominion is apparently anxious to see the Samoans treated fairly, if only to show how capable New Zealand is of such a trust. The causes of failure are but dimly discerned. It is far easier to blame a few conspirators, especially when their actions are clearly culpable in many respects, than to search for the hidden but real weaknesses primarily responsible. The fact is that New Zealand has combined an easy good nature towards Samoa with very little effort to appreciate its responsibility and the necessity for providing trained specialists to undertake a difficult task. It is not the only case in which the Dominion has demonstrated good intentions, while at the same time clearly displaying a decided lag in intellectual grasp and understanding.

The Mother-Complex

By the very circumstances of its foundation, New Zealand was destined to play a leading rôle in combating the centrifugal tendencies which in the mid-nineteenth century appeared to be hastening the dissolution of the British Empire. The essence of Wakefield's theories of colonisation was a protest against the prevailing apathy towards colonial development. In later years Gladstone took occasion of Mr. Seddon's presence among the colonial Premiers in attendance at the Jubilee celebrations of 1897 to pay a well-deserved tribute to the followers of Wakefield, nearly all of whom were actively connected with the foundation and early administration of New Zealand.

There was a time [he said] when statesmen considered that when the Colonies grew in strength, importance, and numbers, they would wish to be severed from the Mother Country. We thought that nothing could be done that would prevent them doing so. But there were those who said, "No, the Colonies will not wish to sever themselves from the parent stock. . . . The more freedom they have, the greater will be their love for the Mother Country and the closer will be the connection." Amongst the men who stood boldly by that position was John Robert Godley, the founder of the Province of Canterbury, in your colony. With him there were four others, and their ideals and aspirations have been fully verified.(51)

Within New Zealand the positive manifestations of this spirit were necessarily confined almost wholly to protests about the activity of foreign Powers in the Pacific, or indeed anywhere where they seemed to threaten the British Empire. Whenever one of the periodical Russian war scares of the period swept across England there was an instant response in New Zealand. The writings of the early colonists abound in patriotic fervour. Sir Charles Bowen's verses, published in 1861, entitled *The Battle of the Free*, foreshadow the ready response which was later to be made to any suggestion that military help from New Zealand might assist the Motherland in a crisis. The almost belligerently imperialist attitude of New Zealand is firmly rooted in tradition.

The first opportunity for the adequate expression of this attitude came at the second Colonial Conference, called upon the occasion of the Jubilee celebrations of 1897. The first Conference, ten years earlier, had hardly envisaged the possibilities of inter-imperial consultation, and is important mainly as a starting-point. That the second Conference attracted more attention was due largely to the effective appearance on the stage of Seddon's picturesque figure. The rôle which he assumed of the bluff democrat who yet was a convinced imperialist ensured him an effective welcome in Britain, where imperialism and radicalism had for so long been regarded as antipathetic. He may be regarded as having created the rôle so effectively played by the Australian Premier, W. M. Hughes, during the world-war. It is one of the curious contradictions of British politics that the fairly even balance of power between the imperialists of Great Britain and their critical opponents should in times of crisis be upset by the irruption into British politics of Dominion statesmen who are reputed to be Radical in their political views, but prove to be more imperialist than the imperialists at Home. No better proof is needed of the small extent to which political beliefs in the Dominions are integrated by a consistent philosophy.

Aroused by his visit to Britain in 1897 (and incidentally by the failure of his representations concerning Hawaii), Seddon took the fullest advantage of the opportunity afforded by the Boer War for a spectacular demonstration of New Zealand's loyalty. Overseas contingents from New South Wales had participated in the Egyptian campaigns of 1885; but the more elaborate voluntary assistance of the Dominions, which was precipitated by Seddon's offer of a contingent from New Zealand to serve in South Africa, went far beyond this precedent. Within New Zealand any criticism that existed was swept aside in a wave of imperialist enthusiasm. Mr. Seddon led the House in the National Anthem after the motion to provide for military assistance had been carried by an overwhelming majority.(52)

On his way home to the Colonial Conference of 1902 Seddon practised his imperialistic speeches in Australia and South Africa. He accepted Lord Kitchener's invitation to visit South Africa, and left with the people there many characteristic bits of advice as to the way in which they should reconstruct the country after the war, mainly along the lines which New Zealand had developed. In England he was received with an amusing mixture of irony and real appreciation. No other colonial statesman was such good "copy", and New Zealand received a liberal advertisement in cartoon, editorial comment, and news. If his understanding of the complexities of international trade was hardly sufficient to enable him to make much real progress with the economic proposals he submitted to the Conference, he at least provided the textbooks on the subject with some excellent illustrations. The "three hundred million gold sovereigns", which he spoke of as leaving Britain annually in consequence of an adverse balance of trade, remain the stock example of the "balance of trade fallacy".

Nor did his defence suggestions meet with any decided response. The proposal to create in the Colonies "imperial service" troops was opposed by Canadian leaders as inconsistent with the sovereignty of the colonial legislatures. The breach between the Canadian nationalist viewpoint and the New Zealand federative attitude was clear. It is true that the appeal of the Home Government for assistance with its naval burden brought a hesitant, and, as events proved, temporary response even from Canada; but the tendency towards decentralisation of imperialistic foreign and defence policy was even then becoming clear.

The most important result of the 1902 Conference was the precipitation of the tariff reform controversy in British politics. Canada had established the principle of imperial preference in 1897, and Mr. Seddon played his full share at the 1902 Conference in pressing for tariff reciprocity, and rather broadly hinting that the Colonies could not be expected to make tariff sacrifices unless they were reciprocated. In 1903 New Zealand followed Canada's lead, and at the next revision of the tariff in 1907, went farther still along the line of imperial preference.

There has been undue magnification of the importance of this gesture. It is true that foreign goods are in many cases charged higher rates of duty than British goods; but this has not meant any reduction of the rates on British imports, but merely an addition of extra duties on those of foreign origin. An inspection of the tariff makes it difficult to resist the conclusion that the reason for the additional duties has been the fact that foreign imports threatened a local industry quite as often as the feeling that they interfered with British imports. In other words, the imperial sentiment has sometimes been used as a stalking-horse for local protection.

Moreover, the United Kingdom as early as 1900 gave a substantial preferential advantage to the Colonial Governments by passing the Colonial Stock Act, which included colonial loans among those for which trust funds may be subscribed. (53) The immediate effect of this measure was to widen the credit and lower the cost of colonial loans. Incidentally those borrowers in Britain who had hitherto enjoyed a monopoly of trust privileges saw the value of their stocks fall appreciably, and have ever since paid substantially higher interest rates than they would otherwise have needed to pay. It is all but impossible to estimate the value of this concession to the Dominion Governments; but it is obviously important, especially to a

Government which borrows heavily, as New Zealand does. Comparison with the value of the preference given by the Dominion to British traders is quite impossible; but the guess may be hazarded that any such preference, granted in the way it has been, has meant far less to British traders than the cheaper borrowing has meant to New Zealand development.

The next incident of importance was Sir Joseph Ward's offer, upon his return from the Defence Conference of 1909, to give a battle-cruiser (or, if necessary, two) on behalf of the Dominion to form part of the British battle-fleet, and be stationed in the North Sea. At the same time, universal military service was introduced, not without opposition, and Lord Kitchener was invited to visit and report upon New Zealand defence. These actions, while no doubt partly prompted by the desire to follow the tradition of initiative and leadership in imperialism built up by Seddon, were not unwelcome to New Zealand opinion. They illustrate clearly also the almost naïve willingness to support and assist British policy without any of the questionings and local independences and nationalisms which Mr. Dafoe has so well described in his study of Laurier, and which took concrete form also in the building of the Australian Navy.

At the 1911 Conference, Sir Joseph Ward attempted a further coup by the proposal of a scheme which does not seem to have clearly distinguished between federation and confederation, but which was based apparently upon a hasty perusal of the Round Table studies then being privately circulated. This proposal met with such scant success and has been so drastically criticised that it may well be left without further comment.

The wholehearted response of New Zealand to the necessities of the Great War is too well known to need emphasis. Next only to Great Britain among the countries of the Empire, the Dominion sent the largest quota of its population, and the casualties were heavy. The Prime Minister, Mr. Massey, and Sir Joseph Ward, who had joined him in a Coalition Cabinet, spent a large part of the war years in London taking their share in the activities of the Imperial War Cabinet. When the Treaty of Versailles was concluded, Mr. Massey signed it under the arrangement worked out by the British Empire delegation at Paris.

At this point, however, a significant divergence of policy from that pursued by the other Dominions begins to emerge. Three years after, in the course of the debate upon Sir John Salmond's report concerning the Washington Conference, Mr. Massey expressed his dislike of the enlargement of the idea of "equality of status". "I am bound to say, Mr. Speaker," he declared, "that I have never liked the arrangement which was made in connection with the League of Nations. There was one dangerous feature in it. I did not agree with everything that has been said, that in signing the Peace Treaty we became independent nations. This is absolute nonsense, and the wish of the people who so expressed themselves was in many cases the father of the thought."(54)

The occasion of this statement was the clear and able presentation, by His Honour Sir John Salmond, of the position which he conceived to be correct concerning Dominion representation at the Washington Conference of 1921–2. It is common knowledge that the Prime Minister of South Africa had endeavoured to get separate invitation to the Conference for the Dominions. Mr. Massey declined emphatically to support his request that a protest should be made. Sir John Salmond went as New Zealand's delegate to the Conference, and his report to the Government upon his return is a classic statement of New Zealand's position. The essential parts of this report are worth reproduction here.(55)

Suggestions have been made in certain quarters, that by permitting the presence of the self-governing dependencies of the Crown at international conventions, such as those of Versailles and Washington, those Dominions have in some manner acquired a new international status—that they are now recognised for international purposes as independent States, although in their constitutional relations they remain portions of the British Empire. It is not easy to attach any definite meaning to this suggestion, but whatever its precise significance may be, there seems no foundation for it in the facts as to the Washington Conference. The true significance of the presence of representatives of the Dominions at that Conference is not that those Dominions have acquired for either international or constitutional purposes any form of independent status, but that they have now been given a voice in the management of the international relations of the British Empire as a single, undivided unity—relations which were formally within the exclusive control of the Government of Great Britain. . . .

The procedure of the Washington Conference was in itself a clear indication that the Dominions were there, not in their own right as quasi-independent States, but merely as constituent portions of an undivided Empire. When any question came to be voted upon, for the purpose of ascertaining whether there existed that unanimous consent which was necessary for a treaty, the question was put to the British delegation as a whole, and was answered "Yes" or "No" by Mr. Balfour, as the head spokesman of that delegation and on behalf of the British Empire as a whole. Although, in the process of discussion and negotiation, the representatives of the Dominions had, and exercised, the same right of audience as any other delegates, they never voted separately on behalf of their own Dominion on any question. The final decision of every case was that of the British Empire as an indivisible unity.

The position of the Dominions at Washington was essentially different from the position which they occupy at an assembly of the League of Nations. By the special and peculiar organisation of that body, self-governing colonies are admitted as members in their own right, as if they were independent States. Although by constitutional and international law such colonies are merely constituent factions of the Empire to which they belong, they are entitled by express agreement to be treated, so far as practicable, as if they were independent. But no such principle was recognised at Washington, or exists except for the special purposes of the League of Nations. . . .

No question ever arose on which it was found impossible to secure complete unanimity of decision within the British delegation. If, unfortunately, it had been otherwise, and if any Dominion delegate, either of his own motion or under the instructions of his Government, had found himself unable to agree with some proposal which commended itself to the delegation, it would then have been necessary for His Majesty's general plenipotentiaries from Great Britain to determine in their own discretion the action to be taken.

If they were of opinion that the matter in dispute was of such minor importance, or related so exclusively to the Dominion itself, that the views of that Dominion ought to be acceded to for the sake of unanimity, this result could have been attained either by a modification of the terms of the proposed treaty or by excluding the dissentient Dominion from its operation unless and until it chose through its Government or Parliament to give it subsequent adherence. If, on the other hand, it was considered that the matter was of such general importance that dissent on the part of a Dominion should be disregarded in the interests of the whole Empire, it would have been within the authority of the plenipotentiaries of Great Britain to assent to the treaty on behalf of the Empire as a whole, without regard to such dissent.

The fact that the delegate of one of the British Dominions had failed to sign the treaty on behalf of that Dominion would have had no effect on the international operation and obligation of the treaty. Any difficulty so unfortunately resulting would have been matter for negotiation and settlement within the borders of the Empire itself, but would have in no way affected the external relations between the Empire and the other contracting Powers. . . .

The Washington treaties, like all others which are negotiations by plenipotentiaries, come into force only on ratification. The ratification required by the constitutional law of the British Empire is that of His Majesty. No action on the part of New Zealand is required. In view, however, of the direct participation of New Zealand in the negotiation and execution of those treaties, it may well be thought expedient that the treaties should be submitted to both Houses of the New Zealand legislature in order that resolutions may be passed approving of their ratification by His Majesty.

Two other important incidents must suffice to illustrate the consistency with which New Zealand has followed the policy so clearly expounded by Sir John Salmond. The first was the procedure adopted in accepting the mandate for the former German territory of Samoa.(56) In the Treaties of Peace Act, 1919, certain authority was given to the Governor-General in Council in case "the League of Nations may be pleased to confer upon His Majesty in right of His Dominion of New Zealand a mandate to govern the said Islands for and on behalf of the said League". Authority was taken under the Foreign Jurisdiction Act, 1890, of the British Parliament, since the New Zealand Court of Appeal in the case "Rex *v.* Lauder", 1919 (*New Zealand Law Reports*, 305), limited the jurisdiction of the New Zealand Parliament to the boundaries of the Dominion. Civil government was established in Western Samoa by an imperial Order-in-Council of March 1920. New Zealand therefore administers the mandated territory through a civil Government, whose constitutional authority is derived, as the Dominion Parliament's authority is derived, from an Act of the British Parliament.

The second incident is the signing of the Locarno Pact. It is no secret that Mr. Massey was strongly opposed to the Geneva Protocol, which was the instrument evolved under the aegis of Mr. Ramsay MacDonald's Labour Ministry to supplement the Covenant of the League.(57) Mr. Massey, indeed, was thoroughly distrustful of the League from many points of view. In replying to Mr. MacDonald's letter in September 1925 on the Singapore base, he said:

You say that your "Government stands for international co-operation through a strengthened and enlarged League of Nations". In reply to that I must say that if the defence of the Empire is to depend upon the League of Nations only, then it may turn out to be a pity that the League was ever brought into being. The very existence of the Empire depends upon the Imperial navy, and if, in the event of war, the navy is to operate successfully, it must have suitable bases from which to work, and where repairs may be effected.(58)

The Locarno Treaty was, however, regarded both by Mr. Massey and by his successor in office, Mr. Coates, as coming under a different category. Both expressed themselves as anxious to have the Treaty submitted to the New Zealand Parliament for ratification in order that the Dominion might stand side by side with Great Britain. This course has not been adopted in view of the expressed divergence of opinion in some of the other Dominions and the desire to avoid any outward appearance of disunity within the Empire.

There is no doubt as to the position of the New Zealand Government, a position which has not varied in essentials since the close of the war. It was compactly put by a very influential leader of the Government, the Hon. W. Downie Stewart, Minister of Finance, in the debate on the Locarno Treaty. He denied the existence of the new status of the Dominions, and claimed that the supposed equality of the nations forming the British Empire had never been real.

No nation [he went on] has more authority than it has power, and for a small democracy like New Zealand to claim the right to make peace or war seems to me to be suicidal. All she asks is the right to be consulted before any decision is made. . . .

If the King attempts to act on the advice of the Ministers in the five Dominions, most hopeless confusion will arise. The British Government therefore consults with the Governments of the Dominions, and the ultimate responsibility for the advice to the King must be taken by the Imperial Ministers in Great Britain.

In the same debate the Prime Minister (the Rt. Hon. J. G. Coates) made an even more emphatic statement:

The method [of consultation] that has been adopted is this: the British Government carries on the negotiations. We express our opinions quite definitely, and if we think the arrangements under consideration are likely not to be in the interests of New Zealand, we say so. But if after this it is decided to go ahead, we say to the British Government, after knowing all the facts of the case: "Very well, if that is the arrangement to be made, we are prepared to stand by it".(59)

It remains only to say that the report of the Inter-Imperial Relations Committee of the Imperial Conference of 1926 has been received with somewhat mixed feelings in New Zealand. The phrases concerning Dominion autonomy and equality of status arouse scepticism in influential quarters. Generally speaking, New Zealand writers and statesmen incline to the view that the less written about an imperial constitution or imperial relationships, the better. The actual contents of the document are not alarming to New Zealand opinion, since they do little more than state the practice of consultation that has been growing up for many years in imperial affairs. Parliament has not debated the document, but Press discussion has on the whole been cautious concerning it.

One thing is certain. The temper of the New Zealand people is such that any dramatic appeal will bring immediate support for the Motherland. When Mr. Lloyd George's famous Chanak telegram was disclosed in such a way as to make it appear that war was likely, Mr. Massey cabled an offer of support if necessary, and over 12,000 volunteers presented themselves without solicitation or any call for services! Included in the number were 300 nurses. This was in striking contrast to the cautious action of the Canadian Prime Minister in refusing to be stampeded into treating the situation as critical and demanding strong measures.

Up till quite recent years there has been little effective opposition to such "robust imperialism" either in Parliament or in the country. There was no particular difference of attitude between Mr. Seddon and Sir Joseph Ward on the one hand and Mr. Massey on the other. But the advent of the Labour Party in 1906, and its growth until it now forms a major factor in Parliament, has added a new element. Generally speaking, the Labour Members are anti-imperialists, but they tend to believe in and support the conception of the British Commonwealth as a free association of nations working in loose international co-operation. Their view therefore tends to parallel the South African and Canadian conceptions of Dominion nationhood. This conception, however, has not penetrated far into New Zealand opinion as yet. It is of interest to notice, on the contrary, that the Prime Minister, after his return from the Imperial Conference of 1926, announced a contribution of £1,000,000, spread over a period of years, for the construction of the Singapore base. This was a bold course to take in a year of severe economic depression, and invited Parliamentary and Press criticism; but public opinion in New Zealand can always be relied upon to respond to a dramatic gesture of imperial loyalty. There is not a great deal of analysis of the ultimate consequences of such gestures. The Dominion is very isolated, and it is difficult to procure full information on which an analysis might rest. The one certain strong factor in every such situation is a deep and abiding emotion of loyalty to the Motherland. There is no reason to believe that this emotion is any stronger in New Zealand than in the other Dominions; but it is certainly more unreasoning and uncritical, betraying a real "mother-complex".

While this remains true, it is apparent that the logic of facts has forced New Zealand into an acceptance of imperial arrangements which differ little in actual practice from those in force in the other Dominions. The outstanding illustration is the post-war development of a tiny New Zealand navy consisting of cruisers permanently stationed in Dominion waters under the command of a Naval Adviser. In foreign policy also there has been some advance towards autonomy. An Imperial Affairs Branch of the Prime Minister's Department has been constituted, and relationships are maintained with the Foreign Office as well as with the Dominions Department in Britain. The clearest example, however, is the trade treaty recently negotiated with Japan, the importance of which can be appreciated only in the light of the past history of the Dominion's relations with the great Asiatic peoples.

New Zealand in the Pacific

The first suggestion for the colonisation of New Zealand was made in 1771, when Dalrymple printed a "Scheme of a Voyage to convey the Conveniences of Life, Domestic Animals, corn, iron, etc., to New Zealand, with Dr. Benjamin Franklin's Sentiments upon the Subject". The scheme was printed again in the *Annual Register* for 1779, where it appears next to a disquisition on Chinese famines. Thus early in New Zealand's history its Pacific situation groups it with the great Powers of Asia. The coincidence of important dates points the moral. The year of New Zealand's colonisation—1840—was the year in which Britain fought the first war to open up the ports of China to European trade and commerce. Twelve years later the infant colony received its constitution of self-government in the same year as the American squadron made forcible entry into Yokohama Bay.

It is no accident also that the first trade treaty which New Zealand has negotiated outside of the British Empire is that which was signed with Japan in 1928. As the westward drift of population continues to people the western coast of Canada and the United States, and the increasing industrialisation both of China and Japan further stimulates trade across the Pacific, a new economic grouping is being formed, a Pacific grouping in which New Zealand cannot help being involved. It is necessary, therefore, to examine with some care the relations that have so far subsisted between the Dominion and the Asiatic peoples.

The first contacts were created by the appearance of Chinese upon the gold-fields in the sixties.(60) Their presence in New Zealand did not cause the rioting which took place under similar circumstances in Australia.(61) Indeed, there was a proposal tentatively put forward to import Chinese labour in the early stages of Vogel's Public Works Policy. The Minister of Works circularised the provincial governments on the subject, but the project was never carried out.

In the meantime protests came from Otago against the concentration of Chinese on the gold-fields there. There were estimated to be 4,215 Chinese in the colony, all but 500 of whom were in Otago. A select committee, set up to consider petitions on the subject, brought in a report favourable to the Chinese, and no action was taken. The agitation for their exclusion steadily increased from this time forward. Similar movements in California and Australia encouraged the agitation, and in 1881 the first Act was passed, largely because Australian legislation was diverting the influx of Chinese to New Zealand. This original Act, as its title, "The Chinese Immigrants Act, 1881," implies, was on a definitely racial basis, imposing a poll-tax on all persons born of Chinese parents, and restricting the numbers to one for every ten tons of ship's tonnage.

By the time amending Acts were passed in 1888 and 1889 New Zealand was in the depths of the severest depression of her history, and it was comparatively easy to raise the restriction to one for every hundred tons of ship's tonnage. This measure was still deemed inadequate, and when the Liberal-Labour Party came into power, pledged to a programme of protective labour legislation, it was inevitable that the restrictions should be still further increased. Mr. Seddon, who became Premier in 1893, himself represented a gold-mining constituency, and had for many years been active in the anti-Chinese agitation. The amendment Act of 1896 therefore raised the poll-tax to £100 and the limit of passengers to one for every two hundred tons of ship's tonnage. In the same year an Asiatic Restriction Act, extending these provisions to all natives of Asia except British Indians, was reserved for the Royal assent, and never came into force.

The matter was discussed at the Colonial Conference of 1897, when the Imperial Government emphasised the undesirability of passing such legislation in racial terms, and recommended the quasi-education test which originated in Natal at this time.

The result in New Zealand was the Immigration Restriction Act, 1899, drawn in general non-racial terms, so as to impose an education test upon every prospective immigrant of other than British birth, and embodying clauses to control the immigration of persons deemed undesirable for physical reasons. At this time Chinese immigration was still subject to the specific discrimination of the earlier Acts, the machinery of which was tightened in 1901 and in 1907, when the education test was imposed on Chinese also. The general immigration Act was also tightened in 1903 and 1906.

By 1908, when all this legislation was consolidated, the policy of immigration restriction had been generally accepted. The arguments used in its favour ran the gamut which similar arguments have run in every country—biological, moral, political, and economic considerations were advanced, usually with more emotion than knowledge. As in other countries, however, it was quite clear that whatever Nationalisations were advanced, and whatever fears were used to work up public opinion, the primary cause of the agitation was economic, the desire to protect the standard of living of workers who feared Chinese competition.

The consolidated statute of 1908 bears a general title—The Immigration Restriction Act—and from this time forward there is traceable a slow but definite advance towards a realisation of the international discourtesy implied in definite racial discrimination. The compilation did not alter the law, so that the specific discriminations against Chinese, particularly the poll-tax, still remained. The amending Acts of 1908 and 1910, and the regulations of 1914 and 1916, had the general effect of improving the restrictive machinery. There was no substantial change in the law until after the war.

In 1919 the Undesirable Immigrants Exclusion Act, directed primarily against ex-enemy aliens and disaffected or disloyal persons, including those even of British nationality, foreshadowed an important change in the law by placing greater discretionary power in the hands of the Government. This change was carried further by the Immigration Restriction Act, 1920, which dropped the education test and substituted a system of individual permits for all immigrants of non-British descent, including British Indians. The result of this change of machinery is very important.

"With the exception of the poll-tax in the case of Chinese there is now no statutory discrimination between race or nationality. All must obtain a permit. The permit is given or withheld at the discretion of the Minister of Customs."(62)

In practice the administration has been such as to restrict still further on economic grounds the immigration of Chinese and Indian coolie labour. Public opinion in New Zealand thoroughly and almost unanimously approves this principle, and this opinion is not weakened by the knowledge that much of the immigration that continues (and the smuggling also) is due to the activities of organisations to whom the immigrant is under an obligation of debt amounting to semi-slavery.

Subsequent amending legislation in 1923, and regulations in 1921 and 1927, did not alter the principle of the 1920 Act. The present position, therefore, is that exclusion of cheap coolie labour is effected without placing the restrictions on a racial basis, the only exception being that certain historical discriminations against Chinese have survived till the present day. There is apparently no desire for immigration on the part of any but Chinese and Indian labourers among the Asiatic peoples. The virtual exclusion of the Indians followed an agreement with the Indian Government after discussions at the Imperial Conference.

Certain irritating and unnecessary racial discriminations survive in other legislation, such as the Old Age Pensions Act, from the provisions of which "Chinese and other Asiatics are excluded, whether naturalised or not, or whether a British subject by birth or not". Even more unfortunately a similar provision was copied into the Family Allowance Act, 1926. It is in the highest degree unlikely that such provisions will ever be necessary, but like the poll-tax, they remain obvious and needless causes of irritation to the Chinese and other Asiatic peoples. The political imagination of New Zealand officials and politicians has apparently not yet reached the point where it will sweep away as useless and needlessly insulting such relics of a historical situation.

Apart from this rather unfortunate negative contact, the relations of New Zealand with the great influential peoples of the Far East have very little reality. As Japan, and now China, enter upon industrial development, their potentialities as markets for New Zealand produce are slowly being realised. Exports to Japan multiplied fivefold between 1914 and 1928, while imports more than doubled.(63) Future possibilities will be greater both in Japan and China. It was a dawning realisation of this fact which caused New Zealand to break through her traditional policy and exchange notes directly with Japan, the net effect of which is to place her butter exporters on a parity with their rivals in Canada, and in a better position than Australian exporters. The exports of butter to Japan are as yet very small, but they may be substantial in the not distant future.

This constructive step in New Zealand's imperial and international policy is of considerable significance. The efforts of the various British colonies to persuade the Colonial Office to recognise their right to pass restrictive immigration legislation are landmarks in the development of colonial nationalism. The national sentiment was naturally expressed on this vital issue, unfortunately of a negative character. The trade agreement which New Zealand negotiated in 1928 with Japan is the Dominion's first hesitant step along the road which Canada has followed in the assertion of her nationalism. It is of good omen that such a first step should be constructive and co-operative rather than restrictive.

New Zealand, together with Canada and Australia, must play a more and more prominent rôle in the Pacific interests of the British Commonwealth. Public opinion in all three Dominions had an unfortunate bias imputed to it by the fact that almost its only basis for judgment regarding Chinese and indeed Asiatic affairs was derived from the presence of coolies in its midst. Market gardeners and laundrymen are not the worthiest representatives of the great civilisations of the Far East. As trade connections develop and travel facilities increase, a truer perspective will be gained. The interest shown by New Zealand in the conferences of the Institute of Pacific Relations is of good augury. As understanding grows and responsibility for positive action is undertaken, the Dominion will tend more and more to grow away from its mother-complex and develop the independent judgments which will make a true and substantial contribution to the common policy of the British Commonwealth.

CHAPTER XIV

AN EXPERIMENT IN DEMOCRACY

The Setting of the Experiment

It is hardly an exaggeration to describe the whole settlement and development of New Zealand as an experiment in democracy. Consider the facts in broad outline. Less than ninety years ago the islands had practically no ordered social life beyond the tribal organisation of the Maoris. The land was empty but fertile, an almost virgin field for the acclimatisation of plants and animals. It would be difficult to imagine any other part of the earth's surface so suitable for a clean start.

It is true that the new settlers could not escape the influence of fundamental geographical conditions. Rainfall, mountains, and forests have played a great part in shaping the destinies of the young community, and isolation has been an even more powerful factor. It should be clear also that the native race complicated the evolution of present-day New Zealand, though in the long run economic progress took the direction which seemed indicated at the very beginning but was hindered and delayed by the Maori wars.

While these facts are to be borne in mind—and with them account must be taken of the external circumstances which dictated the colonising activities of the Wakefield group settlements, the Australian pioneers in the sheep-raising industry, and the assisted immigrants in the Vogel period—it may still be argued that New Zealand presented as clear a field for social experiment as can well be imagined. New Zealand to-day is what the colonists have made it. Working within the broad limits of its geographical situation and the economic circumstances of their period, they have built from the foundations. This is literally true, even of the importation of commercial plants and animals into the country. The farming industries, which are the mainstay of the Dominion, utilise animals which were never known in New Zealand before the advent of the settlers, and depend also in increasing degree upon imported grasses and methods of cultivation.

Just as the settlers could only import the animals and plants with which they were familiar, so they brought to this virgin land the social institutions and ideas which they had known in the lands from which they came. Even within the Wakefield settlements themselves there was diversity, particularly between the aristocratic English settlement of Canterbury and the more democratic Scots settlement of Dunedin (1); but if these settlements had continued for long to dominate the social order it is probable that the experiment might have been less complicated. The gold-miners, however, and following them assisted immigrants, imported social ideas of very different varieties. It is difficult to trace with exactitude the influence of such sectional influences in the thought of present-day New Zealand, but there can be no reasonable doubt that chartists among the gold-miners and trade unionists among the Vogel immigrants contributed a great deal to the formation of State Socialist ideas which were later to have important influence in the difficult times of the eighties and nineties. (2)

There was one important advantage in the new country. While the settlers brought with them familiar notions of law and especially of property, they were able to adapt these notions freely to the different conditions of life in the new land. In such important matters as the registration of land-ownership, in personal relations such as divorce, in the machinery of law, there were important deviations from the established practice of older lands.

Moreover, the colonists, by emigrating to a new country, freed themselves altogether from the accumulated material results of these notions. They came to a country where all the land was Crown property, to be disposed of as seemed best to the sovereign people. It was not encumbered with a land-owning class or property rights. The economic castes inseparable from feudal ownership did not exist and have not been reproduced except in very modified imitative form. In the same way, there were no cities with their urban property rights and slums. What an English writer has called "the heavy hand of an effete ancestralism" could not "fall with a resounding thud on the living hopes of to-day" (3) unless the colonists willed the possibility of its doing so.

Most important of all in the long run, the remoteness and inaccessibility of New Zealand, supplemented by unusual precautions in selecting immigrants, delivered it from the depressing burden of the "residuum" of population.(4) The failures of generations of breeding were not among those selected for colonisation. The long ocean voyage required an effort of imagination, courage, and some resources, especially as it ended by landing the colonists in a country of fierce savages, where conditions of life were hard and success was to be won only by prolonged effort. Many of the early settlers turned back from such harsh conditions.

New Zealand, therefore, was uncommonly lucky in its first colonists. They were men and women of imagination, courage, more than average strength, and considerably more than average ability. Among their numbers were many idealists and men of learning. Moreover, the level of the population has been kept high. There have always been elective influences at work restricting the immigration of the unfit, if only because of the remoteness of New Zealand from the great centres of population. To this day also, the Dominion receives among her immigrants a large proportion of the educated middle class. Once a tradition of this type is established it becomes a powerful factor in its own perpetuation.

A further important factor to be noted is the homogeneity of the immigration and consequently of the population. There has been no melting-pot in New Zealand. Just as the first colonists fought vigorously and successfully against the proposal to bring in convicts, so later generations have fought to keep the population as purely British as possible. Their efforts have been successful. The Dominion is too far away to have been affected by the mass-emigration from Europe which flooded America and Canada in the last quarter of the nineteenth century. The immigration barriers, originally put down firmly against Asiatic immigration, are capable now of being used against any immigrant thought by the responsible officials to be undesirable by reason of his economic status, his political opinions, or any other attribute. The number of race aliens in the country is therefore remarkably small, but even so is watched with a jealous eye.

It is customary to give the proportion of the population who claim British citizenship as high as 99 per cent., but such a high figure can be obtained only by including all naturalised aliens. Apart from the Maoris there are substantial numbers of persons whose descent somewhat complicates the homogeneity of the population. The very effort to exaggerate this homogeneity is, however, indicative of the importance which is placed upon it. Exclusive of Maoris, the proportion of the population which claims descent from white sections of the British Empire is probably well over 90 per cent. Even within this group there is a further tendency towards homogeneity in the fact that so large a proportion of them have been born either in the British Isles or in New Zealand itself, where the tradition of the British Isles is so persistent, rather than in other sections of the Empire.

The scope of the experiment in democracy which is represented by the colonisation of New Zealand should therefore be clear. For rather less than a century, selected and homogeneous colonists have been at work in a virgin land building not only the material but also the social structure of a new community. The past has trammelled them less than in most ventures of this kind. They have therefore had a considerable measure of freedom in their experiment, a fact which makes all the more pertinent their refusal to embark upon revolutionary courses of political or economic reconstruction. They have followed steadily the methods of constitutional democracy and of capitalistic development which they derived from their British tradition. The results of their efforts should throw light upon the strengths and weaknesses of the Parliamentary system of government for the people by the people.

The Striving for Equality

The political structure of the Dominion lacks some of the newest expedients of democracy. Experiments with proportional representation have not gone far and there is only a limited use of the referendum, while no use is made at all of the initiative and recall. On the other hand, there are in New Zealand a few relics of undemocratic practices, such as a nominated Upper House and the country quota. Even with these qualifications, however, it is clear that the outstanding principle of social organisation in the Dominion is democracy. New Zealand, indeed, was a pioneer in many fields of electoral reform, including the important field of woman suffrage. Voting by ballot has been universal and free of plural or property voting rights or any other important limitation since the granting of woman suffrage in 1893.

The means of forming public opinion are also fairly adequate. There is next to no illiteracy in the Dominion, and the average elector is capable of independent decision on the issues presented to him. He reads newspapers which are surprisingly good, both in their presentation of news and in their editorial criticism. Indeed, the standard achieved by the Dominion's numerous newspapers is a matter of comment by most interested visitors. As far as current political issues are concerned there is no lack either of information or of interest. Nor are the newspapers followed blindly. The success of the Labour Party, which in recent years has built itself up into a strong minority position, is proof enough of this.

New Zealand is in consequence a good example of political democracy. The majority rules. Certain very clear consequences flow from this fact. One of the clearest is the humanitarian trend of recent legislation, the ultimate result of which is to maximise the already high standard of physical welfare. This is a matter of basic importance. There would in any case be every reason to expect that with the selected stock from which present-day New Zealand has been bred, and with a favourable environment, the standard of physical welfare should be high. The strongest factor in keeping it high is the remarkable productivity of the population and the equitable distribution of the rewards of industry. There can be no doubt, however, that political power has been used in addition, not only to influence the distribution of wealth, but also to provide from the public purse services which are designed to improve the physical health of the whole community.

The whole arbitration system, for example, rests ultimately upon the theory that it is legitimate to use the power of the State to protect the workers' standard of living. The elaborate code of labour laws has the same object. In the same way a series of measures have built up a code of preventive social legislation. Old-age and widows' pensions, family allowances, outdoor charitable relief, State maternity homes, hospitals and mental asylums, school medical and dental services, are examples of the use of the public purse to provide health services. Against one or other of these measures the argument is often used that productivity and the accumulation of wealth are checked by undue State activity and interference with private business enterprise. It is probable that this argument is occasionally valid, but even if it is, it carries little weight with the majority, which is convinced that the preventive system as a whole maximises physical welfare, and in the long run ought to increase productivity. Macaulay's famous defence of the early Factory Acts, and especially his thesis that nothing which safeguards human life and welfare can in the long run decrease the wealth of a community, would be accepted as axiomatic in New Zealand. The electoral influence of women has greatly emphasised this acceptance of humanitarian standards. There may be occasional grumblings among the business community concerning some of the more debatable fringes of social legislation; but the main body of that legislation is practically immune from serious criticism and still more from any prospect of curtailment or repeal. Any criticism of such measures as old-age pensions would be regarded as an anachronism.

There are abundant signs of physical welfare in New Zealand. The very appearance of the children, the unusually low rate of infant mortality, the sturdy appearance of the average man and woman, and the lowest death-rate of any country in the world, attest the physical vitality of the community. The most striking impression left on the mind of an observant Chinese visitor to the Dominion was the health and happiness of nearly everyone he met. The concern manifested over disease, and the effort to eradicate such scourges as consumption and cancer, are indicative of widespread appreciation of the importance of physical well-being. The large place in public interest taken by outdoor sports and amusements is also significant. Such games as Rugby football are played not by schools or classes, but by the youth of every section of the country, rich and poor, town-dwellers and countrymen, schoolboys and labourers. This democracy of sport is carried further in New Zealand than in any other British community with the possible exception of Australia, and even in the sister Dominion the growth of cities restricts the sporting opportunities of young people and tends to encourage attendance at spectacles instead of participation in contests.

It is obvious that physical effort of this type has a double dependence upon high standards of economic welfare. Without adequate food, good housing, and abundant leisure there could not be the vitality which seeks an outlet in sport. Nor could the average worker indulge in sporting activities without a sufficient margin of income over the pressing necessities of existence to pay for them. The multiplicity of sporting facilities is equal proof with the detached suburban houses and gardens of a more equitable distribution of wealth and leisure than exists in most countries.

There is some reason to believe that the people of New Zealand have approximated fairly closely to the happier of the alternative solutions to the population problem. Instead of a high birth-rate pressing down the margin of subsistence and involving the necessity for an almost equally high death-rate in order to maintain a balance of population, the Dominion has progressed far along the opposite cycle. The average age at marriage is high, girls come to marriage mature and physically strong, the birth-rate is controlled and low; but the infant death-rate is so very low that the natural increase of population is comparatively high. This economy of human life and energy is of the first importance. It is both cause and effect of the high standard of physical welfare which is so obvious in New Zealand. It may fairly be claimed that democratic government has contributed to the maintenance of this high standard by consistently placing humanitarian considerations above private economic gain.

In such a democracy, also, it is natural to find that the whole educational system is based upon the principle of universal, free, and compulsory instruction in the elements of knowledge, together with abundant opportunities for any child in the community to take advantage of higher education.(5) The provision of educational opportunity is as much the duty of the State as the preventive control and relief of poverty, the safeguarding of the standards of living of the economically weak, and the elimination of preventable physical weakness and disease. This whole programme is consistent and economically sound. Free education is accompanied by dental and medical inspection and advice, orphaned and neglected children are cared for by a branch of the Education Department, the children of widows are pensioned and their mothers are given pensions also so that they need not be thrust into the necessity of work outside the home.

Neither physical nor educational attainment can be readily measured for a whole community, but there is little room to doubt the high average standard of either in New Zealand. The provision of universal free and compulsory education is costly but inevitable in a democracy. New Zealand spends large sums on education, by far the greater part of which is spent in maintaining the primary-school system. The pressure of the constituencies upon the local Members of Parliament is too strong to allow any serious neglect of the external facilities for elementary education. The provision of schools has in many districts been carried to an absurd degree of decentralisation because of local pressure. Altogether it is apparent that the expenditure on the elementary branches of the educational system has been greater than the time and thought given to its planning and direction.

There is no need here to give a detailed and exhaustive history of educational developments in the Dominion.(6) The provinces varied a great deal in their educational activities. The wealthier south island provinces had fairly satisfactory systems of primary schools; but in some of the northern provinces the situation was bad. Even before the abolition of the provincial legislatures there was an agitation for a national system. When the provincial councils were abolished a national system was unavoidable. The Education Act of 1877, however, showed foresight and imagination, placing New Zealand for the time being in the forefront of educational progress. Fifty years ago it needed courage as well as imagination to establish a purely secular, free, and compulsory system of primary instruction.

It was many years before substantial amendments were made to this system. The official record, indeed, notes only two important changes before 1914. The introduction of manual and technical subjects into the primary curriculum in 1900, and the introduction of physical drill in 1901, can hardly be regarded as revolutionary changes. Indeed, it may be said that with the exception of the administrative changes noted below, and some inevitable minor changes in the curriculum, primary education still follows in essentials the principles laid down in 1877. Changes are now being suggested, but have not yet been carried out in any large degree.

It is of course possible to argue that this consistency is a tribute to the wisdom of those who laid down the principles of the first Act; but a truer and less flattering explanation is that New Zealand has not kept pace with educational progress. Essentially the primary schools aim at elementary instruction in the rudiments of knowledge. There is little doubt that this aim is successfully accomplished. The average standard of knowledge is higher in New Zealand than in most communities; but the very uniformity of the standard, the disproportionate time and attention given to the tricks of arithmetic and the rules of grammar, the extraordinary importance attached even in the primary schools to examination results, and the almost total lack until very recently of experimental methods, all betoken adherence to educational ideals which have long since been discarded in other countries.

These rigidities and uniformities were greatly emphasised by the centralising tendencies that first found legislative sanction in 1914. The original Act of 1877 left a large place for local interest and control. The most important bodies created were the twelve education boards, which had virtual control over the schools within their districts. Even the local school committees had definite and important responsibilities. The natural result was a fair degree of local interest. Unfortunately this often took the form of undue interference with the appointment, and even the work, of teachers. The professional organisations of teachers pressed strongly for national control, and their expert and continuous interest encouraged the natural centralising tendencies of the department. The Act of 1914, therefore, greatly enlarged the powers of the department and, significantly enough, transferred the inspectors from the control of the education boards to that of the central authority. At the same time, provision was made for a national grading scheme by which all teachers were to be rated by the inspectors in accordance with uniform principles laid down by the department. In 1916 this grading list was published, and since that time teaching appointments have depended almost wholly upon relative positions in the list.

There is a spurious efficiency in centralisation against which educational idealism struggles in vain. More and more the whole system, from the primary schools to the university, has tended to pass into the control of the bureaucrats and to be administered upon bureaucratic principles. The natural result has been a stereotyping of routine. All over New Zealand, teachers are trained with almost no variation in the four training colleges (which are located in the four cities) and instruct children according to a uniform syllabus based upon prescribed textbooks. Their work is judged by inspectors who make short visits to the classes and give tests which can at best yield only sample indications of the external validity of the teaching. The teachers are graded by the inspectors' brief observations of their work. The temptation for them to play up to this system is almost irresistible. Experimental departures from routine are risky and may, if the inspector does not like them, be damning. Quite clearly the best inspectors are able to take a co-operative encouraging attitude, helpful to isolated teachers; but their visits are restricted, and only too often a premium is set upon safe adherence to the well-tried coaching methods that give examination results at the cost of originality. A very clear illustration of this fact came under the notice of university teachers who had occasion to support the claims of their returned soldier comrades for more generous treatment in the grading list. The argument of the inspectors was that by their absence for some years from practical teaching many if not most of these men had lost ground in the technique of teaching. It was extremely difficult to get any but the most grudging recognition of the fact that widened experience and travel, supplemented in many cases by specialist courses overseas, had greatly improved their teaching powers. As a result the men who for various reasons had not served abroad received an advantage in the grading list which in turn gave them wider responsibilities and experience which tended to make the advantage cumulative.

There is a subtlety in the cramping effect of routine uniformity which is heightened by centralisation, but which escapes the notice of all but the comparatively few idealists to whom the encouragement of initiative and intelligence means more than mere efficiency of instruction. Such idealists are easily discounted by the "practical" people, whether the latter be teachers with a professionalised outlook or business men seeking office-boys who can write a good hand and add up a column of figures. There is, however, a widespread uneasiness among those best qualified to judge of the ultimate results of educational systems. One feels that this lack of experiment, of freshness, of variety of approach, of creative thought, tends to result in a stereotyped uniformity not only of educational practice, but also of citizenship.

It is argued below that New Zealand is singularly unfortunate in having few possibilities of counteracting such tendencies to standardisation of thought. With no strongly entrenched institutions embodying generations of tradition such as exist in older lands, a great lack of voluntary associations, and a university which is weak in precisely the same points as the elementary system of education, the influence of the primary schools is predominant in the democracy. There is an indubitable connection between these facts and New Zealand's loss of intellectual initiative and leadership in the past generation. The lowering of Parliamentary standards which has been noted by successive observers with viewpoints as diverse as those of Lord Bryce and Mr. Sidney Webb, (7) the hardening of patriotism into unreasoning imperialism, the failure to apprehend the true significance of imperial and international movements or even to be interested in them, the paucity of educated leaders of political, business, and social life—all these are in striking contrast with the earliest periods of New Zealand history and all of them became noticeable in the period of prosperity which began in the nineties, the period in which the first generation which had gone through the State system of education came definitely into democratic control of the country. An unchecked and unbalanced system of elementary instruction has been the fundamental reason for turning New Zealand into the paths of satisfied mediocrity and provincialism.

Attention may perhaps be drawn to one very significant illustration of the unreality which creeps into an educational system which is bound to uniformity prescribed authoritatively by a centralised administration and one, therefore, in which experiment is necessarily minimised. The whole tenor of instruction in New Zealand remains to-day as it was prescribed in 1877 in imitation and emulation of the best British models then available, a system of instruction in facts derived from and designed to fit children for work in industrialised and urban communities. The best educational practice in older lands has long since shifted the emphasis from instruction to the encouragement of creative endeavour. Music, drama, the graphic arts, and co-operative effort in social studies have come to overshadow the routine instruction and drilling in arithmetical and grammatical rules. Not all schools, even in the most advanced countries, can claim to have achieved even an approximation to these new standards, and it is probable that the average efficiency of instruction in New Zealand remains higher than in most countries; but there is an almost complete failure on the part of the educational authorities, as distinct from a minority of teachers, to realise the possibilities of the new creative methods of education.

In the same way, only after persistent effort has it been possible to embody in the primary school syllabus even partial and grudging recognition of those local backgrounds which should be the basis of interest in the school. New Zealand history and geography are still lodged in an inferior position to arithmetic and grammar, music has received a new stimulus by the importation of specialist instructors from Britain; but any recognition of the fundamental importance of rural interests and scientific agriculture is very recent. Such recognition as there is, forced by the demand of practical farmers for practical instruction, consists for the most part of mere amateurish dabbling in the technique of farming.

The fundamental difficulty, again, is the bureaucratic conception of the necessity for uniformity. It is obviously desirable and necessary to have town schools to fit boys and girls for town life; but the whole school system has to fit into one mould laid down by one set of administrative regulations, and the same training for teachers in the same syllabus is imposed on town and country schools alike. There are a few isolated experiments, mainly in secondary schools, where there is apt to be more permanence of staff and more school spirit, though the control of the department extends to all but the private (mainly Church) secondary schools with only a degree less efficiency. At Rangiora, Oxford, and Feilding, different types of secondary schools, under the guidance of enthusiastic and far-seeing teachers, have devised systems of training based upon the needs of their rural constituencies. It is difficult to fit these promising experiments into a tidy system of departmental control, and any progress has been achieved against the steady apathy and even hostility of the bureaucrats. Already, however, there is ample evidence to show what might be achieved if the New Zealand country-side could be studded with such schools adapted to the needs of their individual districts and staffed by young teachers with freedom to experiment.

One final comment seems to be necessary. The bureaucratic tendencies which are so much in evidence are those of senior men and women, mainly teachers seconded to departmental duties of an administrative or inspectorial character. It is rare for promotion to return an inspector or an administrative official to teaching duties. The planning and control of the system is therefore in the hands of the older men and women; and in the same way the teachers' professional organisations tend to be controlled by the senior members of the service. There is no department where the evils of promotion by seniority are so dangerous, but the grading list makes such a system of promotion almost imperative. It is anomalous that the destinies of the youth of a young country should be entrusted almost wholly to seniority. High education authority can always be found in defence of the existing system, the expert critics of which must speak softly in view of their subordination.

It should be said also that although the secondary schools of the Dominion share increasingly with the elementary schools the difficulties arising from centralised administration, they are in the nature of the work freer and more independent. There is, in the first place, a greater variety of schools, many of them privately financed and some of them successfully reproducing the traditional English public school atmosphere. Even among the secondary schools of the State system there is a greater degree of local interest and support, more school spirit, and more permanence of staff. The best of these schools, under capable head masters, have greater freedom of experiment, pay less regard to examinations, and in consequence achieve a considerable measure of true success.

The Neglect of Higher Education

The anonymous official who wrote the section on education in the official year-book probably intended to be congratulatory when he opened his review with the statement that "the inception and establishment of educational facilities in New Zealand is the history of civilisation and progress in this part of the British Dominions".(8) Such a statement, however, has illuminating meanings immediately one begins to look critically into the facilities which have been established. This is especially true when the limited facilities for "higher education" are considered. There is, for example, a table at the end of this same section of the official year-book showing the items of expenditure which make up New Zealand's total of £3,769,969 spent upon educational purposes in the year 1927-8.(9) More than two-thirds of this large total sum was devoted to elementary education. The one separate item of expenditure upon training colleges (which are dominated almost exclusively by the needs of the elementary schools) is substantially more than the total sum spent from the public purse upon the university, with its four colleges and two agricultural colleges, together with all their professional schools.

These figures are the best possible indication of the relative importance attached to primary and university education by the New Zealand democracy. It follows naturally that a lecturer in a training college, and even a primary school teacher, will probably have to accept a substantial reduction in salary if his academic attainments obtain for him the offer of a lectureship in one of the university colleges.(10) In the same way, it is infinitely easier to obtain a grant for building a primary school than it is to establish a university library. In the last generation it has been all but impossible to extract grants for university purposes from a Parliament dominated by the representatives of farming constituencies. Private gifts to the colleges have been pitiably small, though there has been improvement in this respect since the war. The two southern colleges—Otago and Canterbury—are better off than the northern colleges; but none is sufficiently endowed to be independent of State support. The first obvious evil of this situation is the poverty of the colleges, which have never been in a position to pay adequate salaries, provide junior staffs, or build libraries and research laboratories. In all these respects, but above all in their ludicrously inadequate library facilities, the colleges have been crippled by lack of funds. Moreover, any appeal to the State for funds carries with it the danger of an increasing degree of control by the Education Department. This fear, which restrains many university leaders from being as importunate as they might otherwise be, is based upon a clear realisation of what has happened to the secondary and technical schools as well as to the elementary schools of the Dominion. Senior members of the professoriate carry very clearly in their minds, also, the drastic action of the Government when one of the university colleges refused to surrender to a newspaper agitation in the early period of the war. A professor of German birth and (doubtfully) of German nationality, though of British residence and training almost from infancy, was retained on the staff of the college despite his proffered resignation. A public agitation failed to force his dismissal by the college authorities, who were satisfied of his loyalty; but the agitation was more successful with the Government, which passed an Alien Enemy Teachers Act (1915), making the professor's dismissal mandatory.(11) Doubtless many similar cases of arbitrary Governmental action of this sort can be cited from other universities in other countries; but the position in New Zealand was definitely that of the Government yielding to a skilfully managed agitation. In doing so it suddenly and without giving any reasons reversed its previous policy, which had, after due investigation, paroled the professor and encouraged the council to retain his services. No clearer case can be imagined of popular agitation forcing a democratic Government to pass legislation interfering with the statutory powers and responsibilities of the university. The shadow of political interference is over the university and makes many university leaders, especially among the professoriate, less enthusiastic than they might otherwise be in advocating its claims to financial support.

Here is a clear declination from the ideals and aspirations of New Zealand's first settlers. The Canterbury colonists, for example, set aside land before the foundation of the province for the establishment of a grammar school (Christ's College) and a university. It is true that later generations have been content to watch the development of the grammar school absorb the funds intended for university purposes, and that only in the last few years has the upper department of the foundation shown signs of developing into a residential college upon the English model. It is, however, equally true that before the provincial system went out of existence the last and greatest superintendent of the province, himself a distinguished graduate of Cambridge, took the initiative in providing Canterbury College (which was newly established in 1873 as an entirely separate institution) with endowed funds which at the present time give it the greatest degree of independence among the colleges of the university.

Even earlier, in 1869, the Scots community at Dunedin had founded the University of Otago in the hope and expectation that it would be the university centre for the whole colony. Provincial rivalries, however, aggravated by the fact that the Presbyterian Church had a large share of control over the University of Otago, made a national university impossible from the very beginning.(12) The alternative system of independent colleges in each of the four centres appeared almost ludicrous in such a small community, but when the problem was definitely raised by the Act of 1874 neither of the two existing colleges was willing to give way, nor was the legislature willing to see one Protestant sect have a dominating influence in a national university. As subsequent developments have proved clearly, it would not have been possible in any case to bind the north island cities not to develop collegiate institutions when the time appeared ripe. The only way out of the dilemma was some system of federation, but unfortunately the model adopted when the university was established in 1870 was that of the University of London, whose federal constitution had been adopted in consequence of a precisely similar conflict of collegiate authority. The compromise reached in this way was never satisfactory. A recent authoritative statement puts the matter bluntly: "The university system as it exists in New Zealand is truly an accident; it was never supposed by the men of the day that it was the proper method of dealing with university education. The circumstances and passions of the times, the lack of vision of the men, and not educational foresight, gave us the system." (13)

The worst consequences of the accident might have been averted if credence had been given to the recommendations of an able Royal Commission which sat in 1879. Their report made many concessions to the popular demand for the democratisation of university facilities, but pointed out quite clearly the necessity of linking the controlling university authority more closely with the life of the colleges. Unfortunately the recommendations, which necessarily involved some additional expenditure, came before Parliament just at the time when it could no longer be hoped that the colony would escape a prolonged period of economic distress. Nothing was done, and the university gradually developed into a purely examining body under predominantly amateur direction and with an unfortunate degree of control over the teaching arrangements of the colleges.

The next authoritative report by an external commission almost half a century later, in 1925, made the scathing comment (which, however, has been accepted complacently by all but limited academic circles in New Zealand) that "the general impression left on our minds is that the New Zealand University offers unrivalled facilities for gaining university degrees, but that it is less successful in providing university education".(14)

In retrospect it seems clear that the chief factors in producing this unfortunate situation have arisen from the effort to provide wholesale instruction upon easy conditions. As in many other new countries, popular pressure, combined with amateur government, has lowered university standards. With the London system of external government and examinations there has been combined a high development of the lecturing system brought to New Zealand mainly from the Scottish universities. At its worst this combination can and does result in the professor coaching large numbers of part-time evening students in such of the rudiments of his subject as will enable them to pass an examination which until very recently was set and marked in Great Britain upon a syllabus prescribed uniformly for all colleges by the external Senate. The idealism and hard labour of many professors, even under such a system, may minimise this degradation of standards. Individual teachers strive for the specialisation which is necessary for modern scholarship and for freedom to conduct and direct research, to make the influence of the university felt in the community, and less often to take a share in the social life of the college. That the level of university teaching has not fallen lower is due not to the system, but to the devotion and sacrifice of the teachers who have rebelled against it.

In 1911 the University Reform Association was formed by the efforts of a group of professors in Wellington with the cordial support of many of their colleagues in the other colleges and also of many representative graduates. The report of their activities made the definite charge that "the University's disregard of the principles of education has led to carelessness in the appointment of teachers, poor facilities for teaching, the absence of adequate libraries, the neglect of research".(15) Their attack was rightly directed against the external Senate, which had been created when the university was constituted and which had wide powers of control over both the business and the academic organisation of the university and its colleges. The main charge was the failure of the Senate to give freedom to the teachers, especially in the important subjects of the arts degrees.

> It must be borne in mind [they wrote] that generally speaking every Senator has learned such subjects as Latin, English, Mathematics, and some others in his own youth; that the whole character and aim and scope of university teaching in these subjects has changed beyond recognition in other universities during the last generation; that the only people who can be expected to keep abreast of such changes are the teachers; that the lay senators naturally imagine that in dealing with these and similar subjects they are dealing with matters they more or less understand, whereas in reality they do not; and this group of subjects has fewest professorial representatives on the Senate.(16)

Since the agitation of the University Reform Association many breaches have been made in the system of external amateur control, and it is only a matter of time before the redistribution of powers between the academic and lay authorities of the university will approximate to the practice of other universities. Though many adjustments and alterations of practice have still to be made, the machinery has already been sufficiently changed to give the responsible teachers a fairly adequate degree of control over the essentials of university management.(17)

The problems that remain are more difficult, since they are derived from the general educational outlook of the community. In the first years of its existence the university drew its teachers from Britain, with the result that they naturally followed the English and Scottish models with which they were familiar. The first teachers appointed were for the most part men of distinction and promise, attracted by the opportunity of establishing in a new country the foundations of university life. As the methods of the university were formalised and the conditions of appointment became less attractive it was difficult to keep up the standards of appointment. Moreover, the inspiration of the methods derived from the older universities in the mid-nineteenth century and stereotyped by the external control of the Senate began to flag. The university failed either to keep pace with modern practice in other universities or to develop its own characteristic methods suitable to the environment of a new country.

As in many of the newer American colleges also, the interest of the outside public and its expression, either in the scanty private gifts or in State grants, was mainly concerned with providing more and easier opportunities for all who wished to take advantage of university education. The natural result is that an absurdly large number of students are catered for by an inadequate staff working with poor equipment. There seems no reason why New Zealand should have, in proportion to her population, more than double the number of university students that Australia has and almost double the highest number of any country, including even the United States. The understaffing of the colleges is pathetic. The number of students per teacher is almost four times the average of other British universities. (18)

The multiplication of opportunities for higher education is to be expected in a democracy, and there are some grounds for pride in the fact that so many young people have these opportunities. There is, however, another and very embarrassing aspect of the situation. In the opinion of the Royal Commission of 1925, "this high proportion may at first sight seem ground for legitimate pride and self-congratulation, but closer scrutiny suggests that it is capable of less favourable interpretation; that it may be a symptom of weakness rather than of strength.

It may mean, and in our opinion does mean, that the University in New Zealand is working at a lower level and with inferior ideals."(19)

One aspect of this lowering of standards is very obvious in the undue amount of evening work which is allowed to dominate university teaching. There is good cause in a new country for concessions to individual students, and some reason for combining instruction in certain subjects with practical experience; but it is unfortunate that the supposed needs of the evening students should control the curriculum. The same lowering of standards in order to cater for as many students as possible has caused classes to be organised in subjects and at stages that are ordinarily regarded as below university standards. Preparatory classes in languages and mathematics, elementary engineering that should be relegated to technical schools, overemphasis of the practical aspects of professional subjects in law, commerce, and hardly less in the arts training for the teaching profession—all absorb the time and energy of the professorial staff to an unwarranted degree. (20) In the training of elementary school teachers, indeed, the university plays a minor rôle. The claims of the training colleges upon the time of the students are such that the university classes are used mainly to fill in courses, students being restricted to subjects and times which do not interfere with what is regarded as the more important "practical" part of their training. This is a powerful factor also in the retention of the evening courses which detract so largely from the efficiency of the university. (21)

The curious system of external examination which has made the university an object of curiosity if not of ridicule wherever it is known throughout the university world, seems at last to be in process of disappearing. If anything were needed to encourage cramming, the system under which students' work was wholly judged by examiners in Great Britain, with no reference to the teachers concerned, was calculated to achieve this object. No responsible teacher has any doubts that this system seriously lowered the standard of the degree work and interfered still more with any attempts to build up university ideals of study and research. One amusing illustration may be cited of an external examiner in economics who was placed in a dilemma by having to set essays on New Zealand economic problems. Having no direct knowledge of those problems he slipped into the habit of setting subjects on which honours dissertations had been presented to him in previous years. This gave him some means of checking facts; but the students, who quickly discovered this habit, had merely to borrow and read the theses of their predecessors in order to achieve remarkably good passes. During his term this external examiner, to the chagrin of the teachers, gave more first-class honours in his subject than have ever been given before or since. The teachers had not been consulted in his appointment and were powerless to interfere with his results or to communicate with him.

After a long, and at times bitter, struggle the increasing power of the professoriate in recent years has at last made breaches in the examination system, though the advanced and honours work is still subject to purely external tests. It will now be a matter of a very few years before a more sensible method of collaboration between the teachers and some external examining authority is worked out. It will take a much longer time, however, to re-establish the principles of university teaching and to free the university from the cramming tradition of the last half-century.

It is only too evident that these traditions and standards will for some time to come present difficult problems in the administration of the university. The machinery of administration is gradually being improved; but it is difficult to build up a new tradition. One of the principal difficulties is to be found in the great number of students and their low standard of preparation, which involve the professorial staffs in the necessity of devoting almost their whole energy to elementary work. The salaries paid, the conditions of work, the small degree of assistance made possible by restricted finance, have in recent years tended to cause an unmistakable tendency for the freer and less contented among the younger members of the staff to leave the university in search of wider opportunities of usefulness. When this fact was drawn to the attention of responsible Ministers the reply was received that New Zealand could not afford to compete with the world for brains. Such a remark, made publicly, gives reason for reflection concerning the ultimate consequences of popular government.

For precisely the same reasons it has not been possible for

the university colleges to get adequate funds for libraries or research equipment. The freedom of the teacher to engage in advanced study is the first essential for research. The understaffing of the colleges, aggravated by the fact that each of them is endeavouring to cover practically the whole range of university functions, is the primary weakness. But it is greatly increased by the lack of funds for equipment, and particularly for libraries and laboratories.

In the brief and fragmentary summary that has been attempted above, there appears nothing which has not been a commonplace of university discussion for many years past. The tragedy of the situation is that such commonplaces, restated politely but emphatically by visiting authorities and royal commissions, are received with such complacency by all but the very limited circle, mainly of professors, who have direct university interests.

The frequent successes of New Zealand students in other countries are often quoted in vindication of the university system. It is fortunately true that a gratifyingly large proportion of the students who go abroad achieve great success. It would be surprising if this were not the case. The mental and physical quality of the students who come to the schools and colleges of New Zealand is as high as one might expect from the high standard of physical welfare, the wide opportunities open to all classes of the community, a solid basis of instruction in facts upon which creative education may be built in a more stimulating environment, and above all, the selected stock from which the population has been built up. It is reasonable to expect an unusual distribution of talent in such a community. The appearance of such talent does not justify or excuse a system of education which is stereotyped in the lower and starved in the higher branches of learning.

The Need for Leadership

Attention has been drawn to the weaknesses of the educational system of New Zealand because it seemed necessary to do so in order to explain the very evident intellectual lag which in the recent period of prosperity has turned its people from the paths of experiment into those of satisfied conservatism and even mediocrity. References to the schools and universities in the existing descriptive accounts of New Zealand life are very sketchy. It is, moreover, very significant that all such accounts have been written either by visiting professors and journalists or by New Zealand laymen. None has been written by a trained university specialist who yet has lived in the Dominion long enough to get a real knowledge of the educational foundations of its social life. In his admirable accounts of New Zealand, Reeves writes of the general level of intelligence, of the wide popular reading, the good newspapers, and similar evidences of an average level of culture beyond that of most communities; but he makes only brief and vague passing references to the university.(22) The only other recent New Zealand writers of standing are even less explicit. Visitors, on the other hand, are naturally cautious and inclined to be polite. Most of those qualified to speak of such matters have been more concerned with specific problems which they were investigating. It is very significant, however, that the visitors of greatest academic authority and widest experience—Bryce, Webb, and Siegfried—should all have put their finger upon the weak spot.(23)

A brief survey of the social institutions of the Dominion will suffice to indicate the justice of this verdict. It would be foolish, indeed, to expect a young community, obsessed with the difficult task of developing the economic resources of a new land, to develop into a community of scholars and artists. Reeves ended his appraisal of New Zealand social life by arguing that it was yet too soon to look for much beyond economic progress.

> Industrious, sensible, strong, it is far too soon to complain of this race because it has not yet produced more men of genius from amongst its scanty numbers. Its mission has not been to do that, but to lay the foundations of a true civilisation in two wild and lonely, though beautiful, islands. This has been a work calling for solid rather than brilliant qualities—for a people morally and physically sound and wholesome, and gifted with "grit" and concentration. There is such a thing as collective ability. The men who will carve statues, paint pictures, and write books will come, no doubt, in good time. The business of the pioneer generation has been to turn a bloodstained or silent wilderness into a busy and interesting, a happy, if not yet a splendid, State.(24)

There is much sound commonsense in this point of view, and comparisons with the matured social life and institutions of older lands are obviously unfair. Yet it is fatally easy to take refuge in such excuses. After all, New Zealand has been a self-governing democracy for three-quarters of a century. Its university is almost sixty years old, and its pioneer age is now well past. Moreover, the first settlers did not regard it as foolish to expect that a leavening of scholarship and creative art should maintain the standards of citizenship and evoke a continuous spirit of public service.

Unlike older lands, which have well-established traditions and institutions, New Zealand has almost no counterpoise to the levelling influences of majority rule. In the earliest days of settlement there was an unusual proportion of men and women of learning and consequently of wide outlook and far-sighted leadership. The whole social life of the provinces was stamped with their influence.

There is a sense in which much the same relationship exists still between individuals in New Zealand and the social life of Great Britain. There are in the Dominion many representatives of the older universities and the great public schools, retired officers from the army and navy and the colonial services, and connections of middle-class and aristocratic families. Such groups not only maintain their connections, but often develop in New Zealand itself a pale imitation of the life they have left behind them. For the most part this tends to preserve the social mannerisms rather than the intrinsic values of British middle-class culture. It provides, indeed, the main buttress of the "colonial snobbery" which Siegfried so caustically and truly describes.(25) In any case it has little to offer to the building up of a characteristic New Zealand outlook. It is, after all, a survival from another land, a way of life alien to that which is being worked out all too slowly by New Zealanders for themselves. Even though the land of its origin be the Motherland, and "alien" a word with somewhat harsh connotations, it remains true that any attempt to reproduce sectional British customs in the very different atmosphere of the Dominion is doomed to failure.

The real life of the Dominion springs from the activities of the small working farmers and of the workers of the towns. They are the ultimate repositories both of economic and of political power. Inevitably the customs and institutions of the new country will be moulded to their necessities and to their outlook. There are no powerful institutions as in older lands —an aristocracy, an established church, powerful learned professions, old-established universities—to modify the working of democracy. The only groups which can do so are economic and business associations, whose standards are necessarily monetary. It is precisely for this reason that the failure of the university to develop independent and critical standards of scholarship is so important. The influence and usefulness of the learned professions depend almost entirely upon the education (as distinct from the professional training) received by lawyers, medical men, clergy, teachers, and not less by dentists, accountants, bankers, agriculturists, architects. As long as the intellectual life of the university is cramped and its standards remain low, so that it fails to develop even a minority spirit of analytical scepticism, so long will the community lack trained leadership in social as well as professional endeavour.

It is abundantly clear that New Zealand has not developed as yet any very keen intellectual life. Many reasons may be advanced to account for this failure. Besides the youth of the country and its obsession with economic progress there is its isolation from centres of great world movements. There is also the homogeneity of its tradition, which lacks the clash of cultures that might in the long run have stimulated intellectual life. It is true that the experience of the United States does not encourage the belief that mere variety of backgrounds is sufficient in itself to encourage artistic expression or creative thought. Rather does it seem to indicate that the various national and racial groups must lose their identity and reduce themselves to a lowest common denominator conforming to the economic and social pattern dictated by the new environment, before any cultural life can be built up. On the other hand, the very homogeneity of the New Zealanders has involved them for a longer period in tutelage to the intellectual traditions of the land from which their forbears came. This fact is abundantly illustrated in the writings, and particularly the poetry, of the Dominion, so much of which is reminiscent of England rather than the antipodes.

It is significant also that three of the four whom Reeves singles out as creative spirits of the recent generation—Rutherford, Salmond, Marris, and Katherine Mansfield—should have found their lifework outside the Dominion in which they were born.

The slow development of the higher branches of intellectual activity follows much the same course as in other agricultural pioneer lands. Though many, if not most, New Zealanders would probably resent the comparison, it remains true that, dialect and mannerisms apart, they are closer in outlook and spirit to the farming communities of the middle west of the United States and still closer to those of the Canadian prairie provinces than they are to either the urban workers or the middle classes of England, whose doings they follow with more respect, if not understanding. There is the same diffused prosperity, a good average standard of intelligence and knowledge, a real appreciation of and craving for such arts as music, even though opportunities for hearing it are rare, combined with the same general contentment and even pride in economic progress, and the same lack of creative artistic or scientific effort.

In such communities scientific work naturally begins with description rather than analysis. The biological sciences and geology offer rare opportunities to do new work without any very great degree of specialised training or exceptionally sustained intellectual analysis and experiment. The New Zealand university, and amateurs also, have made good use of this field. Until recently, however, the very similar opportunities in the social sciences, perhaps because they call for a degree more of analysis and imagination, have been neglected. Economic analysis has in the last decade made fair progress; but the kindred fields of political science, sociology, law, and comparative religion have hardly been explored. In anthropology there has been careful recording of material culture mainly by officials in the Government services; but little effort has been made to analyse or interpret the material recorded. New Zealand is strategically placed in one of the richest fields for anthropological research, and is almost unique in the possession of able Maori leaders competent to interpret native lore and thought; but the university has only one part-time lectureship in the subject, and that is located in the college most remote from Maori material.

Reeves very rightly emphasises the comparative poverty of literary expression, even in conversation, and just as rightly draws attention to pioneer efforts now being made. The one outstanding writer of stories, Katherine Mansfield, did most of her work abroad, and drew pictures of bourgeois life in New Zealand that can hardly be considered flattering. Much of the novel-writing which is beginning to appear rings false, as when the unflattering contrast between the rough New Zealanders and the cultured immigrant family is made the turning-point of the heroine's development. There is some reason, however, to hope that the more frequent attempts both at verse and at novels and short stories betoken a young school of writers going through an apprenticeship. Their efforts are hampered by the fact that except for the encouragement of certain daily newspapers they can have little outlet for their work. There are no literary journals in the Dominion, and the university magazines tend to resemble school journals rather than organs of literary expression.

If fiction and verse are still backward, it is to be expected that drama is in even worse condition. There is a very recent interest in reading modern plays, and the first efforts are being made to establish repertory theatres; but only one volume of New Zealand plays has been produced. The pictorial arts are more developed, with characteristic work already beginning to appear. Sculpture and architecture are almost non-existent, though an indication of the decorative value of the Maori designs may be seen in the use of Maori *motifs* in the friezes and panels of the new War Memorial Museum at Auckland. There is, moreover, almost no background of crafts. The middle-class conception of cultural education for children rarely goes beyond lessons on the pianoforte. The striking absence of such craft-work as gives the means of expression in older peasant communities is one of the reasons for the slow development of the arts. Here, again, there is an interesting neglect of the Maori example.

If one turns to consider the ideas and concepts which govern citizenship, there is much the same story to tell. Largely because of the failure of the university to develop even a minority which shall be critical, sceptical, eager, enquiring, and acutely conscious of ideas, the concepts of social behaviour remain nebulous, conservative, and largely negative. There is little real freedom of opinion, public opinion is intolerant, and the rebel or even the radical tends to have an uncomfortable time. There are many evidences of failure to evince any very real trust in freedom of thought and expression. As in most democracies, this was, of course, most evident in the emotional stress of the war period. In New Zealand many of the wartime restrictions have carried over into the normal routine of social life. A maternal Government still maintains, for example, a fairly drastic censorship upon the importation of books. There is no published list of prohibited books; but it is an offence to import those which in the wisdom of the censor are held to transgress economic or sexual morality. Thus a perfectly objective description of international labour organisations, imported years after the war for the economics department of a university library, was prohibited until the offer of the professor concerned to give evidence if a case should be brought safeguarded the bookseller and presumably removed the book from the dangerous list. The reason given for its offensiveness was that an appendix contained the text of the constitution of the Third International. In the same way, though birth-control is widely practised in the Dominion, certain books which sell freely both in Britain and Australia are prohibited in New Zealand. So alert are the Customs officials on this point that a badly written invoice has been known to cause the detention for examination of a case containing a book on obesity entitled *Girth Control*.

Just as the wartime censorship of dangerous publications survives in modified form, so the extension of restrictive legislation against dangerous immigrants, particularly ex-enemy aliens or suspected Communists, has been retained. Occasionally this legislation has been enforced; but its very retention on the statute-books is evidence of New Zealand's conservative point of view regarding the liberty of the subject. It is not the province of the economic historian to decide whether this point of view is evidence of sound judgment and firm government, or evidence of stagnant timidity. It is merely necessary to record the facts.

There can be little doubt that the influence of the women of New Zealand is essentially conservative in these and most other respects. The integrity of family life persists in New Zealand and is less shaken by new and disturbing ideas of sexual morality and human relationships than in most countries. A glance at the long list of legislative measures to which women's organisations have lent their support will indicate that these measures are protective rather than destructive of the family institution. There seems little overt demand for expressive freedom. Entry into clerical and professional occupations is free; but there is far less advantage taken of these opportunities than one might expect in a country of universal education and sex equality. Women lawyers, doctors, and dentists are still rare; there is only one woman professor (of Home Science) in the whole university; women preachers are rarer still; and though women have entered local politics, the central Government is still closed to them, not by law, but by the will of the electorate. The social tradition of the Dominion regards the home as woman's sphere and frowns upon extra-domestic activities. This may be seen, for instance, in the repeated declarations of policy against the employment of married women in the teaching profession. The obverse of this situation is that with many housewives, especially in the country districts, the burden of domestic occupations and conventional social duties preclude any great development of intellectual interests. In this respect the women of New Zealand are at least a generation behind the women of America.

It is perhaps inevitable that the religious life of the Dominion should show most clearly of all the stagnating influence of an educational system which aims at uniformity and fails to produce sceptical leadership. Despite the distinctly adventurous religious tone of the earlier pioneer settlements it is difficult to point to any outstanding achievement distinctly due to Christian citizenship since Dr. Waddell led the crusade against sweating nearly forty years ago. There are, of course, individuals among the clergy and laymen who have striven to awaken or keep alive a social conscience; but almost the whole of their energy has gone into the movement for the prohibition of alcoholic liquors. Puritan ideals tend to seek expression also in crusades against gambling; but there are few evidences of organised effort to build a Christian commonwealth as "the expression of the City of God in the political sphere".

One of the most obvious examples that could be wished, both of the distinct time-lag before social movements reach the

Dominion and of the lack of modern thought in its religious life, is to be found in the very recent recrudescence of activity among the powerful fundamentalist groups within the churches and particularly the effort, apparently well-financed and carefully planned, to work up an agitation against the teaching of evolutionary theories in the State schools. This effort, moreover, like the related efforts to spread quack psychologies, food fads, medical treatments, and revival movements, is added evidence of the tendency to follow American movements some years after they have reached the peak of popularity in the land of their birth. That an anti-Darwinian agitation should be launched on Biblical grounds, even though it be doomed to early failure, indicates that substantial support exists for a view of life which educated people abandoned half a century ago.(26) It is obviously of the same order as the agitation some few years ago among extreme Protestant circles condemning the League of Nations as a Catholic institution because the majority of the adherent countries were Catholic.

If one turns from such futilities to review the social and political organisation based upon the concepts indicated above, there is abundant confirmation of the fact that lack of leadership has led to timidity and conservatism. This is notably true of the trade union movement, which is numerically strong and buttressed by a remarkable code of labour legislation. Since Reeves placed this labour code upon the statute-books the contact between the labour movement and the intelligentsia has been so slight as to be almost non-existent. There has not been, as in the British movement, a friendly alliance with the intellectuals. The unions are efficiently led along routine lines by men who rise from the ranks of unionism; but new ideas are scarce and experiment almost unknown. There has been nothing to parallel the guild movement, the shop-stewards' agitation, or the Whitley Council movement in Britain, and still less the banking experiments, efficiency committees, and collaboration with management of certain American unions. Neither is there the ingenious exploitation of the possibilities of the arbitration system devised by Australian unions. Communism, syndicalism, and other left-wing movements are negligible. It is true that the Alliance of Labour gathers together elements that are vaguely militant, and that its programme embodies a scheme for an industrial Parliament which is compounded of elements derived eclectically from almost all revolutionary programmes; but this is almost wholly fantasy, the only reality in which is a rather redder, belligerent spirit among these industrial unions.

The only labour experiments of a constructive type have been made by individual leaders with union sympathy but upon their own responsibility and initiative. Miners have contracted to take over workings abandoned by the State and have opened up retail organisations in certain cities. Some public works have been carried out by organised contract parties of skilled miners. The most notable case was the construction of a tunnel near Wellington, under the leadership of Mr. R. Semple, who was formerly the organiser of the Federation of Labour. His party underbid private contracting firms, paid high wages, provided excellent working conditions, and finished the job in good time with substantial profit. The success of this venture and of the essentially similar co-operative contracts which are a feature of public works construction proves that there is ample room in New Zealand for experiment if the unions were experimentally minded. There is, however, a great deal of apathy and little real strength in the movement. Mr. Ramsay MacDonald was right when he said that arbitration had taken the steel out of the unions. Their members are slack in their interest, and the leaders tend easily to slip into the rôle of advocates before the Court. The flutter caused by the recent suggestions that the Court might be abolished was indicative of their weak position.

If the trade unions lack enterprise, the same statement is true of other economic organisations. Seddon tried hard to enlist the active co-operation of the friendly societies in his early efforts to promote old-age pension schemes; but they did not respond. It is difficult to generalise concerning the more important private businesses. Sheltered from overseas competition by great shipping distances and a substantial tariff, they are further sheltered by the difficulties of communication hindering inter-provincial competition. They are necessarily organised on a small scale because of the limited local markets, and this again safeguards them from overseas competition setting up branches within the Dominion. While generalisations must inevitably be wrong in detail, it is safe to venture the conjecture that profit-margins tend to be higher, sheltering more routine traditional methods than could survive under fiercer competition. This seems to be especially true of the distributive businesses such as drapery. The system of wholesale and retail businesses breaks down slowly and there is a great number of small retail shops. The revolution in retail trading methods which other countries have been experiencing has not yet reached the Dominion in any marked degree. There are far more profit-sharing, co-partnership, and pension schemes than is obvious until after careful personal enquiry. These reinforce the argument, since they are essentially of a paternalistic nature, introduced privately by individual employers and conducted without publicity.

The chief cause of the comparative lack of new ideas in business is due largely to the small degree in which university graduates have sought business leadership. The imaginative planning upon which modern business depends is the result of combining practical experience with a high degree of mental training. Few banking or business houses in New Zealand employ trained specialists for research or functional duties. Only recently have minor positions been created for industrial chemists and other scientists. Still fewer firms are controlled by men who have been highly trained theoretically before undertaking large practical responsibilities. Business opinion in New Zealand, in fact, still distrusts and discounts the value of theoretical training. No training in economic theory, for instance, has been considered necessary for those who undertake the direction of banking business.

In the same way, the farming industries of the Dominion are only now at the threshold of realising what scientific research may do to help them. They have tried almost every short-cut out of the depression, except the utilisation of trained brains to help them solve large problems of production which depend essentially upon scientific processes.

At the risk of criticism and perhaps with wearisome iteration one must extend the story to include many departments of the public service and also the professional organisations. The lack of specialised training within the Civil Service has been commented on elsewhere. It remains only to point out how greatly the professional associations, such as the legal and medical societies, are preoccupied with purely occupational concerns. This is particularly true of the medical association, which rarely breaks through its rigid etiquette to give public consideration to social problems. The recent Royal Commission on university education reported drastically that the training for the legal profession was such that conventional references to "my learned friend" were in some danger of being regarded as satire.

The final expression of the tendencies which have been traced throughout the social organisation of the Dominion is to be found in what both Lord Bryce and Sidney Webb referred to as the vulgarity of political life. Some attention has been paid in an earlier chapter to the atrophy of local institutions and to the supersession in the central legislature of political issues, which in the eighties and nineties gave place to economic contentions. Economic problems do not necessarily involve lower standards of idealism or of intelligence; but they are more complicated and more mundane, and, moreover, lend themselves more easily to sectional squabbles. Since the greater part of this book has dealt in some detail with the recent development of the more important economic problems of the Dominion, practically all of which have at some time involved Parliamentary action of one kind or another, there is no need to recapitulate the story.

It is in its dealings with the large problems of imperial and foreign policy that the public opinion of New Zealand stands revealed most clearly as based upon negative and non-co-operative principles. Though the major problems necessarily involve Governmental action, there has been little Parliamentary discussion concerning them. Executive action has rested in the hands of a small group of civil servants and politicians, and has had a remarkable continuity because of the long-lived Governments which New Zealand has enjoyed. The lack of Parliamentary discussion correctly reflects public apathy concerning world and even imperial politics. If the policies followed had been subjected to keen critical examination in and out of Parliament, the principles upon which they are based would at least have been exposed to democratic judgment. This has not been the case, and the decisions taken have consistently reflected the perfectly intelligible and defensible attitudes of men to whom the maintenance of the *status quo* in imperial relationships—and especially defence—has been of far greater importance than co-operation in a new order of world politics.

The more detailed discussion of imperial policy in the previous chapter, together with the description of events in Samoa, will have outlined the main features of the policy undertaken. Such a discussion needs only to be supplemented by the bare mention of such important matters as school training in citizenship, the continuance of compulsory military training, and New Zealand's very hesitant and distrustful, if coldly correct, attitude to the League of Nations and the International Labour Office.

In all three related matters there is an increasing volume of criticism. Compulsory military training was introduced in 1909 in the face of strong Radical opposition, which, however, evoked stronger popular resentment. It has been continued into the post-war period, despite increasing criticism, which now questions its utility rather than its desirability. Such criticism is perhaps not as articulate as in the first years of its introduction; but the younger generation, upon whom the burden of service falls, increasingly questions the efficiency of the training which is given. Whatever justice there may be in this criticism, it is at least clear that in a world which is eagerly discussing disarmament New Zealand stands stoutly by its system of compulsory military training. It is equally clear that the territorial battalions lack much of the enthusiasm which characterised the earlier volunteer movement.

Lukewarmness towards the League of Nations and its works is perhaps not quite as evident since responsible statesmen and officials have themselves participated in the activities of the League. But the Dominion shares with Ethiopia and two or three other countries of equal rank the unenviable distinction of having neglected to send any representatives to the conferences of the International Labour Organisation, and of having equally neglected to ratify (a mere formality in most cases) any of the conventions arising from the conferences.

It is impossible to resist the conclusion that this imperviousness to current happenings in the outside world is due primarily to the conception of patriotism and citizenship taught in the schools. Patriotism was, and for the most part still is, conceived almost wholly in imperial terms, and instruction in civics, dictated by examination prescriptions, was in most schools and until recently a curious mixture of the dry bones of constitutional procedure together with objurgations concerning imperialism. It is true that many teachers rise above these limitations; but the time allowed in the curriculum for such social studies as geography and history is utterly inadequate, and it is difficult even for the most idealistic of teachers to convey to their pupils a true idea of the rapid development of international relationships since the war. This is one of the most important illustrations of the time-lag in New Zealand's intellectual life.

The passages just preceding will undoubtedly cause resentment in many quarters as exaggerated carping criticism. One must plead that they could have been written only by a New Zealander. They record the conclusions arrived at after twenty-five years' practically continuous residence in the Dominion, during most of which the writer was engaged in university study and teaching. Even then the writing of this final chapter was deferred until, after an absence of two years mainly spent in travel, a further visit to New Zealand confirmed or modified earlier judgments. All of the illustrations given have come under personal observation. The criticism must therefore stand as an individual judgment which may at least serve to balance the indiscriminating eulogies in which, only too often, New Zealanders deem it their duty to indulge when writing of their country and its institutions.

That it is not solely an individual opinion may perhaps be judged from the fact that at the time of writing a single issue (June 4, 1929) of the *New Zealand News*, published in London, reported three separate important criticisms of the New Zealand educational system. The first is a quotation from a leading daily newspaper.

This is not the first or the second time that we have had to deplore New Zealand's neglect of men of first-class talent—if neglect is a strong enough word. In Australia and America, to which so many of our ablest men have gone, it perhaps appears that we not only neglect men of ability, but almost despise them, since we are willing to let any country outbid us for their services. In this case there is the additional reproach that the scientist concerned has never at any time been treated much better financially than a first-class mechanic, though the Department does not now know where to find another man in the Dominion "without robbing other important lines of work". Unless it can be shown that he is not leaving us for financial reasons, his departure is a reproach not only to the Government, but to the public at large.

The second criticism is quoted from a Commemoration Day address by the Senior Professor of Canterbury College. After surveying the poverty of the university and its colleges, he drew attention to the fact that his own college in three years had lost four of its younger professors; that when one of the colleges advertised in 1928 for a new professor not a single application was received from Great Britain; and that opportunities for professors to return Home were so small that no men of distinction or great promise were likely to apply for chairs in New Zealand. Included in his speech was the very significant paragraph:

The relations between the Government and the University of New Zealand are most unsatisfactory, being based on mutual distrust. While the University can only look to the Government for any substantial improvement in its financial position, it is, like other Universities, anxious to feel itself free from outside control of any kind, and bitterly resents any tendency to bring it under the Education Department. At the same time we have the spectacle of the Government accusing the University of being too rich. Here we seem to have a real dilemma, and one which immensely complicates any attempt to improve the methods or the financial position of the University. The crux of our problem will be found, I think, just here.

The Rector of the College emphasised the position of the library.

We have at Canterbury College two-thirds of the number of matriculated students there are at the University of Leeds. In 1926 Leeds added 7,000 volumes to its library, equal to about half the total number of books in our library. This does not include 7,000 periodical numbers. Leeds expends on books £3,500 a year, as against our £500; on salaries £2,300, as against our sum of something under £300—in the general library ten full-time salaried officers and employees. The reproach implied in this comparison affects not only our Government, but individuals and local bodies, which in other lands contribute so much to universities. It is not relevant to plead the youth or the newness of the Dominion in mitigation. Having established its University Colleges to do the real work of a university, having opened their doors wide to its young people, and proclaiming itself as one of the most prosperous countries in the world—all this with justice—New Zealand is estopped from such a plea in defence of its refusal to shoulder the financial responsibilities involved in its action.

These statements, it must be remembered, were made concerning the best endowed of the four university colleges in New Zealand.

It is the comparative failure to provide high training for potential leadership that is the most discouraging feature of New Zealand's democratic experiment. The material for leadership exists, the average standard is remarkably high, and wherever opportunity offers there is no lack of individuals ready to take responsibility. But the mental training necessary to bring out and sustain effective initiative in politics, business, and social life generally, has been thwarted by an ill-devised educational system.

The stereotyped uniformity of a highly centralised State system of primary education is bad enough. There is no reason to accept its development as inevitable; but it is easy to understand how it has come into existence. It could not have reached its present stage of development if there had been a lively spirit of critical scholarship in the university. It is to the recent developments of promise in the university, therefore, that one must look for a way out of this difficult situation. There are fortunately signs that the long and gallant struggle waged by individual teachers within the colleges is beginning to be rewarded. Young New Zealanders, many of them fortified by additional training and experience in other lands, are beginning to make effective protests of their discontent. As the university colleges make use of their widening powers, there is reason to expect that such protests will become more frequent and effective.

New Zealand presents as fair a field for democratic education as exists anywhere. There is no reason to feel that the temporary and partial failure of the educational system to yield the best qualitative as well as quantitative results is either irremediable or a necessary consequence of democratic rule. New Zealand has recently passed through a period in which economic prosperity came with fair ease to those who took advantage of the exceptionally favourable conditions. It was not to be expected that small working farmers would be lavish in support of a university to which they owed almost nothing and which was to them merely a little-known institution training men and women for the urban professions. The numbing effect of two generations of stereotyped education in the primary schools has also to be remembered. But there are not wanting signs that the temporary worsening of economic conditions is causing a slow change of attitude. The somewhat misdirected interest in agricultural education, culminating in the creation of a new agricultural college in the north island, is evidence that the farmers realise the need for more specialist training and research. Such interest in the practical economic aspects of education leads naturally to support of education for its own sake.

Reform needs to start lower down also. The limited experiments already made have proved the value of consolidating small country schools, bringing pupils together in one centre instead of distributing teachers to work single-handed and ineffectively in isolation. Such school-centres grouped around high-schools organised with a rural instead of an urban bias make possible, also, university extension work which reaches right out into the remote country districts. There seems no reason why New Zealand should not develop as sound and beneficial a system of rural education as Denmark or any other land. It may even be hoped that in the future greater freedom of experiment and emphasis upon creative activity may develop the efforts which have so far been lacking at the expression of thought on social problems in literary and dramatic form.

In the towns there is evidence also of a growing appreciation of the part that the university may play in social life. The greatest evidence comes naturally from the professions which are seeking support in the effort to raise their own standards. The body of graduates is now becoming both more powerful and more interested in the welfare of the university. The extension work carried on through the agency of the Workers' Educational Association, though it has departed somewhat from its original purpose, has at least popularised the university and gained for its teachers a wider appreciation which will bear fruit in popular support.

There is ground for hoping, therefore, that New Zealand may have passed through its worst phase of democratic obscurantism; but in the meantime it has lost at least a generation of intellectual progress, and has only too often provided a happy hunting-ground for quacks,

The final word must, however, be one of optimism. The people of New Zealand come of good stock. They may have missed the turning that led by the most direct route to the goal of their best and fullest development, but they come of a persistent race which has retrieved worse mistakes in the past and which has sound instincts and traditions. There are possibilities in the Dominion of exceptional social and intellectual achievement. Froude wrote of them many years since when he imagined the New Zealand of the future.(27)

The chief danger confronting the people of New Zealand at the present time is that, resting content with their achievements and good fortune, they may lose the vision of the high destiny which the great pioneers of their country set before them.

APPENDIX I

NOTES AND REFERENCES

CHAPTER I

1. THE literature of New Zealand history, especially in its earliest phases, is very voluminous. In the present volume emphasis has been thrown upon the most recent period of economic development. No attempt has been made at historical description except as such seemed necessary to provide a background for current problems. The abundance of excellent secondary authorities for the early period has rendered unnecessary any continuous historical narrative. References to original early sources have also been omitted.

   The best narrative chronological account of New Zealand political, social, and economic development is *The Long White Cloud*, by the Hon. W. Pember Reeves. This well-known work has recently been revised and is incomparable for the whole period of New Zealand history, with the exception of the most recent period.

   For the period before colonisation the most valuable sources are summarised in the painstaking volumes of the Hon. Robert McNab:

   Historical Records of New Zealand, Vol. I, Wellington, 1908; Vol. II, 1914.
   Murihiku and the Southern Island, Invercargill, 1907; Wellington, 1914.
   Old Whaling Days, Christchurch, 1913.
   From Tasman to Marsden, Dunedin, 1914.

   The missionary movement is described in Martin, *Missionaries in the Pacific*, Oxford, 1924, Chap. III.

   Bishop of Waiapu, *Christianity among the New Zealanders*, London, 1867.
   Purchas, *New Zealand Church History*, Christchurch, 1914.
   Carleton, *The Life of Henry Williams*, 2 vols., Auckland, 1874.
   Tucker, *The Life and Episcopate of G. A. Selwyn, D.D.*, 2 vols., London, 1879.
   Buller, *Forty Years in New Zealand*, London, 1878.
   J. B. Marsden, *Life of the Rev. Samuel Marsden*, London, 1857.

   The Maori wars of the early nineteenth century are treated by:

   S. Percy Smith, *Wars of the Northern against the Southern Tribes of New Zealand in the Nineteenth Century*, Wellington, 1904.

2. The earliest trade statistics relating to New Zealand are given by Thomson, *Story of New Zealand*, Vol. II, p. 324, as follows:

Year.	Value of Exports to New South Wales.	Value of Imports from New South Wales.
	£	£
1826	30,000	1,735
1827	63,000	4,926
1828	125,862	5,845
1829	135,486	12,692
1830	60,356	15,597
1831	68,804	60,354
1832	47,895	63,934
1833	—	—
1834	—	—
1835	35,542	39,984
1836	32,155	36,184
1837	42,886	39,528
1838	53,943	46,924
1839	71,707	95,173
1840	54,192	215,486
1841	45,659	114,980
1842	37,246	131,784

McNab adds the following details for the first eight months of 1830:

Imports..	£18,426	Exports..	£9,591
	£		£
Flax (500 tons)	12,513	Muskets (2,120)	2,938
Seal-skins ..	4,480	Gunpowder	862
		Flour ..	787
		Hardware ..	639
		Slops ..	458
		Rum and Whisky	424

3. Cf. Hight and Bamford, *The Constitutional History and Law of New Zealand*, Christchurch, 1914.
   Mills, *The Colonisation of Australia, 1829–1842*, London, 1915.
   Harrop, *England and New Zealand*, London, 1926.
   Marais, *The Colonisation of New Zealand*, London, 1927.
   Beaglehole, *Captain Hobson and the New Zealand Company*, Northampton, Mass., 1928.
4. Cf. Bedford, "Monetary Difficulties of Early Colonisation in New Zealand", *Economic Journal*, June 1916.
5. Saunders, *History of New Zealand*, Christchurch, 1896, Vol. I, p. 266.
6. Pyke, *History of the Early Gold Discoveries in Otago*, Dunedin, 1887, p. 47.
7. For previous attempts at borrowing policies see Gisborne, *New Zealand*, p. 170.
   "Many persons are under the impression that the public works policy of 1870 was altogether original, and that a policy of the kind

had never been proposed in New Zealand. That impression is incorrect, for on three occasions previously a policy similar in principle, though differing in degree, had been proposed. Mr. Domett, when he was Prime Minister of the colony in 1863, drew up a statesmanlike scheme for the settlement and self-defence of the North Island based on the principle of borrowing money for immigration and public works. Mr. Reader Wood, when he was Colonial Treasurer in 1864, proposed a modified scheme to a like effect. Mr. William Fitzherbert, in 1868, when, as a member of the Stafford Ministry, he was in England on a financial mission, recommended to his colleagues a policy in which immigration and public works were distinguishing features. But these three proposals were stillborn. 'The trail of the serpent' was 'over them all'; the war absorbed all attention and interposed insuperable obstacles to the proper undertaking of colonisation. The hour and the man came in 1870."

Vogel himself had published a pamphlet as early as 1865, stressing the imperial aspects of such a policy.

8. Cf., e.g., Carter, *New Zealand Loans,* Wellington, 1886.

   A considered and favourable estimate of Vogel is given, however, in Reeves, *The Long White Cloud,* London, 1924, pp. 237–9.
9. Reeves, *op. cit.*, p. 244.
10. Cf. Gisborne, *New Zealand,* pp. 174–86.
11. Le Rossignol and Stewart, *State Socialism in New Zealand,* London, 1912, p. 60. The mileage open for traffic in 1873 was 145.
12. Condliffe and Tocker, "The Effect of Changing Price-Levels upon the Economic Development of New Zealand" (reprinted from the *New Zealand Accountants' Journal,* 1924). The supporting statistics are to be found in *Transactions of the New Zealand Institute* for 1926, Vol. 56, pp. 722–32.
13. Copland, *Wheat Production in New Zealand,* Christchurch, 1920, pp. 97–107.
14. Findlay, *Labour and the Arbitration Act,* Wellington, 1908.
15. Condliffe and Tocker, *op. cit.* Cf. similar evidence in Benham, *The Prosperity of Australia,* London, 1928. An article by Fawcett and Paton, "Live Stock Production", in *New Zealand Official Year Book,* 1929, pp. 990–1000, gives estimates of production uncorrected for population increase and dealing only with the main primary industries in which there have been large gains. Correction of these figures for population shows that the increase in productivity per head slackened from 25 per cent. in the decade 1901–2 to 1910–11, to 7 per cent. in the following decade. The fact that productivity of all industries, rural and urban, shows a greater slackening is evidence that the transference of resources from rural to urban industry in this period caused a lowering of productivity.
16. Wickens, "Australian Population: Its Nature and Growth", *Economic Record,* Vol. I, No. 1, November 1925.
17. Tocker, "Monetary Standards in Australia and New Zealand", *Economic Journal,* December 1924.

18. Rodwell, "Land Values in Canterbury, New Zealand, 1914–1926", *Economic Record*, May 1927.
19. Belshaw, "The Economic Position of the Farmer in New Zealand", *Economic Record*, May 1928.

CHAPTER II

In preparing this chapter the author is greatly indebted to Mr. F. M. Keesing, M.A., who undertook a special journey through several Maori districts to collect material concerning the effects of land confiscations after the wars and of land-purchase policies. Mr. Keesing also made available an advance copy of his manuscript *Maori Progress on the East Coast.* The author's thanks are due to Maori leaders, and especially to Sir Apirana Turupa Ngata, for ready assistance given to Mr. Keesing, and also to Dr. Peter H. Buck (Te Rangihiroa) for constant friendly criticism. The author regrets that Mr. Raymond W. Firth's book on *The Primitive Economics of the Maori*, London, 1928, was received too late for him to make any considerable use of it.

1. The best general book on the origin of the Maori race is still S. Percy Smith's *Hawaiki: the Home of the Maori*, Christchurch, 1898 (4th edition, 1921).

General books on Maori culture, most of which contain references to the migrations, are:

Elsdon Best, *The Maori*, 2 vols., Wellington, 1924.
James Cowan, *The Maoris of New Zealand*, Christchurch, 1910.
Edward Tregear, *The Maori Race*, Wanganui, 1904.
T. G. Hammond, *The Story of Aotea*, Christchurch, 1924.
Johannes Andersen, *Maori Life in Aotea Roa*, Christchurch, 1907.

The *Journal of the Polynesian Society*, published quarterly from April 1892, is a mine of information for the anthropologist.

Other materials for a study of the social and economic development of the Maoris are found in the various publications of Elsdon Best, particularly in the bulletins and monographs of the Dominion Museum, Wellington. Special attention may be drawn to Bulletin No. 9, on "Maori Agriculture", and the *New Zealand Board of Science and Art Manual*, No. 4, "The Maori as He Was". The Economic History Supplement, No. 1 (January 1926), of the *Economic Journal* contains an article by Raymond W. Firth on "Some Features of Primitive Industry".

The Polynesian Society has also published a valuable series of memoirs, the latest of which, No. 7, *The Evolution of Maori Clothing*, by Te Rangihiroa (P. H. Buck), is of value in showing the adaptation of the Maoris to the different conditions of life in New Zealand.

The Board of Maori Ethnological Research is also publishing a series of memoirs, of which the following are already available:

Vol. 1. *The Material Culture of the Cook Islands* (*Aitutaki*), by Te Rangihiroa (P. H. Buck).
Vol. 2. *Maori String Figures*, by Johannes C. Andersen.

Vol. 3. *Maori Artistry*, by W. Page Rowe.

Vol. 4. *The Changing Maori*, by Felix M. Keesing.

There is a voluminous literature concerning the first contacts of the Maoris with the white settlers, the most important books being:

Grey, *Polynesian Mythology and Ancient Traditional History of the Maoris as furnished by their Priests and Chiefs*, London, 1855.

Thomson, *The Story of New Zealand*, London, 1859.

Maning, *Old New Zealand*, Auckland, 1863.

An important paper relating to this and later periods is Sir A. T. Ngata's "Anthropology and the Government of Native Races in the Pacific", *Australasian Journal of Psychology and Philosophy*, Vol. VI, No. 1, March 1928, reprinted in *New Zealand Affairs*, I.P.R., Wellington, 1929.

There is an important document on the legal aspects of Maori land tenure hidden away as a Memorandum preparatory to the Native Land Act, 1909 (*New Zealand Bills*, 1909, p. 537). It is entitled, "Notes on the History of Native Land Legislation", and was prepared by Sir John Salmond when he was Counsel to the Law Drafting Office.

2. Thomson, *The Story of New Zealand*, Vol. II, p. 338.

3. The best discussion of this subject is a paper by Dr. P. H. Buck, "The Passing of the Maori", in *Transactions of New Zealand Institute*, Vol. 55 (1924), pp. 362–75. This paper reviews the previous literature, and is specially interesting as giving a Maori criticism of the psychological explanations of depopulation advanced by Rivers in *Essays on the Depopulation of Melanesia*. Dr. Buck also deals significantly with the rapid increase of miscegenation. The following table is reproduced from his paper. The interpolations are Dr. Buck's.

Authority.	Year.	Population.
Captain Cook	1769–74	100,000 (400,000)
Nicholas	1814	150,000
Rev. W. Williams	1835	200,000 (120,000)
Sir George Grey..	1849	120,000
Sir Donald McLean	1855	60,000
Judge Fenton	1858	55,970
Official estimate	1867	38,540
Official estimate	1871	37,520
Colonial Government	1874	45,470
Colonial Government	1891	41,993
Colonial Government	1896	39,854
Colonial Government	1901	43,101
Colonial Government	1906*	47,731
Colonial Government	1911	49,844
Colonial Government	1916	49,776
Colonial Government	1921	52,751

* First Maori Census.

The corresponding figure for the census of 1926, including all half-castes, is 63,670.

4. Reeves, *The Long White Cloud*, pp. 142–3.
5. Cf. Harrop, *England and New Zealand*, Chap. IV.
6. Buick, *The Treaty of Waitangi*, Wellington, 1914.
7. The literature of the Maori wars is very voluminous and controversial. Omitting official documents and Parliamentary debates, the most significant references are:

    Martin, *The Taranaki Question*, London, 1860.

    Notes by the Governor on Sir William Martin's pamphlet entitled *The Taranaki Question*, Wellington, 1860.

    Gorst, *The Maori King*, London, 1864.

    Fox, *The War in New Zealand*, London, 1866.

    Cowan, *The Maori Wars and the Colonising Period*, Wellington, 2 vols., 1922–3.

    A typical colonist's point of view is that of Hursthouse, *New Zealand: the Britain of the South*, London, 2nd edition, 1861, Chap. XIX and Appendix.

    The most recent and the most authoritative statement of the controversy is contained in *Report of the Royal Commission on Confiscated Lands and other Grievances*, I—G 7 (1928).

8. Buick, *New Zealand's First War*, Wellington, 1926.
9. See 1928 Report on Confiscated Lands, *op. cit. passim.*
10. Cf. Keith, *Responsible Government in the British Dominions*, London, 1928, Vol. II, pp. 788–92. The references to early Maori administration in this section are very summary, and pass over the complicated and at times embittered relationships between the Governor and the Ministers. Professor Keith states that the Governor, who "was supposed to manage native affairs, had no real touch with them", but there is another side to this statement, and the colonists always regarded the war of 1860 as a "governor's war". Formal control was handed over on the date mentioned as a result of correspondence with the Colonial Office, initiating Weld's "self-reliant policy".
11. Cf. review of native land legislation in "Report of Royal Commission on Native Lands and Native Land Tenure, 1891" (Appendix to *Journal, House of Representatives*, Sess. II, Vol. II, 1891, 9–1), and précis in *Report of Royal Commission*, 1907–9 (9–1c).
12. Lord Jellicoe in preface to Harrop, *England and New Zealand.*
13. See debates in House on the Commission's recommendations (October 6, 1928).
14. Scholefield, *New Zealand in Evolution*, London, 1909, Chap. XXIV.
15. Cf. Buck, "The Passing of the Maoris", *op. cit.*
16. Keesing, *The Changing Maori*, New Plymouth, 1928, gives an illuminating analysis of the psychological phases through which the Maoris have passed.

CHAPTER III

1. McNab, *Historical Records of New Zealand*, Vol. I, p. 40.
2. *Ibid.*, p. 712.
3. *Ibid.*, p. 547. This transaction does not seem to have been completed.
4. Harrop, *England and New Zealand*, pp. 68–9.
5. Jourdain, *History of Land Legislation and Settlement in New Zealand*, Wellington, 1925, p. 9.
6. *Ibid.*, pp. 55–6.
7. *Ibid.*, pp. 57–8 (date misprinted as 1844).
8. Hight and Bamford, *Constitutional History and Law of New Zealand*, Christchurch, 1914, Chap. XVI.
9. I.e. New Munster as defined in the constitution of 1846, comprising the whole of the south island and that part of the north island south of a line drawn due east from the mouth of the Patea River, taking in the Wanganui and Wellington Settlements.
10. Harrop, *op. cit.*, pp. 252–7.
11. *Report on the Statistics of New Zealand*, 1890, p. 214.
12. Reeves, *State Experiments in Australia and New Zealand*, London, 1902, Vol. I, p. 227.
13. Vogel, *Handbook of New Zealand*, p. 185 (2nd edition).
14. The statistics are given as follows for the year 1853 in Thomson's *Story of New Zealand*, Vol. II, p. 325:

Province.	Area.	Purchased from Natives (including Reserves).
Auckland	14,000,000	800,000
Wellington	9,728,000	3,500,000
New Plymouth . .	1,994,240	60,000
Nelson	9,600,000	9,000,000
Canterbury	13,152,000	13,152,000
Otago	15,670,400	15,670,400

15. Cf. the table of revenue (p. 484), remembering that the two provinces, Canterbury and Otago, received the bulk of the territorial revenue from land sales.
16. Jourdain, pp. 63–4.
17. Rees, *Life and Times of Sir George Grey*, Auckland, 1892.
18. *Ibid.*, p. 159.
19. Jourdain, p. 64.
20. *Ibid.*, pp. 64–6.
21. *Ibid.*, p. 20.
22. *Ibid.*, p. 66.
23. *Ibid.*, pp. 68–90.
24. *Ibid.*, p. 23.

COLONIAL AND PROVINCIAL REVENUE (Note 15 above)

000s *omitted*

Year.	Colonial.		Provincial.	
	Ordinary.	Territorial.	Ordinary.	Territorial.
	£	£	£	£
1864	694	8	132	717
1865	825	25	109	460
1866	942	10	142	737
1867	1,090	16	150	509
1868	981	7	122	418
1869	1,043	6	153	377
1870	970	10	148	328
1871	948	2	129	377
1872	1,040	5	139	619
1873	1,251	53	267	1,226

25. *Report on Statistics of New Zealand*, 1890. In the Province of Canterbury the total area sold was approximately 2,115,000 acres for £3,517,000, while the free grants were so small as to be practically negligible. These figures contrast more than favourably with the statistics for the colony as a whole.
26. Reeves, *State Experiments*, Vol. I, pp. 233–7. Le Rossignol and Stewart, *State Socialism in New Zealand*, pp. 36–7.
27. Reeves, *State Experiments*, Vol. I, p. 214.
28. Cf. Hight and Bamford, *Constitutional History and Law of New Zealand*, pp. 292–300; also Morrell, *The Provincial System of Government in New Zealand* (unpublished).
29. Cf. Gisborne, *New Zealand*, pp. 171–2.
30. Drummond, *The Life and Work of Richard John Seddon*, Christchurch, 1906, Chaps. II–III.
31. Jourdain, pp. 91–7.
32. *Ibid.*, p. 27.
33. Reeves, *The Long White Cloud* (3rd edition), Chap. XX.
34. Jourdain, pp. 98–102.
35. To be distinguished from the lease-in-perpetuity introduced by John Mackenzie in 1892.
36. Jourdain, p. 28.
37. *Ibid.*, pp. 103–13.
38. *Ibid.*, p. 29.
39. *Ibid.*, p. 29.
40. For a description of the village settlement schemes see *Official Year Book*, 1894; also Reeves, *State Experiments*, Vol. I, pp. 312–16.
41. Jourdain, p. 30.
42. *Ibid.*, pp. 30 and 115–16.
43. *New Zealand Official Year Book*, 1928, p. 423.

44. *New Zealand Official Year Book*, 1892, Appendix.
45. *Ibid.*, 1928, p. 421.
46. *Ibid.*, 1892 (Appendix); and 1928, p. 420.
    In the year 1926–7, 11,276 acres were sold for cash, and 26,810 acres converted from various leaseholds into freehold tenure (*New Zealand Official Year Book*, 1928, p. 422).
47. Freehold land in 1927 totalled 22,165,582 acres; the corresponding figure in 1892 was 20,364,209 acres.

CHAPTER IV

1. The best description is given by McNab in *Murihiku* and *Old Whaling Days*. Carrick, *Historical Records of New Zealand South*, Dunedin, 1903, pp. 87–9 and 116–34, puts together scattered items concerning the early trade, some of them of considerable interest and value. The history of the American whaling industry has recently been written by E. H. Holman, *The American Whaleman*, New York, 1928. For the recent development of the Antarctic whaling industry based on South Georgia under Norwegian enterprise using mechanical inventions, see *New York Times*, November 4, 1928. For the importance of the sea industries in American Colonial development see Beard, *The Rise of American Civilisation*, New York, 1928, Vol. I, Chap. II.
2. McNab, *Historical Records of New Zealand*, Vol. I, p. 169. The official correspondence of the early governors of New South Wales abounds in references to the possibilities of New Zealand flax.
3. Carrick, *op. cit.*, pp. 75–81.
4. Scholefield, *New Zealand in Evolution*, London, 1909, Chap. V, contains a good account of the vicissitudes of the industry. The table below brings his figures up to date.

Decennial Periods.	Exports.	Value.
	Tons.	£
1858–67	411	10,401
1868–77	27,347	606,318
1878–87	12,600	219,965
1888–97	95,693	1,684,626
1898–1907	195,941	4,931,514
1908–17	210,577	5,776,028
1918–27	143,073	5,177,654

These statistics are for dressed fibre. In recent periods the production of tow adds about 10 per cent. to the value of the exports. In 1925–6 there were 71 works, employing 1,241 hands.

5. L. MacIntosh Ellis, *The Progress of Forestry in New Zealand*. Paper prepared for the Australian Association for the Advancement of Science, January 1923, p. 7.

This paper, by the head of the State Forest Service, together with other publications of the department, provides the most useful summary of the history and present position of forest policy. A full bibliography is given in the paper by the same author, prepared for the Imperial Forestry Conference held at Ottawa in 1923, entitled "Forests and Forestry in New Zealand". See also the annual reports of the department (C—3), especially the first, 1920, which lays down the forest policy to be adopted, and the fifth, 1925, which summarises the results of the first five years' working. Up-to-date statistics are contained in the sections of the *New Zealand Official Year Book* entitled "Forestry".

6. See scattered references in McNab, *Historical Records of New Zealand, passim.*
7. Carrick, *Historical Records of New Zealand South*, p. 83.
8. Ellis, *op. cit.*, p. 8.
9. *Ibid.*, p. 11.
10. See "Deer in New Zealand", Parliamentary Paper C—3A, 1922; and Thomson, *The Naturalisation of Animals and Plants in New Zealand*, pp. 40–51.
11. Ellis, *Forests and Forestry in New Zealand*, p. 24.
12. *New Zealand Official Year Book*, 1928, pp. 486–90.
13. A peculiar by-product of timber, the fossilised resin of former kauri forests in the Auckland Province, known as kauri gum, provides an export peculiar to New Zealand. The area upon which gum is found was estimated by a Royal Commission in 1898 as 814,000 acres, of which 724,000 were in the peninsula north of Auckland. The gum occurs in several layers, the richest deposits, like alluvial gold, being found nearest the surface. Export began in 1847, and despite frequent predictions of exhaustion has continued and expanded to the present time, as the following table will show.

EXPORT OF KAURI GUM, 1853–1926

Year.	Quantity.	Value.
	Tons.	£
1853	800	16,000
1863	1,400	27,000
1873	2,800	86,000
1883	6,500	337,000
1893	8,300	511,000
1903	9,400	631,000
1913	8,800	549,000
1923	6,600	596,000
1926	4,900	333,000

The total amount of gum exported to the end of 1926 was 399,299 tons, valued at £21,855,751.

The gum is used partly as a substitute for amber, but mainly as a basis for varnish, being peculiarly assimilable with oil. The chief markets are London and the United States, but as the outbreak of war proved in 1914, Germany was a large customer in these markets. State assistance had to be rendered to the industry in that year, and in 1925 an export control system was inaugurated. The actual digging of the gum is largely in the hands of Dalmatians and other Slavic immigrants, who form, however, a comparatively small community, which at greatest has numbered about fifteen hundred, and is readily absorbed by naturalisation.

See special article in *New Zealand Official Year Book*, 1900, summarising report of Royal Commission of 1898.

14. McNab, *From Tasman to Marsden*, Preface, p. xii. A contrary opinion is, however, expressed by Thomson, *The Naturalisation of Animals and Plants in New Zealand*, Cambridge, 1922, pp. 19, 33–9.
15. Carrick, *op. cit.*, p. 84. The effect on Maori economic life of the introduction of the pig and the potato was also considerable. Cf. Keesing, *The Changing Maori*, p. 41.
16. There is a good deal of evidence of agricultural ignorance and neglect on the part of some of the missionaries. See McNab, *Historical Records of New Zealand*, Vol. I, pp. 348, 520–1; and Saunders, *History of New Zealand*, Vol I, pp. 84–5. By 1830, however, most of these troubles were over, the sheep had increased to 180, 40 acres were in wheat, and the mill ground 48,000 lbs. of flour, some from wheat grown by distant natives (Saunders, Vol. I, p. 94).
17. Darwin, *A Naturalist's Voyage Round the World*, London, 1845.
18. The export of flour, never very considerable, reached 193 tons, valued at £4,000, in 1856; but was completely checked by the gold discoveries within New Zealand. It began to build up again in the late sixties, but was subject to great fluctuations. In 1883, the same year as the peak of wheat export, it reached 10,932 tons, valued at £120,000. Thereafter it declined, except for peaks in 1889 and 1897, due to special circumstances in the Australian market. The protective policy initiated in 1907, after federation, caused by the general acceptance of a high tariff, quickly killed the New Zealand export trade.
19. Vogel, *Handbook of New Zealand*, London, 1875, 2nd edition, p. 229.
20. Carrick, *op. cit.*, p. 75.
21. *Canterbury Old and New*, Christchurch, 1900, p. 25. For the early introduction of sheep and cattle, see Thomson, *op. cit.*, pp. 51–6. The introduction of merinos into Australia is described in Roberts, *History of Australian Land Settlement*, 1924, Chap. XIII.
22. *Ibid.*, p. 50. Also Scholefield, *Who's Who in New Zealand*, Wellington, 1924, p. 23.
23. E. J. Wakefield, *Handbook for New Zealand*, London, 1848.

    See also Southey, *The Rise, Progress, and Present State of Colonial Sheep and Wools to 1851*, London; and Alice, Lady Lovat, *The Life of Sir Frederick Weld*, London, 1914.
24. *Canterbury, Old and New*, p. 84. See also Roberts, *op. cit.*, p. 171.

25. Samuel Butler, *A First Year in the Canterbury Settlement*, London, 1863 (republished 1923). The author of *Erewhon* lived in New Zealand from 1859 to 1864, taking up a sheep station, "Mesopotamia", in the Rangitata Valley, South Canterbury. The opening chapters of *Erewhon*, which was built from articles originally contributed to the *Christchurch Press*, describe the gorge of the Rangitata. *A First Year in the Canterbury Settlement* was Butler's first published work.
26. Hocken, *Contributions to the Early History of New Zealand*, London, 1898, pp. 300 and 304.
27. The statistics are given in the *Official Year Book* for 1928, p. 412, as follows:

	Acres.
In grain and pulse crops	680,348
In grasses and clovers (for hay and seed), and green and root crops..	1,098,058
In fallow	124,003
In grasses and clovers not cut for hay or seed ..	16,680,348
In vineyards and orchards	25,686
In market-gardens, nurseries, and seed-gardens	5,566
In private gardens and pleasure grounds ..	64,783
In plantations	160,188
	18, 830,436

28. Saunders, *History of New Zealand*, Vol. I, p. 376.
29. The flocks of the Dominion are classified in the *New Zealand Official Year Book*, 1928, p. 461.

    For the extermination of a physical defect in sheep see Thomson, p. 54. Legislative measures which successfully stamped out the disease known as scab are detailed by the same author, p. 542.
30. See Holford, *The New Zealand Corriedale*, Auckland, 1925. Also article on "Cross-breeding" in *New Zealand Official Year Book*, 1894.
31. Thomson, *op. cit.*, traces the introduction of plants and animals, and also (Chap. XVI) legislation controlling pests, particularly noxious weeds such as thistles, blackberries, gorse, and orchard pests.
32. The proportion of the clip taken by the local woollen industry is shown in the following table.

Year.	Export.	Local Consumption.
	lbs.	lbs.
1883	68·1	0·8 (in 1881)
1893	119·6	2·6
1903	160·9	5·3
1913	193·4	6·8
1923	214·8	9·1
1927	219·8	6·3

33. For further detail, see Condliffe, "The External Trade of New Zealand", Appendix to *Official Year Book*, 1915.
34. Copland, *Wheat Production in New Zealand*, Christchurch, 1920.
35. Critchell and Raymond, *History of the Frozen Meat Industry*, London, 1912, Chap. I.
36. The efforts made by various sportsmen and acclimatisation societies to introduce rabbits are detailed in Thomson, *op. cit.*, pp. 84–96. The apparent failure to increase was probably due at first to wide scattering. About 1866 the increase first became noticeable. The ferrets, stoats, and weasels introduced to prey on the rabbits also became pests (*ibid.*, pp. 70–5). For the efforts made by the acclimatisation societies to introduce the house-sparrow, see p. 164 *seq.*
37. The idea dates back at least to the experiments made by Lord Bacon, which led to his death from a chill. See *Novum Organon*, Book II, Par. 50, Sec. 3.
38. Quoted Knowles, *The Industrial and Commercial Revolutions in Great Britain during the Nineteenth Century*, London, 1921, p. 199.
39. Critchell and Raymond, *op. cit.*, p. 12.
40. *Ibid.*, Chap. II.
41. *Ibid.*, pp. 39–45.
42. *Ibid.*, Chap. IV.
43. C. and M. Beard, *The Rise of American Civilisation*, Vol. II, p. 412.
44. Critchell and Raymond, *op. cit.*, Chap. IX. See also *New Zealand Official Year Book*, 1892, pp. 137–9.
45. *Ibid.*, Chap. X.

CHAPTER V

1. Siegfried, *Le Démocratie en Nouvelle Zélande*, Paris, 1904, translated, with an introduction by W. Downie Stewart, London, 1913, pp. 144–5 (French edition).
2. Cf. Blair, *The Industries of New Zealand*, address to the Industrial Association of Canterbury, Christchurch, 1887, p. 74.

   "The cheap production of corn in large quantities is not a permanent industry. It needs fresh fields at short intervals."
3. Knowles, *Industrial and Commercial Revolutions in Great Britain in the Nineteenth Century*, London, 1921, pp. 322–5.
4. Jenks, *The Migration of British Capital*, London, 1927, pp. 328–36.
5. Cf. Callaghan, *The Course of Land Values in Canterbury, 1870–1912* (unpublished). The index-numbers of land values recalculated by H. R. Rodwell in 1926 were:

1870	17	1877	58	1884	107
1871	25	1878	128	1885	92
1872	16	1879	75	1886	108
1873	25	1880	87	1887	79
1874	25	1881	103	1888	—
1875	45	1882	87	1889	103
1876	61	1883	99	1890	91

1891	89	1899	133	1907	161
1892	108	1900	127	1908	203
1893	101	1901	212	1909	176
1894	81	1902	133	1910	186
1895	85	1903	157	1911	206
1896	98	1904	144	1912	208
1897	87	1905	159	1913	202
1898	121	1906	167	1914	214

The course of land values in Canterbury from 1914–26 is analysed in *The Economic Record*, May 1927.

6. Reeves, *State Experiments in Australia and New Zealand*, Vol. I, pp. 270–1. It is noteworthy that the area of new land taken up fell steadily between 1881–90 (*Statistics of New Zealand*, 1890, p. 129).
7. Vogel, *Handbook of New Zealand*, Introduction, pp. 13–14. A general survey of development before 1870 is contained in Hamilton, "On the Economic Progress of New Zealand", *Statistical Journal*, 1869, pp. 293–307.
8. *Ibid.*, p. 137.
9. Northcott, *Australian Social Development*, New York, 1918, p. 54.
10. Cf. historical introduction to the winning essay on the mining industry, at the Christchurch Exhibition of 1906, reprinted in *Three Prize Essays on the Mineral Resources of New Zealand*, Wellington, 1907, pp. 4–11.
11. *Official Catalogue of the New Zealand International Exhibition*, Christchurch, 1882, pp. xxi–xxii.
12. Blair, *op. cit.*, p. 6.
13. Stout, *Notes on the Progress of New Zealand, 1864–1884*, Wellington, 1886, pp. 27–31, and Diagrams XXI (reprinted from *Statistical Journal*, London, Vol. XLIX).
14. *Report on the Statistics of New Zealand*, 1890, pp. 149–50.
15. Cf. also a pamphlet by Fellows, *The Finances of New Zealand*, Dunedin, 1872, and a vitriolic attack on Vogel by W. L. Rees in a pamphlet entitled *The Coming Crisis*, Auckland, 1874. Bull, *Public Works in New Zealand from 1870 to 1877*, Christchurch, 1877, gives a competent criticism by a civil engineer of the faulty methods of construction followed in many works.
16. Published in London in 1886 without publisher's imprint; but officially catalogued along with other works by Carter among the publications of the New Zealand Institute.
17. Summarised from the official *Report on the Statistics of New Zealand*, 1890. The footnote refers to the expedient adopted by the Stout-Vogel Ministry in 1884 to avoid raising the necessary increments to the sinking funds by taxation, an expedient which is the primary cause of the weak condition of the sinking funds at the present day.
18. *Ibid.*, p. 34. See also Drummond, *Life and Work of Richard John Seddon*, Christchurch, 1906, pp. 92–3.
19. For a detailed account of the acute financial situation at the moment of crisis in 1880 and of the cables that passed between the Premier and

Vogel, then Agent-General in London, see Bateman, *The Colonist*, Christchurch, 1881, pp. 95–9.

20. *Ibid.*, pp. 230–8. Also Saunders, *History of New Zealand*, Vol. II, pp. 428–30. Saunders was chairman of the Civil Service Commission.
21. Cf. H. D. Bedford, *History of Banking in New Zealand* (unpublished). Also Teare, *Australian Banking, Currency, and Exchange*, Chap. XVII; and *A Digest of Australian and New Zealand Banking and Currecny Legislation*, Sydney, 1926.
22. Banking statistics for this period are inadequate. The figures quoted represent the average of the returns of deposits and assets furnished by the banks at the close of each quarter of the year, and published in the *Official Year Books* and statistical volumes.
23. This situation is discussed more fully below, Chapter X.
24. For similar developments in the post-war boom, see Condliffe and Belshaw, "A Brief Survey of Rural Credit," *New Zealand Journal of Science and Technology*, Vol. VII, No. 6, pp. 334–52 (1925).

    Larksworthy, *Ninety-one Years*, London, 1924, pp. 351–411, recounts the involved quarrel between the author and the directors of the Bank of New Zealand, and throws light on the extension of credit through subsidiary companies.
25. For much of the information concerning labour problems in this section the author is indebted to Mr. J. D. Salmond, of the University of Otago, who placed at his disposal materials collected for a history of trade unionism in New Zealand.
26. Appendix to *Journals House of Representatives*, H. 5, 1890.

    See also Drummond, *Life and Work of Richard John Seddon*, pp. 103–5; and Reeves, *State Experiments in Australia and New Zealand*, Vol. II, pp. 27–32.
27. Reeves, *State Experiments*, Vol. II, pp. 37–8. See also Drummond, pp. 224–37.
28. For the establishment of the principle of the eight-hour day, see Drummond, pp. 229–32; and Parsons, *The Story of New Zealand*, Chap. 54.
29. Paul, *Trade Unionism in Otago, 1881–1912*, Dunedin, 1912.
30. *A Bone to Pick for Freetraders: A Dialogue*. Reprinted by the Colonists' Protection League Society, Auckland, 1872.
31. "Protection of Native Industries". A paper read before the Colonists' Protection League Society, Auckland, 1873.
32. E.g. Cawkwell, *Local Industry and the New Zealand Government*, Auckland, 1874.
33. Report of the Colonial Industries Commission, R 22, 1881. See also a scathing review of the protectionist claims before the Commission in Bateman, *The Colonist*, Chap. XII.
34. Otago *Daily Times*, Dunedin, June 30 and August 4, 1877. Lyttelton *Times*, Christchurch, August 17, 1877.
35. Drummond, *op. cit.*, pp. 93–100.
36. Reeves's phrase, quoted by Siegfried, p. 98.
37. Cf. Reeves, *State Experiments*, Vol. I, Chap. I.

38. Cf. Beer, *History of British Socialism*, Vol. II, Chap. XII.
39. "Pharos" (W. P. Reeves). "Some Historical Articles on Communism and Socialism: Their dreams, their experiments, their aims, their influence." Reprinted from the Lyttelton *Times*, Christchurch, 1890.
40. Cf. *Letters of John Stuart Mill*, edited by Hugh Elliott, 2 vols., London, 1910.
41. He did, however, characterise the graduated land taxation of certain Australian States as "a mild form of robbery".
42. Gisborne, *New Zealand Rulers and Statesmen, 1840–1897*, London, 1897, pp. 239–40.

    "The dominant principle to be preserved is that the State should not interfere with individual liberty, unless the circumstances of the case call for such interference for the general good of the whole community; and care should be taken not to interfere with the freedom of the citizen unless when it is injurious to the State, or to society, or unless an enlightened majority, after due deliberation, is of opinion that such restraint is for the general permanent advantage."
43. Siegfried, *op. cit.*, p. 290 *seq.*
44. John Stuart Mill, *Autobiography*, Chap. VII.
45. Siegfried, *op. cit.*, Part II.
46. *Ibid.*, pp. 61–2.
47. Stout, *Leasing State Lands*, Dunedin, 1875.

CHAPTER VI

1. Reeves, *The Long White Cloud*, Chaps. XX–XXV (3rd edition), gives by far the best general account of the aims and achievements of the Liberal-Labour Party. With these chapters may be compared: Drummond, *The Life and Work of Richard John Seddon*, Chaps. IX–XX; Siegfried, *Democracy in New Zealand*, Chaps. V–XVIII; Parsons, *The Story of New Zealand*, Philadelphia, 1904, Chaps. XXXV–LXXIII.
2. Cf., e.g., Parsons, *The Story of New Zealand*, Chap. LXXVI; C. E. Russell, *The Uprising of the Many*, London, 1907, Chaps. XXVIII–XXXVI; H. Demarest Lloyd, *Newest England*, New York, 1901.
3. Drummond, *op. cit.*, p. 133.
4. *Ibid.*, Chap. VI.
5. Cf. the very careful and illuminating character portraits in Reeves, *The Long White Cloud, passim.*
6. Reeves, *State Experiments in Australia and New Zealand*, Vol. I, Chap. II.
7. W. T. Charlewood, "Labour Troubles in New Zealand", *Economic Journal*, Vol. I, No. 1, December 1891.
8. The constitution of 1852 provided a property qualification for electors, an Act of 1879 created a residential qualification irrespective of property; but did not abolish the property qualification. The Act of 1889 established the principle of "one man, one vote", but the property qualification was not abolished till 1896. The "country quota" is still in force (1928).

9. W. Sidney Smith, *The Women's Franchise Movement in New Zealand*, Christchurch, 1905.
10. Reeves, *State Experiments*, Vol. I, Chap. III; and Vol. II, Chap. III.
11. Drummond, *op. cit.*, pp. 134–7.
12. *Ibid.*, p. 133.
13. *Ibid.*, Chap. XI. Keith, *Responsible Government in the Dominions*, Vol. I, pp. 456–60.
14. *New Zealand Official Year Book*, 1893, pp. 419–24. See also Cd. 3191 (1906) and 4750 (1909).
15. *New Zealand Official Year Book*, 1893, pp. 425–6.
16. Parsons, *The Story of New Zealand*, p. 203.
17. Cf. Young, *The Single-tax Movement in the United States*, Princeton, 1916, p. 157.
18. *New Zealand Official Year Book*, 1895, pp. 264–7. Also *The Cheviot Estate: Particulars, Terms, and Conditions of Disposal and Occupation*, Wellington, 1893.
19. Le Rossignol and Stewart, *State Socialism in New Zealand*, pp. 117–37.
20. Jourdain, *op. cit.*, pp. 115–16.

    There were amendments to the Lands Act in 1893, 1895, and to the Lands for Settlements Act in 1895, 1896, 1897, 1899. The latter was consolidated in 1900.
21. P. 201 *seq.* This article is repeated in subsequent issues.
22. *New Zealand Official Year Book*, 1892 and 1903.
23. The village-homestead legislation passed by Ballance in 1885 also contained compulsory provisions.
24. Jourdain, *loc. cit.*
25. Le Rossignol and Stewart, *op. cit.*, p. 45.
26. Reeves, *State Experiments in Australia and New Zealand*, Vol. I, pp. 359–86.
27. *Ibid.*, Vol. I, Chap. I. Also *The Long White Cloud*, pp. 290–2 and 314–23.
28. *The Labour Laws of New Zealand* (latest edition), 1925. Also *New Zealand Official Year Book*, 1929, pp. 823–36.
29. Reeves, *The Long White Cloud*, pp. 282–3.
30. The best description of this system is contained in a special article written for the *New Zealand Official Year Book*, 1894 (pp. 234–42), by H. J. H. Blow, Under-Secretary for Public Works.
31. The history of this line is contained in two pamphlets of considerable interest, *East and West Coast and Nelson Railway*, compiled and published by the Executive Committee of the Railway League, Christchurch, 1886; and *East and West: the Story of the Midland Railway*, published by the Canterbury Progress League, Christchurch, 1923. The case of the company against the Government is contained in *Report to the Shareholders: A Brief Account of the New Zealand Midland Railway, 1885 to 1895*, London, 1896.
32. Wyoming (in 1869).
33. Parsons, *The Story of New Zealand*, pp. 274 fn.
34. Cf., e.g., Siegfried, *Democracy in New Zealand*, pp. 284–8; and Bryce, *Modern Democracies*, London, 1921, Vol. II, p. 308. "Woman suffrage

has—so I am everywhere told—made no practical difference to politics, and has not led to the introduction of legislation intended specially to benefit women."

35. *The Long White Cloud*, p. 314.
36. *The White Ribbon*, organ of the W.C.T.U., claimed (February 1903) the following measures as partly due to the first ten years of woman suffrage:

"A law making the conditions of divorce equal for both sexes; a Testator's Family Maintenance Act, by which the economic rights of wife and family are protected; an Infant Life Protection Act (to prevent baby-farming); an Act which admits women to the profession of law; amendments in the Industrial Schools Act; Slander of Women Act; an Act to provide Legal Separation without expense; an Act to regulate the adoption of children; an Act to bring Servants' Registry Offices under regulation; amendments made in the Municipal Act, giving wives a vote in virtue of the qualifications held by their husbands; Technical Schools established; an Act granting Old Age Pensions to both sexes; amendments to Factory Acts which give girl apprentices better wages, and by which the health and interests of shop-girls are safeguarded; an Act to raise the Age of Protection (consent)."

CHAPTER VII

1. The statistical estimates quoted in this section are taken from the 1928 and preceding issues of the *New Zealand Official Year Book*.
2. "Agriculture in New Zealand", by M. Murphy, *New Zealand Official Year Book*, 1894.
3. *New Zealand Official Year Book*, 1928, p. 97.
4. *Ibid.*, p. 468.
5. The technical aspects of these changes were discussed by Mr. A. H. Cockayne in his presidential address to the Agricultural Science Section of the New Zealand Association for the Advancement of Science (Dunedin, January 1926).
6. Statistics in *New Zealand Official Year Books*.
7. See, however, the studies of dairy-farm organisation by E. J. Fawcett, Economist to the Department of Agriculture.
8. Following a report by Sir Frank Heath on "The Organisation of Scientific and Industrial Research in New Zealand" (I—H 27), 1926, a Department of Scientific and Industrial Research was created which has already done valuable work.
9. *Trade Statistics of New Zealand, passim.* Many important products, such as sheep-skins, pelts, and hides, have been omitted from the table for the sake of simplicity.
10. Belshaw, *History and Economics of the Dairy Industry in New Zealand* (unpublished). Also "The Dairying Industry of New Zealand", *Economic Geography*, Vol. III, No. 3, July 1927.
11. Russell and Macklin, *Intensive Dairying in New Zealand and Wisconsin*,

Bulletin 377, Agricultural Experiment Station, University of Wisconsin, May 1925.

12. Hall, "The Co-operative Movement in New Zealand Agriculture", *International Review of Agricultural Economics*, November 1916.
13. Russell and Macklin, *op. cit.*
14. Jourdain, *History of Land Legislation and Settlement in New Zealand*, p. 202.
15. The best statistical measurements of prices are the Government Statistician's index-numbers, *Official Year Book*, 1928, pp. 762–84. Earlier calculations are given in McIlraith's, *The Course of Prices in New Zealand*, Wellington, 1911; and *Royal Commission on the Cost of Living*, H—18, 1912.
16. Cf. Shanahan, *Animal Food-stuffs: Their Production and Consumption*, London.
17. See also Canterbury Chamber of Commerce Bulletin, No. 22, November 1926.
18. *New Zealand Official Year Book*, 1928, p. 895.
19. Summarised from official statistics of industrial production.
20. *New Zealand Official Year Book*, 1928, pp. 341–4.
21. Wickens, "Australian Population: Its Nature and Growth", *Economic Record*, Vol. I, No. 1, November 1925. Also diagram in *New Zealand Official Year Book*, 1928, p. 77.
22. *New Zealand Official Year Book*, 1928, p. 894.
23. *Ibid.*, p. 895.
24. Authoritative theoretical support for this conclusion is contained in Professor Allyn A. Young's presidential address to the Economics Section of the British Association for the Advancement of Science, reprinted under the title "Increasing Returns and Economic Progress", *Economic Journal*, December 1928.
25. *New Zealand Official Year Book*, 1929, p. 80.

CHAPTER VIII

1. *New Zealand Official Year Book*, 1928, p. 421.
2. W. Downie Stewart, "Land Tenure and Land Monopoly in New Zea land", *Journal of Political Economy*, Vol. XVII, Nos. 2 and 3, February and March 1909. Also Chap. II in Le Rossignol and Stewart's *State Socialism in New Zealand*.
3. Jourdain, *History of Land Legislation*, pp. 38–9. Also *Report of Royal Commission*, C—4, 1905.
4. Stewart, *op. cit.*, pp. 44–5.
5. Jourdain, *op. cit.*, pp. 39–41 and 142–3.
6. Stewart, *op. cit.*, p. 28.
7. *New Zealand Official Year Book*, 1928, p. 421.
8. Jourdain, *op. cit.*, pp. 39–40.
9. *New Zealand Official Year Book*, 1928, p. 421.
10. Jourdain, *op. cit.*, pp. 146–7.
11. *New Zealand Official Year Book*, 1928, p. 421.

12. *New Zealand Official Year Book*, p. 424; Jourdain, *op. cit.*, pp. 147–9; and *New Zealand Official Year Book*, 1915, pp. 510–13.
13. Jourdain, *op. cit.*, pp. 41–2, 155–7.
14. Details of this legislation may be found in successive editions of the *Year Book*, and are summarised up to 1924 in Jourdain, *op. cit.*, pp. 155–89. The main steps taken were:

"The owners of leases-in-perpetuity of ordinary Crown lands were permitted to purchase the freehold by paying therefor the original capital value of the land, together with the difference between the rent of 4 per cent. that they had been paying from the date of selection, and 5 per cent. which was the rate fixed for the rent of land acquired under the occupation with right-of-purchase tenure. Renewable lessees of settlement land could obtain the fee-simple by paying the original capital value plus the present value of the difference between the original and present capital values, less value of improvements (1912). Licensees of pastoral lands in the Hauraki Mining District, holders of leases of small grazing-runs taken up under the Lands for Settlements Act, holders of leases of small grazing-runs selected under the Land Act, 1885, as well as holders of small grazing-runs taken up under the Lands for Settlement Act, holders of leases-in-perpetuity of settlement lands, holders of renewable leases in several townships, owners of perpetual leases under the Land Act, 1885 (in cases where their leases gave no former right of purchase), together with lessees of Native land, the freehold of which had subsequently been acquired by the Crown from the Native owners (1913). Licensees of pastoral runs who were allowed to purchase the fee-simple of one of the subdivisions of their runs in cases where such runs were subdivided on expiry of the original license, and holders of renewable leases in other townships (1914); lessees or licensees under the Mining Districts Land Occupation Act, or corresponding provisions of the Land Act, 1908, as well as licensees of pastoral lands in the Westland and Karamea Mining Districts (by legislation in 1915); licensees selecting land under the Waste Lands Development system (in 1919); lessees of national-endowment land disposed of under the Discharged Soldiers Settlement Act; lessees of national-endowment land disposed of under the endowment land disposed of under the Land Acts, 1892 or 1908; unoccupied national-endowment land up to the aggregate of 20,000 acres; lessees of business and residence sites in Te Aroha Township; lessees of Crown land in Rotorua Township, and holders of renewable leases of lands set apart under the Hauraki Plains Act, 1908 (in 1920); lessees of lands acquired by the Crown in Native townships (in 1921); licensees of pastoral runs containing areas not greater than are sufficient for the maintenance of themselves and families, and owners of renewable leases of small lots in Horopito Township (in 1921–2); lessees of national-endowment land within the Hauraki Mining District, and small grazing-run lessees were permitted to acquire the freehold of runs in excess of the prescribed limit of area, provided that such excess area was not suitable for a separate holding (in 1922)" (Jourdain, pp. 41–2).

See also Land Laws Amendment Act, 1926, extending the right of purchase to lessees of national-endowment lands.

15. Jourdain, *op. cit.*, pp. 42–3.
16. Cf. W. D. Hunt, *Land Tenure in New Zealand*, Dunedin, 1917.
17. *Ibid.*, p. 6.
18. *Report of Southern Pastoral Lands Commission*, C—15, 1920. For the legislation, see Jourdain, *op. cit.*, pp. 163–5.
19. Summarised from *New Zealand Official Year Books*, 1913, pp. 505–6, and 1928, p. 421.
20. Jourdain, *op. cit.*, p. 27.
21. *New Zealand Official Year Books*, 1926, 1927, and 1928. Fuller details are given in the successive Blue books, *Agricultural and Pastoral Statistics of New Zealand*.
22. Calculated from *New Zealand Official Year Books*, 1897, 1913, and 1928.
23. *Ibid.*, 1913, pp. 495–9; 1928, pp. 422–4.
24. *Ibid.*, pp. 424–6. Also annual reports on Discharged Soldiers Settlement by the Department of Lands and Survey, 1—C 9.
25. Le Rossignol and Stewart, *State Socialism in New Zealand*, p. 45. An excellent historical summary is given by Scheftel, *The Taxation of Land Values*, New York, 1916. See also a sound estimate by Reeves, *Land Taxes and Rates and the Valuation of Land in New Zealand*, pp. 67–79, Cd. 4750 (1909). Pages 134–56, reprinting official documents, including the taxing Acts then in force, are identical with pp. 24–47 of Cd. 3191 (1906).
26. The present system of land and income taxation is lucidly summarised in the *New Zealand Official Year Book*, 1928, pp. 583–5. Statistics of land valuation are given in pp. 659–66, and illuminating details of income and landownership, as disclosed by the tax returns, in pp. 738–47 and pp. 749–61. The author has also been able to use an unpublished thesis by H. L. Wise, M. Com., on "Income Taxation in New Zealand". The principal alteration in the land-tax system before 1917 was in the mortgage tax. Originally a mortgage was liable to tax at the same rate as the land on which it was secured, but in 1902 the rate was reduced to ¾d. in the £. In 1915 this was increased to 1d as a war measure. In the following year land-tax was abolished on mortgages, the receipts from which became subject to income-tax.

    For the gradual reduction of exemption on account of mortgages, see *New Zealand Official Year Book*, 1928, p. 584.
27. The maximum rate of income-tax at this time was 8s. 9⅜d. in the £. Calculating returns from the land at 7½ per cent., the land-tax was approximately equal to the maximum rate of income-tax at 44 per cent. of the annual income. If super-tax is added, plus the income-tax to which farmers were then liable, the total would be more than the annual income. Actually this was far from the case, because of the disparity between land values as reflecting market prices and the official valuations.

    In the valuable comparative tables prepared by the Tax Department for the 1924 Commission (pp. 12–15) income-tax was shown to be heavier than land-tax if the return on capital invested was taken at 5 per cent. or less; but the reverse was true if it was calculated at 7½ per cent. or more. The calculations, moreover, do not allow for any lag in valuations. The tables submitted by the Sheep-owners' Federation (pp. 116–17) to show the contrary result are invalidated because they make no allowance in comparing the investment either for the valuation lag or for the fact that some of the investment was represented by untaxed improvements. Moreover, the rate of return was taken throughout at 5 per cent.

28. Official estimate by Dr. (Sir) John Findlay, quoted in Le Rossignol and Stewart's *State Socialism in New Zealand*, p. 131. Cf. Scheftel, *op. cit.*, Chap. III. Rodwell, "The Course of Rural Land Values in New Zealand, 1914–1925" (*Economic Record*, May 1927), gives the following table of land values, prices, and farm production:

Year.	A. Land Values.	B.* Wholesale Prices.	C.† Volume of Production.
1914	100	100	100
1915	111	129	113
1916	113	132	112
1917	115	140	100
1918	115	148	101
1919	133	152	106
1920	160	158	108
1921	143	121	110
1922	135	104	121
1923	114	121	110
1924	108	134	102
1925	141	135	115

* Index-number compiled from the index-numbers of wholesale prices of farm products published in the *New Zealand Monthly Abstract of Statistics* for July 1926, p. 45.

† Compiled from the total amount of production of each of the items included in Column B, published in the *New Zealand Official Year Books* under the heading "Agricultural and Pastoral Productions".

Cf. also *Report of British Oversea Settlement Delegation to New Zealand* (Cd. 2167), 1923, p. 19, giving examples of the prices at which typical farm lands changed hands, ranging up to £205 per acre.

The best official description of the methods of valuation is by G. F. C. Campbell, *An Explanatory Memorandum on Valuation*, pp. 146–56, Cd. 4750 (1909).

29. For the practical effects of this system, see a pamphlet entitled *The Excessive Income-Tax Charged to Large Companies in New Zealand and its Effects* (issued by several farm, stock, and station companies, 1921); also *Taxation: Readjustment and Reduction: National Needs* (Taxpayers'

Federation, 1924). The most thorough analysis of the system is contained in the *Report of the Royal Commission on Land and Income Taxation* (1—B 5), 1924. See also *Report of the Committee on Taxation*, 1922; and *Round Table*, September 1922, p. 929, and March 1923, pp. 448–50.
30. Report, *op. cit.*, p. 4.
31. Cf. also Belshaw, "The Economic Position of the Farmer in New Zealand", *Economic Record*, May 1928.
32. Summarised from *New Zealand Official Year Book*, 1928, pp. 738–47.
33. *Ibid.*, pp. 645–6; also *New Zealand Local Authorities Handbook* 19, pp. 118–21. Cf. Scheftel, *op. cit.*, pp. 50–2 and 106–20.
34. The number of freeholders holding 10,000 acres and upwards was: 1883, 259; 1889, 250; 1892, 262; 1902, 216; 1906, 204, 1910, 171. See evidence of Commissioner of Taxes, *Report of Royal Commission*, 1924, *op. cit.*, p. 32. No statistical return of freeholders since 1910 is available.
35. Canterbury Chamber of Commerce Bulletins, Nos. 36–7, January and February 1928.
36. Scheftel, *op. cit.*, pp. 420–1.
37. See special article by G. B. Davy, Registrar-General of Land, in *New Zealand Official Year Book*, 1894, pp. 213–30; also *New Zealand Official Year Book*, 1928, pp. 412–16.
38. This correlation is illustrated diagrammatically in Copland, *Wheat Production in New Zealand*.
39. Henry Ford, *My Life and Work*, New York, 1923, p. 144.
40. Cf. Scheftel, *op. cit.*, pp. 368–87.
41. A penalty of 50 per cent. was added to the land-tax in the case of such land in 1924–5 (*Evidence of Commissioner of Taxes before Royal Commission*, pp. 33–6).
42. Belshaw, "The Economic Position of the Farmer in New Zealand", *op. cit.* Cf. also criticisms of this estimate and Professor Belshaw's defence, *Report of the National Industrial Conference*, 1928.
43. Condliffe and Belshaw, "A Brief Survey of Rural Credit", *New Zealand Journal of Science and Technology*, Vol. VII, No. 6, pp. 334–52, 1925.
44. Cf. evidence of Commissioner of Taxes, *Report*, *op. cit.*, pp. 32–3; also evidence of Sir John Findlay, pp. 214–15.
45. *New Zealand Official Year Book*, 1928, p. 426.
46. *Ibid.*, pp. 718–25.
47. *Ibid.*, 1925, p. 582; 1928, p. 615.
48. *Report of Royal Commission*, 1924, *op. cit.*, pp. 22–4.
49. Cf. Condliffe and Belshaw, *op. cit.*
50. *New Zealand Official Year Book*, 1924, p. 711. See also legislation protecting the existing credit commitments embodied in the Mortgages and Deposit Extension Act, 1921, and amendments (*New Zealand Official Year Book*, 1923, pp. 638–9).
51. *Report of the Royal Commission on Rural Credits*, I—B 5, 1926.
52. *New Zealand Official Year Book*, 1927, p. 953, and 1928, pp. 618–19.

53. *New Zealand Official Year Book*, 1927, pp. 953–4. Cf. also the most recent summary of these measures by T. D. Hall, "A Brief Review of Rural Credit Facilities in New Zealand", *Economic Record*, November 1928.
54. The only direct extension of State aid to industry in recent years was by the Fishing Industry Promotion Act, 1919 (*New Zealand Official Year Book*, 1921–2, p. 562; 1929, p. 649).
55. The operations of the Department of Imperial Supplies are described by Lawson, *Foodships for Britain*, Wellington, 1918. A summary of essential information is contained in the *Official Year Book*, 1917, pp. 714–17; 1918, pp. 412–37; 1919, pp. 447–54; 1920, pp. 16–59; 1923, pp. 304–8.
56. *New Zealand Official Year Book*, 1919, p. 450; 1920, p. 167.
57. Cf. Dyason, "Bawra", supplement to *Economic Record*, February 1928, pp. 51–67.
58. *New Zealand Official Year Book*, 1923, pp. 644–5. The general aspects of export control are canvassed in *Round Table*, September 1926, pp. 877–8.
59. *Round Table*, December 1921, pp. 224–6.
60. *New Zealand Official Year Book*, 1928, p. 471 *seq*. See also R. M. Campbell, "Export Control Boards in the Produce Trades", *Manchester Guardian Commercial*, February 9, 1928.
61. *New Zealand Official Year Book*, 1926, p. 851; and 1927, p. 941.
62. Rodwell, "The Wheat Tariff of 1927", paper read to the Economic Society of Australia and New Zealand, Auckland Branch, 1928.

CHAPTER IX

1. The primary source of information in regard to public works is the annual Public Works Statement (D—1). This is supplemented by the annual Railways Statement (D—2). A special report (D—2A) of the session 1924 gives the "Programme of Railway Improvements and New Works". The report of the latest Royal Commission, "Enquiry into the Railway Service" (1924), was also printed as a separate paper (D—2A) for the session 1925. The evidence appended to this report contains detailed technical information from prominent railway and public works officials, including a valuable series of statements by the Engineer-in-Chief of the Public Works Department.

   For the graph of public works expenditure the author is indebted to the Rt. Hon. J. G. Coates, formerly Prime Minister, and Minister of Public Works.
2. "For the north island it is proposed to develop the power at three main stations—viz. Mangahao (24,000 h.p.), Lake Waikaremoana (40,000 h.p., capable of extension to 130,000 h.p.), and the Arapuni Rapids on the Waikato River (96,000 h.p., capable of extension to 160,000 h.p.). These three power-stations are to be ultimately interconnected by a complete system of 110,000-volt lines for a total length of 1,112 miles, with

309 miles of branch mains at 50,000 and 33,000 volts." (*New Zealand Official Year Book*, 1928, p. 862). A similar scheme for the south island, developing 110,000 h.p., is based upon the three existing stations at Lake Monowai (16,000 h.p.), Waipori Falls (25,000 h.p.), and Lake Coleridge (36,000 h.p.). Preliminary surveys have been made also of supplementary schemes. The total water-power available for development in New Zealand is estimated on a 50 per cent. load factor as 776,080 h.p. (582,650 kw.) in the north island and 4,110,950 h.p. (3,074,430 kw.) in the south island. (*New Zealand Official Year Book*, 1928, pp. 862–84.)

3. *New Zealand Official Year Book*, 1984, pp. 386-9; 1896, pp. 381. See also Le Rossignol and Stewart, *State Socialism in New Zealand*, pp. 62–3, and Scholefield, *New Zealand in Evolution*, pp. 268–80.
4. *New Zealand Official Year Book*, 1895, pp. 381–4; Le Rossignol and Stewart, *op. cit.*, pp. 61–2; and Scholefield, *op. cit.*, p. 263.
5. Full statistics are given in the official *Local Authorities Handbook*, Wellington, 1926. See also *New Zealand Official Year Book*, 1928, pp. 643–58.
6. *Report of Railway Commission*, 1924, p. 169.
7. Cf. references in Chap. VI, Note 31 above.
8. A handy summary is contained in *New Zealand Official Year Book*, 1928, pp. 576–80.
9. *Ibid.*, p. 595.
10. *Ibid.*, pp. 652 and 869. The composition of this sum is roughly as follows:

	£ (millions).
General Purposes Account, Public Works Department ..	101·1
Land Settlement and Forests	25·5
Advances to Settlers	19·3
Hydro-electric works	8·9
Local Body Assets	53·6
	£208·4

11. *New Zealand Official Year Book*, 1913, p. 787.
12. *Ibid.*, pp. 789–90.
13. It is also significant that the table showing railway lines authorised for which money was never voted should show south island lines authorised in 1911 as the first lines to lapse after those of 1879 previously noted (*Report of 1924 Railway Commission*, p. 169).
14. Compiled from *New Zealand Official Year Books.*
15. For the mechanism of these transferences, see Tocker, "The Monetary Standards of Australia and New Zealand", *Economic Journal*, December 1924; also "The Measurement of Business Conditions in New Zealand", *Economic Record*, Vol. I, No. 1; and Canterbury Chamber of Commerce Bulletins on "The Trend of Business" (quarterly).
16. Calculated from *New Zealand Official Year Books*. The details of expenditure from the Consolidated Fund Surpluses are given in the *Year Book*, 1928, as follows:

Year ending March 31st.	£ (millions).
1921	15·0
1922	0·9
1923	3·1
1924	2·6
1925	2·5
1926	1·1
	25·1

17. Calculated as follows:

Year.	Total. Expenditure.	Population.	Prices.	Index.
	£ (millions).	Thousands.		
1914	27·0	114	110	100
1920	75·0	124	178	158
1927	64·0	144	162	127

18. Financial Statement (2—B 6), 1928, p. 9.
19. *New Zealand Official Year Book*, 1911, p. 701.
20. *New Zealand Official Year Book*, 1928, pp. 628–32.
21. *Ibid.*, pp. 689–95.
22. There has been more discussion of Australian than New Zealand overseas borrowing. See, e.g., Cooke and Davenport, *Australian Finance*, London, 1926; Rt. Hon. S. M. Bruce, *The Financial and Economic Position of Australia*, Adelaide, 1927; and E. C. Dyason, "The Australian Public Debt", *Economic Record*, November 1927. Also Mills, Portus, and Campbell, *Studies in Australian Affairs*, Melbourne, 1928, Chap. V. on "Australian Loan Policy", by R. C. Mills.
23. Canterbury Chamber of Commerce Bulletins, No. 36, January 1928.
24. *Report of Royal Commission*, 1924, p. 228.
25. *New Zealand Official Year Book*, 1928, pp. 369–74.
26. *Ibid.*, pp. 862–84.
27. *Ibid.*, pp. 893–5.
28. The pertinent statistics are summarised below:

RAILWAY STATISTICS ILLUSTRATING PRODUCTIVITY, 1890–1 TO 1925–6

Year.	Train Mileage.	Passengers.	Goods Tonnage.	Population.	Tonnage per Head.
	Millions.	Millions.	Millions.	Thousands.	
1890–1	2·9	3·4	2·1	667	3·1
1895–6	3·3	4·2	2·2	754	2·9
1900–1	4·6	6·2	3·5	808	4·3
1905–6	6·4	8·8	4·4	926	4·8
1910–11	8·1	11·2	5·9	1,050	5·6
1915–16	9·4	14·2	6·4	1,153	5·5
1920–1	9·3	15·3	6·5	1,258	5·2
1925–6	10·3	11·8	7·3	1,401	5·2

29. Stamp, *On Stimulus in the Economic Life*, Cambridge, 1927.
30. Wise, *The Income Tax in New Zealand* (unpublished M. Commerce thesis).
31. Dyason, *op. cit.*, *Economic Record*, November 1927, p. 174.
32. *Financial Times*' Banking Supplement, March 25, 1929, p. 17.

CHAPTER X

1. *New Zealand Official Year Book*, 1928, p. 893.
2. *Ibid.*, also 1915, pp. 833–9.
3. Cf. Keynes, *The End of Laisser-Faire*, London, 1926.
4. Parsons, *The Story of New Zealand*, p. 115.
5. J. W. Dowling, *The Public Trust Office of New Zealand* (unpublished), Christchurch, 1924. Cf. also annual reports of the Public Trustee.
6. Cf. *Report of Royal Commission on University Education in New Zealand* (E—7A), 1925, pp. 11–20.
7. Le Rossignol and Stewart, *State Socialism in New Zealand*, Chap. XII.
8. *Ibid.*, pp. 167–70.
9. *Ibid.*, Chap. IX; *New Zealand Official Year Book*, 1928, pp. 690–3.
10. *Ibid.*, Chap. X; and *New Zealand Official Year Book*, 1928, pp. 708–9.
11. Cf information slips issued by the New Zealand Labour Party Information Bureau, August and September 1928, compiled from the official report on Insurance Statistics, 1926. Summaries of the main statistics are given in the *New Zealand Official Year Book*, 1928, *op. cit.* See also annual reports of Government Insurance Commissioner and the General Manager of the State Fire Insurance Office, I—6, 6A, 8 and 8A.
12. *New Zealand Official Year Books*, 1902, *et seq.*, also annual reports on State Coal Mines (C—2A).
13. *New Zealand Official Year Book*, 1928, pp. 505–8.
14. *Ibid.*, pp. 193–201.
15. Canterbury Chamber of Commerce Bulletin, No. 16, May 1926.
16. J. W. Jenks, *The Trust Problem*, New York, 1919, pp. 465–9.
17. *Report of Royal Commission on Cost of Living*, 1912 (H—18).
18. *New Zealand Official Year Book*, 1916, pp. 362–3. See also annual reports of the Department of Industries and Commerce (H—44). The general aspects of the Board of Trade's work are discussed in Condliffe, "New Zealand during the War", *Economic Journal*, June, 1919; Findlay, "Industrial Peace in New Zealand", *International Labour Review*, October 1921; and Condliffe, "Experiments in State Control in New Zealand", *ibid.*, March 1924.
19. Cf. the different course of land values in New Zealand and the United States as disclosed in Rodwell, "The Course of Rural Land Values in New Zealand, 1914–25", *Economic Record*, May 1927.
20. Cf. *Round Table*, December 1924, p. 212.
21. Cf. argument and evidence printed in the Case on Appeal to the Supreme Court, Christchurch, 1920.
22. Cf. Findlay, *op. cit.*, and Condliffe, *op. cit.*, *International Labour Review*,

October 1921 and March 1924. *New Zealand Official Year Book*, 1925, pp. 790–1.

23. Cf. *Royal Commission on the Cost of Living*, 1912.
24. Cf. annual reports of the control boards, and also *Round Table*, March 1924, p. 426; March 1925, p. 412; and September 1926, p. 877.
25. Drummond, *Life of Seddon*, Chap. XIII; H. D. Lloyd, *New England*, New York, 1901, Chap. XI.
26. Cf. sup., Chap. V.
27. H. E. Teare, *Australian Banking Currency and Exchange*, Sydney, 1926, pp. 18–21.
28. Cf. recent criticism by Nash, *Financial Power in New Zealand*, Labour Party, Wellington, 1925, pp. 4–5.
29. Cf. Lloyd, *op. cit.*
30. For an earlier example cf. Saunders, *History of New Zealand*, Vol. II, pp. 226–34.
31. The report of this Committee and proceedings in the House are separately printed as *Bank of New Zealand: Parliamentary Debate, Session 1895.*
32. *New Zealand Official Year Book*, 1908, p. 525.
33. Cf. Nash, *op. cit.*
34. *New Zealand Official Year Book*, 1927, pp. 953–4.
35. *Ibid.*, 1928, p. 668.
36. Cf. Teare, *op. cit.*, Chap. XVII; and *A Digest of Australian and New Zealand Banking and Currency Legislation*, by the same author.
37. Cf. Tocker, "The Monetary Standards of Australia and New Zealand", *Economic Journal*, December 1924.
38. Cf., e.g., *Proceedings of Imperial Economic Conference*, 1923, Cmd. 2009, pp. 439–79; including report of special banking committee and British Treasury Memorandum.

CHAPTER XI

1. The best description of the introduction of the Act and its surrounding circumstances is that given by its author, the Hon. W. P. Reeves, *The Long White Cloud*, pp. 317–20, and *State Experiments in Australia and New Zealand*, Vol. II, Chap. I. The awards of the Court are published regularly in bound volumes from 1900 onwards. There is also a consolidated digest of the awards, 1913–17. The annual reports of the Labour Department also contain useful material. The *Journal of the Department of Labour*, which was published from 1894 to 1917, is very useful.

   The following official reports upon the working of the arbitration system are available:

   Backhouse, *Report of Enquiry into the Working of Compulsory Conciliation and Arbitration Laws*, New South Wales Royal Commission, 1901.

   Aves, *Report on the Wages Boards and Industrial Conciliation and Arbitration Acts of Australia and New Zealand*, Cmd. 4167, 1908.

   California Commissioners' Report on New Zealand Arbitration System, 1910.

   Report of Proceedings of the National Industrial Conference, 1928.

2. Cf. Le Rossignol and Stewart, *State Socialism in New Zealand*, p. 250.
3. Siegfried, *Democracy in New Zealand*, p. 89.
4. Scholefield, *New Zealand in Evolution*, Chap. XVI; also H. E. Holland, "Ballot Box", and R. S. Ross, *The Tragic Story of the Waihi Strike*, Wellington, 1913.
5. Condliffe, "Experiments in State Control in New Zealand", *International Labour Review*, Vol. IX, No. 3, March 1924, pp. 336–8.
6. *Report of National Industrial Conference*, 1928, p. 408.
7. Broadhead, *State Regulation of Labour and Labour Disputes in New Zealand*, Christchurch, 1908, pp. 105–26.
8. *Awards*, 1906, p. 50; 1922, p. 1002.
9. *Report*, *op. cit.*, pp. 23 and 176.
10. MacGregor, *Industrial Arbitration in New Zealand*, Dunedin, 1901.
11. The best summary of present-day opinion in New Zealand on arbitration is contained in the report of the 1928 Conference, *op. cit.* Cf. also the summary of this report by W. H. Cocker, "Industrial Arbitration in New Zealand", *Economic Record*, November 1928.
12. Cf. Reeves, *op. cit.*; also Lloyd, *A Country without Strikes*, New York, 1901; and *Newest England*, New York, 1901. Metin, *Le Socialisme sans Doctrines*, Paris, 1901; Siegfried, *La Démocratie en Nouvelle Zélande*, Paris, 1904, English edition, London, 1914; Clark, *The Labour Movement in Australasia*, London, 1906; Broadhead, *State Regulation of Labour and Labour Disputes in New Zealand*, Christchurch, 1908. See also two Fabian Tracts written by Reeves: No. 74, *The State and its Functions in New Zealand* (1896), and No. 83, *State Arbitration and the Living Wage* (1898); and V. S. Clark, *New Zealand Labour Conditions*, U.S. Labour Bulletins, No. 49, November 1903.
13. Scholefield, *New Zealand in Evolution*, Chap. XVI; Le Rossignol and Stewart, *State Socialism in New Zealand*, Chap. XV. See also Hancox and Hight, "The Labour Movement and the Strike of 1913 in New Zealand", *Economic Journal*, June 1914.
14. The detailed report of the first case was printed by the bootmakers' trade union in a substantial pamphlet by J. F. Arnold, *The Boot Trade Dispute*, Dunedin, 1897.
15. See Broadhead, *op. cit.*, Chap. XVI, for a trenchant criticism of the pro-Labour and Socialist opinions freely expressed by Mr. Tregear.
16. Reeves, *op. cit.*, p. 123.
17. Broadhead, *op. cit.*, Chap. VI.
18. Hammond, "The Regulation of Wages in New Zealand", *Quarterly Journal of Economics*, Vol. XXXI, May 1917, p. 423. See also Broadhead, pp. 58–61.
19. *Book of Awards*, Vol. IX, p. 517; Vol. XX, p. 1405; and XXV, p. 771. See also statement of Farmers' Union before National Industrial Conference, 1928, pp. 145–7, demanding statutory assurance that the primary industries shall remain exempt.
20. Cf. tables of wages and prices quoted by Hammond (p. 420) from *New Zealand Official Year Book*, 1908, p. 540.
21. Cf. Siegfried, *Democracy in New Zealand*, Chap. XII.

22. Broadhead, Chap. XIV.
23. Scholefield, p. 231.
24. F. V. Frazer, Judge, *Pronouncements of the Court* re *Cost of Living and General Order Amending Awards,* May 1922, p. 11.
25. Cf. J. T. Paul, *Labour and the Future,* Dunedin, 1911.
26. *National Industrial Conference,* 1928, p. 194.
27. Findlay, *Labour and the Arbitration Act,* Wellington, 1908.
28. The account of the revolutionary movement which follows is based largely upon the authorised statement in Holland, Ross, and "Ballot Box"—*The Tragic Story of the Waihi Strike,* Wellington, 1913.
29. *Ibid.,* p. 13.
30. *Ibid.,* p. 189.
31. *Ibid.,* p. 14.
32. *Report of National Industrial Conference,* 1928, pp. 230–1. For a summary of the early strikes, see Le Rossignol and Stewart, *op. cit.,* Chap. XV.
33. *The Tragic Story of the Waihi Strike, passim.*
34. *Ibid.,* Chaps. XII–XVII.
35. *The United Labour Party: Its Constitution and Platform,* with introduction by Walter Thomas Mills, National Organiser, Wellington, 1912.
36. Hight and Hancox, "The Labour Movement and the Strike of 1913 in New Zealand", *Economic Journal,* June 1914, pp. 183–5.
37. *Ibid.,* pp. 185–99.
38. *New Zealand Official Year Book,* 1929, p. 831.
39. *Awards,* Vol. XX, p. 403.
40. *Ibid.,* Vol. XXI, p. 513.
41. *Ibid.,* Vol. XXI, pp. 22–33.
42. Cf. statistical evidence of this brought forward by the representatives of the Freezing Workers' Union, *Report,* 1928, pp. 211–15.
43. *Awards,* Vol. XXII, p. 804 and p. 938.
44. *Pronouncements of the Court* re *Cost of Living and General Order Amending Awards,* May 1922.
45. *Awards,* Vol. XXII, p. 804.
46. *Ibid.*
47. *Report,* 1928, pp. 45–101, 133–53.
48. *Ibid.,* pp. 36–45 and 267–94.
49. See, e.g., an able theoretical criticism by the Senior Professor of Economics of the University of New Zealand, *ibid.,* pp. 12–25.
50. *Awards,* Vol. XXIV, p. 122.
51. Cf. Adam, *An Australian Looks at America,* London, 1928. Cf. also the verdict of the employers' spokesman on the small effect of the Court's regulations as compared with collective bargaining, *Report,* 1928, p. 229.
52. *Report,* 1928, pp. 12–25.

CHAPTER XII

1. Cf., e.g., plans for schools, churches, university, and hospitals in the *Canterbury Papers.*

2. Hight and Bamford, *Constitutional History and Law of New Zealand*, Chap. XXV.
3. *Ibid.*, pp. 372–3.
4. App. House of Representatives, 1909, H—16B.
5. *New Zealand Official Year Book*, 1928, Section IX.
6. *Women of the Pacific: Proceedings of the First Pan-Pacific Women's Conference*, Honolulu, 1928, pp. 210–12.
7. Siegfried, *Democracy in New Zealand*, pp. 284–96.
8. *Women of the Pacific*, pp. 86–9.
9. *Annual Report of the Royal New Zealand Society for the Health of Women and Children*, 1928. Cf. R. M. Woodbury, *Infant Mortality and Preventive Work in New Zealand*, U.S. Department of Labour, Children's Bureau, No. 105 (1922); also Dr. Margaret Harper, *Report on the Work of the Royal New Zealand Society for the Health of Women and Children*, Sydney, 1920; and *New Zealand Society for the Health of Women and Children: An Example of Methods of Baby-Saving Work in Small Towns and Rural Districts*, U.S. Children's Bureau, No. 6 (1914).

   Dr. Woodbury's work was later utilised for his *Causal Factors in Infant Mortality*, U.S. Children's Bureau, No. 6 (1925).
10. *New Zealand Official Year Book*, 1928, pp. 150–5. See also E. P. Neale, "A New Zealand Study of Natality" and "A New Study in Infant Mortality," *Journal of the American Statistical Association*, December 1924 and September 1925.
11. *Women of the Pacific*, pp. 134–42.
12. *New Zealand Official Year Book*, 1928, pp. 200–1.
13. *Ibid.*, pp. 236–7.
14. C. E. Montague, *Disenchantment*, London, 1922, Chap. XI.
15. *New Zealand Official Year Book*, 1928, p. 205.
16. *Ibid.*, pp. 272–4.
17. *Ibid.*, pp. 899–900, and previous issues for details of legislation regarding early closing, employment of women, prohibition of drunkenness, etc.
18. Reeves, *State Experiments*, Vol. II, Chap. III; *The Long White Cloud*, pp. 266–9. Also Siegfried, *op. cit.*, Chap. XXIII.
19. A detailed account of these changes is given in Dr. Fenwick's *The History of the Christchurch Hospital*, Christchurch, 1925. The author has also had access to an unpublished *History of the Hospital and Charitable Aid System of New Zealand*, by Miss E. M. Higgins, M.A.
20. *New Zealand Official Year Book*, 1928, p. 202. See also annual reports of the Department of Health (H—31).
21. *New Zealand Official Year Book*, 1928, pp. 214–18; also annual reports of the Inspector-General of Mental Hospitals (H—7).
22. Cf. the acute criticisms contained in the annual reports of Dr. MacGregor as head of the Department of Health in the early nineties.
23. For the historical account of early pensions discussions the author is indebted to a comprehensive paper prepared by Mesdames C. A. Fraer, H. A. Atkinson, and Miss E. M. Hyndman, for a W.E.A. advanced tutorial class held in Christchurch in 1925.
24. Clapham, *Economic Development of France and Germany, 1815–1914*,

Cambridge, 1921, pp. 333–8. The salient features of this programme are outlined in a pamphlet by J. W. Frost, *Old Age Pensions*, published by the Canterbury Progressive Liberal Association in 1894.

25. Cf. *Report of Committee on Old Age Pensions*, 1894 (App. H.R. I—11).
26. Cf. detailed report in *Christchurch Press*, March 21, 1883.
27. Cf. quotations in Le Rossignol and Stewart, *State Socialism in New Zealand*, Chap. XI.
28. See especially W. T. Leys, "An Old Age Pension Scheme for the Colonists of New Zealand: A Lecture delivered before the members of the Auckland Liberal Association, November 15, 1893".
29. Reprinted from Lyttelton *Times*, March 1, 1895.
30. Reeves, *State Experiments*, Vol. II, Chap. II.
31. For the details of these events see Drummond, *The Life and Work of Richard John Seddon*, Chap. XX; and Reeves, *op. cit.*
32. See H. D. Lloyd, *Newest England*, Chap. XIV, for a description of the first applicants under the Act.
33. Cf. estimates by H. W. Segar in "The Population of New Zealand," *Transactions New Zealand Institute*, 1900, p. 445.
34. *New Zealand Official Year Book*, 1928, Section XXV, "Pensions, Superannuations", gives the present status of all the various schemes now in operation. Cf. also annual reports of the Pensions Department (H—18).
35. *Ibid.*; also R. M. Campbell, "Family Allowances in New Zealand," *Economic Journal*, September 1927.
36. Cf. D. T. Sawkins, "The Australian Standard of Living", Chap. II in *Studies in Australian Affairs* (edited by Mills, Portus, and Campbell), Melbourne, 1928.
37. Cf., e.g., *Report on the Standard of Living in Various Countries*, League of Nations, Geneva, 1926.
38. Cf. *supra*, p. 369.
39. *New Zealand Official Year Book*, 1924, pp. 751–4, contains a summary of the 1921 census figures relating to dwellings.
40. Cf. Chap. XI.
41. *New Zealand Official Year Book*, 1929, pp. 647–8.
42. *Ibid.*, 1923, p. 506.
43. *Ibid.*, 1929, pp. 644–6.
44. *Ibid.*, 1929, p. 752.

CHAPTER XIII

1. C. D. Allin, *Australian Preferential Tariffs*, Minneapolis, 1929, p. 135 *seq.*
2. G. H. Scholefield, *The Pacific: Its Past and Future*, London, 1920, p. 149.
3. H. Duncan Hall, *The British Commonwealth of Nations*, London, 1920, Chap. IV–V.
4. Cf., e.g., *The Book of Canterbury Rhymes*, Christchurch, 1866.
5. Hall, *op. cit.*, p. 60.
6. Cf. W. T. G. Airey, *New Zealand: A Nation*, Christchurch, 1928.
7. Cf. Drummond, *Life of Seddon*.

8. Bowman, *The New World* (4th edition), New York, 1928.
9. Tucker, *Life and Episcopate of G. A. Selwyn, D.D.*, 2 vols., London, 1879. Vol. I, pp. 73–86, gives the origins of Selwyn's missionary activity, and Chap. VII records his first voyages.
10. Rees, *Life and Time of Sir George Grey*, Chap. XIV.
11. Scholefield, *op. cit.*
12. Cf. Seddon's views quoted in *Round Table*, "New Zealand Notes", p.70.
13. Siegfried, *Democracy in New Zealand*, p. 351.
14. Scholefield, p. 149 *seq.*
15. *Ibid.*, p. 152 *seq.*
16. *Ibid.*, p. 155 *seq.*
17. *Ibid.*, p. 209 *seq.*
18. Drummond, *op. cit.*, pp. 326–7.
19. *Ibid.*
20. The primary sources of information are the annual *Reports of the Cook and other Islands* (A—3). See also *New Zealand Official Year Book*, 1929, pp. 954–60.
21. Cf. *New Zealand Official Year Book*, 1929, pp. 960–4; also annual *Reports on Western Samoa* (A—4) and *Report of Department of Health on Western Samoa* (A—4a). See also *Mandated Territory of Western Samoa*, Eighth Report (for the year ended March 31, 1928), New Zealand Government Printing Office, Wellington, 1928.
22. The best historical account is to be found in Scholefield, *op. cit.*
23. Mandate for German Samoa, League of Nations, 21/31/14B.
24. *Round Table*, September 1921, pp. 96–7.
25. The legal history of the mandate is summarised in the *Report of the Royal Commission on Western Samoa* (1927), pp. iv–v.
26. *Round Table*, December 1927, pp. 191–210.
27. Reprinted, together with reports of preceding Samoan meetings and the Administrator's review thereof, in Royal Commission's *Report*, pp. xliv–lxxii. An account of the Minister's visit was separately printed in 1927 as "Mandated Territory of Western Samoa: Report of Visit by Hon. W. Nosworthy, together with Representations of Citizens' Committee and Replies thereto, etc." (A—4B), 1927.
28. *Round Table, op. cit.* The legality of this Order-in-Council was subsequently challenged, but the Samoa Amendment Act, 1927, definitely gave the Administrator power of deportation.
29. *New Zealand Parliamentary Debates*, 2nd Session, 1927, Nos. 9 and 10, pp. 831–907, 911–31.
30. Statement of Prime Minister issued to Press, January 24, 1928.
31. The case of the Samoan Administration is to be found in the files of the *Samoa Times*. The *Samoa Guardian*, organ of the Citizens' Committee, was published at Apia from May 1927 to March 1929, and has restarted publication at Auckland from May 9, 1929. Mr. Nelson has set forth his case in a pamphlet entitled *The Truth About Samoa*, Auckland, 1928. The position of the Labour Party is set forth in the files of the *Maoriland Worker*, published at Wellington, and also in two pamphlets by H. E. Holland, the present leader of the party—*Samoa: A*

Story that Teems with Tragedy (1918), and *The Revolt of the Samoans* (1928). The official view of the New Zealand Government is contained in the annual reports to the Council of the League of Nations, and may be followed also in the official statements released to the New Zealand Press. A convenient summary from a sympathetic viewpoint is A. B. Chappell's *The Stir in Samoa*, Auckland, 1928.

32. *Proceedings before the Permanent Mandates Commission at Geneva*, separately printed as "Extract from the Minutes of the 13th Session concerning the examination of the Report of the Royal Commission on the administration of Western Samoa", League of Nations, C. 341, M. 99, 1928, VI.
33. Blakeslee, "The Pacific Mandates", *Foreign Affairs*, September 1922.
34. Cf. also "Notes on Certain Aspects of the Work of the League of Nations of interest to Pacific Countries", prepared for the Institute of Pacific Relations and reprinted in *Problems of the Pacific*, Chicago, 1928.
35. Blakeslee, *op. cit.*
36. First *Report* of New Zealand Government to League of Nations (C. 480, 1922, V—I).
37. Cf. statement in *Samoa Guardian*, November 15, 1928.
38. *Report of Royal Commission*, pp. x–xii. The evidence is printed in New Zealand Parliamentary Paper A—4B (1927), pp. 5–13, and the official comments thereon appear in *Report*, pp. 487–90.
39. *Ibid.*, p. vi.
40. Cf. editorial in *Sydney Morning Herald*, December 14, 1927.

    "New Zealand's administration of the mandate has in general been carried out with praiseworthy regard for the interests of the people and with disinterestedness. For what has been done to improve their health conditions, Samoans cannot but be grateful; but the very rapidity with which reforms have been effected has caused dissatisfaction. Attachment to old and harmful customs dies hard among Pacific natives, and much tact must be brought to bear in the handling of them."
41. *Report on Western Samoa*, 1924 (A—4A), p. 37. See also other medical authorities quoted in *Report of Royal Commission*, p. xiv.
42. Blakeslee, *op. cit.*
43. *Report of Royal Commission*, Exhibit No. 63, p. 490. Also Holland, *The Revolt of the Samoans*.
44. *Ibid.*, pp. xx–xxviii.
45. *Ibid.*, pp. xxviii–xliii.
46. *Round Table*, December 1927, pp. 191–210.
47. *Report*, pp. xxxv–xli.
48. *New Zealand Parliamentary Debates*, 2nd Session, 1927, No. 10, pp. 928–31.
49. Cf. criticism in *Headway*, July 1928, p. 128, and *Manchester Guardian Weekly*, June 8, 1928. The New Zealand delegates at Versailles were strenuously opposed to the mandate system. Cf. van Maanen-Helmer, *The Mandates System in Relation to Africa and the Pacific Islands*, London, 1929, p. 36.

50. *New Zealand Herald*, July 25, 1927. Cf. also Miller, "The Origin of the Mandates System", *Foreign Affairs*, January 1928.
51. Drummond, *Life of Seddon*, p. 305.
52. Cf., however, the protest of Mr. J. Grattan Grey, a journalist on the Hansard staff, who was penalised for expressing pro-Boer opinions. Correspondence between him and Mr. Seddon was published in two pamphlets as *Freedom of Thought and Speech in New Zealand*, No. 1 and No. 2, Wellington, 1900.
53. Cf. estimate of effect of this financial preference in *Round Table*, "New Zealand Notes", pp. 34–5.
54. *Round Table*, No. 49, December 1922. An example of the identification of New Zealand policies with those of Britain is to be found in the League of Nations document, "Bases of Discussion drawn up for the Conference for the Codification of International Law". Vol. I, *Nationality*, Geneva, 1929. Page 185 gives a telegram received on October 20th, stating, "New Zealand Government desire to associate themselves with the views expressed by His Majesty's Government in Great Britain on subject of nationality and territorial waters".

    Page 169 gives in detail the British views contained in a letter dated three weeks after the New Zealand telegram was received.
55. "Conference on the Limitation of Armament: Report of the New Zealand Delegate" (New Zealand Parliamentary Paper A 5, 1922).
56. *Round Table*, September 1921 and March 1920.
57. "Protocol for the Pacific Settlement of International Disputes". Correspondence relating to the position of the Dominions (I—A 5c), 1925. See also statement by the Prime Minister (A—5B).
58. *Round Table*, No. 56, September 1924.
59. *Ibid.*
60. Cf. G. H. Scholefield and T. D. Hall, "Asiatic Immigration in New Zealand: Its History and Legislation" (preliminary paper prepared for the Institute of Pacific Relations, Honolulu, 1927); also T. D. Hall, "New Zealand and Asiatic Immigration", *Economic Record*, November 1907, and Chap. V by the same author in *New Zealand Affairs*, 1929. An account of the earlier legislation is contained in Reeves, *State Experiments*, Vol. II, Chap. IV.
61. Cf. Willard, *History of the White Australia Policy*, Melbourne, 1923.
62. Scholefield and Hall, *op. cit.*
63. Scholefield, "Japan and New Zealand: An Interesting Trade Agreement", *Pacific Affairs*, March 1929.

CHAPTER XIV

1. Cf. Moss, *A School History of New Zealand*, Auckland, 1889.
2. Cf. Beard, *The Rise of American Civilisation*, Macmillan, New York, 1928, Vol. I, pp. 544–53; and Portus, "The Labour Movement in Australia, 1788 to 1914", in Atkinson (Editor), *Australia—Economic and Political Studies*, Macmillan, Melbourne, 1920, for similar developments in the United States and Australia.

3. Laski, *Authority in the Modern State*, London.
4. Marshall, *Principles of Economics*, Macmillan, London, 8th edition, 1925, p. 2.
5. Cf. *New Zealand Official Year Book*, 1929, pp. 223–44; also the annual series of official reports on education:
   Report of Minister of Education, E. 1.
   Report on Primary Education, E. 2.
   Report on Education of Native Children, E. 3.
   Report on Child Welfare, State Care of Children, Special Schools, and Infant Life Protection, E. 4.
   Report on Technical Education, E. 5.
   Report on Secondary Education, E. 6.
   Report on Higher Education, E. 7.

   The results of recent independent investigations have been printed as follows:
   Tate, *Investigation into Certain Aspects of Post-Primary Education in New Zealand*, Wellington, 1925.
   Report of Royal Commission on University Education in New Zealand, E—7A (1925).
   Report of Committee on Primary Syllabus, 1928.
6. An outline of the provincial systems of education is given in the *New Zealand Official Year Book*, 1927, pp. 231–4, and of the national system, pp. 235–6. See also A. G. Butchers, *Young New Zealand*, Dunedin, 1929.
7. Bryce, *Modern Democracies*, Vol. II, p. 318. Siegfried, *Democracy in New Zealand*, p. 75, quotes the emphatic statement of Mr. Sidney Webb:

   "The great reproach which can be made against the New Zealand Government is without doubt its complete vulgarity. It is a failing common to all New Zealanders, although it appears under different forms with different people. With few exceptions, and without distinction of parties, there is a vulgarity of ideas and an absence of refinement among politicians which is the result of the pioneer life that they have led. What is more serious is the absence throughout the colony of serious economic study, of scientific investigation of those industrial and social problems which the politicians themselves attempt to solve."
8. *New Zealand Official Year Book*, 1929, p. 223.
9. *Ibid.*, p. 244.
10. *Some Aspects of University Teaching in New Zealand*, Christchurch, 1926.
11. The correspondence in this case was printed for permanent record by the Victoria University College Council as *Report concerning the Case of Professor von Zedlitz*, Wellington, 1915.
12. *Report of Royal Commission on University Education in New Zealand*, 1925, pp. 4–11.
13. Professor T. A. Hunter's evidence, quoted *Report*, p. 13.
14. *Report*, p. 11.
15. *University Reform in New Zealand*, Wellington, 1911, p. 12.
16. *Ibid.*, p. 32.
17. New Zealand University Amendment Act (1926, No. 70).

18. Cf. the statistics recently prepared in 1929 for the Professorial Board of the Auckland University College.

Proportion of Students to Each Member of Staff

University.	Staff.	Students.	Proportion.
Leeds	273	1,610	5·9
Liverpool	286	2,020	7·1
Aberdeen	137	1,399	10·2
Edinburgh	301	3,850	12·7
Belfast..	129	1,338	10·4
Johannesburg	132	1,351	10·2
Pretoria	83	811	9·8
Alberta	130	1,020	7·8
McGill	262	2,325	8·9
Queensland	34	205	6·0
Sydney	199	1,989	10·0
Average for 11 British Universities	—	—	9·1
Auckland	36	1,248	34·7

19. *Report of Royal Commission*, 1925, p. 11.
20. *Ibid.*, p. 31.
21. *Ibid.*, pp. 32–9.
22. Reeves, *The Long White Cloud*, pp. 361–73.
23. Bryce, *Modern Democracies*, Vol. II, p. 279.
24. Reeves, *op. cit.*, p. 378.
25. Siegfried, *Democracy in New Zealand*, Chap. XXI.
26. The agitation apparently met with more immediate success than might have been expected. The *New Zealand Herald*, August 2, 1929, quoted a public statement of the Minister of Education (Hon. H. Atmore), which reads in part:

    "There is no intention that the theory of evolution, in its connection with the ancestry of man, should be taught in our schools. The subject of the theory of evolution is highly controversial and touches the religious beliefs of a large section of the community, and for those reasons is quite unsuitable for a school subject."
27. G. A. Froude, *Oceana: England and her Colonies*, London, 1886.

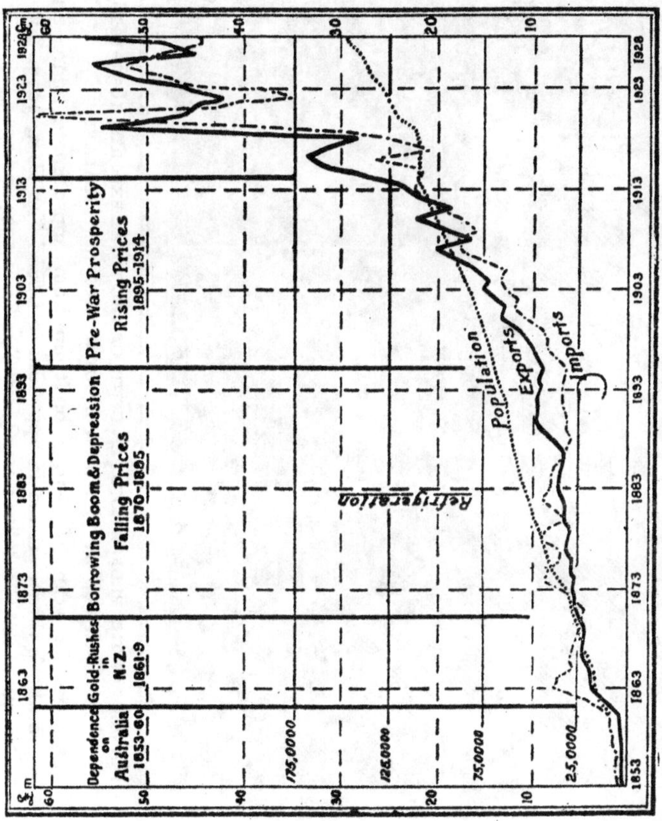

DIAGRAM OF EXTERNAL TRADE AND POPULATION OF NEW ZEALAND, 1853–1928

(Statistics taken from official publications.)

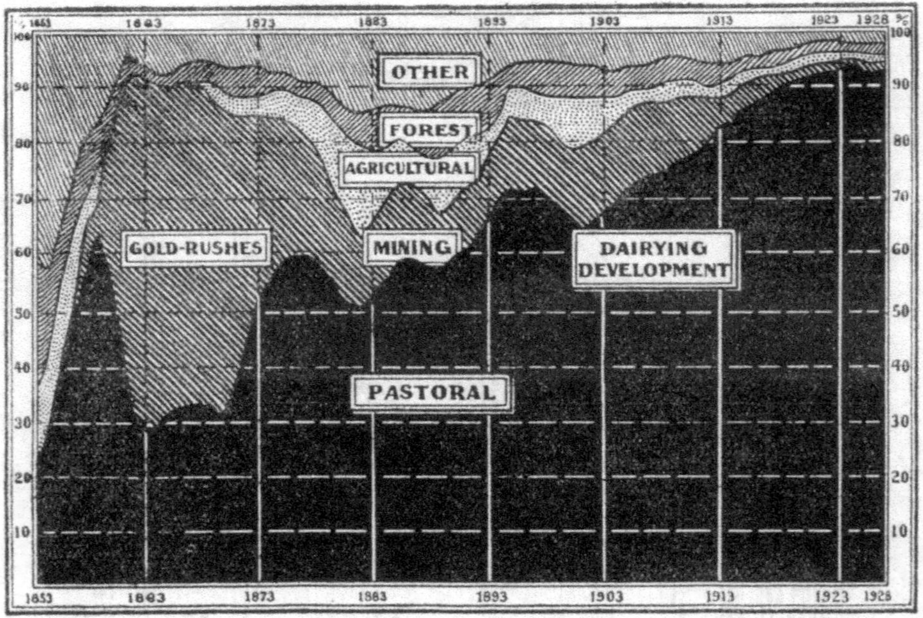

DIAGRAM OF THE PROPORTIONS PER CENT. OF THE TOTAL EXPORTS, 1853–1928, PROVIDED BY THE MAIN INDUSTRIES OF NEW ZEALAND

(Statistics for years 1851–1900 built up from approximate figures in author's thesis, printed in appendix to *Official Year Book*, 1915. Subsequent statistics taken from *Official Year Books*, 1924 and 1929.)

APPENDIX II

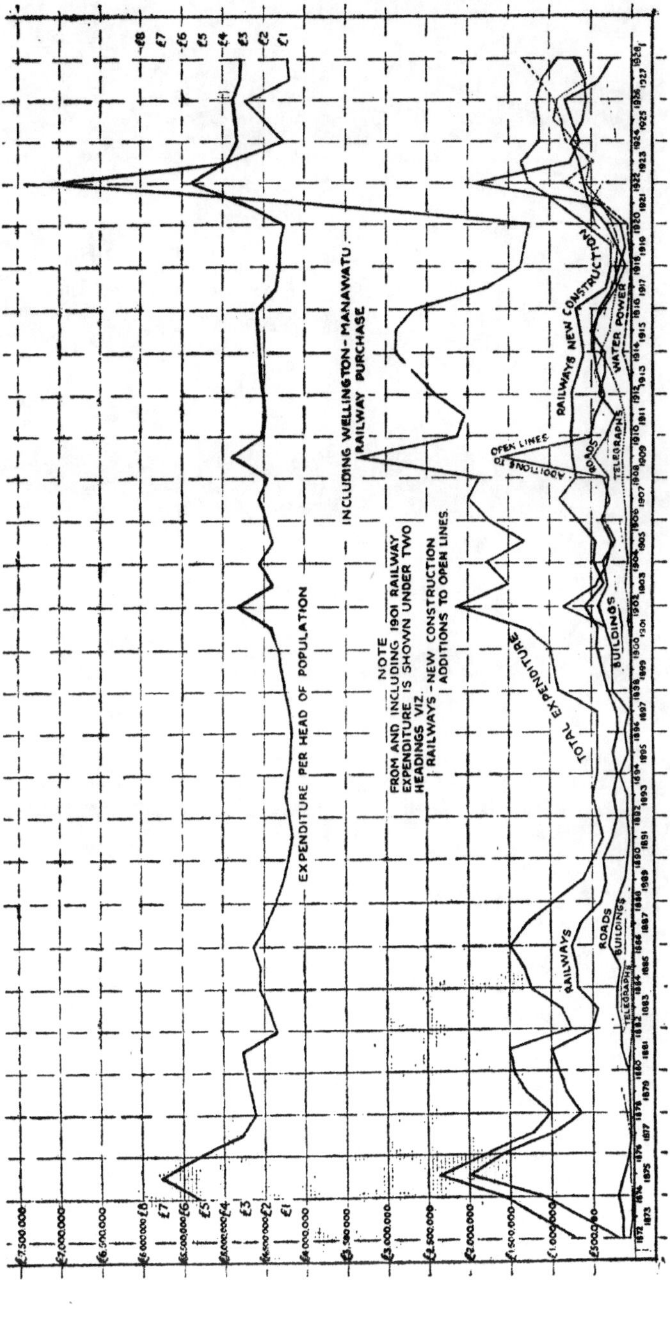

PUBLIC WORKS EXPENDITURE IN NEW ZEALAND, 1872–1928

(Original Diagram lent by Rt. Hon. J. G. Coates, formerly Minister of Public Works.)

INDEX

For Product Safety Concerns and Information please contact our EU representative GPSR@taylorandfrancis.com
Taylor & Francis Verlag GmbH, Kaufingerstraße 24, 80331 München, Germany

www.ingramcontent.com/pod-product-compliance
Lightning Source LLC
LaVergne TN
LVHW011101300926
849160LV00008B/247
* 9 7 8 1 0 3 2 5 2 5 3 3 4 *